KT-526-228

CONCURRENCY CONTROL AND RECOVERY IN DATABASE SYSTEMS

Philip A. Bernstein
Wang Institute of Graduate Studies

Vassos Hadzilacos
University of Toronto

Nathan Goodman
Kendall Square Research Corporation

Park Learning Centre
University of Gloucestershire
Cheltenham
GL50 2RH
01242 714333

ADDISON-WESLEY PUBLISHING COMPANY

Reading, Massachusetts ■ Menlo Park, California
Don Mills, Ontario ■ Wokingham, England ■ Amsterdam ■ Sydney
Singapore ■ Tokyo ■ Madrid ■ Bogotá ■ Santiago ■ San Juan

OXSTALLS CAMPUS LIBRARY
CHELT... & GLOUCE...R
COLLEGE OF HIGHER EDUCATION
OXSTALLS LANE
GLOUCESTER GL2 9HW

6717

18.3.91   £24-95

004.35 BER

This book is in the Addison-Wesley Series in Computer Science
Michael A. Harrison, Consulting Editor

Library of Congress Cataloging-in-Publication Data

Bernstein, Philip A.
   Concurrency control and recovery in database systems.

   Includes index.
   1. Data base management.   2. Parallel
processing (Electronic computers)
I. Hadzilacos, Vassos.   II. Goodman, Nathan.
III. Title.
QA76.9.D3B48   1987   004.3   86-14127
ISBN 0-201-10715-5

Copyright © 1987 by Addison-Wesley Publishing Company

All rights reserved. No part of this publication may be reproduced, stored in a retrieval system, or transmitted, in any form or by any means, electronic, mechanical, photocopying, recording, or otherwise, without the prior written permission of the publisher. Printed in the United States of America. Published simultaneously in Canada.

ABCDEFGHIJ-MA-8987

Serializability Theory

Whether by its native capabilities or the way we educate it, the human mind seems better suited for reasoning about sequential activities than concurrent ones. This is indeed unfortunate for the study of concurrency control algorithms. Inherent to the study of such algorithms is the need to reason about concurrent executions.

Over the years, researchers have developed an abstract model that simplifies this sort of reasoning. The model, called *serializability theory*, provides two important tools. First, it provides a notation for writing down concurrent executions in a clear and precise format, making it easy to talk and write about them. Second, it gives a straightforward way to determine when a concurrent execution of transactions is serializable. Since the goal of a concurrency control algorithm is to produce serializable executions, this theory helps us determine when such an algorithm is correct.

To understand serializability theory, one only needs a basic knowledge of directed graphs and partial orders. A comprehensive presentation of this material appears in most undergraduate textbooks on discrete mathematics. We briefly review the material in the Appendix.

We mainly use serializability theory to express example executions and to reason abstractly about the behavior of concurrency control and recovery algorithms. However, we also use the theory to produce formal correctness proofs of some of the algorithms. Although we feel strongly about the importance of understanding such proofs, we recognize that not every reader will want to take the time to study them. We have therefore isolated the more complex proofs in separate sections, which you can skip without loss of continuity. Such sections are marked by an asterisk (*). Less than 10 percent of the book is so marked.

Chapter Organization

Chapter 1 motivates concurrency control and recovery problems. It defines correct transaction behavior from the user's point of view, and presents a model for the internal structure of the database system that implements this behavior — the model we will use throughout the book. Chapter 2 covers serializability theory.

The remaining six chapters are split into two parts: Chapters 3–5 on concurrency control and Chapters 6–8 on recovery.

In Chapter 3 we cover two phase locking. Since locking is so popular in commercial systems, we cover many of the variations and implementation details used in practice. The performance of locking algorithms is discussed in a section written for us by Dr. Y.C. Tay. We also discuss non–two-phase locking protocols used in tree structures.

In Chapter 4 we cover concurrency control techniques that do not use locking: timestamp ordering, serialization graph testing, and certifiers (i.e., optimistic methods). These techniques are not widely used in practice, so the chapter is somewhat more conceptual and less implementation oriented than Chapter 3. We show how locking and non-locking techniques can be integrated into hundreds of variations.

In Chapter 5 we describe concurrency control for multiversion databases, where the history of values of each data object is maintained as part of the database. As is discussed later in Chapter 6, old versions are often retained for recovery purposes. In this chapter we show that they have value for concurrency control too. We show how each of the major concurrency control and recovery techniques of Chapters 3 and 4 can be used to manage multiversion data.

In Chapter 6 we present recovery algorithms for centralized systems. We emphasize undo-redo logging because it demonstrates most of the recovery problems that all techniques must handle, and because it is especially popular in commercial systems. We cover other approaches at a more conceptual level: deferred updating, shadowing, checkpointing, and archiving.

In Chapter 7 we describe recovery algorithms for distributed systems where a transaction may update data at two or more sites that only communicate via messages. The critical problem here is *atomic commitment*: ensuring that a transaction's results are installed either at all sites at which it executed or at none of them. We describe the two phase and three phase commit protocols, and explain how each of them handles site and communications failures.

In Chapter 8 we treat the concurrency control and recovery problem for replicated distributed data, where copies of a piece of data may be stored at multiple sites. Here the concurrency control and recovery problems become closely intertwined. We describe several approaches to these problems: quorum consensus, missing writes, virtual partitions, and available copies. In this chapter we go beyond the state-of-the-art. No database systems that we know of support general purpose access to replicated distributed data.

Chapter Prerequisites

This book is designed to meet the needs of both professional and academic audiences. It assumes background in operating systems at the level of a one semester undergraduate course. In particular, we assume some knowledge of the following concepts: concurrency, processes, mutual exclusion, semaphores, and deadlocks.

We designed the chapters so that you can select whatever ones you wish with few constraints on prerequisites. Chapters 1 and 2 and Sections 3.1, 3.2, 3.4, and 3.5 of Chapter 3 are all that is required for later chapters. The subsequent material on concurrency control (the rest of Chapter 3 and Chapters 4–5) is largely independent of the material on recovery (Chapters 6–8). You can go as far into each chapter sequence as you like.

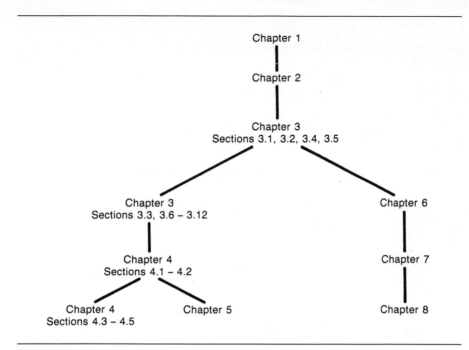

FIGURE 1
Dependencies between Chapters

A minimal survey of centralized concurrency control and recovery would include Sections 3.1–3.7, 3.12, and 3.13 of Chapter 3 and Sections 6.1–6.4 and 6.8 of Chapter 6. This material covers the main techniques used in commercial database systems, namely, locking and logging. In length, it's about a quarter of the book.

You can extend your survey to distributed (nonreplicated) data by adding Sections 3.10 and 3.11 (distributed locking) and Chapter 7 (distributed recovery). You can extend it to give a more complete treatment of centralized systems by adding the remaining sections of Chapters 3 and 6, on locking and recovery, and Chapter 5, on multiversion techniques (Section 5.3 requires Section 4.2 as a prerequisite). As we mentioned earlier, Chapter 4 covers nonlocking concurrency control methods, which are conceptually important, but are not used in many commercial products.

Chapter 8, on replicated data, requires Chapters 3, 6, and 7 as prerequisites; we also recommend Section 5.2, which presents an analogous theory for multiversion data. Figure 1 summarizes these prerequisite dependencies.

We have included a substantial set of problems at the end of each chapter. Many problems explore dark corners of techniques that we didn't have the space to cover in the chapters themselves. We think you'll find them interesting reading, even if you choose not to work them out.

For Instructors

We designed the book to be useful as a principal or supplementary textbook in a graduate course on database systems, operating systems, or distributed systems. The book can be covered in as little as four weeks, or could consume an entire course, depending on the breadth and depth of coverage and on the backgrounds of the students.

You can augment the book in several ways depending on the theme of the course:

☐ Distributed Databases — distributed query processing, distributed database design.

☐ Transaction Processing — communications architecture, applications architecture, fault-tolerant computers.

☐ Distributed Computing — Byzantine agreement, network topology maintenance and message routing, distributed operating systems.

☐ Fault Tolerance — error detecting codes, Byzantine agreement, fault-tolerant computers.

☐ Theory of Distributed Computing — parallel program verification, analysis of parallel algorithms.

In a theoretical course, you can augment the book with the extensive mathematical material that exists on concurrency control and recovery.

The exercises supply problems for many assignments. In addition, you may want to consider assigning a project. We have successfully used two styles of project.

The first is an implementation project to program a concurrency control method and measure its performance on a synthetic workload. For this to be workable, you need a concurrent programming environment in which processing delays can be measured with reasonable accuracy. Shared memory between processes is also very helpful. We have successfully used Concurrent Euclid for such a project [Holt 83].

The second type of project is to take a concurrency control or recovery algorithm described in a research paper, formalize its behavior in serializability theory, and prove it correct. The bibliography is full of candidate examples. Also, some of the referenced papers are abstracts that do not contain proofs. Filling in the proofs is a stimulating exercise for students, especially those with a theoretical inclination.

Acknowledgments

In a sense, work on this book began with the SDD-1 project at Computer Corporation of America (CCA). Under the guidance and support of Jim Rothnie, two of us (Bernstein and Goodman) began our study of concurrency control in database systems. He gave us an opportunity that turned into a career. We thank him greatly.

We wrote this book in part to show that serializability theory is an effective way to think about practical concurrency control and recovery problems. This goal required much research, pursued with the help of graduate students, funding agencies, and colleagues. We owe them all a great debt of gratitude. Without their help, this book would not have been written.

Our research began at Computer Corporation of America, funded by Rome Air Development Center, monitored by Tom Lawrence. We thank Tom, and John and Diane Smith at CCA, for their support of this work, continuing well beyond those critical first years. We also thank Bob Grafton, at the Office for Naval Research, whose early funding helped us establish an independent research group to pursue this work. We appreciate the steady and substantial support we received throughout the project from the National Science Foundation, and more recently from the Natural Sciences and Engineering Research Council of Canada, Digital Equipment Corporation, and the Wang Institute of Graduate Studies. We thank them all for their help.

Many colleagues helped us with portions of the research that led to this book. We thank Rony Attar, Catriel Beeri, Marco Casanova, Ming-Yee Lai, Christos Papadimitriou, Dennis Shasha, Dave Shipman, Dale Skeen, and Wing Wong.

We are very grateful to Dr. Y.C. Tay of the University of Singapore for writing an important section of Chapter 3 on the performance of two phase locking. He helped us fill an important gap in the presentation that would otherwise have been left open.

We gained much from the comments of readers of early versions of the chapters, including Catriel Beeri, Amr El Abbadi, Jim Gray, Rivka Ladin, Dan Rosenkrantz, Oded Shmueli, Jack Stiffler, Mike Stonebraker, and Y.C. Tay. We especially thank Gordon McLean and Irv Traiger, whose very careful reading of the manuscript caught many errors and led to many improvements. We also thank Ming-Yee Lai and Dave Lomet for their detailed reading of the final draft.

We are especially grateful to Jenny Rozakis for her expert preparation of the manuscript. Her speed and accuracy saved us months. We give her our utmost thanks.

We also thank our editor, Keith Wollman, and the entire staff at Addison-Wesley for their prompt and professional attention to all aspects of this book.

We gratefully acknowledge the Association for Computing Machinery for permission to use material from "Multiversion Concurrency Control — Theory and Algorithms," *ACM Transaction on Database Systems* 8, 4 (Dec. 1983), pp. 465–483 (© 1983, Association for Computing Machinery, Inc.) in Chapter 5; and "An Algorithm for Concurrency Control and Recovery in Replicated Distributed Databases," *ACM Transactions on Database Systems* 9, 4 (Dec. 1984), pp. 596–615 (© 1984, Association for Computing Machinery, Inc.) in Chapter 8. We also acknowledge Academic Press for allowing us to use material from "Serializability Theory for Replicated Databases," *Journal of Computer and System Sciences* 31, 3 (1986) (© 1986, Academic Press) in Chapter 8; and Springer-Verlag for allowing us to use material from "A Proof Technique for Concurrency Control and Recovery Algorithms for Replicated Databases," *Distributed Computing* 2, 1 (1986) in Chapter 8.

Finally, we thank our families, friends, and colleagues for indulging our bad humor as a two-year project stretched out to six. Better days are ahead.

Tyngsboro, Mass.　　　　　　　　　　　　　　　　　　　　P.A.B.
Toronto, Canada　　　　　　　　　　　　　　　　　　　　V.H.
Cambridge, Mass.　　　　　　　　　　　　　　　　　　　　N.G.

CONTENTS

3

TWO PHASE LOCKING 47

4

NON-LOCKING SCHEDULERS 113

5

MULTIVERSION CONCURRENCY CONTROL 143

6

CENTRALIZED RECOVERY   167

7

DISTRIBUTED RECOVERY   217

8

REPLICATED DATA   265

PREFACE

The Subject

For over 20 years, businesses have been moving their data processing activities on-line. Many businesses, such as airlines and banks, are no longer able to function when their on-line computer systems are down. Their on-line databases must be up-to-date and correct at all times.

In part, the requirement for correctness and reliability is the burden of the application programming staff. They write the application programs that perform the business's basic functions: make a deposit or withdrawal, reserve a seat or purchase a ticket, buy or sell a security, etc. Each of these programs is designed and tested to perform its function correctly. However, even the most carefully implemented application program is vulnerable to certain errors that are beyond its control. These potential errors arise from two sources: concurrency and failures.

Multiprogramming is essential for attaining high performance. Its effect is to allow many programs to interleave their executions. That is, they execute *concurrently*. When such programs interleave their accesses to the database, they can interfere. Avoiding this interference is called the *concurrency control problem*.

Computer systems are subject to many types of failures. Operating systems fail, as does the hardware on which they run. When a failure occurs, one or more application programs may be interrupted in midstream. Since the program was written to be correct only under the assumption that it executed in its entirety, an interrupted execution can lead to incorrect results. For example, a money transfer application may be interrupted by a failure after debiting one account but before crediting the other. Avoiding such incorrect results due to failures is called the *recovery problem*.

Systems that solve the concurrency control and recovery problems allow their users to assume that each of their programs executes atomically — as if no other programs were executing concurrently — and reliably — as if there were no failures. This abstraction of an atomic and reliable execution of a program is called a *transaction*.

A *concurrency control algorithm* ensures that transactions execute atomically. It does this by controlling the interleaving of concurrent transactions, to give the illusion that transactions execute serially, one after the next, with no interleaving at all. Interleaved executions whose effects are the same as serial executions are called *serializable*. Serializable executions are correct, because they support this illusion of transaction atomicity.

A *recovery algorithm* monitors and controls the execution of programs so that the database includes only the results of transactions that run to a normal completion. If a failure occurs while a transaction is executing, and the transaction is unable to finish executing, then the recovery algorithm must wipe out the effects of the partially completed transaction. That is, it must ensure that the database does not reflect the results of such transactions. Moreover, it must ensure that the results of transactions that do execute are never lost.

This book is about techniques for concurrency control and recovery. It covers techniques for centralized and distributed computer systems, and for single copy, multiversion, and replicated databases. These techniques were developed by researchers and system designers principally interested in transaction processing systems and database systems. Such systems must process a relatively high volume of short transactions for data processing. Example applications include electronic funds transfer, airline reservation, and order processing. The techniques are useful for other types of applications too, such as electronic switching and computer-aided design — indeed any application that requires atomicity and reliability of concurrently executing programs that access shared data.

The book is a blend of conceptual principles and practical details. The principles give a basic understanding of the essence of each problem and why each technique solves it. This understanding is essential for applying the techniques in a commercial setting, since every product and computing environment has its own restrictions and idiosyncrasies that affect the implementation. It is also important for applying the techniques outside the realm of database systems. For those techniques that we consider of most practical value, we explain what's needed to turn the conceptual principles into a workable database system product. We concentrate on those practical approaches that are most often used in today's commercial systems.

1
THE PROBLEM

1.1 TRANSACTIONS

Concurrency control is the activity of coordinating the actions of processes that operate in parallel, access shared data, and therefore potentially interfere with each other. Recovery is the activity of ensuring that software and hardware failures do not corrupt persistent data. Concurrency control and recovery problems arise in the design of hardware, operating systems, real time systems, communications systems, and database systems, among others. In this book, we will explore concurrency control and recovery problems in database systems.

We will study these problems using a model of database systems. This model is an abstraction of many types of data handling systems, such as database management systems for data processing applications, transaction processing systems for airline reservations or banking, and file systems for a general purpose computing environment. Our study of concurrency control and recovery applies to any such system that conforms to our model.

The main component of this model is the *transaction*. Informally, a transaction is an execution of a program that accesses a shared database. The goal of concurrency control and recovery is to ensure that transactions execute *atomically*, meaning that

1. each transaction accesses shared data without interfering with other transactions, and
2. if a transaction terminates normally, then all of its effects are made permanent; otherwise it has no effect at all.

The purpose of this chapter is to make this model precise.

1

In this section we present a user-oriented model of the system, which consists of a database that a user can access by executing transactions. In Section 1.2, we explain what it means for a transaction to execute atomically in the presence of failures. In Section 1.3, we explain what it means for a transaction to execute atomically in an environment where its database accesses can be interleaved with those of other transactions. Section 1.4 presents a model of a database system's concurrency control and recovery components, whose goal is to realize transaction atomicity.

Database Systems

A *database* consists of a set of named *data items*. Each data item has a *value*. The values of the data items at any one time comprise the *state* of the database.

In practice, a data item could be a word of main memory, a page of a disk, a record of a file, or a field of a record. The size of the data contained in a data item is called the *granularity* of the data item. Granularity will usually be unimportant to our study and we will therefore leave it unspecified. When we leave granularity unspecified, we denote data items by lower case letters, typically x, y, and z.

A *database system* $(DBS)^1$ is a collection of hardware and software modules that support commands to access the database, called *database operations* (or simply *operations*). The most important operations we will consider are Read and Write. Read(x) returns the value stored in data item x. Write(x, *val*) changes the value of x to *val*. We will also use other operations from time to time.

The DBS executes each operation *atomically*. This means that the DBS behaves as if it executes operations *sequentially*, that is, one at a time. To obtain this behavior, the DBS might *actually* execute operations sequentially. However, more typically it will execute operations *concurrently*. That is, there may be times when it is executing more than one operation at once. However, even if it executes operations concurrently, the final effect must be the same as some sequential execution.

For example, suppose data items x and y are stored on two different devices. The DBS might execute operations on x and y in this order:

1. execute Read(x);

2. after step (1) is finished, concurrently execute Write(x, 1) and Read(y);

3. after step (2) is finished, execute Write(y, 0).

Although Write(x, 1) and Read(y) were executed concurrently, they may be regarded as having executed atomically. This is because the execution just

---

[1] We use the abbreviation *DBS*, instead of the more conventional *DBMS*, to emphasize that a DBS in our sense may be much less than an integrated database management system. For example, it may only be a simple file system with transaction management capabilities.

given has the same effect as a sequential execution, such as Read(x), Write(x, 1), Read(y), Write(y, 0).

The DBS also supports *transaction operations*: Start, Commit, and Abort. A program tells the DBS that it is about to begin executing a new transaction by issuing the operation *Start*. It indicates the termination of the transaction by issuing either the operation *Commit* or the operation *Abort*. By issuing a Commit, the program tells the DBS that the transaction has terminated normally and all of its effects should be made permanent. By issuing an Abort, the program tells the DBS that the transaction has terminated abnormally and all of its effects should be obliterated.

A program must issue each of its database operations on behalf of a particular transaction. We can model this by assuming that the DBS responds to a Start operation by returning a unique transaction identifier. The program then attaches this identifier to each of its database operations, and to the Commit or Abort that it issues to terminate the transaction. Thus, from the DBS's viewpoint, a transaction is defined by a Start operation, followed by a (possibly concurrent) execution of a set of database operations, followed by a Commit or Abort.

A transaction may be a *concurrent* execution of two or more programs. That is, the transaction may submit two operations to the DBS before the DBS has responded to either one. However, the transaction's last operation *must* be a Commit or Abort. Thus, the DBS must refuse to process a transaction's database operation if it arrives after the DBS has already executed the transaction's Commit or Abort.

Transaction Syntax

Users interact with a DBS by invoking programs. From the user's viewpoint, a *transaction* is the execution of one or more programs that include database and transaction operations.

For example, consider a banking database that contains a file of customer accounts, called Accounts, each entry of which contains the balance in one account. A useful transaction for this database is one that transfers money from one account to another.

Procedure Transfer **begin**
    Start;
    input(fromaccount, toaccount, amount);
    /* This procedure transfers "amount" from "fromaccount" into "toaccount." */
    temp : = Read(Accounts[fromaccount]);
    if temp < amount **then begin**
        output("insufficient funds");
        Abort
    end

```
        else begin
            Write(Accounts[fromaccount], temp − amount);
            temp := Read(Accounts[toaccount]);
            Write(Accounts[toaccount], temp + amount);
            Commit;
            output("transfer completed");
        end;
        return
end
```

"Transfer" illustrates the programming language we will use in examples. It includes the usual procedure declaration (**Procedure** procedure-name **begin** procedure-body **end**), assignment statement (variable := expression), a conditional statement (**if** Boolean-expression **then** statement **else** statement), **input** (which reads a list of values from a terminal or other input device and assigns them to variables), **output** (which lists values of constants or variables on a terminal or other output device), **begin-end** brackets to treat a statement list as a single statement (**begin** statement-list **end**), a statement to return from a procedure (**return**), and brackets to treat text as a comment (/* comment */). We use semicolons as statement separators, in the style of Algol and Pascal.

The choice of language for expressing transactions is not important to our study of concurrency control and recovery. In practice, the language could be a database query language, a report writing language, or a high level programming language augmented with database operations. No matter how the transaction is expressed, it must eventually be translated into programs that issue database operations, since database operations are the only way to access the database. We therefore assume that the programs that comprise transactions are written in a high level language with embedded database operations.

Transfer is an unrealistic program in that it doesn't perform any error checking, such as testing for incorrect input. Although such error checking is essential if application programs are to be reliable, it is unimportant to our understanding of concurrency control and recovery problems. Therefore, to keep our example programs short, we will ignore error checking in those programs.

Commit and Abort

After the DBS executes a transaction's Commit (or Abort) operation, the transaction is said to be *committed* (or *aborted*). A transaction that has issued its Start operation but is not yet committed or aborted is called *active*. A transaction is *uncommitted* if it is aborted or active.

A transaction issues an Abort operation if it cannot be completed correctly. The transaction itself may issue the Abort because it has detected an error from which it cannot recover, such as the "insufficient funds" condition in Transfer.

Or the Abort may be "imposed" on a transaction by circumstances beyond its control.

For example, suppose a system failure interrupts the execution of a Transfer transaction after it debited one account but before it credited the other. Assuming Transfer's internal state was lost as a consequence of the failure, it cannot continue its execution. Therefore, when the system recovers, the DBS should cause this execution of Transfer to abort. In such cases, we still view the Abort to be an operation of the *transaction*, even though the *DBS* actually invoked the operation.

Even in the absence of system failures, the DBS may decide unilaterally to abort a transaction. For example, the DBS may discover that it has returned an incorrect value to transaction T in response to T's Read. It may discover this error long after it actually processed the Read. (We'll see some examples of how this may happen in the next section.) Once it discovers the error, it's too late to change the incorrect value, so it must abort T.

When a transaction aborts, the DBS wipes out all of its effects. The prospect that a transaction may be aborted calls for the ability to determine a point in time after which the DBS guarantees to the user that the transaction will *not* be aborted and its effects will be permanent. For example, in processing a deposit through an automatic teller machine, a customer does not want to leave the machine before being assured that the deposit transaction will not be aborted. Similarly, from the bank's viewpoint, in processing a withdrawal the teller machine should not dispense any money before making certain that the withdrawal transaction will not be aborted.

The Commit operation accomplishes this guarantee. Its invocation signifies that a transaction terminated "normally" and that its effects should be permanent. Executing a transaction's Commit constitutes a guarantee by the DBS that it will not abort the transaction and that the transaction's effects will survive subsequent failures of the system.

Since the DBS is at liberty to abort a transaction T until T commits, the user can't be sure that T's output will be permanent as long as T is active. Thus, a user should not trust T's output until the DBS tells the user that T has committed. This makes Commit an important operation for read-only transactions (called *queries*) as well as for transactions that write into the database (called *update transactions* or *updaters*).

The DBS should guarantee the permanence of Commit under the weakest possible assumptions about the correct operation of hardware, systems software, and application software. That is, it should be able to handle as wide a variety of errors as possible. At least, it should ensure that data written by committed transactions is not lost as a consequence of a computer or operating system failure that corrupts main memory but leaves disk storage unaffected.

Messages

We assume that each transaction is self-contained, meaning that it performs its computation without any direct communication with other transactions. Transactions do communicate indirectly, of course, by storing and retrieving data in the database. However, this is the *only* way they can affect each other's execution.

To ensure transaction atomicity, the DBS must control all of the ways that transactions interact. This means that the DBS must mediate each transaction's operations that can affect other transactions. In our model, the only such operations are accesses to shared data. Since a transaction accesses shared data by issuing database operations to the DBS, the DBS can control all such actions, as required.

In many systems, transactions are allowed to communicate by sending messages. We allow such message communication in our model, provided that those messages are stored in the database. A transaction sends or receives a message by writing or reading the data item that holds the message.

This restriction on message communication only applies to messages *between* transactions. Two or more processes that are executing on behalf of the same transaction can freely exchange messages, and those messages need not be stored in the database. In general, a transaction is free to control its internal execution using any available mechanism. Only interactions between different transactions need to be controlled by the DBS.

1.2 RECOVERABILITY

The recovery system should make the DBS behave as if the database contains all of the effects of committed transactions and none of the effects of uncommitted ones. If transactions never abort, recovery is rather easy. Since all transactions eventually commit, the DBS simply executes database operations as they arrive. So to understand recovery, one must first look at the processing of Aborts.

When a transaction aborts, the DBS must wipe out its effects. The effects of a transaction T are of two kinds: effects on data, that is, values that T wrote in the database; and effects on other transactions, namely, transactions that read values written by T. Both should be obliterated.

The DBS should remove T's effects by restoring, for each data item x updated by T, the value x would have had if T had never taken place. We say that the DBS *undoes* T's Write operations.

The DBS should remove T's effects by aborting the affected transactions. Aborting these transactions may trigger further abortions, a phenomenon called *cascading abort*.

For example, suppose the initial values of x and y are 1, and suppose transactions T_1 and T_2 issue operations that the DBS executes in the following order:

$Write_1(x, 2)$; $Read_2(x)$; $Write_2(y, 3)$.

The subscript on each Read and Write denotes the transaction that issued it. Now, suppose T_1 aborts. Then the DBS undoes $Write_1(x, 2)$, restoring x to the value 1. Since T_2 read the value of x written by T_1, T_2 must be aborted too, a cascading abort. So, the DBS undoes $Write_2(y, 3)$, restoring y to 1.

Recall that by committing a transaction, the DBS guarantees that it will not subsequently abort the transaction. Given the possibility of cascading aborts, the DBS must be careful when it makes that guarantee. Even if a transaction T issues its Commit, the DBS may still need to abort T, because T may yet be involved in a cascading abort. This will happen if T read a data item from some transaction that subsequently aborts. Therefore, T cannot commit until all transactions that wrote values read by T are guaranteed not to abort, that is, are themselves committed. Executions that satisfy this condition are called *recoverable*.

This is an important concept so let's be more precise. We say a *transaction T_j reads x from transaction T_i in an execution*, if

1. T_j reads x after T_i has written into it;
2. T_i does not abort before T_j reads x; and
3. every transaction (if any) that writes x between the time T_i writes it and T_j reads it, aborts before T_j reads it.

A *transaction T_j reads from T_i* if T_j reads some data item from T_i. An execution is *recoverable* if, for every transaction T that commits, T's Commit follows the Commit of every transaction from which T read.

Recoverability is required to ensure that aborting a transaction does not change the semantics of committed transactions' operations. To see this, let's slightly modify our example of cascading aborts:

$Write_1(x, 2)$; $Read_2(x)$; $Write_2(y, 3)$; $Commit_2$.

This is not a recoverable execution, because T_2 read x from T_1 and yet the Commit of T_2 does *not* follow the Commit of T_1 (which is still active). The problem is what to do if T_1 now aborts. We can leave T_2 alone, which would violate the semantics of T_2's $Read(x)$ operation; $Read_2(x)$ actually returned the value 2, but given that T_1 has aborted, it should have returned the value that x had before $Write_1(x, 2)$ executed. Alternatively, we can abort T_2, which would violate the semantics of T_2's Commit. Either way we are doomed. However, if the DBS had delayed $Commit_2$, thus making the execution recoverable, there would be no problem with aborting T_2. The system, not having processed T_2's Commit, never promised that it would not abort T_2. In general, delaying the processing of certain Commits is one way the DBS can ensure that executions are recoverable.

Terminal I/O

Intuitively, an execution is recoverable if the DBS is always able to reverse the effects of an aborted transaction on other transactions. The definition of recoverable relies on the assumption that all such effects are through Reads and Writes. Without this assumption, the definition of recoverable does not correspond to its intuition.

There is one other type of interaction between transactions that calls the definition into question, namely, interactions through users. A transaction can interact with a terminal or other user-to-computer I/O device using **input** and **output** statements. Since a user can read the output of one transaction and, using that information, select information to feed as input to another transaction, **input** and **output** statements are another method by which transactions can indirectly communicate.

For example, suppose a transaction T_1 writes output to a terminal before it commits. Suppose a user reads that information on the terminal screen, and based on it decides to enter some input to another transaction T_2. Now suppose T_1 aborts. Indirectly, T_2 is executing operations based on the output of T_1 Since T_1 has aborted, T_2 should abort too, a cascading abort. Unfortunately, the DBS doesn't know about this dependency between T_1 and T_2, and therefore isn't in a position to ensure automatically that the cascading abort takes place.

In a sense, the error here is really the user's. Until the DBS writes the message "Transaction T_1 has committed" on the user's terminal, the user should not trust the output produced by T_1. Until that message appears, the user doesn't know whether T_1 will commit; it may abort and thereby invalidate its terminal output. In the previous paragraph, the user incorrectly assumed T_1's terminal output would be committed, and therefore prematurely propagated T_1's effects to another transaction.

The DBS can prevent users from prematurely propagating the effects of an uncommitted transaction T by *deferring* T's output statements until after T commits. Then the user will only see committed output.

It is often acceptable for the DBS to adopt this deferred output approach. In particular, it works well if each transaction requests all of its input from the user before it produces any output. But if a transaction T writes a message to a terminal and subsequently requests input from the user, deferring output puts the user in an untenable position. The user's response to T's input request may depend on the uncommitted output that he or she has not yet seen. In this case, the DBS must release the output to the terminal before T commits.

Suppose the DBS does release T's output and the user then responds to T's input request. Now suppose T aborts. Depending on the reason why T aborted, the user may choose to try executing T again. Since other transactions may have executed between the time T aborted and was restarted, T's second execution may be reading a different database state than its first execution. It may therefore produce different output, which may suggest to the user that different input is required than in T's first execution. Therefore, in reexecuting T, the DBS *cannot* reuse the terminal input from T's first execution.

Avoiding Cascading Aborts

Enforcing recoverability does not remove the possibility of cascading aborts. On the contrary, cascading aborts may have to take place precisely to guarantee that an execution is recoverable. Let's turn to our example again:

$Write_1(x, 2)$; $Read_2(x)$; $Write_2(y, 3)$; $Abort_1$.

This is a recoverable execution. T_2 must abort because if it *ever* committed, the execution would no longer be recoverable.

However, the prospect of cascading aborts is unpleasant. First, they require significant bookkeeping to keep track of which transactions have read from which others. Second, and more importantly, they entail the possibility of uncontrollably many transactions being forced to abort because some other transaction happened to abort. This is very undesirable. In practice, DBSs are designed to avoid cascading aborts.

We say that a DBS *avoids cascading aborts* (or is *cascadeless*) if it ensures that every transaction reads only those values that were written by committed transactions. Thus, only committed transactions can affect other transactions.

To achieve cascadelessness, the DBS must delay each $Read(x)$ until all transactions that have previously issued a $Write(x, val)$ have either aborted or committed. In doing so, recoverability is also achieved: a transaction must execute its Commit after having executed all its Reads and therefore after all the Commits of transactions from which it read.

Strict Executions

Unfortunately, from a practical viewpoint, avoiding cascading aborts is not always enough. A further restriction on executions is often desirable. To motivate this, consider the question of undoing a transaction's Writes. Intuitively, for each data item x that the transaction wrote, we want to restore the value x would have had if the transaction had never taken place. Let's make this more precise. Take any execution involving a transaction T that wrote into x. Suppose T aborts. If we assume that the execution avoids cascading aborts, no other transaction needs to be aborted. Now erase from the execution in question all operations that belong to T. This results in a new execution. "The value that x would have had if T had never occurred" is precisely the value of x in this new execution.

For example, consider

$Write_1(x, 1)$; $Write_1(y, 3)$; $Write_2(y, 1)$; $Commit_1$; $Read_2(x)$; $Abort_2$.

The execution that results if we erase the operations of T_2 is

$Write_1(x, 1); Write_1(y, 3); Commit_1.$

The value of y after this execution is obviously 3. This is the value that should be restored for y when T_2 aborts in the original execution.

The *before image* of a Write(x, val) operation in an execution is the value that x had just before this operation. For instance, in our previous example the before image of $Write_2(y, 1)$ is 3. It so happens that this is also the value that should be restored for y when T_2 (which issued $Write_2(y, 1)$) aborts. It is very convenient to implement Abort by restoring the before images of all Writes of a transaction. Many DBSs work this way. Unfortunately, this is not always correct, unless some further assumptions are made about executions. The following example illustrates the problems.

Suppose the initial value of x is 1. Consider the execution

$Write_1(x, 2); Write_2(x, 3); Abort_1.$

The before image of $Write_1(x, 2)$ is 1, the initial value of x. Yet the value of x that should be "restored" when T_1 aborts is 3, the value written by T_2. This is a case where aborting T_1 should not really affect x, because x was overwritten after it was written by T_1. Notice that there is no cascading abort here, because T_2 wrote x without having previously read it.

To take the example further, suppose that T_2 now aborts as well. That is, we have

$Write_1(x, 2); Write_2(x, 3); Abort_1; Abort_2.$

The before image of $Write_2(x, 3)$ is 2, the value written by T_1. However, the value of x after $Write_2(x, 3)$ is undone should be 1, the initial value of x (since both updates of x have been aborted). In this case the problem is that the before image was written by an aborted transaction.

This example illustrates discrepancies between the values that should be restored when a transaction aborts and the before images of the Writes issued by that transaction. Such discrepancies arise when two transactions, neither of which has terminated, have both written into the same data item. Note that if T_1 had aborted before T_2 wrote x (that is, if $Abort_1$ and $Write_2(x, 3)$ were interchanged in the previous example) there would be no problem. The before image of $Write_2(x, 3)$ would then be 1, not 2, since the transaction that wrote 2 would have already aborted. Thus when T_2 aborts, the before image of $Write_2(x, 3)$ would be the value that should be restored for x. Similarly, if T_1 had committed before T_2 wrote x, then the before image of $Write_2(x, 3)$ would be 2, again the value that should be restored for x if T_2 aborts.

We can avoid these problems by requiring that the execution of a Write(x, val) be delayed until all transactions that have previously written x are either committed or aborted. This is similar to the requirement that was needed to avoid cascading aborts. In that case we had to delay all Read(x) operations until all transactions that had previously written x had either committed or aborted.

Executions that satisfy *both* of these conditions are called *strict*. That is, a DBS that ensures strict executions delays both Reads and Writes for x until all transactions that have previously written x are committed or aborted. Strict executions avoid cascading aborts and are recoverable.

The requirement that executions be recoverable was born out of purely semantic considerations. Unless executions are recoverable, we cannot ensure the integrity of operation semantics. However, pragmatic considerations have led us to require an even stronger condition on the executions, namely, strictness. In this way cascading aborts are eliminated and the Abort operation can be implemented using before images.[2]

1.3 SERIALIZABILITY

Concurrency Control Problems

When two or more transactions execute concurrently, their database operations execute in an *interleaved* fashion. That is, operations from one program may execute in between two operations from another program. This interleaving can cause programs to behave incorrectly, or *interfere*, thereby leading to an inconsistent database. This interference is entirely due to the interleaving. That is, it can occur even if each program is coded correctly and no component of the system fails. The goal of concurrency control is to avoid interference and thereby avoid errors. To understand how programs can interfere with each other, let's look at some examples.

Returning to our banking example, suppose we have a program called Deposit, which deposits money into an account.

Procedure Deposit **begin**
    Start;
    input(account#, amount);
    temp := Read(Accounts[account#]);
    temp := temp + amount;
    Write(Accounts[account#], temp);
    Commit
end

Suppose account 13 has a balance of $1000 and customer 1 deposits $100 into account 13 at about the same time that customer 2 deposits $100,000 into account 13. Each customer invokes the Deposit program thereby creating a transaction to perform his or her update. The concurrent execution of these Deposits produces a sequence of Reads and Writes on the database, such as

---

[2]In [Gray et al. 75], strict executions are called *degree 2 consistent*. *Degree 1 consistency* means that a transaction may not overwrite uncommitted data, although it may read uncommitted data. *Degree 3 consistency* roughly corresponds to serializability, which is the subject of the next section.

$Read_1(Accounts[13])$ returns the value \$1000
$Read_2(Accounts[13])$ returns the value \$1000
$Write_2(Accounts[13], \$101,000)$
$Commit_2$
$Write_1(Accounts[13], \$1100)$
$Commit_1$

The result of this execution is that Accounts[13] contains \$1100. Although customer 2's deposit was successfully accomplished, its interference with customer 1's execution of Deposit caused customer 2's deposit to be lost. This *lost update* phenomenon occurs whenever two transactions, while attempting to modify a data item, both read the item's old value before either of them writes the item's new value.

Another concurrency control problem is illustrated by the following program, called PrintSum, which prints the sum of the balances of two accounts.

Procedure PrintSum **begin**
     Start;
     input(account1, account2);
     temp1 : = Read(Accounts[account1]);
     output(temp1);
     temp2 : = Read(Accounts[account2]);
     output(temp2);
     temp1 : = temp1 + temp2;
     output(temp1);
     Commit
end

Suppose accounts 7 and 86 each have a balance of \$200, and customer 3 prints the balances in accounts 7 and 86 (using PrintSum) at about the same time that customer 4 transfers \$100 from account 7 to account 86 (using Transfer, discussed previously under Transaction Syntax). The concurrent execution of these two transactions might lead to the following execution of Reads and Writes.

$Read_4(Accounts[7])$ returns the value \$200
$Write_4(Accounts[7], \$100)$
$Read_3(Accounts[7])$ returns the value \$100
$Read_3(Accounts[86])$ returns the value \$200
$Read_4(Accounts[86])$ returns the value \$200
$Write_4(Accounts[86], \$300)$
$Commit_4$
$Commit_3$

Transfer interferes with PrintSum in this execution, causing PrintSum to print the value $300, which is not the correct sum of balances in accounts 7 and 86. Printsum did not capture the $100 in transit from account 7 to 86. Notice that despite the interference, Transfer still installs the correct values in the database.

This type of interference is called an *inconsistent retrieval*. It occurs whenever a retrieval transaction reads one data item before another transaction updates it and reads another data item after the same transaction has updated it. That is, the retrieval only sees some of the update transaction's results.

Serializable Executions

In the preceding examples, the errors were caused by the interleaved execution of operations from different transactions. The examples do not exhaust *all* possible ways that concurrently executing transactions can interfere, but they do illustrate two problems that often arise from interleaving. To avoid these and other problems, the kinds of interleavings between transactions must be controlled.

One way to avoid interference problems is not to allow transactions to be interleaved at all. An execution in which no two transactions are interleaved is called serial. More precisely, an execution is *serial* if, for every pair of transactions, all of the operations of one transaction execute before any of the operations of the other. From a user's perspective, in a serial execution it looks as though transactions are operations that the DBS processes atomically. Serial executions are correct because each transaction individually is correct (by assumption), and transactions that execute serially cannot interfere with each other.

One could require that the DBS actually process transactions serially. However, this would mean that the DBS could not execute transactions concurrently, for concurrency means interleaved executions. Without such concurrency, the system may make poor use of its resources, and so might be too inefficient. Only in the simplest systems is serial execution a practical way to avoid interference.

We can broaden the class of allowable executions to include executions that have the same effect as serial ones. Such executions are called serializable. More precisely, an execution is *serializable* if it produces the same output and has the same effect on the database as some serial execution of the same transactions. Since serial executions are correct, and since each serializable execution has the same effect as a serial execution, serializable executions are correct too.

The executions illustrating lost updates and inconsistent retrievals are not serializable. For example, executing the two Deposit transactions serially, in either order, gives a different result than the interleaved execution that lost an update, so the interleaved execution is not serializable. Similarly, the interleaved execution of Transfer and PrintSum has a different effect than every serial execution of the two transactions, and so is not serializable.

Although these two interleaved executions are not serializable, many others are. For example, consider this interleaved execution of Transfer and PrintSum.

$Read_4(Accounts[7])$ returns the value \$200
$Write_4(Accounts[7], \$100)$
$Read_3(Accounts[7])$ returns the value \$100
$Read_4(Accounts[86])$ returns the value \$200
$Write_4(Accounts[86], \$300)$
$Commit_4$
$Read_3(Accounts[86])$ returns the value \$300
$Commit_3$

This execution has the same effect as serially executing Transfer followed by PrintSum. In such a serial execution, $Read_3(Accounts[7])$ immediately follows $Write_4(Accounts[86], \$300)$. Although the order of execution of operations in this serial execution is different from the interleaved execution, the effect of each operation is exactly the same as in the interleaved execution. Thus, the interleaved execution is serializable.

Serializability is the definition of correctness for concurrency control in DBSs. Given the importance of the concept, let us explore its strengths and weaknesses.

Most importantly, a DBS whose executions are serializable is easy to understand. To its users, it looks like a sequential transaction processor. A programmer can therefore write each transaction as if it will execute all by itself on a dedicated machine. Potential interference from other transactions is precluded and hence can be ignored.

A DBS that produces serializable executions avoids the kind of interference illustrated by the earlier examples of lost updates and inconsistent retrievals. A lost update occurs when two transactions both read the old value of a data item and subsequently both update that data item. This cannot happen in a serial execution, because one of the transactions reads the data item value written by the other. Since every serializable execution has the same effect as a serial execution, serializable executions avoid lost updates.

An inconsistent retrieval occurs when a retrieval transaction reads some data items before an update transaction updates them and reads some other data items after the update transaction updates them. This cannot happen in a serial execution, because the retrieval transaction reads all of the data items either before the update transaction performs any updates, or after the update transaction performs all of its updates. Since every serializable execution has the same effect as some serial execution, serializable executions avoid inconsistent retrievals too.

Consistency Preservation

The concept of consistent retrieval can be generalized to apply to the entire database, not just to the data items retrieved by one transaction. This generalization provides another explanation of the value of serializability.

Assume that some of the states of the database are defined to be *consistent*. The database designer defines *consistency predicates* that evaluate to true for the consistent states and false for the other (*inconsistent*) states. For example, suppose we augment the banking database of Accounts to include a data item, Total, which contains the sum of balances in all accounts. A consistency predicate for this database might be "Total is the sum of balances in Accounts." The database state is consistent if and only if (*iff*) the predicate is true.

As part of transaction correctness, we then require that each transaction *preserve database consistency*. That is, whenever a transaction executes on a database state that is initially consistent, it must leave the database in a consistent state after it terminates. For example, Transfer preserves database consistency, but Deposit does not, because it does not update Total after depositing money into an account. To preserve database consistency, Deposit needs to be modified to update Total appropriately.

Notice that each Write in Transfer, taken by itself, does not preserve database consistency. For example, Write(Accounts[oldaccount], temp − amount) unbalances the accounts temporarily, because after it executes, Accounts and Total are inconsistent. Such inconsistencies are common after a transaction has done some but not all of its Writes. However, as long as a transaction fixes such inconsistencies before it terminates, the overall effect is to preserve consistency, and so the transaction is correct.

Consistency preservation captures the concept of producing database states that are meaningful. If each transaction preserves database consistency, then any serial execution of transactions preserves database consistency. This follows from the fact that each transaction leaves the database in a consistent state for the next transaction. Since every serializable execution has the same effect as some serial execution, serializable executions preserve database consistency too.

Ordering Transactions

All serializable executions are equally correct. Therefore, the DBS may execute transactions in *any* order, as long as the effect is the same as that of *some* serial order. However, not all serial executions produce the same effect. Sometimes a user may prefer one serial execution of transactions over another. In such a case, it is the *user's* responsibility to ensure that the preferred order actually occurs.

For example, a user may want her Deposit transaction to execute before her Transfer transaction. In such a case, she should not submit the transactions at the same time. If she does, the DBS can execute the transactions' operations in any order (e.g., the Transfer before the Deposit). Rather, she should first submit the Deposit transaction. Only after the system acknowledges that the Deposit transaction is committed should she submit the Transfer transaction. This guarantees that the transactions are executed in the desired order.[3]

We will be constructing schedulers that only guarantee serializability. If users must ensure that transactions execute in a particular order, they must secure that order by mechanisms outside the DBS.

Limitations of Serializability

In many types of computer applications, serializability is not an appropriate goal for controlling concurrent executions. In fact, the concept of transaction may not even be present. In these applications, methods for attaining serializability are simply not relevant.

For example, a statistical application may be taking averages over large amounts of data that is continually updated. Although inconsistent retrievals may result from some interleavings of Reads and Writes, such inconsistencies may only have a small effect on the calculation of averages, and so may be unimportant. By not controlling the interleavings of Reads and Writes, the DBS can often realize a significant performance benefit — at the expense of serializability.

As another example, process control programs may execute forever, each gathering or analyzing data to control a physical process. Since programs never terminate, serial executions don't make sense. Thus, serializability is not a reasonable goal.

A common goal for concurrency control in systems with nonterminating programs is *mutual exclusion*. Mutual exclusion requires the section of a program that accesses a shared resource to be executed by at most one program at a time. Such a section is called a *critical section*. We can view a critical section as a type of transaction. Mutual exclusion ensures that critical sections (i.e., transactions) that access the same resource execute serially. This is a strong form of serializability.

---

[3]If two transactions do not interact, then it is possible that the user cannot control their effective order of execution. For example, suppose the user waits for T_1 to commit before submitting T_2, and suppose no data item is accessed by both transactions. If other transactions were executing concurrently with T_1 and T_2, it is still possible that the only serial execution equivalent to the interleaved execution that occurred is one in which T_2 precedes T_1. This is odd, but possibly doesn't matter since T_1 and T_2 don't interact. However, consider the discussion of Terminal I/O in Section 1.2. If the user uses the output of T_1 to construct the input to T_2, then T_1 *must* effectively execute before T_2. This incorrect behavior is prevented by the most popular concurrency control method, two phase locking (see Chapter 3), but not by all methods. This rather subtle point is explored further in Exercises 2.12 and 3.4.

Many techniques have been developed for solving the mutual exclusion problem, including locks, semaphores, and monitors. Given the close relationship between mutual exclusion and serializability, it is not surprising that some mutual exclusion techniques have been adapted for use in attaining serializability. We will see examples of these techniques in later chapters.

1.4 DATABASE SYSTEM MODEL

In our study of concurrency control and recovery, we need a model of the internal structure of a DBS. In our model, a DBS consists of four *modules* (see Fig. 1–1): a *transaction manager*, which performs any required preprocessing of database and transaction operations it receives from transactions; a *scheduler*, which controls the relative order in which database and transaction operations are executed; a *recovery manager*, which is responsible for transaction commitment and abortion; and a *cache manager*, which operates directly on the database.[4]

Database and transaction operations issued by a transaction to the DBS are first received by the transaction manager. The operations then move down through the scheduler, recovery manager, and cache manager. Thus, each module sends requests to and receives replies from the next lower level module.

We emphasize that this model of a DBS is an *abstract* model. It does not correspond to the software architecture of any DBS we know of. The modules themselves are often more tightly integrated, and therefore less clearly separable, than the model would suggest. Still, for pedagogical reasons, we believe it is important to cleanly separate concurrency control and recovery from other functions of a DBS. This also makes the model a good tool for thought. In later chapters, we will discuss more realistic software architectures for performing the functions of the model.

For most of this section, we will assume that the DBS executes on a *centralized* computer system. Roughly speaking, this means the system consists of a central processor, some main memory, secondary storage devices (usually disks), and I/O devices. We also consider any multiprocessor configuration in which each processor has direct access to all of main memory and to all I/O devices to be a centralized system. A system with two or more processors that do not have direct access to shared main memory or secondary storage devices is called a *distributed* computer system. We extend our model of a centralized DBS to a distributed environment in the final subsection.

---

[4][Gray 78] uses "transaction manager" to describe what we call the scheduler and recovery manager, and "database manager" to describe what we call the transaction manager and cache manager.

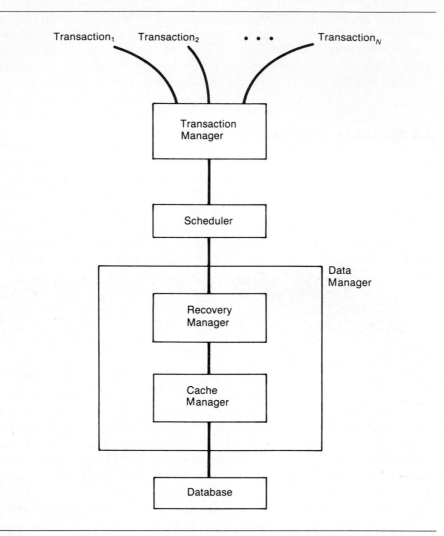

FIGURE 1–1
Centralized Database System

The Cache Manager

A computer system ordinarily offers both volatile and stable storage. *Volatile storage* can be accessed very efficiently, but is susceptible to hardware and operating system failures. Due to its relatively high cost, it is limited in size. *Stable storage* is resistant to failures, but can only be accessed more slowly. Due to its relatively low cost, it is usually plentiful. In today's technology, volatile storage is typically implemented by semiconductor memory and stable storage is implemented by disk devices.

Due to the limited size of volatile storage, the DBS can only keep part of the database in volatile storage at any time. The portion of volatile storage set aside for holding parts of the database is called the *cache*. Managing the cache is the job of the *cache manager (CM)*. The CM moves data between volatile and stable storage in response to requests from higher layers of the DBS.

Specifically, the CM supports operations Fetch(x) and Flush(x). To process Fetch(x), the CM retrieves x from stable storage into volatile storage. To process Flush(x), the CM transfers the copy of x from volatile storage into stable storage.

There are times when the CM is unable to process a Fetch(x) because there is no space in volatile storage for x. To solve this problem, the CM must make room by flushing some other data item from volatile storage. Thus, in addition to supporting the Flush operation for higher levels of the DBS, the CM sometimes executes a Flush for its own purposes.

The Recovery Manager

The *recovery manager (RM)* is primarily responsible for ensuring that the database contains all of the effects of committed transactions and none of the effects of aborted ones. It supports the operations Start, Commit, Abort, Read, and Write. It processes these operations by using the Fetch and Flush operations of the CM.

The RM is normally designed to be resilient to failures in which the entire contents of volatile memory are lost. Such failures are called *system failures*. After the computer system recovers from a system failure, the RM must ensure that the database contains the effects of all committed transactions and no effects of transactions that were aborted or active at the time of the failure. It should eliminate the effects of transactions that were active at the time of failure, because those transactions lost their internal states due to the loss of main memory's contents and therefore cannot finish executing and commit.

After a system failure, the only information the RM has available is the contents of stable storage. Since the RM never knows when a system failure might occur, it must be very careful about moving data between volatile and stable storage. Otherwise, it may be caught after a system failure in one of two unrecoverable situations: (1) stable storage does not contain an update by some committed transaction, or (2) stable storage contains the value of x written by some uncommitted transaction, but does not contain the last value of x that was written by a committed transaction. To avoid these problems, the RM may need to restrict the situations in which the CM can unilaterally decide to execute a Flush.

The RM may also be designed to be resilient to failures of portions of stable storage, called *media failures*. To do this, it needs to keep redundant copies of data on at least two different stable storage devices that are unlikely to fail at the same time. To cope with media failures, it again needs to be able to return the database to a state that contains all of the updates of committed transactions and none of the updates of uncommitted ones.

It will frequently be useful to deal with the RM and CM as if it were a single module. We use the term *data manager* (DM) to denote that module. The interface to this module is exactly that of the RM. That is, CM functions are hidden from higher levels.

Schedulers

A scheduler is a program or collection of programs that controls the concurrent execution of transactions. It exercises this control by restricting the order in which the DM executes Reads, Writes, Commits, and Aborts of different transactions. Its goal is to order these operations so that the resulting execution is serializable and recoverable. It may also ensure that the execution avoids cascading aborts or is strict.

To execute a database operation, a transaction passes that operation to the scheduler. After receiving the operation, the scheduler can take one of three actions:

1. Execute: It can pass the operation to the DM. When the DM finishes executing the operation, it informs the scheduler. Moreover, if the operation is a Read, the DM returns the value(s) it read, which the scheduler relays back to the transaction.

2. Reject: It can refuse to process the operation, in which case it tells the transaction that its operation has been rejected. This causes the transaction to abort. The Abort can be issued by the transaction or by the transaction manager.

3. Delay: It can delay the operation by placing it in a queue internal to the scheduler. Later, it can remove the operation from the queue and either execute it or reject it. In the interim (while the operation is being delayed), the scheduler is free to schedule other operations.

Using its three basic actions — executing an operation, rejecting it, or delaying it — the scheduler can control the order in which operations are executed. When it receives an operation from the transaction, it usually tries to pass it to the DM right away, if it can do so without producing a nonserializable execution. If it decides that executing the operation may produce an incorrect result, then it either delays the operation (if it may be able to correctly process the operation in the future) or reject the operation (if it will never be able to correctly process the operation in the future). Thus, it uses execution, delay, and rejection of operations to help produce correct executions.

For example, let's reconsider from the last section the concurrent execution of two Deposit transactions, which deposit $100 and $100,000 into account 13:

$Read_1(Accounts[13])$;
$Read_2(Accounts[13])$;
$Write_2(Accounts[13], \$101,000)$;
$Commit_2$;
$Write_1(Accounts[13], \$1100)$;
$Commit_1$.

To avoid this nonserializable execution, a scheduler might decide to reject $Write_1$, thereby causing transaction T_1 to abort. In this case, the user or transaction manager can resubmit T_1, which can now execute without interfering with T_2. Alternatively, the scheduler could prevent the above execution by delaying $Read_2$ until after it receives and processes $Write_1$. By delaying $Read_2$, it avoids having to reject $Write_1$ later on.

The scheduler is quite limited in the information it can use to decide when to execute each operation. We assume that it can only use the information that it obtains from the operations that transactions submit. The scheduler does *not* know any details about the programs comprising the transactions, except as conveyed to it by operations. It can predict neither the operations that will be submitted in the future nor the relative order in which these operations will be submitted. When this type of advance knowledge about programs or operations is needed to make good scheduling decisions, the transactions must explicitly supply this information to the scheduler via additional operations. Unless stated otherwise, we assume such information is not available.

The study of concurrency control techniques is the study of scheduler algorithms that attain serializability and either recoverability, cascadelessness, or strictness. Most of this book is devoted to the design of such algorithms.

Transaction Manager

Transactions interact with the DBS through a *transaction manager* (*TM*). The TM receives database and transaction operations issued by transactions and forwards them to the scheduler. Depending on the specific concurrency control and recovery algorithms that are used, the TM may also perform other functions. For example, in a distributed DBS the TM is responsible for determining which site should process each operation submitted by a transaction. We'll discuss this more in a moment.

Ordering Operations

Much of the activity of concurrency control and recovery is ensuring that operations are executed in a certain order. It is important that we be clear and precise about the order in which each module processes the operations that are presented to it. In the following discussion, we use the generic term *module* to describe any of the four DBS components: TM, scheduler, RM, or CM.

At any time, a module is allowed to execute *any* of the unexecuted operations that have been submitted to it. For example, even if the scheduler submits operation p to the RM before operation q, the RM is allowed to execute q before p.

When a module wants two operations to execute in a particular order, it is the job of the module that *issues* the operations to ensure that the desired order is enforced. For example, if the scheduler wants p to execute before q, then it should first pass p to the RM and wait for the RM to acknowledge p's execution; after the acknowledgment, it can pass q, thereby guaranteeing that p executes before q. This sequence of events — pass an operation, wait for an acknowledgment, pass another operation — is called a *handshake*. We assume that each module uses handshaking whenever it wants to control the order in which another module executes the operations it submits.

As an alternative to handshaking, one could enforce the order of execution of operations by having modules communicate through *first-in–first-out queues*. Each module receives operations from its input queue in the same order that the operations were placed in the queue, and each module is required to process operations in the order they are received. For example, if the CM were to use an input queue, then the RM could force the CM to execute p before q by placing p in the queue before q.

We do not use queues for intermodule communication for two reasons. First, they unnecessarily force a module to process operations strictly sequentially. For example, even if the RM doesn't care in what order p and q are executed, by placing them in the CM queue it forces the CM to process them in a particular order. In our model, if the RM doesn't care in which order p and q are processed, then it would pass p and q without handshaking, so the CM could process the operations in either order.

Second, when three or more modules are involved in processing operations, queues may not be powerful enough to enforce orders of operations. For example, suppose two modules perform the function of data manager, say DM_1 and DM_2. (DM_1 and DM_2 might be at different sites of a distributed system.) And suppose the scheduler wants DM_1 to process p before DM_2 processes q. The scheduler can enforce this order using handshaking, but not using queues. Even if DM_1 and DM_2 share an input queue, they need a handshake to ensure the desired order of operations.

Except when we explicitly state otherwise, we assume that handshaking is used for enforcing the order of execution of operations.

Distributed Database System Architecture

A *distributed database system* (or *distributed DBS*) is a collection of *sites* connected by a communication network (see Fig. 1–2). We assume that two

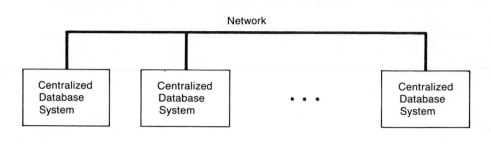

FIGURE 1–2
Distributed Database System

processes can exchange messages whether they are located at the same site or at different sites (in which case the messages are sent over the communication network).

Each site is a centralized DBS, which stores a portion of the database. We assume that each data item is stored at exactly one site.[5] Each transaction consists of one or more processes that execute at one or more sites. We assume that a transaction issues each of its operations to whichever TM is most convenient (e.g., the closest). When a TM receives a transaction's Read or Write that cannot be serviced at its site, the TM forwards that operation to the scheduler at another site that has the data needed to process the operation. Thus, each TM can communicate with every scheduler by sending messages over the network.

BIBLIOGRAPHIC NOTES

Research publications on transaction management began appearing in the early to mid 1970s [Bjork 72, Davies 72], [Bjork 73] [Chamberlin, Boyce, Traiger 74], and [Davies 73], although the problem was probably studied even earlier by designers of the first on-line systems in the 1960s. By 1976, it was an active research area with a steady stream of papers appearing. Some of the early influential ones include [Eswaran et al. 76], [Gray et al. 75], and [Stearns, Lewis, Rosenkrantz 76].

Concurrency control problems had been treated in the context of operating systems beginning in the mid 1960s. [Ben-Ari 82], [Brinch Hansen 73], and [Holt et al. 78] survey this work, as do most textbooks on operating systems.

Recovery was first treated in the context of fault-tolerant hardware design, and later in general purpose program design. Elements of the transaction concept appeared in the

---

[5]In Chapter 8, on replicated data, we will allow a data item to be stored at multiple sites.

"recovery block" proposal of [Horning et al. 74]. Atomic actions (transactions) in this context were proposed in [Lomet 77b]. Surveys of hardware and software approaches to fault tolerance appear in [Anderson, Lee 81], [Shrivastava 85], and [Siewiorek 82].

An interesting extension of the transaction abstraction is to allow transactions to be nested as subtransactions within larger ones. Several forms of nested transactions have been implemented [Gray 81], [Liskov, Scheifler 83], [Moss 85], [Mueller, Moore, Popek 83], and [Reed 78]. Theoretical aspects of nested transactions are described in [Beeri et al. 83], [Lynch 83b], and [Moss, Griffeth, Graham 86]. We do not cover nested transactions in this book.

EXERCISES

1.1   For each of the example executions in Section 1.2, determine if it is serializable, assuming each active transaction ultimately commits.

1.2   Explain why each example execution in Section 1.3 is or is not recoverable, cascadeless, or strict.

1.3   Suppose transaction T_1 reads x, then reads y, then writes x, and then writes y. Suppose T_2 reads y and then writes x. Give example executions of T_1 and T_2 that are serializable and

    a. recoverable but not cascadeless;

    b. cascadeless but not strict; and

    c. strict.

    Now, give example executions that are *not* serializable and satisfy (a), (b), and (c).

1.4   We assumed that transactions only interact through their accesses to the database. We can weaken this assumption slightly by allowing transactions to exchange messages that are not part of the database in the following case: A transaction T_1 can receive a message from transaction T_1 provided that the DBS processed T_1's Commit before it processed T_2's Read of T_1's message. Explain why this weakened assumption is still satisfactory by analyzing its effects on recoverability and serializability.

1.5   Using the banking database of this chapter, write a program that takes two account numbers as input, determines which account has the larger balance, and replaces the balance of the smaller account by that of the larger. What are the possible sequences of Reads and Writes that your program can issue?

1.6   Give an example program for the banking application that, when executed as a transaction, has terminal output that cannot be deferred.

2
SERIALIZABILITY THEORY

2.1 HISTORIES

Serializability theory is a mathematical tool that allows us to prove whether or not a scheduler works correctly. In the theory, we represent a concurrent execution of a set of transactions by a structure called a history. A history is called serializable if it represents a serializable execution. The theory gives precise properties that a history must satisfy to be serializable.

Transactions

We begin our development of serializability theory by describing how transactions are modelled. As we said in Chapter 1, a transaction is a particular execution of a program that manipulates the database by means of Read and Write operations. From the viewpoint of serializability theory, a transaction is a representation of such an execution that identifies the Read and Write operations and indicates the order in which these operations execute. For each Read and Write, the transaction specifies the name, but not the value, of the data item read and written (respectively). In addition, the transaction contains a Commit or Abort as its last operation, to indicate whether the execution it represents terminated successfully or not.

For example, an execution of the following program

Procedure P **begin**
    Start;
    temp : = Read(x);
    temp : = temp + 1;
    Write(x, temp);
    Commit
end

OXSTALLS
CAMPUS LIBRARY
C&G C.H.E, Oxstalls Lane,
Gloucester, GL2 9HW
Tel (0452) 426718

may be represented as: $r_1[x] \rightarrow w_1[x] \rightarrow c_1$. The subscripts identify this particular transaction and distinguish it from other transactions that happen to access the same data items in the same order—for instance, other executions of the same program.

In general, we use $r_i[x]$ (or $w_i[x]$) to denote the execution of a Read (or Write) issued by transaction T_i on data item x. To keep this notation unambiguous, we assume that no transaction reads or writes a data item more than once. None of the results in this chapter depend on this assumption (see Exercise 2.10). We use c_i and a_i to denote T_i's Commit and Abort operations (respectively). In a particular transaction, only one of these two can appear. The arrows indicate the order in which operations execute. Thus in the example, $w_1[x]$ follows ("happens after") $r_1[x]$ and precedes ("happens before") c_1.

As we saw in Chapter 1, a transaction may be generated by concurrently executing programs. For example, a program that reads data items x and y and writes their sum into z might issue the two Reads in parallel. This type of execution is modelled as a *partial* order. In other words, the transaction need not specify the order of every two operations that appear in it. For instance, the transaction just mentioned would be represented as:

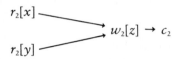

This says that $w_2[z]$ must happen after both $r_2[x]$ and $r_2[y]$, but that the order in which $r_2[x]$ and $r_2[y]$ take place is unspecified and therefore arbitrary.

If a transaction both reads and writes a data item x, we require that the partial order specify the relative order of Read(x) and Write(x). This is because the order of execution of these operations necessarily matters. The value of x returned by Read(x) depends on whether this operation precedes or follows Write(x).

We want to formalize the definition of a transaction as a partial ordering of operations. In mathematics, it is common practice to write a partial order as an ordered pair $(\Sigma, <)$, where Σ is the set of elements being ordered and $<$ is the ordering relation.[1] In this notation, we would define a transaction T_i to be an ordered pair $(\Sigma_i, <_i)$, where Σ_i is the set of operations of T_i and $<_i$ indicates the execution order of those operations.

This notation is a bit more complex than we need. We can do away with the symbol Σ by using the name of the partial order, in this case T_i, to denote *both* the partial order and the set of elements (i.e., operations) in the partial order. The meaning of a symbol that denotes both a partial order and its elements, such as T_i, will always be clear from context. In particular, when we write $r_i[x] \in T_i$, meaning that $r_i[x]$ is an element (i.e., operation) of T_i, we are

---

[1] The definition of partial orders is given in Section A.4 of the Appendix.

using T_i to denote the set of operations in the partial order. We are now ready to give the formal definition.

A *transaction* T_i is a partial order with ordering relation $<_i$ where

1. $T_i \subseteq \{r_i[x], w_i[x] \mid x \text{ is a data item}\} \cup \{a_i, c_i\};$

2. $a_i \in T_i$ iff $c_i \notin T_i;$

3. if t is c_i or a_i (whichever is in T_i), for any other operation $p \in T_i$, $p <_i t;$ and

4. if $r_i[x], w_i[x] \in T_i$, then either $r_i[x] <_i w_i[x]$ or $w_i[x] <_i r_i[x]$.

In words, condition (1) defines the kinds of operations in the transaction. Condition (2) says that this set contains a Commit or an Abort, but not both. $<_i$ indicates the order of operations. Condition (3) says that the Commit or Abort (whichever is present) must follow all other operations. Condition (4) requires that $<_i$ specify the order of execution of Read and Write operations on a common data item.

We'll usually draw transactions as in the examples we've seen so far, that is, as directed acyclic graphs[2] (dags) with the arrows indicating the ordering defined by $<_i$. To see the relationship between the two notations, consider the following transaction.

$$r_2[x] \searrow$$
$$w_2[z] \to c_2$$
$$r_2[y] \nearrow$$

Formally, this says that T_2 consists of the operations $\{r_2[x], r_2[y], w_2[z], c_2\}$ and $<_2 = \{(r_2[x], w_2[z]), (r_2[y], w_2[z]), (w_2[z], c_2), (r_2[x], c_2), (r_2[y], c_2)\}$.[3] Note that we generally do not draw arcs implied by transitivity. For example, the arc $r_2[x] \to c_2$ is implied by $r_2[x] \to w_2[z]$ and $w_2[z] \to c_2$.

Our formal definition of a transaction does not capture every observable aspect of the transaction execution it models. For example, it does not describe the initial values of data items or the values written by Writes. Moreover, it only describes the database operations, and not, for example, assignment or conditional statements. Features of the execution that are not modelled by transactions are called *uninterpreted*, meaning unspecified. When analyzing transactions or building schedulers, we must be careful not to make assumptions about uninterpreted features. For example, we must ensure that our analysis holds for all possible initial states of the database and for all possible computations that a program might perform in between issuing its Reads and Writes. Otherwise, our analysis may be incorrect for some database states or computations.

---

[2]The definition of dags and their relationship to partial orders is given in Sections A.3 and A.4 of the Appendix.

[3]A standard notation for a binary relation $<_2$ is the set of pairs (x, y) such that $x <_2 y$.

For example, in the transaction $r_i[x] \rightarrow w_i[x] \rightarrow c_i$, we cannot make any assumptions about the initial value of x or the computation performed by T_i in between the Read and Write. In particular, we cannot tell whether or not the value written into x by the Write depends on the value of x that was read. To ensure that our analysis is valid for all interpretations of a transaction, we assume that each value written by a transaction depends on the values of all the data items that it previously read. To put it more formally, for every transaction T_i and for all data items x and y, the value written by $w_i[x]$ is an arbitrary function of the values read by all $r_i[y] <_i w_i[x]$.

You may object that the value written by $w_i[x]$ might also depend on information supplied to T_i by input statements executed before $w_i[x]$. This is true and is a good reason for including input statements in transactions. But we can take care of this without expanding the repertoire of operations by modelling input statements as Reads and output statements as Writes. Each such Read or Write operates on a *unique* data item, one that is referenced by no other operation. These data items must be unique to accurately model the fact that a value read from or written to a terminal or similar I/O device by one transaction isn't read or written by any other transaction. For example, a Write to a terminal produces a value that is not read by any subsequent Read on that terminal. In this way we can incorporate input and output statements in our model of executions without complicating the model.

The choice of what information to incorporate in a formal model of a transaction and what information to leave out is based on the scheduler's view of the system. Our model includes only those aspects of a transaction that we choose to allow the DBS's scheduler to exploit when trying to attain a serializable execution. Of course, we must give the scheduler enough information to successfully avoid nonserializable executions. As we will see, we have defined transactions in a way that satisfies this requirement.

Histories

When a set of transactions execute concurrently, their operations may be interleaved. We model such an execution by a structure called a history. A history indicates the order in which the operations of the transactions were executed relative to each other. Since some of these operations may be executed in parallel, a history is defined as a *partial* order. If transaction T_i specifies the order of two of its operations, these two operations must appear in that order in any history that includes T_i. In addition, we require that a history specify the order of all *conflicting operations* that appear in it.

Two operations are said to *conflict* if they both operate on the same data item and at least one of them is a Write. Thus, Read(x) conflicts with Write(x), while Write(x) conflicts with both Read(x) and Write(x). If two operations conflict, their order of execution matters. The value of x returned by Read(x) depends on whether or not that operation precedes or follows a particular

Write(x). Also, the final value of x depends on which of two Write(x) operations is processed last.

Formally, let $T = \{T_1, T_2, ..., T_n\}$ be a set of transactions. A *complete history* H over T is a partial order with ordering relation $<_H$ where:

1. $H = \bigcup_{i=1}^{n} T_i$;

2. $<_H \supseteq \bigcup_{i=1}^{n} <_i$; and

3. for any two conflicting operations $p, q \in H$, either $p <_H q$ or $q <_H p$.

Condition (1) says that the execution represented by H involves precisely the operations submitted by $T_1, T_2, ..., T_n$. Condition (2) says that the execution honors all operation orderings specified within each transaction. Finally, condition (3) says that the ordering of every pair of conflicting operations is determined by $<_H$. When the history under consideration is clear from the context, we drop the H subscript from $<_H$.

A *history* is simply a prefix of a complete history.[4] Thus a history represents a possibly incomplete execution of transactions. As we mentioned in Chapter 1, we'll be interested in handling various types of failures, notably failures of the DBS. Such a failure may interrupt the execution of active transactions. Therefore our theory of executions must accommodate arbitrary histories, not merely complete ones. We draw histories as dags, employing the same conventions as for transactions.

To illustrate these definitions consider three transactions.

$$T_1 = r_1[x] \rightarrow w_1[x] \rightarrow c_1$$
$$T_3 = r_3[x] \rightarrow w_3[y] \rightarrow w_3[x] \rightarrow c_3$$
$$T_4 = r_4[y] \rightarrow w_4[x] \rightarrow w_4[y] \rightarrow w_4[z] \rightarrow c_4$$

A complete history over $\{T_1, T_3, T_4\}$ is

$$
\begin{array}{ll}
& r_3[x]\rightarrow w_3[y]\rightarrow w_3[x]\rightarrow c_3 \\
& \quad\uparrow \qquad\quad \uparrow \\
H_1 = & r_4[y] \rightarrow w_4[x]\rightarrow w_4[y]\rightarrow w_4[z]\rightarrow c_4 \\
& \quad\uparrow \\
& r_1[x] \rightarrow w_1[x]\rightarrow c_1
\end{array}
$$

A history over the same three transactions (that also happens to be a prefix of H_1) is

$$
\begin{array}{ll}
& r_3[x]\rightarrow w_3[y] \\
& \quad\uparrow \qquad\quad \uparrow \\
H_1' = & r_4[y] \rightarrow w_4[x]\rightarrow w_4[y] \\
& \quad\uparrow \\
& r_1[x] \rightarrow w_1[x]\rightarrow c_1
\end{array}
$$

---

[4]See Section A.4 of the Appendix for the definition of prefix of a partial order.

As usual we do not draw all arrows implied by transitivity.

We will often deal with histories that are total orders of operations, such as:

$$r_1[x] \rightarrow r_3[x] \rightarrow w_1[x] \rightarrow c_1 \rightarrow w_3[y] \rightarrow w_3[x] \rightarrow c_3.$$

We will normally drop the arrows when writing such histories, as in:

$$r_1[x] \; r_3[x] \; w_1[x] \; c_1 \; w_3[y] \; w_3[x] \; c_3.$$

A transaction T_i is *committed* (or *aborted*) in history H if $c_i \in H$ (or $a_i \in H$). T_i is *active* in H if it is neither committed nor aborted. Of course a complete history has no active transactions. Given a history H, the *committed projection of H*, denoted $C(H)$, is the history obtained from H by deleting all operations that do not belong to transactions committed in H.[5]

Note that $C(H)$ is a complete history over the set of committed transactions in H. If H represents an execution at some point in time, $C(H)$ is the only part of the execution we can count on, since active transactions can be aborted at any time, for instance, in the event of a system failure.

2.2 SERIALIZABLE HISTORIES

Histories represent concurrent executions of transactions. We are now ready to characterize serializable histories, that is, histories that represent serializable executions. Recall that an execution is serializable if it's equivalent to a serial execution of the same transactions. Our plan is to

□ define conditions under which two histories are equivalent;

□ define conditions under which a history is serial; and

□ define a history to be serializable if it is equivalent to a serial one.

Equivalence of Histories

We define two histories H and H' to be *equivalent* ($\equiv$) if

1. they are defined over the same set of transactions and have the same operations; and

2. they order conflicting operations of nonaborted transactions in the same way; that is, for any conflicting operations p_i and q_j belonging to transactions T_i and T_j (respectively) where $a_i, a_j \notin H$, if $p_i <_H q_j$ then $p_i <_{H'} q_j$.[6]

---

[5]More formally, $C(H)$ is the restriction of H on domain $\cup_{c_i \in H} T_i$ (cf. Section A.4 of the Appendix.)

[6]Note that this implies: $p_i <_H q_j$ iff $p_i <_{H'} q_j$ (why?).

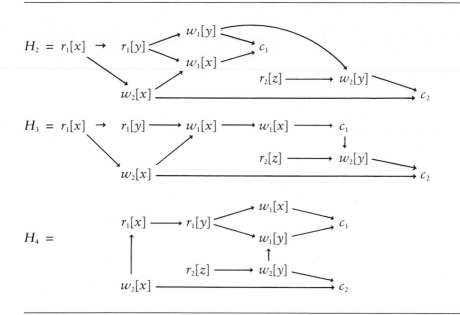

FIGURE 2–1
Example Histories
H_2 and H_3 are equivalent, but H_4 is not equivalent to either.

The idea underlying this definition is that the outcome of a concurrent execution of transactions depends only on the relative ordering of conflicting operations. To see this observe that executing two nonconflicting operations in either order has the same computational effect. Conversely, the computational effect of executing two conflicting operations depends on their relative order.

For example, given the three histories shown in Fig. 2-1, $H_2 \equiv H_3$ but H_4 is not equivalent to either. (Keep in mind the orderings implied transitively by the arrows shown.)

Serializable Histories

A complete history H is *serial* if, for every two transactions T_i and T_j that appear in H, either all operations of T_i appear before all operations of T_j or vice versa. Thus, a serial history represents an execution in which there is no interleaving of the operations of different transactions. Each transaction executes from beginning to end before the next one can start.

We'll often denote a serial history over $\{T_1, T_2, .., T_n\}$ as $T_{i_1} T_{i_2} \ldots T_{i_n}$ where $i_1, i_2, \ldots, i_n$ is a permutation of 1, 2, ..., n. This means that T_{i_1} appears first in the serial history, T_{i_2} second, and so on.

At this point we would like to define a history H to be serializable if it is equivalent to some serial history H_s. This would be a perfectly reasonable definition if H were a *complete* history. Otherwise there are problems. First, there is an artificial problem in that a partial history can never be equivalent to a serial one. This is because serial histories must be complete by definition, and two histories can be equivalent only if they contain the same set of operations. But even assuming for the moment that we did not insist on serial histories being complete, we would still have a problem—a problem of substance and not mere definition. Namely, an incomplete execution of a transaction does not necessarily preserve the consistency of the database. Thus, serializability would be an inappropriate correctness condition if it merely stated that a history be computationally equivalent to a serial execution of some possibly partial transactions, since such a history does not necessarily represent a consistency preserving execution.

We are therefore led to a slightly more complex definition of serializability. Although more complex, the definition is still natural and, most importantly, sound. A history H is *serializable* (*SR*) if its committed projection, $C(H)$, is equivalent to a serial history H_s.

This takes care of the problems, because $C(H)$ is a *complete* history. Moreover, it is not an arbitrarily chosen complete history. If H represents the execution so far, it is really only the *committed* transactions whose execution the DBS has unconditionally guaranteed. All other transactions may be aborted.

2.3 THE SERIALIZABILITY THEOREM

We can determine whether a history is serializable by analyzing a graph derived from the history called a serialization graph. Let H be a history over $T = \{T_1, ..., T_n\}$. The *serialization graph* (*SG*) for H, denoted $SG(H)$, is a directed graph whose nodes are the transactions in T that are committed in H and whose edges are all $T_i \rightarrow T_j$ $(i \neq j)$ such that one of T_i's operations precedes and conflicts with one of T_j's operations in H. For example:

$$H_s = \begin{array}{c} r_3[x] \rightarrow w_3[x] \rightarrow c_3 \\ \nearrow \\ r_1[x] \rightarrow w_1[x] \rightarrow w_1[y] \rightarrow c_1 \\ \nearrow \qquad \nearrow \\ r_2[x] \rightarrow w_2[y] \rightarrow c_2 \end{array}$$

$$SG(H_s) = \quad T_2 \rightarrow T_1 \rightarrow T_3$$

The edge $T_1 \rightarrow T_3$ is in $SG(H_s)$ because $w_1[x] < r_3[x]$, and the edge $T_2 \rightarrow T_3$ is in $SG(H_s)$ because $r_2[x] < w_3[x]$. Notice that a single edge in $SG(H_s)$ can be present because of more than one pair of conflicting operations. For instance, the edge $T_2 \rightarrow T_1$ is caused both by $r_2[x] < w_1[x]$ and $w_2[y] < w_1[y]$.

In general, the existence of edges $T_i \rightarrow T_j$ and $T_j \rightarrow T_k$ in an SG does not necessarily imply the existence of edge $T_i \rightarrow T_k$. For instance, with $w_3[z]$ replacing $w_3[x]$ in T_3, $SG(H_s)$ becomes

$$T_2 \rightarrow T_1 \rightarrow T_3$$

since there is no conflict between T_2 and T_3.[7]

Each edge $T_i \rightarrow T_j$ in SG(H) means that at least one of T_i's operations precedes and conflicts with one of T_j's. This suggests that T_i should precede T_j in any serial history that is equivalent to H. If we can find a serial history, H_s, consistent with all edges in SG(H), then $H_s \equiv H$ and so H is SR. We can do this as long as SG(H) is acyclic.

In our previous example, SG(H_s) is acyclic. A serial history where transactions appear in an order consistent with the edges of SG(H_s) is $T_2 \, T_1 \, T_3$. Indeed this is the only such serial history. You can easily verify that H_s is equivalent to $T_2 \, T_1 \, T_3$ and is therefore SR. We formalize this intuitive argument in the following theorem—the fundamental theorem of serializability theory.

Theorem 2.1: (The Serializability Theorem) A history H is serializable iff SG(H) is acyclic.

Proof: (if) Suppose H is a history over $T = \{T_1, T_2, ..., T_n\}$. Without loss of generality, assume $T_1, T_2, ..., T_m \, (m \leq n)$ are all of the transactions in T that are committed in H. Thus $T_1, T_2, ..., T_m$ are the nodes of SG(H). Since SG(H) is acyclic it may be topologically sorted.[8] Let $i_1, ..., i_m$ be a permutation of 1, 2, ..., m such that $T_{i_1}, T_{i_2}, ..., T_{i_m}$ is a topological sort of SG(H). Let H_s be the serial history $T_{i_1} \, T_{i_2} \, ... \, T_{i_m}$. We claim that C($H$) $\equiv H_s$. To see this, let $p_i \in T_i$ and $q_j \in T_j$, where T_i, T_j are committed in H. Suppose p_i, q_j conflict and $p_i <_H q_j$. By definition of SG(H), $T_i \rightarrow T_j$ is an edge in SG(H). Therefore in any topological sort of SG(H), T_i must appear before T_j. Thus in H_s all operations of T_i appear before any operation of T_j, and in particular, $p_i <_{H_s} q_j$. We have proved that any two conflicting operations are ordered in C(H) in the same way as H_s. Thus C(H) $\equiv H_s$ and, because H_s is serial by construction, H is SR as was to be proved.

(only if) Suppose history H is SR. Let H_s be a serial history equivalent to C(H). Consider an edge $T_i \rightarrow T_j$ in SG(H). Thus there are two conflicting operations p_i, q_j of T_i, T_j (respectively), such that $p_i <_H q_j$. Because C(H) $\equiv H_s, p_i <_{H_s} q_j$. Because H_s is serial and p_i in T_i precedes q_j in T_j, it follows that T_i appears before T_j in H_s. Thus, we've shown that if $T_i \rightarrow T_j$ is in SG(H) then T_i appears before T_j in H_s. Now suppose there is a cycle in SG(H), and without loss of generality let that cycle be $T_1 \rightarrow T_2 \rightarrow ... \rightarrow T_k \rightarrow T_1$. These edges imply that in H_s, T_1 appears before T_2 which appears before T_3 which appears ... before T_k which appears before T_1. Thus, the existence of the cycle implies that each of $T_1, T_2, ..., T_k$ appears before

---

[7] We say that *two transactions conflict* if they contain conflicting operations.

[8] See Section A.3 of the Appendix for a definition of "topological sort of a directed acyclic graph."

itself in the serial history H_s, an absurdity. So no cycle can exist in $SG(H)$. That is, $SG(H)$ is an acyclic directed graph, as was to be proved. □

From the proof of the "if" part of this theorem we see that if a complete history H has an acyclic $SG(H)$, then H is equivalent to *any* serial history that's a topological sort of $SG(H)$. Since the latter can have more than one topological sort, H may be equivalent to more than one serial history. For instance,

$$H_6 = w_1[x]\ w_1[y]\ c_1\ r_2[x]\ r_3[y]\ w_2[x]\ c_2\ w_3[y]\ c_3$$

has the serialization graph

$$SG(H_6) = \quad T_1 \rightarrow T_3 \qquad T_2$$

which has two topological sorts, T_1, T_2, T_3 and T_1, T_3, T_2. Thus H_6 is equivalent to both $T_1\ T_2\ T_3$ and $T_1\ T_3\ T_2$.

2.4 RECOVERABLE HISTORIES

In Chapter 1, we saw that to ensure correctness in the presence of failures the scheduler must produce executions that are not only SR but also recoverable. We also discussed some additional requirements that may be desirable— preventing cascading aborts and the loss of before images—leading us to the idea of strict executions. Like serializability, these concepts can be conveniently formulated in the language of histories.

A transaction T_i reads data item x from T_j if T_j was the transaction that had last written into x but had not aborted at the time T_i read x. More precisely, we say that T_i *reads x from T_j* in history H if

1. $w_j[\mathrm{x}] < r_i[x\ ]$;

2. $a_j \not< r_i[x]$[9] and

3. if there is some $w_k[x]$ such that $w_j[x] < w_k[x] < r_i[x]$, then $a_k < r_i[x]$.

We say that T_i *reads from T_j* in H if T_i reads some data item from T_j in H. Notice that it is possible for a transaction to read a data item from itself (i.e., $w_i[x] < r_i[x]$).

A history H is called *recoverable* (*RC*) if, whenever T_i reads from T_j $(i \neq j)$ in H and $c_i \in H$, $c_j < c_i$. Intuitively, a history is recoverable if each transaction commits after the commitment of all transactions (other than itself) from which it read.

A history H *avoids cascading aborts* (*ACA*) if, whenever T_i reads x from T_j $(i \neq j)$, $c_j < r_i[x]$. That is, a transaction may read only those values that are written by committed transactions or by itself.

---

[9]$p \not< q$ denotes that operation p does not precede q in the partial order.

A history H is *strict* (ST) if whenever $w_j[x] < o_i[x]$ $(i \neq j)$, either $a_j < o_i[x]$ or $c_j < o_i[x]$ where $o_i[x]$ is $r_i[x]$ or $w_i[x]$. That is, no data item may be read or overwritten until the transaction that previously wrote into it terminates, either by aborting or by committing.

We illustrate these definitions using the following four histories, over transactions:

$$T_1 = w_1[x] \, w_1[y] \, w_1[z] \, c_1 \qquad T_2 = r_2[u] \, w_2[x] \, r_2[y] \, w_2[y] \, c_2$$

$$H_7 = w_1[x] \, w_1[y] \, r_2[u] \, w_2[x] \, r_2[y] \, w_2[y] \, c_2 \, w_1[z] \, c_1$$

$$H_8 = w_1[x] \, w_1[y] \, r_2[u] \, w_2[x] \, r_2[y] \, w_2[y] \, w_1[z] \, c_1 \, c_2$$

$$H_9 = w_1[x] \, w_1[y] \, r_2[u] \, w_2[x] \, w_1[z] \, c_1 \, r_2[y] \, w_2[y] \, c_2$$

$$H_{10} = w_1[x] \, w_1[y] \, r_2[u] \, w_1[z] \, c_1 \, w_2[x] \, r_2[y] \, w_2[y] \, c_2$$

H_7 is not an RC (i.e., recoverable) history. To see this, note that T_2 reads y from T_1, but $c_2 < c_1$. H_8 *is* RC but not ACA (i.e., does not avoid cascading aborts), because T_2 reads y from T_1 before T_1 is committed. H_9 is ACA but not ST (i.e., strict), because T_2 overwrites the value written into x by T_1 before the latter terminates. H_{10} is ST.

In the remainder of this section, we will use RC, ACA, ST, and SR to denote the set of histories that are recoverable, avoid cascading aborts, are strict, and are serializable (respectively). Our next theorem says that recoverability, avoiding cascading aborts, and strictness are increasingly restrictive properties.

Theorem 2.2: ST $\subset$ ACA $\subset$ RC

Proof: Let $H \in ST$. Suppose T_i reads x from T_j in H $(i \neq j)$. Then we have $w_j[x] < r_i[x]$ and $a_j \not< r_i[x]$. Thus, by definition of ST, $c_j < r_i[x]$. Therefore $H \in ACA$. This shows that ST $\subseteq$ ACA. History H_9 (above) avoids cascading aborts but isn't strict, implying ST $\neq$ ACA. Hence ST $\subset$ ACA.

Now let $H \in ACA$, and suppose T_i reads x from T_j in H $(i \neq j)$ and $c_i \in H$. Because H avoids cascading aborts, we must have $w_j[x] < c_j < r_i[x]$. Since $c_i \in H$, $r_i[x] < c_i$ and therefore $c_j < c_i$, proving $H \in RC$. Thus ACA $\subseteq$ RC. History H_8 (above) is in RC but not in ACA, proving ACA $\neq$ RC. Hence ACA $\subset$ RC. $\square$

SR intersects all of the sets RC, ACA, and ST, but is incomparable to each of them.[10] The relationships among the four sets are illustrated in Fig. 2–2 by a Venn diagram. The diagram shows where histories $H_7 - H_{10}$ belong. All inclusions shown in Fig. 2–2 are proper (see Exercise 2.7).

---

[10]Two sets are *incomparable* if neither is contained in the other.

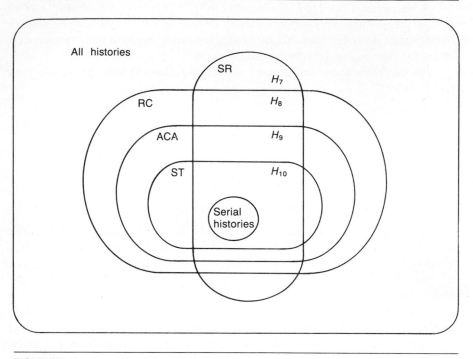

FIGURE 2–2
Relationships between Histories that are SR, RC, ACA, and ST

Figure 2–2 illustrates that there exist histories that are SR but not RC. In a DBS that must correctly handle transaction and system failures (as most must do), the scheduler must enforce recoverability (or the even stronger properties of cascadelessness or strictness) *in addition to* serializability.

We conclude this section with an important observation. A property of histories is called *prefix commit-closed* if, whenever the property is true of history H, it is also true of history $C(H')$, for any prefix H' of H. A correctness criterion for histories that accounts for transaction and system failures *must* be described by such a property. To see this, suppose that H is a "correct" history, that is, one that could be produced by a correct scheduler. Hence, any prefix H' of H could also be produced by the scheduler. But suppose at the time H' had been produced, the DBS failed. Then, at recovery time, the database should reflect the execution of exactly those transactions that were committed in H' that is, it should reflect the execution represented by $C(H')$. If the DBS is to handle transaction and system failures, $C(H')$ had better be a "correct" history too.

It is easy to verify that RC, ACA, and ST are indeed prefix commit-closed properties (Exercise 2.9). As shown in the following theorem, serializability is too.

Theorem 2.3: Serializability is a prefix commit-closed property. That is, if H is an SR history, then for any prefix H' of H, $C(H')$ is also SR.

Proof: Since H is SR, $SG(H)$ is acyclic (from the "only if" part of Theorem 2.1). Consider $SG(C(H'))$ where H' is any prefix of H. If $T_i \rightarrow T_j$ is an edge of this graph, then we have two conflicting operations p_i, q_j belonging to T_i, T_j (respectively) with $p_i <_{C(H')} q_j$. But then clearly $p_i <_H q_j$ and thus the edge $T_i \rightarrow T_j$ exists in $SG(H)$ as well. Therefore $SG(C(H'))$ is a subgraph of $SG(H)$. Since the latter is acyclic, the former must be too. By the "if" part of Theorem 2.1, it follows that $C(H')$ is SR, as was to be proved. $\square$

2.5 OPERATIONS BEYOND READS AND WRITES

In Chapter 1 we assumed that Read and Write are the only operations that transactions can perform on the database. However, neither the theoretical nor practical results presented in this book depend very much on this assumption. To help us understand how to treat a more general set of operations, let's reexamine serializability theory with new operations in mind.

Suppose we allow other database operations in addition to Read and Write. If transactions can interact through these operations, then these operations must appear in histories. Since every pair of conflicting operations in a history must be related by $<$, we must extend the definition of conflict to cover the new operations. The definition should be extended so that it retains the essence of conflict. Namely, two operations must be defined to conflict if, *in general*, the computational effect of their execution depends on the order in which they are processed.[11] The computational effect of the two operations consists of both the value returned by each operation (if any) and the final value of the data item(s) they access. If we extend the definition of conflict in this way, the definition of equivalent histories will remain valid in that only histories with the same computational effect will be defined to be equivalent.

The definition of SG remains unchanged. Moreover, since the proof of Theorem 2.1 only depends on the notion of conflict, not on the nature of the operations, it remains unchanged too. That is, a history is SR iff its SG is acyclic.

So, to add new operations in addition to Read and Write, the only work we need to do is to extend the definition of conflict.

For example, suppose we add Increment and Decrement to our repertoire of operations. Increment(x) adds 1 to data item x and Decrement(x) subtracts 1 from x. (This assumes, of course, that x's value is a number.) An Increment or Decrement does *not* return a value to the transaction that issued it. We abbreviate these operations by $inc_i[x]$ and $dec_i[x]$, where the subscript denotes the transaction that issued the operation. Since transactions can interact

---

[11]Note the qualification "in general" in this phrase. For example, one can think of *particular* Write operations that access the same data item and do not conflict, such as two Writes that write the same value. However, *in general*, two Writes on the same data item do conflict.

	Read	Write	Increment	Decrement
Read	y	n	n	n
Write	n	n	n	n
Increment	n	n	y	y
Decrement	n	n	y	y

FIGURE 2–3
A Compatibility Matrix

through Increments and Decrements (via Reads and Writes), Increments and Decrements must appear in histories.

We define two operations to *conflict* if they operate on the same data item and either at least one of them is a Write, or one is a Read and the other is an Increment or Decrement. We can conveniently express which combinations of operations conflict by a table called a *compatibility matrix*. The compatibility matrix for Read, Write, Increment, and Decrement is shown in Fig. 2–3. A "y" entry indicates that the operations in the corresponding row and column are compatible (i.e., do *not* conflict), while an "n" indicates that they are incompatible (i.e., conflict). Take a moment to convince yourself that the computational effect of executing two operations (as defined previously) depends on the order in which they were processed iff there is an "n" in the row and column combination corresponding to the operations.

A history that uses these operations is given below along with its SG.

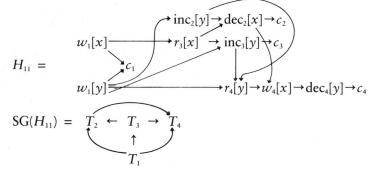

Since $SG(H_{11})$ is acyclic, the generalized Serializability Theorem says that H_{11} is SR. It is equivalent to the serial history $T_1\ T_3\ T_2\ T_4$, which can be obtained by topologically sorting $SG(H_{11})$.

2.6 VIEW EQUIVALENCE

This section explores another notion of history equivalence. To introduce it, let's rethink the concept from first principles.

We want to define equivalence so that two histories are equivalent if they have the same effects. The effects of a history are the values produced by the Write operations of unaborted transactions.

Since we don't know anything about the computation that each transaction performs, we don't know much about the value written by each Write. All we *do* know is that it is *some* function of the values read by each of the transaction's Reads that preceded the Write. Thus, if each transaction's Reads read the same value in two histories, then its Writes will produce the same values in both histories. From this observation and a little careful thought, we can see that (1) if each transaction reads each of its data items from the same Writes in both histories, then all Writes write the same values in both histories, and (2) if for each data item x, the final Write on x is the same in both histories, then the final value of all data items will be the same in both histories. And if all Writes write the same values in both histories and leave the database in the same final state, then the histories must be equivalent.

This leads us to the following definition of history equivalence. The *final write* of x in a history H is the operation $w_i[x] \in H$, such that $a_i \notin H$ and for any $w_j[x] \in H$ $(j \neq i)$ either $w_j[x] < w_i[x]$ or $a_j \in H$. Two histories H, H' are *equivalent* if

1. they are over the same set of transactions and have the same operations;
2. for any T_i, T_j such that $a_i, a_j \in H$ (hence $a_i, a_j \notin H'$) and for any x, if T_i reads x from T_j in H then T_i reads x from T_j in H' and
3. for each x, if $w_i[x]$ is the final write of x in H then it is also the final write of x in H'.

As we'll see later, this definition of equivalence is somewhat different from the one we've used so far, so to distinguish it we'll give it a different name, *view equivalence* (since, by (2), each Read has the same view in both histories). For clarity, we'll call the old definition *conflict equivalence* (since it says that two histories are equivalent if conflicting operations of unaborted transactions appear in the same order in both histories).

View equivalence will be very useful in Chapters 5 and 8 for our formal treatment of concurrency control algorithms for multicopy data.

*View Serializability[12]

In Section 2.2 we defined a history H to be serializable if its committed projection, $C(H)$, is (conflict) equivalent to some serial history. We can use the definition of view equivalence in a similar manner to arrive at a new concept of

---

[12]The asterisk before this section title means that the rest of this section goes deeper into serializability theory than is needed to understand succeeding nontheoretical sections (cf. the Preface).

serializability. Specifically, we define a history H to be *view serializable* (VSR) if for any prefix H' of H, $C(H')$ is view equivalent to some serial history. For emphasis we'll use *conflict serializable* (CSR) for what we have thus far simply called serializable.

The reason for insisting that the committed projection of *every prefix* of H (instead of just the committed projection of H itself) be view equivalent to a serial history is to ensure that view serializability is a prefix commit-closed property. Consider, for instance,

$$H_{12} = w_1[x]\ w_2[x]\ w_2[y]\ c_2\ w_1[y]\ c_1\ w_3[x]\ w_3[y]\ c_3.$$

$C(H_{12}) = H_{12}$ and is view equivalent to $T_1\ T_2\ T_3$. However, if we take H'_{12} to be the prefix of H_{12} up to and including c_1, we have that $C(H'_{12})$ is not view equivalent to either $T_1\ T_2$ or $T_2\ T_1$. Thus we wouldn't get a prefix commit-closed property if we had defined view serializability by requiring only that the committed projection of that history itself be equivalent to a serial history.[13] As discussed at the end of Section 2.2, this would make view serializability an inappropriate correctness criterion in an environment where transactions or the system are subject to failures.

The two "versions" of serializability are not the same. In fact, as the following theorem shows, view serializability is a (strictly) more inclusive concept.

Theorem 2.4: If H is conflict serializable then it is view serializable. The converse is not, generally, true.

Proof: Suppose H is conflict serializable. Consider an arbitrary prefix H' of H. By assumption, $C(H')$ is conflict equivalent to some serial history, say H_s. We claim that $C(H')$ is view equivalent to H_s. Clearly, $C(H')$ and H_s are over the same set of transactions and have the same operations (since they are conflict equivalent). It remains to show that $C(H')$ and H_s have the same reads-from relationships and final writes for all data items. Suppose T_i reads x from T_j in $C(H')$. Then, $w_j[x] <_{C(H')} r_i[x]$ and there is no $w_k[x]$ such that $w_j[x] <_{C(H')} w_k[x] <_{C(H')} r_i[x]$. Because $w_j[x]$, $r_i[x]$ conflict with each other and $w_k[x]$ conflicts with both, and because $C(H')$ and H_s order conflicting operations in the same way, it follows that $w_j[x] <_{H_s} r_i[x]$ and there is no $w_k[x]$ such that $w_j[x] <_{H_s} w_k[x] <_{H_s} r_i[x]$. Hence T_i reads x from T_j in H_s. If T_i reads x from T_j in H_s, then the same argument implies T_i reads x from T_j in $C(H')$. Thus $C(H')$ and H_s have the same reads-from relationships. Because Writes on the same data item conflict and $C(H')$ and H_s order conflicting operations in the same way, the

---

[13] In case of *conflict* serializability, however, requiring that the committed projection of the history be conflict equivalent to a serial history was sufficient to ensure prefix commit closure (see Theorem 2.3).

two histories must also have the same final write for each data item. $C(H')$ and H_s are therefore view equivalent. Since H' is an arbitrary prefix of H, it follows that H' is view serializable.

To show that the converse is not, generally, true, consider

$$H_{13} = w_1[x]\ w_2[x]\ w_2[y]\ c_2\ w_1[y]\ w_3[x]\ w_3[y]\ c_3\ w_1[z]\ c_1.$$

H_{13} is view serializable. To see this, consider any prefix H'_{13} of H_{13}. If H'_{13} includes c_1 (i.e. $H'_{13} = H_{13}$, it is view equivalent to $T_1\ T_2\ T_3$; if H'_{13} includes c_3 but not c_1, it is view equivalent to $T_2\ T_3$; if H'_{13} includes c_2 but not c_3, it is view equivalent to T_2; finally, if H'_{13} does not include c_2 it is view equivalent to the empty serial history. However, H_{13} is not conflict serializable because its SG, shown below, has a cycle.

$$SG(H_{13}) =$$

Even though view serializability is more inclusive than conflict serializability, there are reasons for keeping the latter as our concurrency control correctness criterion. From a practical point of view, all known concurrency control algorithms are *conflict based*. That is, their goal is to order *conflicting* operations in a consistent way, and as a result produce only conflict serializable histories. From a theoretical standpoint, it is hopeless to expect efficient schedulers to be based on view serializability. Technically, it can be shown that an efficient scheduler that produces exactly the set of all view serializable histories can only exist if the famous $P = NP$? problem has an affirmative answer. This is considered very unlikely, as it would imply that a wide variety of notoriously difficult combinatorial problems would be solvable by efficient algorithms.

Thus, in the rest of the book we continue to use the terms equivalent and serializable (histories) to mean *conflict* equivalent and *conflict* serializable (histories), unless otherwise qualified.

BIBLIOGRAPHIC NOTES

Virtually all rigorous treatments of concurrency control use some form of the history model of executions. See [Bernstein, Shipman, Wong 79], [Gray et al. 75], [Papadimitriou 79], and [Stearns, Lewis, Rosenkrantz 76]. An extensive treatment of serializability theory appears in [Papadimitriou 86].

The definition of equivalence and serializability used here and the Serializability Theorem are from [Gray et al. 75]. View equivalence and view serializability are defined in [Yannakakis 84]. Recoverability, avoidance of cascading aborts, and strictness are defined in [Hadzilacos 83] and [Hadzilacos 86]. See also [Papadimitriou, Yannakakis 85].

[Papadimitriou 79] proves that no efficient scheduler can output all view serializable histories, unless $P = NP$. (For the $P = NP$? question see [Garey, Johnson 79].)

EXERCISES

2.1 Let H_1 and H_2 be *totally ordered* histories. Define a (symmetric) relation $\sim$ between such histories as follows:

$$H_1 \sim H_2 \text{ iff } H_1 = p_1 p_2 \cdots p_{i-1} \, p_i \, p_{i+1} \cdots p_n \text{ and}$$
$$H_2 = p_1 p_2 \cdots p_{i-1} \, p_{i+1} \, p_i \, p_{i+2} \cdots p_n$$

where p_i, p_{i+1} are operations such that either the operations do not conflict or (at least) one of the two transactions issuing the operations is aborted in H_1 (and hence in H_2). Extend $\sim$ to arbitrary (not necessarily totally ordered) histories as follows:

$H_1 \sim H_2$ iff there exist totally ordered histories
$\quad$ H'_1, H'_2 compatible with H_1, H_2 (respectively), such that $H'_1 \sim H'_2$.

(H' is compatible with H if they have the same operations and $p <_H q$ implies $p <_{H'} q$). Finally, define $\approx$ to be the transitive closure of $\sim$. That is,

$H \approx H'$ iff there exist histories $H_1, H_2, \ldots, H_k$ $(k \geq 1)$ such that
$H = H_1 \sim H_2 \sim \cdots \sim H_k = H'$.

Prove that $H' \equiv H$ iff $H \approx H'$.

2.2 Prove that if two histories are equivalent then their serialization graphs are identical.

2.3 The converse of Exercise 2.2 is obviously not true. For example, the histories $w_1[x] \, w_2[x]$ and $w_1[y] \, w_2[y]$ have the same serialization graph but are clearly not equivalent. Is the following, stronger version of the converse in Exercise 2.2 true: If histories H and H' are over the same set of transactions, have the same operations, and have the same serialization graphs, then $H \equiv H'$.

2.4*14 A *blind write* is a Write on some data item x by a transaction that did not previously read x. Suppose we insist that transactions have no blind writes. Formally, this means replacing condition (4) in the definition of transaction (cf. Section 2.1) by the stronger

$(4')$ if $w_i[x] \in T_i$ then $r_i[x] \in T_i$ and $r_i[x] <_i w_i[x]$.

Prove that under this assumption a history is view serializable iff it is conflict serializable.

---

[14]Starred exercises are not necessarily difficult, but require knowledge of starred sections in the text.

2.5* Prove that if H and H' are complete, recoverable, and view equivalent histories then they are conflict equivalent. Also prove that the requirements "complete and recoverable" are necessary for the truth of this statement.

2.6* A *view graph* of history H is a directed graph with nodes corresponding to the committed transactions in H and edges defined as follows:

    a. if T_i, T_j are committed transactions such that T_j reads from T_i then $T_i \rightarrow T_j$ is an edge in the view graph, and

    b. if T_i, T_j, T_k are committed transactions, T_j reads x from T_i and T_k writes x then either $T_k \rightarrow T_i$ or $T_j \rightarrow T_k$ is an edge in the view graph.

As can be seen from (b), there may be several view graphs corresponding to the history H. Prove that H is view serializable iff for every prefix H' of H, $C(H')$ has some acyclic view graph.

2.7* The following Venn diagram summarizes the relationships among the five sets of histories defined in Chapter 2.

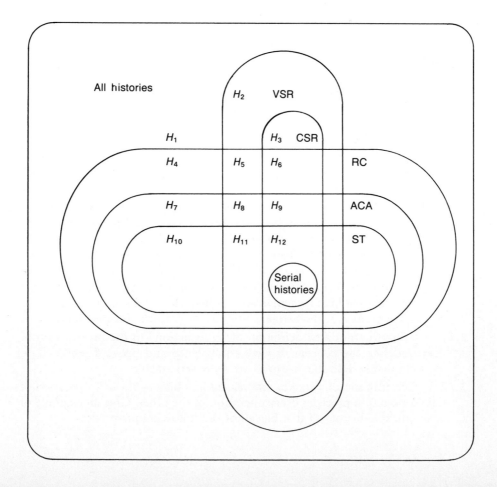

Prove that all regions in the diagram represent non-empty sets by providing example histories $H_1 - H_{12}$.

2.8   In a draft of a proposed standard on commitment, concurrency and recovery (ISO, "Information Processing—Open Systems Interconnection—Definition of Common Application Service Elements—Part 3: Commitment, Concurrency and Recovery," Draft International Standard ISO/DIS 8649/3) the following definition of concurrency control correctness is given (p. 6):

> Concurrency control [ensures] that an atomic action is not committed unless
>
> 1. all atomic actions which have changed the value of a datum prior to its period of use by this atomic action have committed; and
> 2. no change has been made to the value of a datum during its period of use, except by [...] this atomic action.

The *period of use* of a datum by an atomic action is defined as "the time from first use of the datum by [...] the atomic action to the last use of that datum by the atomic action."

In our terminology an atomic action is a transaction and a datum is a data item.

a. What did we call condition (1) in this chapter?
b. Express this definition of concurrency control as conditions on histories.
c. How does the above definition of concurrency control relate to serializability and recoverability? (Is it equivalent, stronger, weaker or unrelated to them?)
d. Suppose we define the period of use of a datum by an atomic action as the time from the first use of the datum by the atomic action to the time of the action's commitment or abortion. How does this change affect your answer to (c)?

2.9   Prove that RC, ACA, and ST are prefix commit-closed properties.

2.10   Redefine the concept of "transaction" in serializability theoretic terms so that each transaction T_i can read or write a data item more than once. To do this, you need to distinguish two Reads or Writes by T_i, say by another subscript, such as $r_{i1}[x]$ and $r_{i2}[x]$. Using this modified definition of "transaction," redefine each of the following terms if necessary: complete history, history, equivalence of histories, and serialization graph. Prove Theorem 2.1, the Serializability Theorem, for this new model.

2.11   Using the modified definition of "transaction" in the previous problem, redefine the concept of view equivalence and prove Theorem 2.4, that conflict serializable histories are view serializable.

2.12   Two transactions are *not interleaved* in a history if every operation of one transaction precedes every operation of the other. Give an example of a serializable history H that has all of the following properties:

a. transactions T_1 and T_2 are not interleaved in H;

b. T_1 precedes T_2 in H; and

c. in any serial history equivalent to H, T_2 precedes T_1.

The history may include more than two transactions.

2.13 Prove or disprove that every history H having the following property is serializable: If p_i, $q_j \in H$ and p_i, q_j conflict, then T_i and T_j are not interleaved in H. (See Exercise 2.12 for the definition of interleaved.)

3
TWO PHASE LOCKING

3.1 AGGRESSIVE AND CONSERVATIVE SCHEDULERS

In this chapter we begin our study of practical schedulers by looking at two phase locking schedulers, the most popular type in commercial products. For most of the chapter, we focus on locking in centralized DBSs, using the model presented in Chapter 1. Later sections show how locking schedulers can be modified to handle a distributed system environment. The final section discusses specialized locking protocols for trees and dags.

Recall from Chapter 1 that when a scheduler receives an operation from a TM it has three options:

1. immediately schedule it (by sending it to the DM);

2. delay it (by inserting it into some queue); or

3. reject it (thereby causing the issuing transaction to abort).

Each type of scheduler usually favors one or two of these options. Based on which of these options the scheduler favors, we can make the fuzzy, yet conceptually useful, distinction between *aggressive* and *conservative* schedulers.

An aggressive scheduler tends to avoid delaying operations; it tries to schedule them immediately. But to the extent it does so, it foregoes the opportunity to reorder operations it receives later on. By giving up the opportunity to reorder operations, it may get stuck in a situation in which it has no hope of finishing the execution of all active transactions in a serializable fashion. At this point, it has to resort to rejecting operations of one or more transactions, thereby causing them to abort (option (3) above).

A conservative scheduler, on the other hand, tends to delay operations. This gives it more leeway to reorder operations it receives later on. This leeway makes it less likely to get stuck in a situation where it has to reject operations to produce an SR execution. An extreme case of a conservative scheduler is one that, at any given time, delays the operations of all but one transaction. When that transaction terminates, another one is selected to have its operations processed. Such a scheduler processes transactions serially. It never needs to reject an operation, but avoids such rejections by sometimes excessively delaying operations.

There is an obvious performance trade-off between aggressive and conservative schedulers. Aggressive schedulers avoid delaying operations and thereby risk rejecting them later. Conservative schedulers avoid rejecting operations by deliberately delaying them. Each approach works especially well for certain types of applications.

For example, in an application where transactions that are likely to execute concurrently rarely conflict, an aggressive scheduler might perform better than a conservative one. Since conflicts are rare, conflicts that require the rejection of an operation are even rarer. Thus, the aggressive scheduler would not reject operations very often. By contrast, a conservative scheduler would needlessly delay operations, anticipating conflicts that seldom materialize.

On the other hand, in an application where transactions that are likely to execute concurrently conflict, a conservative scheduler's cautiousness may pay off. An aggressive scheduler might output operations recklessly, frequently placing itself in the undesirable position where rejecting operations is the only alternative to producing incorrect executions.

The rate at which conflicting operations are submitted is not the only factor that affects concurrency control performance. For example, the load on computer resources other than the DBS is also important. Therefore, this discussion of trade-offs between aggressive and conservative approaches to scheduling should be taken with a grain of salt. The intent is to develop some intuition about the operation of schedulers, rather than to suggest precise rules for designing them. Unfortunately, giving such precise rules for tailoring a scheduler to the performance specifications of an application is beyond the state-of-the-art.

Almost all types of schedulers have an aggressive and a conservative version. Generally speaking, a conservative scheduler tries to anticipate the future behavior of transactions in order to prepare for operations that it has not yet received. The main information it needs to know is the set of data items that each transaction will read and write (called, respectively, the *readset* and *writeset* of the transaction). In this way, it can predict which of the operations that it is currently scheduling may conflict with operations that will arrive in the future. By contrast, an aggressive scheduler doesn't need this information, since it schedules operations as early as it can, relying on rejections to correct mistakes.

A very conservative version of any type of scheduler can usually be built if transactions *predeclare their readsets and writesets*. This means that the TM begins processing a transaction by giving the scheduler the transaction's readset and writeset. Predeclaration is more easily and efficiently done if transactions are analyzed by a preprocessor, such as a compiler, before being submitted to the system, rather than being interpreted on the fly.

An impediment to building very conservative schedulers is that different executions of a given program may result in transactions that access different sets of data items. This occurs if programs contain conditional statements. For example, the following program reads either x and y, or x and z, depending on the value of x that it reads.

Procedure Fuzzy-readset **begin**
    Start;
    $a := \text{Read}(x)_i$
    if $(a > 0)$ **then** $b := \text{Read}(y)$ **else** $b := \text{Read}(z)$;
    Commit
end

In this case the transaction must predeclare the set of all data items it *might* read or write. This often causes the transaction to overstate its readset and writeset. For example, a transaction executing Fuzzy-readset would declare its readset to be $\{x, y, z\}$, even though on any single execution it will only access two of those three data items. The same problem may occur if transactions interact with the DBS using a high level (e.g., relational) query language. A high level query may *potentially* access large portions of the database, even though on any *single* execution it only accesses a small portion of the database. When transactions overstate readsets and writesets, the scheduler ends up being even more conservative than it has to be, since it will delay certain operations in anticipation of others that will never be issued.

3.2 BASIC TWO PHASE LOCKING

Locking is a mechanism commonly used to solve the problem of synchronizing access to shared data. The idea behind locking is intuitively simple. Each data item has a *lock* associated with it. Before a transaction T_1 may access a data item, the scheduler first examines the associated lock. If no transaction holds the lock, then the scheduler obtains the lock on behalf of T_1. If another transaction T_2 does hold the lock, then T_1 has to wait until T_2 gives up the lock. That is, the scheduler will not give T_1 the lock until T_2 releases it. The scheduler thereby ensures that only one transaction can hold the lock at a time, so only one transaction can access the data item at a time.

Locking can be used by a scheduler to ensure serializability. To present such a locking protocol, we need some notation.

Transactions access data items either for reading or for writing them. We therefore associate *two* types of locks with data items: read locks and write locks. We use $rl[x]$ to denote a read lock on data item x and $wl[x]$ to denote a write lock on x. We use $rl_i[x]$ (or $wl_i[x]$) to indicate that transaction T_i has obtained a read (or write) lock on x. As in Chapter 2, we use the letters o, p, and q to denote an arbitrary type of operation, that is, a Read (r) or Write (w). We use $ol_i[x]$ to denote a lock of type o by T_i on x.

Locks can be thought of as entries in a lock table. For example, $rl_i[x]$ corresponds to the entry $[x, r, T_i]$ in the table. For now, the detailed data structure of the table is unimportant. We'll discuss those details in Section 3.6.

Two locks $pl_i[x]$ and $ql_j[y]$ *conflict* if $x = y$, $i \neq j$, and operations p and q are of conflicting type. That is, two locks conflict if they are on the same data item, they are issued by different transactions, and one or both of them are write locks.[1] Thus, two locks on different data items do not conflict, nor do two locks that are on the same data item and are owned by the same transaction, even if they are of conflicting type.

We also use $rl_i[x]$ (or $wl_i[x]$) to denote the *operation* by which T_i *sets* or *obtains* a read (or write) lock on x. It will always be clear from the context whether $rl_i[x]$ and $wl_i[x]$ denote locks or operations that set locks.

We use $ru_i[x]$ (or $wu_i[x]$) to denote the operation by which T_i *releases* its read (or write) lock on x. In this case, we say T_i *unlocks* x (the u in ru and wu means unlock).

It is the job of a two phase locking (2PL) scheduler to manage the locks by controlling when transactions obtain and release their locks. In this section, we'll concentrate on the *Basic* version of 2PL. We'll look at specializations of 2PL in later sections.

Here are the rules according to which a Basic 2PL scheduler manages and uses its locks:

1. When it receives an operation $p_i[x]$ from the TM, the scheduler tests if $pl_i[x]$ conflicts with some $ql_j[x]$ that is already set. If so, it delays $p_i[x]$, forcing T_i to wait until it can set the lock it needs. If not, then the scheduler sets $pl_i[x]$, and then sends $p_i[x]$ to the DM.[2]

2. Once the scheduler has set a lock for T_i, say $pl_i[x]$, it may not release that lock *at least* until after the DM acknowledges that it has processed the lock's corresponding operation, $p_i[x]$.

3. Once the scheduler has released a lock for a transaction, it may not subsequently obtain *any* more locks for that transaction (on *any* data item).

---

[1]We will generalize the notion of lock conflict to operations other than Read and Write in Section 3.8.

[2]The scheduler must be implemented so that setting a lock is atomic relative to setting conflicting locks. This ensures that conflicting locks are never held simultaneously.

Rule (1) prevents two transactions from concurrently accessing a data item in conflicting modes. Thus, conflicting operations are scheduled in the same order in which the corresponding locks are obtained.

Rule (2) supplements rule (1) by ensuring that the DM processes operations on a data item in the order that the scheduler submits them. For example, suppose T_i obtains $rl_i[x]$, which it releases before the DM has confirmed that $r_i[x]$ has been processed. Then it is possible for T_j to obtain a conflicting lock on x, $wl_j[x]$, and send $w_j[x]$ to the DM. Although the scheduler has sent the DM $r_i[x]$ before $w_j[x]$, without rule (2) there is no guarantee that the DM will receive and process the operations in that order.

Rule (3), called the *two phase rule*, is the source of the name *two phase locking*. Each transaction may be divided into two phases: a *growing phase* during which it obtains locks, and a *shrinking phase* during which it releases locks. The intuition behind rule (3) is not obvious. Roughly, its function is to guarantee that *all* pairs of conflicting operations of two transactions are scheduled in the same order. Let's look at an example to see, intuitively, why this might be the case.

Consider two transactions T_1 and T_2:

$$T_1: r_1[x] \rightarrow w_1[y] \rightarrow c_1 \qquad T_2: w_2[x] \rightarrow w_2[y] \rightarrow c_2$$

and suppose they execute as follows:

$$H_1 = rl_1[x]\ r_1[x]\ ru_1[x]\ wl_2[x]\ w_2[x]\ wl_2[y]\ w_2[y]\ wu_2[x]\ wu_2[y]\ c_2\ wl_1[y]$$
$$w_1[y]\ wu_1[y]\ c_1$$

Since $r_1[x] < w_2[x]$ and $w_2[y] < w_1[y]$, $SG(H_1)$ consists of the cycle $T_1 \rightarrow T_2 \rightarrow T_1$. Thus, H_1 is not SR.

The problem in H_1 is that T_1 released a lock ($ru_1[x]$) and subsequently set a lock ($wl_1[y]$), in violation of the two phase rule. Between $ru_1[x]$ and $wl_1[y]$, another transaction T_2 wrote into both x and y, thereby appearing to follow T_1 with respect to x and precede it with respect to y. Had T_1 obeyed the two phase rule, this "window" between $ru_1[x]$ and $wl_1[y]$ would not have opened, and T_2 could not have executed as it did in H_1. For example, T_1 and T_2 might have executed as follows.

1. Initially, neither transaction owns any locks.

2. The scheduler receives $r_1[x]$ from the TM. Accordingly, it sets $rl_1[x]$ and submits $r_1[x]$ to the DM. Then the DM acknowledges the processing of $r_1[x]$.

3. The scheduler receives $w_2[x]$ from the TM. The scheduler can't set $wl_2[x]$, which conflicts with $rl_1[x]$, so it delays the execution of $w_2[x]$ by placing it on a queue.

4. The scheduler receives $w_1[y]$ from the TM. It sets $wl_1[y]$ and submits $w_1[y]$ to the DM. Then the DM acknowledges the processing of $w_1[y]$.

5. The scheduler receives c_1 from the TM, signalling that T_1 has terminated. The scheduler sends c_1 to the DM. After the DM acknowledges processing c_1, the scheduler releases $rl_1[x]$ and $wl_1[y]$. This is safe with respect to rule (2), because $r_1[x]$ and $w_1[y]$ have already been processed, and with respect to rule (3), because T_1 won't request any more locks.

6. The scheduler sets $wl_2[x]$ so that $w_2[x]$, which had been delayed, can now be sent to the DM. Then the DM acknowledges $w_2[x]$.

7. The scheduler receives $w_2[y]$ from the TM. It sets $wl_2[y]$ and sends $w_2[y]$ to the DM. The DM then acknowledges processing $w_2[y]$.

8. T_2 terminates and the TM sends c_2 to the scheduler. The scheduler sends c_2 to the DM. After the DM acknowledges processing c_2, the scheduler releases $wl_2[x]$ and $wl_2[y]$.

This execution is represented by the following history.

$$H_2 = rl_1[x]\ r_1[x]\ wl_1[y]\ w_1[y]\ c_1\ ru_1[x]\ wu_1[y]\ wl_2[x]\ w_2[x]\ wl_2[y]\ w_2[y]\ c_2$$
$$wu_2[x]\ wu_2[y].$$

H_2 is serial and therefore is SR.

An important and unfortunate property of 2PL schedulers is that they are subject to *deadlocks*. For example, suppose a 2PL scheduler is processing transactions T_1 and T_3

$$T_1: r_1[x] \rightarrow w_1[y] \rightarrow c_1 \qquad T_3: w_3[y] \rightarrow w_3[x] \rightarrow c_3$$

and consider the following sequence of events:

1. Initially, neither transaction holds any locks.

2. The scheduler receives $r_1[x]$ from the TM. It sets $rl_1[x]$ and submits $r_1[x]$ to the DM.

3. The scheduler receives $w_3[y]$ from the TM. It sets $wl_3[y]$ and submits $w_3[y]$ to the DM.

4. The scheduler receives $w_3[x]$ from the TM. The scheduler does not set $wl_3[x]$ because it conflicts with $rl_1[x]$ which is already set. Thus $w_3[x]$ is delayed.

5. The scheduler receives $w_1[y]$ from the TM. As in (4), $w_1[y]$ must be delayed.

Although the scheduler behaved exactly as prescribed by the rules of 2PL schedulers, neither T_1 nor T_3 can complete without violating one of these rules. If the scheduler sends $w_1[y]$ to the DM without setting $wl_1[y]$, it violates rule (1). Similarly for $w_3[x]$. Suppose the scheduler releases $wl_3[y]$, so it can set $wl_1[y]$ and thereby be allowed to send $w_1[y]$ to the DM. In this case, the scheduler will never be able to set $wl_3[x]$ (so it can process $w_3[x]$), or else it would violate rule (3). Similarly if it releases $rl_1[x]$. The scheduler has painted itself into a corner.

This is a classic deadlock situation. Before either of two processes can proceed, one must release a resource that the other needs to proceed.

Deadlock also arises when transactions try to strengthen read locks to write locks. Suppose a transaction T_i reads a data item x and subsequently tries to write it. T_i issues $r_i[x]$ to the scheduler, which sets $rl_i[x]$. When T_i issues $w_i[x]$ to the scheduler, the scheduler must upgrade $rl_i[x]$ to $wl_i[x]$. This upgrading of a lock is called a lock *conversion*. To obey 2PL, the scheduler must not release $rl_i[x]$. This is not a problem, because locks set by the same transaction do not conflict with each other. However, if two transactions concurrently try to convert their read locks on a data item into write locks, the result is deadlock.

For example, suppose T_4 and T_5 issue operations to a 2PL scheduler.

$$T_4: r_4[x] \rightarrow w_4[x] \rightarrow c_4 \qquad T_5: r_5[x] \rightarrow w_5[x] \rightarrow c_5$$

The scheduler might be confronted with the following sequence of events:

1. The scheduler receives $r_4[x]$, and therefore sets $rl_4[x]$ and sends $r_4[x]$ to the DM.

2. The scheduler receives $r_5[x]$, and therefore sets $rl_5[x]$ and sends $r_5[x]$ to the DM.

3. The scheduler receives $w_4[x]$. It must delay the operation, because $wl_4[x]$ conflicts with $rl_5[x]$.

4. The scheduler receives $w_5[x]$. It must delay the operation, because $wl_5[x]$ conflicts with $rl_4[x]$.

Since neither transaction can release the $rl[x]$ it owns, and since neither can proceed until it sets $wl[x]$, the transactions are deadlocked. This type of deadlock commonly occurs when a transaction scans a large number of data items looking for data items that contain certain values, and then updates those data items. It sets a read lock on each data item it scans, and converts a read lock into a write lock only when it decides to update a data item.

We will examine ways of dealing with deadlocks in Section 3.4.

3.3 *CORRECTNESS OF BASIC TWO PHASE LOCKING

To prove that a scheduler is correct, we have to prove that all histories representing executions that could be produced by it are SR. Our strategy for proving this has two steps. First, given the scheduler we characterize the properties that all of its histories must have. Second, we prove that any history with these properties must be SR. Typically this last part involves the Serializability Theorem. That is, we prove that for any history H with these properties, $SG(H)$ is acyclic.

To prove the correctness of the 2PL scheduler, we must characterize the set of *2PL histories*, that is, those that represent possible executions of transactions that are synchronized by a 2PL scheduler. To characterize 2PL histories, we'll find it very helpful to include the Lock and Unlock operations. (They were not in our formal model of Chapter 2.) Examining the order in which Lock and Unlock operations are processed will help us establish the order in which Reads and Writes are executed. This, in turn, will enable us to prove that the SG of any history produced by 2PL is acyclic.

To characterize 2PL histories, let's list all of the orderings of operations that we know must hold. First, we know that a lock is obtained for each database operation before that operation executes. This follows from rule (1) of 2PL. That is, $ol_i[x] < o_i[x]$. From rule (2) of 2PL, we know that each operation is executed by the DM before its corresponding lock is released. In terms of histories, that means $o_i[x] < ou_i[x]$. In particular, if $o_i[x]$ belongs to a committed transaction (all of whose operations are therefore in the history), we have $ol_i[x] < o_i[x] < ou_i[x]$.

> **Proposition 3.1:** Let H be a history produced by a 2PL scheduler. If $o_i[x]$ is in $C(H)$, then $ol_i[x]$ and $ou_i[x]$ are in $C(H)$, and $ol_i[x] < o_i[x] < ou_i[x]$. □

Now suppose we have two operations $p_i[x]$ and $q_j[x]$ that conflict. Thus, the locks that correspond to these operations also conflict. By rule (1) of 2PL, only one of these locks can be held at a time. Therefore, the scheduler must release the lock corresponding to one of the operations before it sets the lock for the other. In terms of histories, we must have $pu_i[x] < ql_j[x]$ or $qu_j[x] < pl_i[x]$.

> **Proposition 3.2:** Let H be a history produced by a 2PL scheduler. If $p_i[x]$ and $q_j[x]$ ($i \neq j$) are conflicting operations in $C(H)$, then either $pu_i[x] < ql_j[x]$ or $qu_j[x] < pl_i[x]$. □

Finally, let's look at the two phase rule, which says that once a transaction releases a lock it cannot subsequently obtain any other locks. This is equivalent to saying that every lock operation of a transaction executes before every unlock operation of that transaction. In terms of histories, we can write this as $pl_i[x] < qu_i[y]$.

> **Proposition 3.3:** Let H be a complete history produced by a 2PL scheduler. If $p_i[x]$ and $q_i[y]$ are in $C(H)$, then $pl_i[x] < qu_i[y]$. □

Using these properties, we must now show that every 2PL history H has an acyclic SG. The argument has three steps. (Recall that $SG(H)$ contains nodes only for the committed transactions in H.)

1. If $T_i \rightarrow T_j$ is in $SG(H)$, then one of T_i's operations on some data item, say x, executed before and conflicted with one of T_j's operations. Therefore, T_i must have released its lock on x *before* T_j set its lock on x.

2. Suppose $T_i \rightarrow T_j \rightarrow T_k$ is a path in SG(H). From step (1), T_i released some lock before T_j set some lock, and similarly T_j released some lock before T_k set some lock. Moreover, by the two phase rule, T_j set all of its locks before it released any of them. Therefore, by transitivity, T_i released some lock before T_k set some lock. By induction, this argument extends to arbitrarily long paths in SG(H). That is, for any path $T_1 \rightarrow T_2 \rightarrow \cdots \rightarrow T_n$, T_1 released some lock before T_n set some lock.

3. Suppose SG(H) had a cycle $T_1 \rightarrow T_2 \rightarrow \cdots \rightarrow T_n \rightarrow T_1$. Then by step (2), T_1 released a lock before T_1 set a lock. But then T_1 violated the two phase rule, which contradicts the fact that H is a 2PL history. Therefore, the cycle cannot exist. Since SG(H) has no cycles, the Serializability Theorem implies that H is SR.

Notice that in step (2), the lock that T_i released does not necessarily conflict with the one that T_k set, and in general they do not. T_i's lock conflicts with and precedes one that T_j set, and T_j released a lock (possibly a different one) that conflicts with and precedes the one that T_k set. For example, the history that leads to the path $T_i \rightarrow T_j \rightarrow T_k$ could be

$$r_i[x] \rightarrow w_j[x] \rightarrow w_j[y] \rightarrow r_k[y].$$

T_i's lock on x does not conflict with T_k's lock on y.

We formalize this three step argument in the following lemmas and theorem. The two lemmas formalize steps (1) and (2). The theorem formalizes step (3).

Lemma 3.4: Let H be a 2PL history, and suppose $T_i \rightarrow T_j$ is in SG(H). Then, for some data item x and some conflicting operations $p_i[x]$ and $q_j[x]$ in H, $pu_i[x] < ql_j[x]$.

Proof: Since $T_i \rightarrow T_j$, there must exist conflicting operations $p_i[x]$ and $q_j[x]$ such that $p_i[x] < q_j[x]$. By Proposition 3.1,

1. $pl_i[x] < p_i[x] < pu_i[x]$, and
2. $ql_j[x] < q_j[x] < qu_j[x]$.

By Proposition 3.2, either $pu_i[x] < ql_j[x]$ or $qu_j[x] < pl_i[x]$. In the latter case, by (1), (2) and transitivity, we would have $q_j[x] < p_i[x]$, which contradicts $p_i[x] < q_j[x]$. Thus, $pu_i[x] < ql_j[x]$, as desired. □

Lemma 3.5: Let H be a 2PL history, and let $T_1 \rightarrow T_2 \rightarrow \cdots \rightarrow T_n$ be a path in SG(H), where $n > 1$. Then, for some data items x *and* y, and some operations $p_1[x]$ and $q_n[y]$ in H, $pu_1[x] < ql_n[y]$.

Proof: The proof is by induction on n. The basis step, for $n = 2$, follows immediately from Lemma 3.4.

For the induction step, suppose the lemma holds for $n = k$ for some $k \geq 2$. We will show that it holds for $n = k + 1$. By the induction hypothesis, the path $T_1 \rightarrow \cdots \rightarrow T_k$ implies that there exist data items x and z, and operations $p_1[x]$ and $o_k[z]$ in H, such that $pu_1[x] < ol_k[z]$. By $T_k \rightarrow T_{k+1}$ and Lemma 3.4, there exists data item y and conflicting operations $o'_k[y]$, and $q_{k+1}[y]$ in H, such that $o'u_k[y] < ql_{k+1}[y]$. By Proposition 3.3, $ol_k[z] < o'u_k[y]$. By the last three precedences and transitivity, $pu_1[x] < ql_{k+1}[y]$, as desired. $\square$

Theorem 3.6:   Every 2PL history H is serializable.

Proof: Suppose, by way of contradiction, that $SG(H)$ contains a cycle $T_1 \rightarrow T_2 \rightarrow \cdots \rightarrow T_n \rightarrow T_1$, where $n > 1$. By Lemma 3.5, for some data items x and y, and some operations $p_1[x]$ and $q_1[y]$ in H, $pu_1[x] < ql_1[y]$. But this contradicts Proposition 3.3. Thus, $SG(H)$ has no cycles and so, by the Serializability Theorem, H is SR. $\square$

3.4 DEADLOCKS

The scheduler needs a strategy for detecting deadlocks, so that no transaction is blocked forever. One strategy is *timeout*. If the scheduler finds that a transaction has been waiting too long for a lock, then it simply guesses that there may be a deadlock involving this transaction and therefore aborts it. Since the scheduler is only guessing that a transaction may be involved in a deadlock, it may be making a mistake. It may abort a transaction that isn't really part of a deadlock but is just waiting for a lock owned by another transaction that is taking a long time to finish. There's no harm done by making such an incorrect guess, insofar as correctness is concerned. There *is* certainly a performance penalty to the transaction that was unfairly aborted, though as we'll see in Section 3.12, the overall effect may be to improve transaction throughput.

One can avoid too many of these types of mistakes by using a long timeout period. The longer the timeout period, the more chance that the scheduler is aborting transactions that are actually involved in deadlocks. However, a long timeout period has a liability, too. The scheduler doesn't notice that a transaction might be deadlocked until the timeout period has elapsed. So, should a transaction become involved in a deadlock, it will lose some time waiting for its deadlock to be noticed. The timeout period is therefore a parameter that needs to be tuned. It should be long enough so that most transactions that are aborted are actually deadlocked, but short enough that deadlocked transactions don't wait too long for their deadlocks to be noticed. This tuning activity is tricky but manageable, as evidenced by its use in several commercial products, such as Tandem.

Another approach to deadlocks is to detect them precisely. To do this, the scheduler maintains a directed graph called a *waits-for graph* (WFG). The nodes of WFG are labelled with transaction names. There is an edge $T_i \rightarrow T_j$, from node T_i to node T_j, iff transaction T_i is waiting for transaction T_j to release some lock.[3]

Suppose a WFG has a cycle: $T_1 \rightarrow T_2 \rightarrow \cdots \rightarrow T_n \rightarrow T_1$. Each transaction is waiting for the next transaction in the cycle. So, T_1 is waiting for itself, as is every other transaction in the cycle. Since all of these transactions are blocked waiting for locks, none of the locks they are waiting for are ever going to be released. Thus, the transactions are deadlocked. Exploiting this observation, the scheduler can detect deadlocks by checking for cycles in WFG.

Of course, the scheduler has to maintain a representation of the WFG in order to check for cycles in it. The scheduler can easily do this by adding an edge $T_i \rightarrow T_j$ to the WFG whenever a lock request by T_i is blocked by a conflicting lock owned by T_j. It drops an edge $T_i \rightarrow T_j$ from the WFG whenever it releases the (last) lock owned by T_j that had formerly been blocking a lock request issued by T_i. For example, suppose the scheduler receives $r_i[x]$, but has to delay it because T_j already owns $wl_j[x]$. Then it adds an edge $T_i \rightarrow T_j$ to the WFG. After T_j releases $wl_j[x]$, the scheduler sets $rl_i[x]$, and therefore deletes the edge $T_i \rightarrow T_j$.

How often should the scheduler check for cycles in the WFG? It could check every time a new edge is added, looking for cycles that include this new edge. But this could be quite expensive. For example, if operations are frequently delayed, but deadlocks are relatively rare, then the scheduler is spending a lot of effort looking for deadlocks that are hardly ever there. In such cases, the scheduler should check for cycles less often. Instead of checking every time an edge is added, it waits until a few edges have been added, or until some timeout period has elapsed. There is no danger in checking less frequently, since the scheduler will never miss a deadlock. (Deadlocks don't go away by themselves!) Moreover, by checking less frequently, the scheduler incurs the cost of cycle detection less often. However, a deadlock may go undetected for a longer period this way. In addition, *all* cycles must be found, not just those involving the most recently added edge.

When the scheduler discovers a deadlock, it must break the deadlock by aborting a transaction. The Abort will in turn delete the transaction's node from the WFG. The transaction that it chooses to abort is called the *victim*. Among the transactions involved in a deadlock cycle in WFG, the scheduler should select a victim whose abortion costs the least. Factors that are commonly used to make this determination include:

---

[3]WFGs are related to SGs in the following sense. If $T_i \rightarrow T_j$ is in the WFG, and both T_i and T_j ultimately commit, then $T_j \rightarrow T_i$ will be in the SG. However, if T_i aborts, then $T_j \rightarrow T_i$ may never appear in the SG. That is, WFGs describe the current state of transactions, which includes waits-for situations involving operations that never execute (due to abortions). SGs only describe dependencies between committed transactions (which arise from operations that actually execute).

□ The amount of effort that has already been invested in the transaction. This effort will be lost if the transaction is aborted.

□ The cost of aborting the transaction. This cost generally depends on the number of updates the transaction has already performed.

□ The amount of effort it will take to finish executing the transaction. The scheduler wants to avoid aborting a transaction that is almost finished. To do this, it must be able to predict the future behavior of active transactions, e.g., based on the transaction's type (Deposits are short, Audits are long).

□ The number of cycles that contain the transaction. Since aborting a transaction breaks all cycles that contain it, it is best to abort transactions that are part of more than one cycle (if such transactions exist).

A transaction can repeatedly become involved in deadlocks. In each deadlock, the transaction is selected as the victim, aborts, and restarts its execution, only to become involved in a deadlock again. To avoid such *cyclic restarts*, the victim selection algorithm should also consider the number of times a transaction is aborted due to deadlock. If it has been aborted too many times, then it should not be a candidate for victim selection, unless all transactions involved in the deadlock have reached this state.

3.5 VARIATIONS OF TWO PHASE LOCKING

Conservative 2PL

It is possible to construct a 2PL scheduler that never aborts transactions. This technique is known as *Conservative 2PL* or *Static 2PL*. As we have seen, 2PL causes abortions because of deadlocks. Conservative 2PL avoids deadlocks by requiring each transaction to obtain *all* of its locks before *any* of its operations are submitted to the DM. This is done by having each transaction predeclare its readset and writeset. Specifically, each transaction T_i first tells the scheduler all the data items it will want to Read or Write, for example as part of its Start operation. The scheduler tries to set *all* of the locks needed by T_i. It can do this providing that none of these locks conflicts with a lock held by any other transaction. If the scheduler succeeds in setting all of T_i's locks, then it submits T_i's operations to the DM as soon as it receives them. After the DM acknowledges the processing of T_i's last database operation, the scheduler may release all of T_i's locks.

If, on the other hand, *any* of the locks requested in T_i's Start conflicts with locks presently held by other transactions, then the scheduler does not grant any of T_i's locks. Instead, it inserts T_i along with its lock requests into a waiting queue. Every time the scheduler releases the locks of a completed transaction, it examines the waiting queue to see if it can grant all of the lock requests of any waiting transactions. If so, it then sets all of the locks for each such transaction and continues processing as just described.

In Conservative 2PL, if a transaction T_i is waiting for a lock held by T_j, then T_i is holding no locks. Therefore, no other transaction T_k can be waiting for T_i, so there can be no WFG edges of the form $T_k \rightarrow T_i$. Since there can be no such edges, T_i cannot be in a WFG cycle, and hence cannot become part of a deadlock. Since deadlock is the only reason that a 2PL scheduler ever rejects an operation and thereby causes the corresponding transaction to abort, Conservative 2PL never aborts a transaction. (Of course, a transaction may abort for other reasons.) This is a classic case of a conservative scheduler. By delaying operations sooner than it has to, namely, when the transaction begins executing, the scheduler avoids abortions that might otherwise be needed for concurrency control reasons.

Strict 2PL

Almost all implementations of 2PL use a variant called *Strict* 2PL. This differs from the Basic 2PL scheduler described in Section 3.2 in that it requires the scheduler to release all of a transaction's locks together, when the transaction terminates. More specifically, T_i's locks are released *after* the DM acknowledges the processing of c_i or a_i, depending on whether T_i commits or aborts (respectively).

There are two reasons for adopting this policy. First, consider when a 2PL scheduler can release some $ol_i[x]$. To do so the scheduler must know that: (1) T_i has set all of the locks it will ever need, and (2) T_i will not subsequently issue operations that refer to x. One point in time at which the scheduler can be sure of (1) and (2) is when T_i terminates, that is, when the scheduler receives the c_i or a_i operation. In fact, in the absence of any information from the TM aside from the operations submitted, this is the earliest time at which the scheduler can be assured that (1) and (2) hold.

A second reason for the scheduler to keep a transaction's locks until it ends, and specifically until *after* the DM processes the transaction's Commit or Abort, is to guarantee a strict execution. To see this, let history H represent an execution produced by a Strict 2PL scheduler and suppose $w_i[x] < o_j[x]$. By rule (1) of 2PL (Proposition 3.1) we must have

1. $wl_i[x] < w_i[x] < wu_i[x]$, and

2. $ol_j[x] < o_j[x] < ou_j[x]$.

Because $wl_i[x]$ and $ol_j[x]$ conflict (whether o is r or w, we must have either $wu_i[x] < ol_j[x]$ or $ou_j[x] < wl_i[x]$ (by Proposition 3.2). The latter, together with (1) and (2), would contradict that $w_i[x] < o_j[x]$ and, therefore,

3. $wu_i[x] < ol_j[x]$.

But because H was produced by a Strict 2PL scheduler we must have that

4. either $a_i < wu_i[x]$ or $c_i < wu_i[x]$.

From (2) - (4), it follows that either $a_i < o_j[x]$ or $c_i < o_j[x]$, proving that H is strict.

Actually, from this argument it follows that it is only necessary to hold *write* locks until after a transaction commits or aborts to ensure strictness. Read locks may be released earlier, subject to the 2PL rules to ensure serializability. Pragmatically, this means that *read locks can be released when the transaction terminates* (i.e., when the scheduler *receives* the transaction's Commit or Abort), *but write locks must be held until after the transaction commits or aborts* (i.e., after the DM *processes* the transaction's Commit or Abort).

Recall that strict histories have nice properties. They are recoverable and avoid cascading aborts. Furthermore, Abort can be implemented by restoring before images. For this reason, 2PL implementations usually take the form of Strict 2PL schedulers, rather than the seemingly more flexible Basic 2PL schedulers.

3.6 IMPLEMENTATION ISSUES

An implementation of 2PL for any particular system depends very much on the overall design of the computer system and on the available operating system facilities. It is therefore difficult to give general guidelines for implementation. However, at the risk of superficiality, we will briefly sketch the issues faced in most implementations of locking.

The scheduler abstraction is usually implemented by a combination of a lock manager (LM) and a TM. The LM services the Lock and Unlock operations. When the TM receives a Read or Write from a transaction, it sends the appropriate Lock operation to the LM. When the LM acknowledges that the lock is set, the TM sends the Read or Write to the DM. Thus, the TM subsumes the scheduler function of ensuring that a lock is set before the corresponding operation is performed.

Notice that the control flow here differs somewhat from the scheduler abstraction. In our DBS model, the TM sends the Read or Write directly to the scheduler. The scheduler sets the appropriate lock and forwards the Read or Write to the DM.

The Lock Manager

The LM maintains a table of locks, and supports the operations Lock(transaction-id, data-item, mode) and Unlock(transaction-id, data-item), where *transaction-id* is the identifier of the transaction requesting the lock,[4] *data-item* is the name of the data item to be locked, and *mode* is "read" or "write." To process a Lock operation, the LM tries to set the specified lock by adding an entry to the lock table. If another transaction owns a conflicting lock, then the LM adds the lock request to a queue of waiting requests for that data item.[5] Unlock releases the specified lock, and grants any waiting lock requests that are no longer blocked.

Lock and Unlock operations are invoked very frequently. In most transaction processing systems (such as airline reservation and on-line banking), each transaction does little computing for each data item it accesses. Therefore, unless locking is very fast, it consumes a significant fraction of the processor's time. As a rule of thumb, it should take on the average no more than several hundred machine language instructions to set or release a lock (including potential overhead for a monitor call, supervisor call, context switch, etc.). To reach this speed, the LM is often optimized carefully for special cases that occur frequently, such as setting a lock that conflicts with no other locks, and releasing all of a transaction's locks at once.

The lock table is usually implemented as a hash table with the data item identifier as key, because hash tables are especially fast for content-based retrieval. An entry in the table for data item x contains a queue header, which points to a list of locks on x that have been set and a list of lock requests that are waiting. Each lock or lock request contains a transaction-id and a lock mode. Since a very large number of data items can potentially be locked, the LM limits the size of the lock table by only allocating entries for those data items that actually *are* locked. When it releases the last lock for a data item x, it deallocates the entry for x.

Since the TM normally releases all of a transaction's read locks as soon as the transaction terminates, releasing a transaction's read locks should be a basic LM operation. Similarly, if the scheduler is strict, the TM releases a transaction's write locks as soon as the DM acknowledges committing the transaction. So releasing write locks should also be a basic LM operation. To make these operations fast, a common practice is to link together in the lock table all of the read lock entries and all of the write lock entries of each transaction. If the Commit operation is very efficient, then it may not be cost effective to release read locks before the Commit and write locks afterwards. Instead, it may be satisfactory to release write *and* read locks after the Commit. This saves the overhead of one call to the LM, at the expense of some lost concurrency by holding read locks a little longer than necessary.

---

[4]This is the transaction identifier discussed in Section 1.1.

[5]One could add another parameter to Lock that specifies whether, in the event that the lock request cannot be granted, the request should be queued or cancelled (i.e., return immediately to the caller).

The lock table should be protected. It should only be accessed by the programs that implement Lock and Unlock, so that it cannot be easily corrupted. Clearly, a stray update to memory that compromises the integrity of the lock table's data structures is likely to cause the entire system to malfunction (by executing in a non-SR manner) or die. This goal of protection may be accomplished by making the LM part of the operating system itself, thereby providing strong protection against corruption by user programs. Alternatively, it might be implemented as a monitor or device driver. The latter technique is a common workaround in systems that do not support shared memory between processes.

Blocking and Aborting Transactions

When the LM releases a lock for x, it may be able to grant other lock requests that are waiting on x's lock queue. If there are such waiting requests, then the LM must schedule them "fairly"; otherwise, it runs the risk of delaying some forever.

For example, suppose there is a queue of lock requests $[rl_2[x], rl_3[x], wl_4[x], rl_5[x]]$ waiting for $wl_1[x]$ to be released, where $rl_2[x]$ is at the head of the queue. After it releases $wl_1[x]$, the LM can now set $rl_2[x]$ and $rl_3[x]$. It can also set $rl_5[x]$. This is unfair, in the sense that $rl_5[x]$ has jumped ahead of $wl_4[x]$. It can also lead to the indefinite postponement of $wl_4[x]$, since a steady stream of read lock requests may continually jump ahead of $wl_4[x]$, preventing it from being set. This danger of indefinite postponement can be avoided by servicing the queue first-come-first-served, thereby never letting a read lock request jump ahead. Or, the LM can allow read lock requests to jump ahead only if no write lock request has been waiting too long, where the maximum waiting time is a tunable parameter.

The mechanism by which the LM causes transaction T_i to wait and later unblocks it depends on the process synchronization primitives provided by the operating system, and on the way transactions and DBS modules are structured. For example, suppose each transaction executes as a process, and the DBS is also a process. The DBS receives Read and Write requests as messages. For each such message, it invokes its LM to set the appropriate lock. By not responding to a transaction T_i's message, the DBS has effectively blocked T_i, if T_i is waiting for the response. It eventually unblocks T_i by sending the response message. Alternatively, suppose T_i calls the DBS as a procedure (e.g., a monitor) that executes in T_i's process context. Then the DBS can block T_i simply by blocking the process in which T_i is executing (e.g., by waiting on a condition that is assigned uniquely to T_i). When the LM executing (in the DBS) in another transaction's context releases the relevant lock, it can signal the event for T_i (e.g., by signaling T_i's condition), thereby unblocking T_i and allowing it to complete the lock request.

Similar issues arise in aborting the victim of a detected deadlock. The TM must be informed of the forced abortion, so it can either notify the transaction or automatically restart it. When processing an Abort (for deadlock or any other reason), the TM must delete the transaction's legacy from the lock table. Performing such activities outside the normal flow of control of the transaction again depends on several factors: how transactions, the TM, the LM, and the deadlock detector are structured as processes; if and how they share memory; and what synchronization and process control primitives they can exercise on each other.

System dependencies are often paramount in designing solutions to these control problems. The quality of those solutions can be among the most important factors affecting the robustness and performance of the concurrency control implementation.

Atomicity of Reads and Writes

A critical assumption in our model of histories is that every operation in the history is atomic. Since our correctness proof of 2PL is built on the history model, our implementation of 2PL must honor its assumptions. There are four operations that we used in histories to argue the correctness of 2PL: Lock, Unlock, Read, and Write. These four operations must be implemented atomically.

To ensure that concurrent executions of Locks and Unlocks are atomic, accesses to the lock table must be synchronized using an operating system synchronization mechanism, such as semaphores or monitors. If accesses to the lock table are synchronized by a single semaphore (or lock, monitor, etc.), then a very high locking rate may cause that semaphore to become a bottleneck. This bottleneck can be relieved by partitioning the lock table into several component tables, with a different semaphore serializing accesses to each component. To insert a lock entry, the Lock operation selects the appropriate component by analyzing its parameters (e.g., by hashing the data item name), and then requesting the semaphore that regulates access to that component.

Since most databases are stored on disk, Reads and Writes on data items are usually implemented by Reads and Writes of fixed-size disk blocks. If the granularity of a data item is a disk block, then it is straightforward to implement Read and Write atomically. Each Read or Write on a data item is implemented as an atomic Read or Write on a disk block. If the granularity of data items is not a disk block, then extra care is needed to ensure that Reads and Writes on data items execute atomically.

For example, suppose the granularity of data items is a record, where many records fit on each disk block, but no record is spread over more than one disk block. A program that implements Read must read the disk block that contains the record, extract the record from that block, and return the record to the calling program. A program that implements Write must read the disk

Accounts	Account#	Location	Balance
	339	Marlboro	750
	914	Tyngsboro	2308
	22	Tyngsboro	1550

Assets	Location	Total
	Marlboro	750
	Tyngsboro	3858

FIGURE 3–1
A Banking Database

block that contains the record, update the relevant record in that block, and then write the block back to disk.[6]

An uncontrolled concurrent execution of two of these operations may not be atomic. For example, suppose that two Writes execute concurrently on different records stored in the same block. Suppose each Write begins by independently and concurrently reading a copy of the block into its local memory area. Each Write now updates the copy of its record in its private copy of the disk block, and then writes that private copy back to disk. Since each Write was working on an independent copy of the block, one of the record updates gets lost. If the two Writes had executed serially (with their associated Reads), then neither update would have been lost. Therefore, the implementation is not atomic.

A solution to this problem is to require that each block be locked while a Write is being applied to a record contained in that block. Depending on how Read and Write are implemented, Reads may need to lock disk blocks as well.

Notice that these locks on blocks that make record operations atomic are generally not the same as the record locks that are used to make transactions serializable. A lock on a block can be released as soon as the operation that was using it completes. A lock on a record must follow the 2PL locking protocol.

3.7 THE PHANTOM PROBLEM

We have been modelling a database as a fixed set of data items, which can be accessed by Reads and Writes. Most real databases can dynamically grow and shrink. In addition to Read and Write, they usually support operations to Insert new data and Delete existing data. Does 2PL extend naturally to support dynamic databases? The answer is yes, but the following example would suggest *no*.

---

[6]As we will see in Chapter 6, the disk Writes do not have to take place physically to complete the transaction.

Suppose we have two files representing banking information (see Fig. 3-1): an Accounts file that, for each account, gives the account number (Account#), the bank branch that holds the account (Location), and the amount of money in the account (Balance); and an Assets file that, for each bank branch (Location) gives the total assets of that branch (Total).

We have two transactions to execute on this database. Transaction T_1 reads all of the accounts in Tyngsboro[7] from the Accounts file, adds up their Balances, and compares that sum to the Total assets in Tyngsboro (in Assets). Transaction T_2 adds a new account [99, Tyngsboro, 50] by inserting a record into the Accounts file and then adding the Balance of that account to the Total assets in Tyngsboro. Here is one possible execution of these transactions:

$Read_1$(Accounts[339], Accounts[914], Accounts[22]);

$Insert_2$(Accounts[99, Tyngsboro, 50]);

$Read_2$(Assets[Tyngsboro]); /* returns 3858 */

$Write_2$(Assets[Tyngsboro]); /* writes 3908 */

$Read_1$(Assets[Tyngsboro]); /* returns 3908 */

This execution could have resulted from an execution in which both T_1 and T_2 were two phase locked. T_1 begins by locking the three Accounts records that it wants to Read. (It has to read all of the Accounts records to determine which ones are in Tyngsboro.) Then T_2 locks the record it is about to insert and, after inserting the record, locks the Tyngsboro record in Assets. After finishing with its update to Assets, T_2 releases both of its locks. Now T_1 can finish up by locking the Tyngsboro record in Assets, reading the Total for that Branch, and terminating.

Unfortunately, the execution is not SR. T_1 reads Accounts 339, 914, and 22, but when it reads the Assets of Tyngsboro, it gets a Total that includes Account 99. If T_1 had executed serially before T_2, then it would have correctly read the old Total for Tyngsboro, 3858. If T_1 had executed serially after T_2, then it would have read all four Accounts records and the correct new Total for Tyngsboro.

The problem is record 99 in Accounts. When T_1 first looks in Accounts, it doesn't find that record. However, when it looks in Assets a little later, it finds a Total that reflects the insertion of record 99. Record 99 is called a *phantom* record, because it seems to appear and disappear like a ghost.

The *phantom problem* is the concurrency control problem for dynamic databases. The example seems to show that 2PL does not guarantee correct executions for dynamic databases. Fortunately, the example is misleading and 2PL actually is a good method for synchronizing accesses to dynamic databases.

---

[7]Rhymes with "Kingsborough."

To see how the example is misleading, let's return to first principles. A basic assumption of our model is that a transaction communicates with other transactions *only* through Reads and Writes, and that all such Reads and Writes are synchronized by the scheduler. In the example under discussion, there is a hidden conflict between a Read from T_1 and a Write from T_2. Since T_1 read *all* of the records in Accounts, it must have *read* some control information that told it which records to read, and since T_2 inserted a record into Accounts, it must have *written* that control information. These Read and Write operations on the control information must be locked, just like any other accesses to shared data.

Suppose we adopt a straightforward implementation that locks control information. For example, suppose each file has an end-of-file marker (EOF) after the last record. To determine which records to read, T_1 reads (and locks) records until it reads (and locks) EOF. To insert a record, T_2 must move EOF, so it write locks it. T_1's and T_2's locks on EOF would prevent the incorrect execution under discussion: if T_1 reads EOF before T_2 tries to write it, then T_2 is unable to insert the new record until after T_1 reads Assets[Tyngsboro]; if T_2 writes EOF before T_1 tries to read it, then T_1 cannot finish scanning records in Accounts until after T_2 adds the new record and updates Assets[Tyngsboro].

Unfortunately, this straightforward implementation may perform poorly. Every transaction that inserts a record locks EOF, thereby preventing any other transaction from scanning or inserting into the file. In some cases this is unavoidable. For instance, in the example T_1 is scanning for Accounts records in Tyngsboro, and T_2 is inserting such a record. However, if T_2 were inserting a record into Marlboro instead of Tyngsboro, then T_1 and T_2 would not be accessing any records in common, so their conflict between accesses to EOF would be unnecessary. We can exploit this observation by using a technique called *index locking*.

Index Locking

Suppose each file has one or more *indices* associated with it. Each index is defined on exactly one field of the file, and contains a set of *index entries*. Each index entry has one value of the field on which it's defined and a list of pointers to the records that have that field value. Indices are commonly used in DBSs to speed up access to sets of records whose fields have given values.[8] In the example database of Fig. 3–1, we might create an index on the Location field of Accounts for this purpose.

When a transaction such as T_1 scans Accounts for records in Tyngsboro, it reads and locks the index entry for Tyngsboro. Since any transaction that

---

[8]Section 3.13 describes locking schedulers that are specialized for synchronizing access to tree-structured indices.

inserts a new record r in Tyngsboro must add a pointer to r in the index entry for Tyngsboro, it will try to lock that index entry and thereby conflict with T_1 as desired. If a transaction inserts a record into any other Location, it will access a different index entry and therefore won't conflict with T_1. Thus, T_1 only conflicts with transactions that insert records that it wants to read.

Recall that data item names are not interpreted by the LM. Therefore, a transaction can set a lock on an index entry even though the index does not physically exist. Thus, we can obtain the benefit of index locking without requiring the indices to exist. Each transaction that scans records sets a lock on an index entry that "covers" all of the records it's reading, and each transaction that inserts a record sets a lock on every index entry that would include the new record (if the index existed) and that may be locked by a scanning transaction. The effect is the same as if the transactions were locking indices that physically exist.

In a sense, a transaction that locks the Tyngsboro index entry is effectively locking all records that satisfy the predicate (Location = "Tyngsboro").

One can generalize index locking by allowing more complex predicates to be locked, such as conjunctions of such predicates. That is, the data item name stored in the lock table is actually a predicate. Two locks conflict if there could be a record that satisfies both predicates, that is, if the lock predicates are mutually satisfiable. This is called *predicate locking*. While more general than index locking, it is also more expensive, since it requires the LM to detect conflicts between arbitrary predicates. It is therefore not widely used.

3.8 LOCKING ADDITIONAL OPERATIONS

In some applications, there are periods with heavy Write traffic on certain data items, called *hot spots*. For example, in the banking database of Fig. 3–1, every deposit and withdrawal transaction for Accounts at a given branch Location requires updating the Assets record for that Location; during periods of peak load, the Assets records may become hot spots. When hot spots are present, many transactions may be delayed waiting for locks on hot spot data items. This performance problem can often be avoided by adding other types of operations to the standard repertoire of Read and Write.

For example, in deposits and withdrawals, Writes are used to add and subtract from the Total assets of Locations. If we implement Increment and Decrement as atomic operations, then most Writes can be replaced by these operations. Since Increment and Decrement commute, they can set weaker locks than Write operations, which do not commute. These weaker locks allow transactions to execute concurrently in situations where ordinary write locks would have them delay one another, thereby helping to relieve the bottleneck created by the hot spot. A version of this scheme is implemented in the Main Storage Data Base (MSDB) feature of IBM's IMS Fast Path.

The generalized locking scheme has four types of operations: Read, Write, Increment, and Decrement. It therefore has four types of locks: read locks, write locks, increment locks, and decrement locks. To define the conflict relation between lock types, we examine the corresponding operation types to determine which ones commute. To determine this, we have to be precise about what Increment and Decrement actually do. Let us define them this way:

Increment(x, val):   add val to data item x.

Decrement(x, val):   subtract val from data item x.

We assume that data item values can be arbitrary positive or negative numbers. To ensure that Increment and Decrement commute, we assume that neither operation returns a value to the transaction that issued it. Therefore, for any data item x and values val_I and val_D, the sequence of operations [Increment(x, val_I), Decrement(x, val_D)] produces exactly the same result as the sequence [Decrement(x, val_D), Increment(x, val_I)]. That is, each operation returns the same result (i.e., nothing) and the two operations leave x in the same final state, independent of the order in which they execute. Since they commute independent of the value of val_I and val_D, we drop the val parameters in what follows.

Increment(x) and Decrement(x) *do* conflict with Read(x) and Write(x). For example, Read(x) returns a different value of x depending on whether it precedes or follows Increment(x). Increment(x) produces a different value depending on whether it precedes or follows Write(x). Lock types should be defined to conflict in the same way that their corresponding operations conflict (we'll explain why in a moment). Therefore, the compatibility matrix for the lock types is as shown in Fig. 3–2. A "y" (yes) entry means that two locks of the types specified by the row and column labels for that entry can be simultaneously held on a data item by two different transactions, i.e., the two lock types do *not* conflict. An "n" (no) entry means that the two lock types cannot be concurrently held on a data item by distinct transactions, i.e., the lock types conflict.

Since increment and decrement locks do not conflict, different transactions can concurrently set these locks, most importantly on hot spot data items. Transactions that use these new lock types will therefore be delayed less frequently than if they had only used write locks, which do conflict.

This technique requires that Increment(x) and Decrement(x) be implemented atomically. Each of these operations must read x, update the value appropriately, and then write the result back into x. To ensure that this read-update-write process is atomic, no other operation can access the data item while the process is going on. Thus, while an Increment or Decrement is operating on a data item, the data item is effectively locked (against any other operations on that data item). This lock is only held for the duration of the Increment or Decrement operation. Once the operation is completed, this lock

	Read	Write	Increment	Decrement
Read	y	n	n	n
Write	n	n	n	n
Increment	n	n	y	y
Decrement	n	n	y	y

FIGURE 3–2
A Compatibility Matrix

can be released. However, the increment or decrement lock must be held until the transaction commits to satisfy the two phase rule and strictness.

To understand why this generalized form of 2PL works correctly, we need to revisit the proof of correctness, Lemmas 3.4 and 3.5 and Theorem 3.6. Relative to this issue, the critical step in the proof is: If $T_i \rightarrow T_j$ is in SG(H), then T_i and T_j had conflicting accesses to some data item, and T_i unlocked that data item before T_j locked it. As long as every pair of conflicting (i.e., noncommutative) operation types have associated lock types that conflict, then this argument is valid. Since we defined the lock types so that this property holds, this generalized form of 2PL is correct. We don't even need to modify the proof to handle this case, since it is expressed in terms of arbitrary conflicting operations, such as p and q.

So, we can easily add new operation types by following these simple rules:

1. Ensure that the implementation of each new operation type is atomic with respect to all other operation types.

2. Define a lock type for each new operation type.

3. Define a compatibility matrix for the lock types (for both the old and new operations) so that two lock types conflict iff the corresponding operation types on the same data item do not commute.

3.9 MULTIGRANULARITY LOCKING

So far we have viewed the database as an unstructured collection of data items. This is a very abstract view. In reality a data item could be a block or page of data, a file, a record of a file, or a field of a record. The *granularity* of a data item refers to that item's relative size. For instance, the granularity of a file is *coarser*, and the granularity of a field *finer*, than that of a record.

The granularity of data items is unimportant as far as correctness is concerned. The granularity *is* important, however, when it comes to performance. Suppose, for instance, that we use some version of 2PL. Using coarse granules incurs low overhead due to locking, since there are fewer locks to

Database
|
Area
|
File
|
Record

FIGURE 3–3
A Lock Type Graph

manage. At the same time, it reduces concurrency, since operations are more likely to conflict. For example, if we lock files, two transactions that update the same file cannot proceed concurrently even if they access disjoint sets of records. Fine granularity locks improve concurrency by allowing a transaction to lock only those data items it accesses. But fine granularity involves higher locking overhead, since more locks are requested.[9]

Selecting a granularity for locks requires striking a balance between locking overhead and amount of concurrency. We can do even better than choosing a uniform "optimal" granule size for all data items by means of *multigranularity locking (MGL)*. MGL allows each transaction to use granule sizes most appropriate to its mode of operation. *Long* transactions, those that access many items, can lock coarse granules. For example, if a transaction accesses many records of a file, it simply locks the entire file, instead of locking each individual record. *Short* transactions can lock at a finer granularity. In this way, long transactions don't waste time setting too many locks, and short transactions don't block others by locking large portions of the database that they don't access.

MGL requires an LM that prevents two transactions from setting conflicting locks on two granules that overlap. For example, a file should not be read locked by a long transaction if a record of that file is write locked by a short transaction. An unsatisfactory solution would be to require that the long transaction look at each record of the file to find out whether it may lock the file. This would defeat the very purpose of locking at coarse granularity — namely, to reduce locking overhead.

A better solution is possible by exploiting the natural hierarchical relationship between locks of different granularity. We represent these relationships by

---

[9]There are other factors that could cause concurrency to actually decrease when finer granularity is used. For a more detailed discussion of the effects of granularity on performance, see Section 3.12.

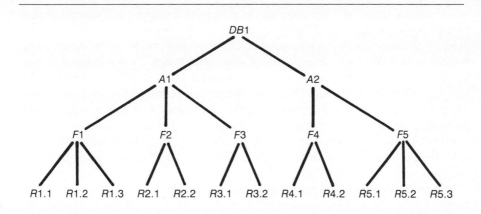

FIGURE 3–4
A Lock Instance Graph

	r	w	ir	iw	riw
r	y	n	y	n	n
w	n	n	n	n	n
ir	y	n	y	y	y
iw	n	n	y	y	n
riw	n	n	y	n	n

FIGURE 3–5
A Compatibility Matrix for Multigranularity Locking

a *lock type graph*. Each edge in the graph connects a data type of coarser granularity to one of finer granularity. For example, in Fig. 3–3 areas (i.e., regions of disks) are of coarser granularity than files, which are of coarser granularity than records.

A set of data items that is structured according to a lock type graph is called a *lock instance graph* (see Fig. 3–4). The graph represents an abstract structure that is used only by the scheduler to manage locks of different granularities. It need not correspond to the physical structure of the data items themselves.

We'll assume that the lock instance graph is a tree. (Later we'll consider more general types of lock instance graphs.) Then a lock on a coarse granule x *explicitly* locks x and *implicitly* locks all of x's proper descendants, which are finer granules "contained in" x. For example, a read lock on an area implicitly read locks the files and records in that area.

It is also necessary to propagate the effects of fine granule locking activity to the coarse granules that "contain" them. To do this, each lock type has an associated *intention lock* type. So, in addition to read and write locks, we have *intention read* (*ir*) *locks* and *intention write* (*iw*) *locks*. Before it locks x, the scheduler must ensure that there are no locks on ancestors of x that implicitly lock x in a conflicting mode. To accomplish this, it sets intention locks on those ancestors. For example, before setting $rl[x]$ on record x, it sets ir locks on x's database, area, and file ancestors (in that order). For any y, $irl[y]$ and $wl[y]$ conflict. Thus, by setting $irl[y]$ on every ancestor y of x, the scheduler ensures that there is no $wl[y]$ that implicitly write locks x. For the same reason, $iwl[x]$ conflicts with $rl[x]$ and $wl[x]$ (see Fig. 3–5).

Suppose a transaction reads every record of a file and writes into a few of those records. Such a transaction needs both a read lock on the file (so it can read all records) and an iw lock (so it can write lock some of them). Since this is a common situation, it is useful to define an riw lock type. An $riwl[x]$ is logically the same as owning both $rl[x]$ and $iwl[x]$ (see Fig. 3–5).

For a given lock instance graph G that is a tree, the scheduler sets and releases locks for each transaction T_i according to the following *MGL protocol*:

1. If x is not the root of G, then to set $rl_i[x]$ or $irl_i[x]$, T_i must have an ir or iw lock on x's parent.

2. If x is not the root of G, then to set $wl_i[x]$ or $iwl_i[x]$, T_i must have an iw lock on x's parent.

3. To read (or write) x, T_i must own an r or w (or w) lock on some ancestor of x. A lock on x itself is an *explicit lock* for x; a lock on a proper ancestor of x is an *implicit lock* for x.

4. A transaction may not release an intention lock on a data item x, if it is currently holding a lock on any child of x.

Rules (1) and (2) imply that to set $rl_i[x]$ or $wl_i[x]$, T_i must first set the appropriate intention locks on all ancestors of x. Rule (3) implies that by locking x, a transaction has implicitly locked all of x's descendants in G. This implicit locking relieves a transaction from having to set explicit locks on x's descendants, which is the main reason for MGL. Rule (4) says that locks should be released in leaf-to-root order, which is the reverse of the root-to-leaf direction in which they were obtained. This ensures that a transaction never owns a read or write lock on x without owning the corresponding intention locks on ancestors of x.

For example, referring to Fig. 3–4, suppose that transaction T_1 wants to set $rl_1[F3]$. It must first set $irl_1[DB1]$, then $irl_1[A1]$, and finally $rl_1[F3]$. Now suppose T_2 tries to set $wl_2[R3.2]$. It must set $iwl_2[DB1]$, $iwl_2[A1]$, and $iwl_2[F3]$. It can obtain the first two locks, but not $iwl_2[F3]$, because it conflicts with $rl_1[F3]$. After T_1 releases $rl_1[F3]$, T_2 can set $iwl_2[F3]$ and $wl_2[R3.2]$. Now suppose T_3 comes along and tries to set $rl_3[A1]$. It must set $irl_3[DB1]$, which it can do immediately, and then set $rl_3[A1]$. It cannot do this before T_2 releases $iwl_2[A1]$.

Correctness

The goal of the MGL protocol is to ensure that transactions never hold conflicting (explicit or implicit) locks on the same data item (i.e., node of the lock instance graph).

Theorem 3.7: Suppose all transactions obey the MGL protocol with respect to a given lock instance data graph, G, that is a tree. If a transaction owns an explicit or implicit lock on a node of G, then no other transaction owns a conflicting explicit or implicit lock on that node.

Proof: It is enough to prove the theorem for *leaf* nodes. For, if two transactions held conflicting (explicit or implicit) locks on a nonleaf node x, they would be holding conflicting (implicit) locks on all descendants and, in particular, all *leaf* descendants of x. Suppose then that transactions T_i and T_j own conflicting locks on leaf x. There are seven cases:

transaction T_i	transaction T_j
1. implicit r lock	explicit w lock
2. implicit r lock	implicit w lock
3. explicit r lock	explicit w lock
4. explicit r lock	implicit w lock
5. implicit w lock	explicit w lock
6. implicit w lock	implicit w lock
7. explicit w lock	explicit w lock

Case 1. By rule (3) of the MGL protocol, T_i owns $rl_i[y]$ for some ancestor y of x. By rule (2) of the MGL protocol (and induction), T_j must own an iw lock on every ancestor of x. In particular, it owns $iwl_i[y]$, which is impossible because the lock types iw and r conflict.

Case 2. By rule (3) of the MGL protocol, T_i owns $rl_i[y]$ for some ancestor y of x, and T_j owns $wl_j[y']$ for some ancestor y' of x. There are three subcases: (a) $y = y'$, (b) y is an ancestor of y', and (c) y' is an ancestor of y. Case (a) is impossible, because T_i and T_j are holding conflicting read and write locks (respectively) on $y = y'$. Case (b) is impossible because T_j must own $iwl_j[y]$, which conflicts with $rl_i[y]$. And case (c) is impossible because T_i must own $irl_i[y']$, which conflicts with $wl_j[y']$. Thus, the assumed conflict is impossible.

Cases (3) and (7) are obviously impossible. Cases (4) and (5) follow the same argument as case (1), and (6) follows the argument of (2).   □

Implementation Issues

Theorem 3.7 says that the MGL protocol prevents transactions from owning conflicting locks. However, this is not sufficient for serializability. To ensure serializability, a scheduler that manages data items of varying granularities must use the MGL protocol *in conjunction with* 2PL. One way of framing the relationship between these two techniques is to say that 2PL gives rules for *when* to lock and unlock data items. The MGL protocol tells *how* to set or release a lock on a data item, given that data items of different granularities are being locked. For example, for a transaction T_i to read a record, 2PL requires that T_i set a read lock on the record. To set that read lock, MGL requires setting *ir* locks on the appropriate database, area, and file, and setting an *r* lock on the record.

Using MGL, the LM services commands to set and release locks in a conventional manner. When it gets a lock request, it checks that no other transaction owns a conflicting lock on the same data item, where the data item could be a database, area, file, or record. If no conflicting locks are set, then it grants the lock request by setting the lock. Otherwise, it blocks the transaction until either the lock request can be granted or a deadlock forces it to reject the request, thereby causing the transaction to abort. The LM need not know about the lock type graph, the lock instance graph, the MGL protocol, or implicit locks. Its only new feature is that it handles more lock types (namely, intention locks) using the expanded compatibility matrix.

Given the larger number of lock types, there are more types of lock conversion than simply converting a read lock to a write lock. For example, one might convert $irl_i[x]$ to $rl_i[x]$ or $riwl_i[x]$. To simplify this lock conversion activity, it is helpful to define the strength of lock types: lock type p is *stronger* than lock type q if for every lock type o, $ol_i[x]$ conflicts with $ql_j[x]$ implies that $ol_i[x]$ conflicts with $pl_j[x]$. For example, *riw* is stronger than *r*, and *r* is stronger than *ir*, but *r* and *iw* have incomparable strengths.

If a transaction owns $pl_i[x]$ and requests $ql_i[x]$, then the LM should convert $pl_i[x]$ into a lock type that is at least as strong as both p and q. For example, if $p = r$ and $q = iw$, then the LM should convert $rl_i[x]$ into $riwl_i[x]$. The strengths of lock types and the lock conversion rules that they imply can be derived from the compatibility matrix. However, this is too inefficient to do at run-time for each lock request. It is better to derive the lock conversion rules statically, and store them in a table that the LM can use at run-time (see Fig. 3–6). The lock conversion problems of deadlocks (cf. Section 3.2) and fair scheduling (cf. Section 3.6) must also be generalized to this expanded set of lock types.

		Old lock type				
		ir	*iw*	*r*	*riw*	*w*
	ir	*ir*	*iw*	*r*	*riw*	*w*
	iw	*iw*	*iw*	*riw*	*riw*	*w*
Requested lock type	*r*	*r*	*riw*	*r*	*riw*	*w*
	riw	*riw*	*riw*	*riw*	*riw*	*w*
	w	*w*	*w*	*w*	*w*	*w*

FIGURE 3–6
Lock Conversion Table
If a transaction has a lock of "old lock type" and requests a lock of "requested lock type," then the table entry defines the lock type into which the "old lock type" should be converted.

Lock Escalation

A system that employs MGL must decide the level of granularity at which a given transaction should be locking data items. Fine granularity locks are no problem. The TM or scheduler simply requests them one by one as it receives operations from the transaction. Coarse granularity locks are another matter. A decision to set a coarse lock is based on a prediction that the transaction is likely to access many of the data items covered by the lock. A compiler may be able to make such predictions by analyzing a transaction's program and thereby generating coarse granularity lock requests that will be explicitly issued by the transaction at run-time. If transactions send high level (e.g., relational) queries to the TM, the TM may be able to tell that the query will generate many record accesses to certain files.

The past history of a transaction's locking behavior can also be used to predict the need for coarse granularity locks. The scheduler may only be able to make such predictions based on the transaction's recent behavior, using a technique called *escalation*. In this case, transactions start locking items of fine granularity (e.g., records). If a transaction obtains more than a certain number of locks of a given granularity, then the scheduler starts requesting locks at the next higher level of granularity (e.g., files), that is, it escalates the granularity of the locks it requests. The scheduler may escalate the granularity of a transaction's lock requests more than once.

In Section 3.2, we showed that a deadlock results when two transactions holding read locks on a data item try to convert them to write locks. Lock escalation can have the same effect. For example, suppose two transactions are holding *iw* locks on a file and are setting *w* locks on records, one by one. If they both escalate their record locking activity to a file lock, they will both try to convert their *iw* lock to a *w* lock. The result is deadlock.

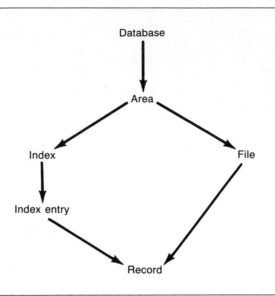

FIGURE 3–7
A Dag Structured Lock Type Graph

In some applications, lock escalations have a high probability of leading to lock conversions that cause deadlocks. In such cases lock escalation may be inappropriate. Instead, if a transaction gets too many fine granularity locks, it should be aborted and restarted, setting coarser granularity locks in its second incarnation. This may be less expensive than lock escalation, which may cause a deadlock.

Generalized Locking Graph

So far, we have assumed that the lock type graph is a tree. This is too restrictive for some applications. In particular, if we use indices, then we would like to be able to lock records of a file by locking indices, index entries, the file, or records. Thus, we are led to the locking type graph of Fig. 3–7, which is a rooted dag,[10] not a tree.

However, we cannot use the MGL protocol's rules for w and iw locks, as illustrated by the following example. Consider the banking database of Fig. 3–1, structured using the lock type graph of Fig. 3–7. Suppose there is an index on Location in Accounts, and that the Location index and the Accounts file are stored in area A1. Suppose T_1 has an ir lock on the database, on A1, and on the Location index for Accounts, and an r lock on the Tyngsboro index

---

[10]See Appendix, Section A.3, for the definition of rooted dag.

entry. Suppose another transaction T_2 has an iw lock on the database and A1 and a w lock on the Accounts file. This is an error, because T_1 has implicitly read locked all records pointed to by the Tyngsboro index entry and T_2 has implicitly write locked those very same records.

One solution to this problem is to require a transaction to set a w or iw lock on x only if it owns an iw lock on *all* parents of x. For example, to obtain a write lock on record 14, a transaction must have an iw lock on (say) the Tyngsboro index entry *and* the Accounts file. To implicitly write lock x, a transaction must explicitly or implicitly write lock *all* parents of x. So, to implicitly write lock the records in the Accounts file, it is not enough to set a write lock on the Accounts file. One must also write lock the Location index (or all of the index's entries). This prevents the problem of the last paragraph; if T_1 has an ir lock on the Location index, then T_2 cannot obtain a w lock on that index and therefore cannot implicitly lock any of the records in the Accounts file.

For a given lock instance graph G that is a dag, the scheduler sets and releases locks for each transaction T_i as follows:

1. If x is not the root of G, then to set $rl_i[x]$ or $irl_i[x]$, T_i must have an ir or iw lock on some parent of x.

2. If x is not the root of G, then to set $wl_i[x]$ or $iwl_i[x]$, T_i must have an iw lock on *all* of x's parents.

3. To read x, T_i must own an r or w lock on *some* ancestor of x. To write x, T_i must own, for every path from the root of G to x, a w lock for some ancestor of x along that path (i.e., it may own different locks for different paths). A lock on x itself is an *explicit lock* for x; locks on proper ancestors of x are *implicit locks* for x.

4. A transaction may not release an intention lock on a data item x if it is currently holding a lock on any child of x.

The proof that this protocol prevents transactions from owning conflicting (explicit or implicit) locks is similar to that of Theorem 3.7 (see Exercise 3.23).

3.10 DISTRIBUTED TWO PHASE LOCKING

Two phase locking can also be used in a distributed DBS. Recall from Section 1.4 that a distributed DBS consists of a collection of communicating sites, each of which is a centralized DBS. Each data item is stored at exactly one site. We say that the scheduler *manages* the data items stored at its site. This means that the scheduler is responsible for controlling access to these (and only these) items.

A transaction submits its operations to a TM. The TM then delivers each Read(x) or Write(x) operation of that transaction to the scheduler that manages x. When (and if) a scheduler decides to process the Read(x) or

Write(x), it sends the operation to its local DM, which can access x and return its value (for a Read) or update it (for a Write). The Commit or Abort operation is sent to all sites where the transaction accessed data items.

The schedulers at all sites, taken together, constitute a *distributed scheduler*. The task of the distributed scheduler is to process the operations submitted by the TMs in a (globally) serializable and recoverable manner.

We can build a distributed scheduler based on 2PL. Each scheduler maintains the locks for the data items stored at its site and manages them according to the 2PL rules. In 2PL, a Read(x) or Write(x) is processed when the appropriate lock on x can be obtained, which only depends on what other locks on x are presently owned. Therefore, each local 2PL scheduler has all the information it needs to decide when to process an operation, without communicating with the other sites. Somewhat more problematic is the issue of when to release a lock. To enforce the two phase rule, a scheduler cannot release a transaction T_i's lock until it knows that T_i will not submit any more operations to it *or any other scheduler*. Otherwise, one scheduler might release T_i's lock and some time later another scheduler might set a lock for T_i, thereby violating the two phase rule (see Exercise 3.26).

It would appear that enforcing the two phase rule requires communication among the schedulers at different sites. However, if schedulers use *Strict* 2PL, then they can avoid such communication. Here is why. As we said previously, the TM that manages transaction T_i sends T_i's Commit to all sites where T_i accessed data items. By the time the TM decides to send T_i's Commit to all those sites, it must have received acknowledgments to all of T_i's operations. Therefore, T_i has surely obtained all the locks it will ever need. Thus, if a scheduler releases T_i's locks after it has processed T_i's Commit (as it must under Strict 2PL), it knows that no scheduler will subsequently set any locks for T_i.

To prove that the distributed 2PL scheduler is correct we simply note that any history H it could have produced satisfies the properties of 2PL histories described in Propositions 3.1–3.3. By Theorem 3.6 then, H is SR. Moreover if the local schedulers use Strict 2PL, H is ST and therefore RC.[11]

The simplicity of this argument is a consequence of the fact that histories model centralized and distributed executions equally well. Since we'll typically specify the properties of histories generated by a scheduler without referring to whether it is a centralized or distributed one, the proof of correctness will apply to both cases.

---

[11]One may question the legitimacy of this argument, given that the Commit or Abort of a distributed transaction is processed by several sites, yet is represented as a single atomic event in a history. For the time being, we can view c_i or a_i as the atomic event corresponding to the moment T_i's TM received acknowledgments of the processing of T_i's Commit or Abort by *all* sites where T_i accessed data items. In Chapter 7 we'll have a lot more to say about why (and how) the commitment and abortion of a distributed transaction can be viewed as an atomic event.

3.11 DISTRIBUTED DEADLOCKS

As in the centralized case, a distributed 2PL scheduler must detect and resolve deadlocks. Timeouts can be used to guess the existence of deadlocks. Or we can explicitly detect deadlocks using WFGs.

The scheduler at site i can maintain a *local* waits-for graph, WFG_i, recording the transactions that wait for other transactions to release a lock on data items managed by that scheduler. Each WFG_i is maintained as described for centralized 2PL. The *global* waits-for graph, WFG, is the union of the local WFG_is.

Unfortunately, it is possible that WFG contains a cycle, and therefore the system is deadlocked, even though each WFG_i is acyclic. For example, consider a distributed scheduler consisting of two 2PL schedulers: scheduler A manages x and scheduler B manages y. Suppose that we have two transactions:

$$T_1 = r_1[x] \rightarrow w_1[y] \rightarrow c_1 \qquad T_2 = r_2[y] \rightarrow w_2[x] \rightarrow c_2$$

Now consider the following sequence of events:

1. Scheduler A receives $r_1[x]$ and sets $rl_1[x]$.

2. Scheduler B receives $r_2[y]$ and sets $rl_2[y]$.

3. Scheduler B receives $w_1[y]$. Since $wl_1[y]$ conflicts with $rl_2[y]$, the scheduler makes $w_1[y]$ wait and adds the edge $T_1 \rightarrow T_2$ to WFG_B.

4. Scheduler A receives $w_2[x]$. That scheduler delays $w_2[x]$ and adds $T_2 \rightarrow T_1$ to WFG_A.

The union of WFG_A and WFG_B contains the cycle $T_1 \rightarrow T_2 \rightarrow T_1$, and we therefore have a deadlock. But this deadlock is not detected by either scheduler's local WFG, since both WFG_A and WFG_B are acyclic. Such a deadlock is called a *distributed deadlock*. To discover such deadlocks, all the schedulers must put their local WFGs together and check the resulting global WFG for cycles.

Global Deadlock Detection

A simple way to do this is for each scheduler to send changes to its WFG_i to a special process, the *global deadlock detector*. The global deadlock detector keeps the latest copy of the local WFG that it has received from each scheduler. It periodically takes the union of these local WFGs to produce a global WFG, and checks it for cycles.

Since the global WFG is only periodically analyzed for cycles, deadlocks may go undetected for a while. As in centralized DBSs, the main penalty for the delay in detecting deadlocks is that deadlocked transactions are holding resources that they aren't using and won't use until the deadlock is broken. The communications delays in shipping around the local WFGs contribute to the delay of distributed deadlock detection, so this delay may be longer than in a centralized DBS.

Once the global deadlock detector finds a deadlock, it must select a victim to abort. This is done based on the same considerations as centralized deadlocks. Therefore, in addition to receiving local WFGs, the global deadlock detector needs information from each site to help it make good victim selections. Moving this information around costs more messages. A technique called *piggybacking* can be used to reduce this message cost.

In piggybacking, n messages that originate at one site and that are all addressed to a common other site are packaged up in one large message. Thus, the number of messages is reduced by a factor of n. Since communication cost is generally a function of the number of messages exchanged (as well as the amount of information), reducing the number of messages in this way can significantly reduce communication cost.

This technique can be applied to global deadlock detection. Each site has its local WFG to send to the global deadlock detector. It also has information for victim selection to send, such as each transaction's resource consumption or abortion cost. Combining this information into one message reduces the cost of sending it to the global deadlock detector.

Phantom Deadlocks

Another problem with distributed deadlock detection relates again to the delay in detecting deadlocks. Clearly, every deadlock will eventually be detected. It may take a while before all of the edges in the deadlock cycle are sent to the global deadlock detector. But since deadlocks don't disappear spontaneously, eventually all of the edges in the cycle will propagate to the deadlock detector, which will then detect the deadlock.

But what about edges in the global WFG that are out-of-date, due to the delay in sending local WFGs to the global deadlock detector? Might the global deadlock detector find a WFG cycle that isn't really a deadlock? Such incorrectly detected deadlocks are called *phantom deadlocks*.

For example, suppose a scheduler sends its local WFG containing some edge $T_i \rightarrow T_j$ to the global deadlock detector. Suppose that shortly after this local WFG is sent, T_j releases its locks, thereby unblocking T_i. Since the scheduler only sends its local WFG periodically, the global detector may use the copy of the graph containing $T_i \rightarrow T_j$ to look for cycles. If it finds a cycle containing that edge, it may believe it has found a genuine deadlock. But the deadlock is a *phantom deadlock*. It isn't real, because one edge in the cycle has gone away, unknown to the global deadlock detector.

Phantom deadlocks can surely happen if a transaction that was involved in a real deadlock spontaneously aborts. For example, a deadlocked transaction might be aborted because some hardware resource (e.g., a terminal) being used by the transaction failed. Although the deadlock wasn't detected, it was broken by the spontaneous abortion. If the global deadlock detector finds the deadlock before it learns of the abortion, it may unnecessarily abort another transaction.

It is interesting that phantom deadlocks can *only* occur due to spontaneous abortions, as long as all transactions are two phase locked. To see this, assume that each lock operation corresponds to a database operation (i.e., no intention locks), and no transaction spontaneously aborts. Suppose the global deadlock detector found a cycle, $T_1 \rightarrow T_2 \rightarrow \cdots \rightarrow T_n \rightarrow T_1$, but there really is no deadlock. Since no transaction spontaneously aborts, and there is no deadlock, all transactions eventually commit. In the resulting execution, since each lock operation corresponds to a database operation, for each edge $T_i \rightarrow T_{i+1}$ in this WFG cycle, there must be an edge $T_{i+1} \rightarrow T_i$ in the SG of the execution. This is true even if the deadlock cycle is a phantom cycle; each edge in the cycle existed at *some* time, so the conflict between the database operations for each edge is real and must produce an SG edge. However, that means that the SG has the same cycle as the WFG, but in the opposite direction. This is impossible, because all transactions were two phase locked. We leave the extension of this argument for intention locks as an exercise (Exercise 3.25).

Distributed Cycle Detection

Most WFG cycles are of length two. To see why, consider how a WFG grows. Suppose we start with all active transactions waiting for no locks, so the WFG has no edges. As transactions execute, they become blocked waiting for locks, so edges begin to appear. Early in the execution, most transactions are not blocked, so most edges will correspond to a transaction's being blocked by a lock owned by an unblocked transaction. But as more transactions become blocked, there is an increased chance that a transaction T_i will be blocked by a lock owned by a blocked transaction T_j. Such an event corresponds to creating a path of length two (i.e., T_i waits for T_j, which is waiting for some other transaction).

Suppose all transactions access the same number of data items, and all data items are accessed with equal probability. Then it can be shown that, on the average, blocked and unblocked transactions own about the same number of locks. This implies that if transactions randomly access data items, then *all* transactions (both blocked and unblocked ones) are equally likely to block a given unblocked transaction. So the probability that an edge creates a path of length two (or three, four, etc.) is proportional to the fraction of blocked transactions that are on the ends of paths of length one (or two, three, etc.). Since initially there are no paths, this must mean that short paths predominate. That is, most transactions are unblocked, many fewer are blocked at the ends of paths of length two, many fewer still are at the ends of paths of length three, and so forth. Hence, an edge that completes a cycle has a much higher chance of connecting an unblocked transaction to one at the end of a path of length one than to one at the end of longer paths. Therefore, most WFG cycles are of length two. For typical applications, over 90% of WFG cycles are of length two.

This observation that cycles are short may make global deadlock detection a less attractive choice than it first appears to be. With global deadlock detection there may be a significant delay and overhead in assembling all of the local WFGs at the global deadlock detector. Thus, a distributed deadlock might go undetected for quite a while. This is especially annoying because most deadlocks involve only two transactions. If the two sites that participate in the deadlock communicate directly, they can detect the deadlock faster by exchanging WFGs with each other. But if every pair of sites behaved this way, then they would all be functioning as global deadlock detectors, leading to much unnecessary communication.

Path pushing is a distributed deadlock detection algorithm that allows all sites to exchange deadlock information without too much communication. Using path pushing, each site looks for cycles in its local WFG *and* lists all paths in its WFG. It selectively sends portions of the list of paths to other sites that may need them to find cycles. Suppose site A has a path $T_i \rightarrow \cdots \rightarrow T_j$. It sends this path to every site at which T_j might be blocked, waiting for a lock. When a site, say B, receives this path, it adds the path's edges to its WFG. Site B's WFG may now have a cycle. If not, B still may find some new and longer paths that neither A nor B had seen before. It lists these paths and sends them to sites that may have more edges to add to the paths.

Every cycle in the global WFG can be decomposed into paths, each of which exists in one local WFG. Using this algorithm, each site sends its paths to other sites that may be able to extend them, by concatenating them with paths that (only) it knows about. Eventually, each path in a cycle will be "pushed" all the way around the cycle and the cycle will be detected by some site.

For example, suppose sites A, B, and C have the following WFGs.

$$\text{WFG}_A = \qquad T_1 \rightarrow T_5 \rightarrow T_3$$
$$\text{WFG}_B = \qquad T_3 \rightarrow T_4$$
$$\text{WFG}_C = \qquad T_4 \rightarrow T_1$$

Site A sends the one and only path in WFG_A to site B, whose graph is now

$$\text{WFG}_B = \qquad T_1 \rightarrow T_5 \rightarrow T_3 \rightarrow T_4$$

Since WFG_B has changed, site B sends its one and only path to C, whose WFG becomes

$$\text{WFG}_C = \qquad T_1 \rightarrow T_5 \rightarrow T_3 \rightarrow T_4 \rightarrow T_1$$

which contains a cycle.

This method usually detects short cycles faster than global deadlock detection. If T_1 is waiting for T_2 at site A and T_2 is waiting for T_1 at site B, then as soon as either A or B sends its paths to the other site, the receiving site will detect the deadlock. By contrast, using global deadlock detection, both A and B would have to wait until both of them send their WFGs to the global deadlock detector, which then has to report the deadlock back to both A and B.

Path pushing sounds fine, as long as each site knows where to send its paths. It could send them to all sites, and in some cases that is the best it can do. But this does involve a lot of communication. The communications cost could easily overshadow the benefit of detecting short cycles more quickly.

One can avoid some of the communication by observing that not all paths need to be sent around. Consider a deadlock cycle that is a concatenation of paths, $p_1, \ldots, p_n$, each of that is local to one site's WFG, say $site_1, \ldots, site_n$ (respectively). So far, we have been pushing all of those paths around the cycle. So to start, $site_1$ sends p_1 to $site_2$, $site_2$ sends p_2 to $site_3$, etc. Now each site knows about longer paths, so $site_1$ sends $[p_n, p_1]$ to site 2, site 2 sends $[p_1, p_2]$ to $site_3$, etc. Using this approach, *every* site will end up detecting the deadlock, which is clearly more than what's necessary. Even worse, two sites that detect the same deadlock might choose different victims.

To reduce the traffic, suppose that (1) each transaction, T_i, has a unique name, $Id(T_i)$, which identifies it, and (2) Ids are totally ordered. In every cycle, at least one path $T_i \rightarrow \cdots \rightarrow T_j$ has $Id(T_i) < Id(T_j)$. (If no path had this property, then $T_i \rightarrow \cdots \rightarrow T_i$ implies $Id(T_i) > Id(T_i)$, a contradiction.) If we only send around paths that have this property, we will still find every cycle. But on average, we will only be sending half as many paths. Therefore, after a site produces a list of paths, it should only send those that have the property.

Communications traffic can be controlled further if each transaction is only active at one site at a time. Suppose that when a transaction T_j executing at site A wants to access data at another site B, it sends a message to B, stops executing at A, and begins executing at B. (Essentially, T_j is making a remote procedure call from A to B.) It does not continue executing at A until B replies to A that it is finished executing its part of the transaction.

When site A finds a path in its WFG from T_i to T_j, it need only send it to B. A knows that B is the only place where T_j could be executing and thereby be blocked waiting for a lock. Of course, T_j at B may have sent a message to C, and so may be stopped at B and now executing at C. But then B will send the path $T_i \rightarrow \cdots \rightarrow T_j$ to C the next time it performs deadlock detection. Eventually, the path $T_i \rightarrow \cdots \rightarrow T_j$ will make its way to every site at which T_j could be waiting for a lock.

In the resulting algorithm, each site, say A, performs the following steps. Site A periodically detects cycles in its local WFG. For each cycle, it selects a victim and aborts it. It then lists all paths not in cycles. For each such path, $T_i \rightarrow \cdots \rightarrow T_j$, if

1. $Id(T_i) < Id(T_j)$, and

2. T_j was formerly active at site A, but is now stopped, waiting for a response from another site B,

then A sends the path to B. When a site receives a list of paths from another site, it adds those edges to its WFG and performs the above steps.

We explore additional simplifications to this algorithm in Exercises 3.27 and 3.28.

Timestamp-based Deadlock Prevention

Deadlock prevention is a cautious scheme in which the scheduler aborts a transaction when it determines that a deadlock might occur. In a sense, the timeout technique described earlier is a deadlock prevention scheme. The system doesn't know that there is a deadlock, but suspects there might be one and therefore aborts a transaction.

Another deadlock prevention method is to run a test at the time that the scheduler is about to block T_i because it is requesting a lock that conflicts with one owned by T_j. The test should guarantee that if the scheduler allows T_i to wait for T_j, then deadlock cannot result. Of course, one could never let T_i wait for T_j. This trivially prevents deadlock but forces many unnecessary abortions. The idea is to produce a test that allows waiting as often as possible without ever allowing a deadlock.

A better test uses a priority that TMs assign to each transaction. Before allowing T_i to wait for T_j, a scheduler compares the transactions' priorities. If T_i has higher priority than T_j, then T_i is allowed to wait; otherwise, it is aborted. In this scheme, T_i waits for T_j only if T_i has higher priority than T_j. Therefore, for each edge $T_i \rightarrow T_j$ in WFG, T_i has higher priority than T_j. The same is true of longer paths that connect T_i to T_j. If there were a cycle in the WFG connecting T_i to itself, then T_i would have a priority higher than itself, which is impossible because each transaction has a single priority. Thus, deadlock is impossible.

However, this scheme may be subject to a different misfortune that prevents a transaction from terminating. If priorities are not assigned carefully, it is possible that every time a transaction tries to lock a certain data item, it is aborted because its priority isn't high enough. This is called *livelock* or *cyclic restart*.

For example, suppose each TM uses a counter to assign a priority to each transaction when it begins executing or when it restarts after being aborted. Suppose a TM supervises the execution of T_i and T_j as follows.

1. The TM assigns T_i a priority of 1.

2. T_i issues $w_i[x]$, causing it to set $wl_i[x]$.

3. The TM assigns T_j a priority of 2.

4. T_j issues $w_j[y]$, causing it to set $wl_j[y]$.

5. T_i issues $w_i[y]$. Since T_j has set $wl_j[y]$, we have to decide whether to allow T_i to wait. Since T_i's priority is lower than T_j's, T_i is aborted.

6. The TM restarts T_i, assigning it a priority of 3.

7. T_i issues $w_i[x]$, causing it to set $wl_i[x]$.

8. T_j issues $w_j[x]$. Since T_i has set $wl_i[x]$ and has a higher priority than T_i, T_j is aborted.

9. The TM restarts T_j, assigning it a priority of 4.

10. T_j issues $w_j[y]$, causing it to set $wl_j[y]$.

We are now in exactly the same situation as step (4). If the transactions follow the same sequence of requests that they did before, they will each cause the other one to abort as before, perhaps forever. They are in a livelock.

Livelock differs from deadlock because it doesn't prevent a transaction from executing. It just prevents the transaction from completing because it is continually aborted. One way to avoid livelock is to ensure that each transaction eventually has a high enough priority to obtain all of the locks that it needs without being aborted. This can be accomplished by using a special type of priority called timestamps.

Timestamps are values drawn from a totally ordered domain. Each transaction T_i is assigned a timestamp, denoted $ts(T_i)$, such that if $T_i \neq T_j$ then either $ts(T_i) < ts(T_j)$ or $ts(T_j) < ts(T_i)$.

Usually, TMs assign timestamps to transactions. If there is only one TM in the entire system, then it can easily generate timestamps by maintaining a counter. To generate a new timestamp, it simply increments the counter and uses the resulting value. If there are many TMs, as in distributed DBSs, then a method is needed to guarantee the total ordering of timestamps generated by different TMs. It is desirable to find a method that doesn't require the TMs to communicate with each other, which would make the timestamp generation activity more expensive.

The following technique is usually used to make this guarantee. Each TM is assigned a unique number (its process or site identifier, for example). In addition, each TM maintains a counter as before, which it increments every time it generates a new timestamp. However, a timestamp is now an ordered pair consisting of the current value of the counter followed by the TM's unique number. The pairs are totally ordered, first by their counter value and second, in case of ties, by their unique TM numbers.

The local counter used by each TM can be an actual clock. If a clock is used, then the TM obviously should not increment it to guarantee uniqueness. Instead, it should simply check that the clock has ticked between the assignment of any two timestamps.

Since timestamps increase monotonically with time and are unique, if a transaction lives long enough it will eventually have the smallest timestamp (i.e., will be the oldest) in the system. We can use this fact to avoid livelock by using a rule for priority-based deadlock prevention that never aborts the oldest active transaction. Every transaction that is having trouble finishing due to livelock will eventually be the oldest active transaction, at which point it is guaranteed to finish.

Suppose we define a transaction's priority to be the inverse of its timestamp. Thus, the older a transaction, the higher its priority. We can then use timestamps for deadlock prevention, without risking livelock, as follows. Suppose the scheduler discovers that a transaction T_i may not obtain a lock because some other transaction T_j has a conflicting lock. The scheduler can use several strategies, two of which are:

Wait-Die: **if** $\text{ts}(T_i) < \text{ts}(T_j)$ **then** T_i waits **else** abort T_i.

Wound-Wait: **if** $\text{ts}(T_i) < \text{ts}(T_j)$ **then** abort T_j **else** T_i waits.

The words *wound*, *wait*, and *die* are used from T_i's viewpoint; T_i wounds T_j, causing T_j to abort; T_i waits; and T_i aborts and therefore dies. In both methods, only the younger of the two transactions is aborted. Thus, the oldest active transaction is never aborted by either method.

To ensure these methods are not subject to livelock, two other restrictions are needed. First, the timestamp generator must guarantee that it only generates a finite number of timestamps smaller than any given timestamp. If this were not true, then a transaction could remain in the system indefinitely without ever becoming the oldest transaction. Second, when an aborted transaction is restarted, it uses its old timestamp. If it were reassigned a new timestamp every time it was restarted, then it might never become the oldest transaction in the system.

Notice that wounding a transaction might not cause it to abort. The definition of Wound-Wait should really be:

if $\text{ts}(T_i) < \text{ts}(T_j)$ **then** *try to* abort T_j **else** T_i waits.

The scheduler can only *try* to abort T_j because T_j may have already terminated and committed before the scheduler has a chance to abort it. Thus, the abort may be ineffective in killing the transaction. That's why it's called *wound* and not *kill*; the scheduler wounds T_j, in a (possibly unsuccessful) attempt to kill it. But this still avoids the deadlock, because the wounded transaction releases its locks whether it commits or aborts.

Wound-Wait and Wait-Die behave rather differently. In Wound-Wait, an old transaction T_i pushes itself through the system, wounding every younger transaction T_j that it conflicts with. Even if T_j has nearly terminated and has no more locks to request, it is still vulnerable to T_i. After T_i aborts T_j and T_j restarts, T_j may again conflict with T_i, but this time T_j waits.

By contrast, in Wait-Die an old transaction T_i waits for each younger transaction it encounters. So as T_i ages, it tends to wait for more younger transactions. Thus, Wait-Die favors younger transactions while Wound-Wait favors older ones. When a younger transaction T_j conflicts with T_i, it aborts. After it restarts, it may again conflict with T_i and therefore abort again — a disadvantage relative to Wound-Wait. However, once a transaction has obtained all of its locks, it will not be aborted for deadlock reasons — an advantage over Wound-Wait.

Comparing Deadlock Management Techniques

Each approach to deadlock management has its proponents. Many centralized DBSs, such as IBM's DB2 and RTI's INGRES, use WFG cycle detection. Each of the distributed techniques we have described is implemented in a commercial product, and each putatively works well: Tandem uses timeout; Distributed INGRES uses centralized deadlock detection; IBM's System R* prototype uses path pushing; and GE's MADMAN uses timestamp-based prevention.

3.12 LOCKING PERFORMANCE[12]

To accept published guidelines on locking performance requires a leap of faith, because the results are derived with simplistic assumptions and the state-of-the-art is unsettled. Nevertheless, an understanding of locking performance is pivotal to quality system design. This section should be read as preliminary results of an immature field.

Throughout this section, we will assume that all transactions require the same number of locks, all data items are accessed with equal probability, and all locks are write locks. The transactions use Strict 2PL: data items are locked before they are accessed, and locks are released only after the transactions commit (or abort). The DBS is centralized, so there is no communication cost. However, the DBS may be running on a machine with two or more tightly coupled processors.

Resource and Data Contention

In any multiprogramming system, the amount of work done on the system cannot increase linearly with the number of users. When there is *resource contention* over memory space, processor time, or I/O channels, queues form and time is wasted waiting in the queues. In DBSs that use locking, queues also form because of delays due to lock conflicts, called *data contention*.

Locking can cause *thrashing*. That is, if one increases the number of transactions in the system, throughput will increase up to a point, then drop. The

---

[12]Written by Dr. Y.C. Tay, Mathemathics Department, National University of Singapore. Unlike other sections, this section mentions results that are not derived in the book. For adequate justifications of these conclusions, we refer the reader to the bibliographic notes.

user usually observes this as a sudden increase in response time. This phenomenon is similar to thrashing in operating systems. There, the throughput drops due to time wasted in page faults when too many processes each have too little space. It is the result of resource contention — too many processes fighting over main memory. In DBSs, thrashing *can be caused by data contention alone*. In an idealized system with unlimited hardware resources, so that transactions queue only for data and never for resources, thrashing may still occur.

We distinguish two forms of thrashing: *RC-thrashing*, which occurs in systems with resource contention and no data contention, and *DC-thrashing*, which occurs in an idealized system with data contention and no resource contention. Although all systems have some resource contention, DC-thrashing is a useful concept.

Thrashing

Resource and data contention produce rather different forms of thrashing. With RC-thrashing, the system is busy transferring pages in and out of memory, so user processes make little progress. This suggests that DC-thrashing may be caused by transaction restarts induced by deadlocks. If the deadlock rate is high, then transactions are busy being repeatedly restarted, so transactions make little progress. However, DC-thrashing is in fact not caused by restarts, but by blocking.

Measurements of experimental and commercial DBSs indicate that deadlocks are much rarer than conflicts. Simulations also show that, up to the DC-thrashing point, transactions spend much more time waiting in lock queues than in being restarted. Moreover, the restart rate can be as low as 1-2% of throughput when DC-thrashing happens. But the most conclusive evidence is that beyond the DC-thrashing point, increasing the number of transactions actually decreases the number of transactions that are not blocked. That is, adding one more transaction causes more than one transaction (on average) to be blocked. Thus, whereas RC-thrashing happens because the system is busy doing wasteful work, DC-thrashing happens because too many transactions are tied up in lock queues, thus reducing system utilization.

It does not even take much blocking to cause DC-thrashing. At the DC-thrashing point, the average length of a lock queue could be less than one, and the average depth of a tree in the waits-for graph less than two. (The latter implies that, up to the DC-thrashing point, most deadlock cycles have only two transactions.) Hence, if half the transactions are blocked, the system is probably thrashing.

Although blocking is the dominant performance factor up to the DC-thrashing point, the effect of deadlocks does increase at a much faster rate than blocking. Beyond the thrashing point, restarts rapidly overtake blocking as the dominant factor.

Blocking and Restarts

Locking resolves conflicts either by blocking a transaction or by aborting and restarting it. Restarts are obviously undesirable, since work is wasted. The way blocking degrades performance is more subtle. Blocking lets a transaction hold locks without doing anything with them, even while other transactions are waiting to acquire those locks. Through DC-thrashing, we have seen how seriously this can affect performance.

Both restarts and blocking are bad for performance. But which is worse? Since Strict 2PL may be thrashing and yet have a very low deadlock rate, it resolves almost all conflicts by blocking. Therefore, let us call Strict 2PL a *blocking policy.* Alternatively, a *pure restart policy* simply aborts a transaction whenever it requests a lock that is already held by another transaction, and restarts the aborted transaction when the other releases the lock. Thus, a pure restart policy resolves all conflicts by restarts. Comparing these two policies is a way of comparing the performance effect of blocking and restarts.

Intuitively, a pure restart policy is very severe. One might expect it to perform badly compared with a blocking policy. Surprisingly, this is not necessarily so. Let the *multiprogramming level* (MPL) refer to the number of active transactions. Since aborted transactions waiting to restart consume minimal resources, we exclude them from MPL. However, since transactions blocked in lock queues by a blocking policy consume resources (mainly, memory space) as transactions in resource queues do, we include them in MPL.

Given the same MPL and under two conditions (see the next paragraph), a pure restart policy has a throughput that is only slightly lower than that of a blocking policy before the latter's DC-thrashing point. Furthermore, when DC-thrashing sets in for the blocking policy, the pure restart policy has a higher throughput. (See Fig. 3–8. Note that this comparison does not take resource contention into account yet; if there were no conflicts, the throughput would increase linearly with MPL in this figure.)

The two required conditions are quick transaction abortion and low resource contention. If abortions take too long, they will slow down the throughput of a pure restart policy, thus making it inferior to a blocking policy, which is only marginally affected by abort time since it has a low deadlock rate. Resource contention also hurts a pure restart policy more than a blocking policy. With the latter, some transactions are blocked in lock queues, so fewer transactions compete for resources. (Thus, data contention alleviates resource contention for a blocking policy.) Since resource contention causes transactions to waste time waiting in resource queues, it degrades the throughput of a blocking policy less than that of a pure restart policy. This too can make a pure restart policy consistently inferior (see Fig. 3–9).

Therefore, our intuition that a pure restart policy has worse throughput than a blocking policy is based on the assumption that restarts either take a long time or add too much resource contention. However, both assumptions

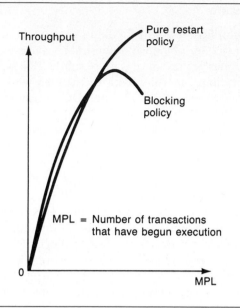

FIGURE 3–8
Throughput of Blocking and Pure Restart Policies with No Resource Contention

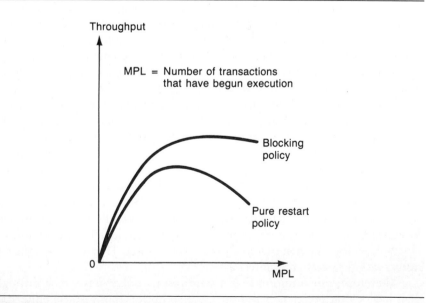

FIGURE 3–9
Possible Effect of Resource Contention on Fig. 3–8

could be violated. A clever implementation can make transaction abortion fast. And resource contention can perhaps be minimized by giving each transaction a dedicated microprocessor, so there is no contention for CPU cycles. Hence, a pure restart policy may be feasible.

Still, a pure restart policy has a longer response time than a blocking policy, even when their throughputs are similar. This is because an aborted transaction must wait for the conflicting transaction to release the lock before restarting, thus increasing its response time.

Therefore, except for the response time difference, blocking a transaction for a conflict may not be better than restarting it. Blocking is selfish. A blocked transaction can preserve what it has done, and prevent transactions that need its locks from making progress. Restarting is self-sacrificing. Since a conflict prevents a transaction from proceeding, restarting it frees its locks, so that it will not hinder others. When data contention becomes intense, altruism is the better policy. This is why a pure restart policy has a higher throughput than a blocking policy when the latter suffers from DC-thrashing, provided the two conditions hold. One may therefore consider restarts as a means of overcoming the upper bound that blocking imposes on the throughput through DC-thrashing.

Predeclaration

Another way to exceed the throughput limit that blocking imposes is to replace *Basic 2PL*, where a transaction sets locks as it needs them, by *Conservative 2PL*, where it obtains them before it begins. As the number of transactions increases, the throughput under Basic 2PL is initially higher than under Conservative 2PL, but eventually becomes lower. However, resource contention can change this. Under light data contention, Basic 2PL delays fewer transactions, and so suffers more resource contention. Its throughput is therefore reduced more, and may become consistently lower than Conservative 2PL.

Resource contention aside, how can Conservative 2PL have a higher throughput than Basic 2PL? Intuitively, since Basic 2PL only sets locks as they are needed, it should have more concurrency and therefore higher throughput than Conservative 2PL. This is true when data contention is light. But when it becomes heavy, as when DC-thrashing sets in, Basic 2PL in fact causes transactions to hold locks longer than under Conservative 2PL, thereby lowering throughput.

Conservative 2PL is sometimes favored because it avoids deadlocks. However, DC-thrashing occurs even if deadlocks are rare. Conservative 2PL should therefore be first considered as a means of bringing throughput above the limit set by blocking through DC-thrashing. Its advantage in deadlock avoidance is secondary.

A Bound on Workload

We have said little about performance beyond the DC-thrashing point. Indeed, we have assumed that a system will not be driven beyond that point, since there is no performance gain to be had. DC-thrashing thus defines an operating region for the combination of parameters that affect the performance. What is this region?

Suppose N is the MPL, k the number of locks a transaction requires, and D the number of data items, where data item is the locking granularity. (Note that, in general, k is less than the number of data accesses a transaction makes. For instance, if a data item is a file, two writes on one particular file would require only one lock.) Then a measure of the data contention is the *DC-workload* $W = k^2N/D$. DC-thrashing occurs at about $W = 1.5$, so the operating region is roughly bounded by $k^2N/D < 1.5$. (This number 1.5 was numerically obtained from a performance model, and confirmed through simulations. It is not known why DC-thrashing occurs at this particular value of W.)

The value 1.5 is almost surely optimistic. It is based on the assumption that accesses are uniform over the database. In reality, access patterns are skewed, which causes DC-thrashing to occur earlier. Furthermore, DC-thrashing does not account for resource contention, which further reduces the throughput. Therefore, real DBSs thrash before the DC-thrashing point. Hence, the value 1.5 only indicates the order of magnitude of the bound on the DC-workload.

MPL, Transaction Length, and Granularity

Bearing the caveat in mind, MPL should therefore be less than $1.5D/k^2$ for given k and D. This bound should only act as a guide in planning a system. The true bound will quickly reveal itself once the system is built.

Other than thrashing, there is another constraint on the MPL. Although throughput increases with N (up to the thrashing point), the deadlock rate increases even faster. If restarts are expensive, they may further reduce the number of active transactions that can be handled.

As expected, increasing the number of locks per transaction reduces the throughput. It also increases the number of deadlocks per transaction completion. Transactions should therefore be kept short. Long transactions should be broken into smaller ones, if possible. For a quantitative but simplistic argument, suppose N transactions requiring k locks each are broken into $2N$ transactions requiring k^2 locks each. The DC-workload then drops from k^2N/D to $(k/2)^2(2N)/D = k^2N/2D$, thus reducing the data contention.

Besides the number of transactions and the number of locks they need, another parameter in the DC-workload is the number of data items D. A small D (coarse granularity) implies more data is covered by each lock. A large D (fine granularity) implies the opposite.

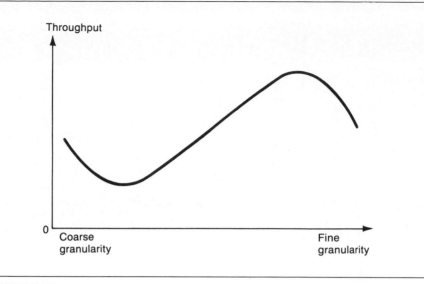

FIGURE 3–10
The General Granularity Curve

Three factors determine the effect of granularity on performance. One is locking overhead. The finer the granularity, the more locks a transaction must set, thus incurring more overhead.

Another factor is data contention. Intuitively, the finer the granularity, the more potential concurrency, so the better the performance. Actually, this intuition is not entirely correct. Finer granularity does reduce the probability of conflict *per request*. However, more locks are needed too, so the number of conflicts a transaction encounters may increase. One can see this from the DC-workload k^2N/D. If an increase in D causes a proportionate increase in k, then the DC-workload increases, so there is more data contention.

The third factor is resource contention. Recall that data contention alleviates resource contention by blocking some transactions. Refining the granularity may therefore release so many transactions from lock queues that they end up spending even more time in resource queues.

These three factors combine to shape the *granularity curve* in Fig. 3–10. The initial drop in throughput as granularity is refined is caused by an increase in k when D is increased, leading to increased locking overhead and data contention. As granules shrink, the number of locks a transaction requires approaches the maximum of one new lock per data access. Now k becomes insensitive to D, the DC-workload decreases, and throughput picks up if granularity is further refined. The final drop in the granularity curve is caused by resource contention. Suppose there are enough transactions in the system to cause RC-thrashing if some transactions are not blocked in lock queues. Then

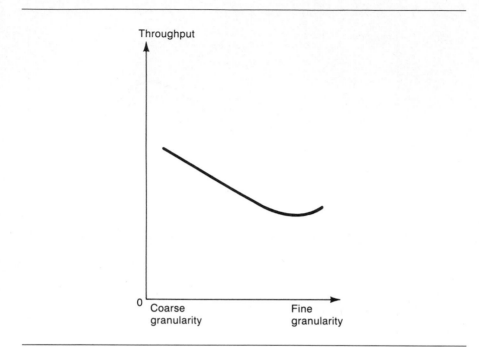

FIGURE 3–11
Possible Granularity Curve for Long Transactions

refining granularity reduces the data contention, unblocks the transactions, and causes a drop in throughput through RC-thrashing.

A given system may not see the entire granularity curve. For instance, for *long* transactions, which access a significant portion of the database, even the finest granularity may not bring the throughput above the initial drop, as in Fig. 3–11. Each transaction should then lock the entire database, thus using the coarsest granularity. For short transactions, k may quickly become insensitive to D, so the initial drop in the granularity curve is minimal. If, in addition, N is not excessive, then the final drop in the granularity curve will not occur, so the curve may look like Fig. 3–12. In this case, the curve suggests that the granularity should be as fine as possible.

Read Locks and Nonuniform Access

We have so far assumed that all locks are write locks. Suppose now that a fraction s of the lock requests are for read locks, and the rest are for write locks. Then the DC-workload drops from k^2N/D to $(1-s^2) k^2N/D$. Equivalently, it is as if the granules have been refined, with D increased to $D/(1-s^2)$.

Contrary to our assumption, transactions do not really access all data with equal probability. In particular, a portion p of the database may contain high-

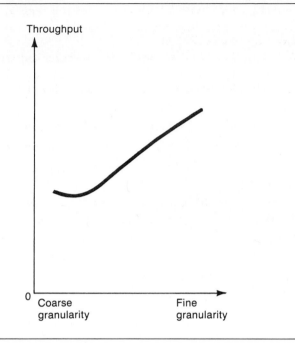

FIGURE 3–12
Possible Granularity Curve for Short Transactions

traffic data that transactions access with a higher probability q than the rest of the database. For example, if $p = 0.2$ and $q = 0.7$, then 70% of a transaction's requests fall within 20% of the database. If we assume uniform access among high-traffic data, and uniform access among the rest of the data as well, then this skewed access pattern increases the DC-workload from k^2N/D to $(1 + (q-p)^2/p(1-p))(k^2N/D)$. Equivalently, it is as if the number of granules has been reduced from D to $D/(1 + (q-p)^2/p(1-p)$.

3.13 TREE LOCKING

Suppose data items are known to be structured as nodes of a tree, and transactions always access data items by following paths in the tree. The scheduler can exploit the transactions' predictable access behavior by using locking protocols that are not two phase. That is, in certain cases, a transaction can release a lock and subsequently obtain another lock. This can lead to better performance.

To simplify the discussion we shall not distinguish between Reads and Writes. Instead we have just one type of operation, "transaction T_i accesses data item x," denoted $a_i[x]$. The Access operation $a_i[x]$ can read and/or write into x. Hence, two Access operations on the same data item conflict.

We associate a lock type a with the operation type a. We use $al_i[x]$ to denote an *access lock* on x by transaction T_i. Since two Access operations on x conflict, two access locks on x also conflict.

In *tree locking* (*TL*), we assume that a hierarchical structure has been imposed on the set of data items.[13] That is, there is a tree DT, called the *data tree*, whose nodes are labelled by the data items. The TL scheduler enforces the following rules:

1. Before submitting $a_i[x]$ to the DM, the scheduler must set $al_i[x]$.

2. The scheduler can set $al_i[x]$ only if no $al_j[x]$ is set, for all $j \neq i$.

3. If x is not the root of DT, then the scheduler can set $al_i[x]$ only if $al_i[y]$ is already set, where y is x's parent in DT.

4. The scheduler must not release $al_i[x]$ until *at least* after the DM has acknowledged that $a_i[x]$ has been processed.

5. Once the scheduler releases a lock on behalf of T_i, it may not subsequently obtain that same lock again for T_i.

Rules (3) and (5) imply that the scheduler can release $al_i[x]$ only after it has obtained the locks T_i needs on x's children. This handshake between locking children and unlocking their parent is called *lock coupling*. Notice that lock coupling implies that locks are obtained in root-to-leaf order.

This leads to the key fact about TL: If T_i locks x before T_j, then for every descendant v of x in DT, if T_i and T_j both lock v, then T_i locks v before T_j. To see this, let $(x, z_1, ..., z_n, v)$ be the path of nodes connecting x to v ($n \geq 0$). By rules (3) and (5), T_i must lock z_1 before releasing its lock on x. Since T_i locks x before T_j, that means T_i must lock z_1 before T_j. A simple induction argument shows that the same must be true for every node on the path. This gives us the following proposition.

Proposition 3.8: If T_i locks x before T_j, then for every descendant v of x in DT, if T_i and T_j both lock v, then T_i locks v before T_j. □

Consider any edge $T_i \rightarrow T_j$ in the SG of some history produced by TL. By the definition of SG, there is a pair of conflicting operations $a_i[x] < a_j[x]$. By rules (1), (2), and (4), T_i unlocked x before T_j locked x. By Proposition 3.8, it immediately follows that T_i locked the root before T_j, since x is a descendant of the root and, by rule (3), all transactions must lock the root. By rule (2), this implies that T_i unlocked the root before T_j locked the root. A simple induction argument shows that this property also holds for paths in the SG. That is, if there is a path from T_i to T_j in SG, then T_i unlocked the root before T_j locked the root.

---

[13]This should not be confused with the lock instance graph, used in connection with multigranularity locking.

Suppose the SG has a cycle $T_1 \rightarrow \cdots \rightarrow T_n \rightarrow T_1$. By the previous paragraph, it follows that T_1 unlocked the root before T_1 locked the root. This violates rule (5), so the cycle cannot exist. Thus, we have proved the following theorem.

Theorem 3.9: The tree locking scheduler produces serializable executions. $\square$

TL scheduling is reminiscent of a scheduling policy used to avoid deadlocks in operating systems where processes must obtain resources in a predefined linear order. TL schedulers share the property of deadlock freedom with this policy. To see this, first note that if T_i is waiting to lock the root, it can't be involved in a deadlock (since it has no locks and therefore no transaction could be waiting for it). Now, suppose T_i is waiting for a lock currently held by T_j on a node other than the root. By the argument just given, T_j unlocks the root before T_i locks it. Thus, by induction, if the WFG has a cycle containing T_i, T_i unlocks the root before it locks the root, a contradiction. So, TL schedulers are not prone to deadlocks.

In addition to deadlock avoidance, another benefit of TL is that locks can be released earlier than in 2PL. For any data item x, once a transaction has locked all of x's children that it will ever lock, it no longer needs $al_i[x]$ to satisfy rule (3), and can therefore release it. The problem is, how does the scheduler know that T_i has locked all of x's children that it needs? Clearly, if T_i has locked *all* children of x, then it has locked all those that it needs. However, other than this special case, the scheduler cannot determine that T_i no longer needs $al_i[x]$ unless it receives some advice from T_i's TM. Without this help, it can only safely release a transaction T_i's locks when the transaction terminates. In this case transactions are (strictly) two phase locked and there is little point in enforcing the additional restriction of tree locking — except that we also get deadlock freedom. Therefore, TL only makes sense in those cases where the TM knows transactions' access patterns well enough to tell the scheduler when to release locks.

Releasing locks earlier than the end of the transaction is valuable for performance reasons. By holding locks for shorter periods, transactions block each other less frequently. Thus transactions are delayed less often due to locking conflicts, and thereby have better response time.

However, this benefit is only realized if transactions normally access nodes in DT in root-to-leaf order. If they don't, then TL is imposing an unnatural ordering on their accesses, thereby forcing them to lock nodes before they're ready to use them or to lock nodes that they don't use at all. In this sense, TL could be reducing the concurrency among transactions.

In addition, we may need to strengthen TL to ensure recoverability, strictness, or avoidance of cascading aborts. For example, to avoid cascading aborts, a transaction should hold its lock on each data item it writes until it commits, which is more than what TL requires. For internal nodes, holding locks for longer periods can have a serious performance impact, since transactions must lock an internal node x to access any of x's descendants. Fortunately, in many practical applications, most updates are to leaves of DT, which transactions can lock until commitment with little performance impact. We'll look at one such application, B-trees, later in the section.

Variations of Tree Locking

TL can be generalized in several ways. First, we need not restrict a transaction to set its first lock on the root of DT. It is safe for it to begin by locking *any* data item in DT. However, once it sets its first lock on some data item x, rule (3) implies that it can subsequently only lock data items in the subtree rooted at x (see Exercise 3.39).

TL can also be generalized to distinguish between read and write locks. If each transaction sets either only read locks or only write locks, then the ordinary conflict rules between these locks are satisfactory for producing SR executions. However, if a transaction can set both read and write locks, then problems can arise, because read locks can allow transactions to "pass" each other while moving down the tree. For example, suppose x is the root of the tree, y is a child of x, and z is a child of y. Consider the following sequence of events:[14]

$$wl_1[x] \ rl_1[y] \ wu_1[x] \ wl_2[x] \ rl_2[y] \ wu_2[x] \ wl_2[z] \ ru_2[y] \ wu_2[z] \ wl_1[z] \ ru_1[y] \ wu_1[z].$$

In this execution, T_1 write locked x before T_2, but T_2 write locked z before T_1, producing a non-SR execution. This was possible because T_2 "passed" T_1 when they both held read locks on y. A solution to this problem is to require that for every path of data items $x_1, \ldots, x_n$, if T_i sets write locks on x_1 and x_n, and sets read locks on the other data items on the path, then it obtains locks on all data items on the path before it releases locks on any of them. By holding locks this long, a transaction ensures that other transactions cannot pass it along this path. Another solution is to require that locks set by a transaction along a path are of nondecreasing strength. (See Exercise 3.40.)

A third generalization of tree locking is *dag locking* (*DL*), in which data items are organized into a partial order rather than a hierarchy. That is, there is a rooted dag whose nodes are labelled by the data items. The DL scheduler must enforce the same rules (1) – (5), the only difference being

3. Unless x is the root, to obtain a lock on x, T_i must be holding (at that time) a lock on *some* parent of x, and there must have been a time at which T_i held locks on *all* parents of x.

---

[14]Recall that $rl_i[x]$, $wl_i[x]$, $ru_i[x]$ and $wu_i[x]$ mean that T_i has set a read lock on x, set a write lock on x, released its read lock on x, and released its write lock on x, respectively.

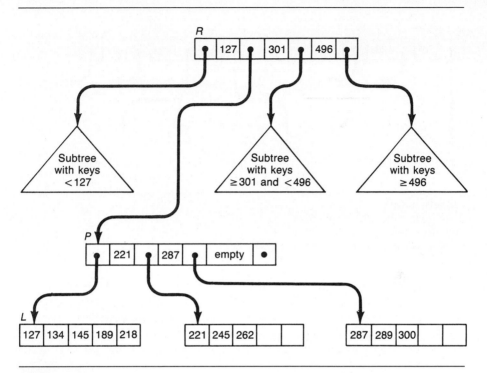

FIGURE 3–13
A B-tree
In this example, there is room for up to three keys in each internal node and up to five keys in each leaf.

As with TL, the DL scheduler produces SR executions and is not prone to deadlocks (see Exercise 3.41). The two previous generalizations apply to this case too.

B-Tree Locking[15]

An important application of tree locking is to concurrency control in tree-structured indices. The most popular type of search tree in database systems is B-trees. There are several specialized tree locking protocols specifically designed for B-trees, some of which we will describe. These protocols can also be applied to other types of search structures, such as binary trees and dynamic hash tables.

---

[15]This subsection assumes a basic knowledge of B-trees; see [Bayer, McCreight 72], and [Comer 79]. We use the B^+-tree variation in this section, which is the variation of choice for commercial products, such as IBM's VSAM.

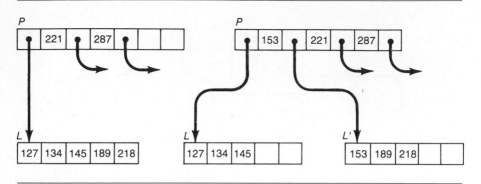

FIGURE 3–14
A B-tree Insertion Causing a Split
(a) Before inserting key 153.
(b) After splitting L to make room for key 153.

A B-tree consists of a set of nodes structured as a tree. Its purpose is to index a set of records of the form [key, data], where the key values are totally ordered and may consist, for example, of numbers or alphanumeric strings.

Each node of a B-tree contains a sorted list of key values. For internal nodes, each pair of consecutive field values defines a range of key values between two keys, k_i and k_{i+1} (see Fig. 3–13). For each such pair of consecutive values, there is a pointer to a subtree that contains all of the records whose key values are in the range defined by that pair. For leaf nodes, each key has the data part of the record associated with that key value (but no pointer). Since the data portion of records is uninterpreted by the B-tree algorithms of interest to us, we will ignore them in the following discussion and examples.

The two B-tree algorithms that are important for this discussion are Search and Insert. (Delete leads to problems similar to those of Insert, so we will not treat it here.) The *search* of a B-tree for a key value begins at the root. Each node has information that directs the search to the appropriate child of that node. The search proceeds down one path until it reaches a leaf, which contains the desired key value. For example, a search for key 134 in Fig. 3–13 (1) finds the key range [127, 301) in the root R, (2) follows the pointer to P, (3) finds the key range [127, 221) in node P, (4) follows the pointer to L, and (5) finds the key 134 in L.[16]

To *insert* a record R in a B-tree, a program first searches for the leaf L that should contain the record. If there is room for R in L, then it inserts R there (properly sequenced). Otherwise, it allocates another node L', moves half of L's records from L to L', and adds the minumum key in L' and a pointer to L'

---

[16]The notation $[a, b)$ means the range of values from a to b that includes the value a but not the value b.

in L's parent (see Fig. 3–14). If L's parent has no room for the extra key and pointer, then the program splits L's parent in the same way that it split L. This splitting activity continues recursively up the tree until it reaches a node that has room for the pointer being added, or it splits the root, in which case it adds a new root.

We want to implement Search and Insert as transactions.[17] We could use 2PL for this purpose. But since Search and Insert begin by accessing the root of the tree, each such operation would effectively lock the entire tree.

We can do somewhat better by using tree locking. Since Search only *reads* nodes, it sets read locks. Since Insert writes into a leaf L, it should certainly set a write lock on L. If L was full before the Insert began, then Insert will also write into some of L's ancestors, and must set write locks on them as well. Unfortunately, Insert cannot determine whether it will need to write into nonleaf nodes until it actually reads L to determine if L is full. Since this happens at the end of its search down the tree, it doesn't know which nodes to write lock until it has read all the nodes it will read. Herein lies the critical problem of B-tree locking.

Exactly which nodes does Insert have to write lock? If L isn't full, then it only write locks L. If L *is* full, then it will write into L's parent, P. If P is full, then it will write into P's parent, and so on. In general, if L is full, then Insert should set write locks on the path $P_1, \ldots, P_n, L$ of ancestors of L ($n \geq 1$) such that P_1 is not full and P_2 through P_n are full.

One way for Insert to do this is to set write locks during its search down the tree. It releases each write lock when it realizes that the lock is not needed. Insert does this as follows. Before reading a node N, it sets a write lock on that node. If N is not full, then N won't be split. It therefore releases all locks it owns on N's ancestors, since the insertion will not cause any of them to be written. After it has read L, it has write locked the appropriate path, and can proceed with its updating activity.

This approach requires setting write locks before they are actually known to be needed. If internal nodes are not full, as is often the case in B-trees, then all of the write locks on internal nodes will be released. These locks needlessly generate conflicts during the search, thereby delaying the transaction. For this reason, it is probably better to delay the acquisition of write locks until it is known that they are needed. This more aggressive approach can be accomplished by doing lock conversions.

---

[17]A user may want to regard Search and Insert as atomic operations nested within a larger transaction. This means that a Search or Insert must be atomic with respect to other Searches or Inserts issued by the same or different transactions. In this sense, Search and Insert are independent transactions. However, larger transactions that invoke multiple Searches and Inserts have other synchronization requirements. This opens a broader collection of issues, that of *nested transactions*, which is not treated in this book. See the Bibliographic Notes in Chapter 1 for references.

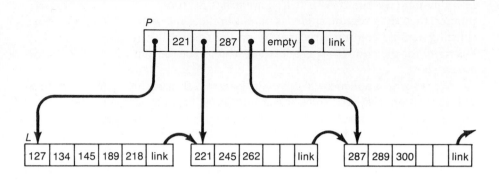

FIGURE 3–15
Links in a B-tree

During its initial search procedure, Insert only sets read locks on internal nodes. It concludes the search by setting a write lock on L. If it discovers that L is full, then it converts the necessary read locks into write locks. So, starting at the node closest to the root that it must write lock, it proceeds down the tree converting its read locks to write locks. In this way, it only sets write locks on nodes that actually have to be written.

Unfortunately, this modified protocol can lead to deadlock. For instance, two transactions may both be holding a read lock on a node and wanting to convert it to a write lock — a deadlock situation. One can avoid such a deadlock by introducing a new lock type, called might-write. A might-write lock conflicts with a write or might-write lock, but not with a read lock. Instead of obtaining read locks on its first pass down the tree, Insert obtains might-write locks. When it reaches a non-full node, it releases its ancestors' locks as before. After it reaches the desired leaf, it converts the might-write locks that it still owns to Write locks. This prevents two Inserts from locking the same node, and therefore prevents deadlocks on lock conversion.

B-Tree Locking Using Links

Lock contention can be reduced even further by departing from the lock coupling requirement of TL. Insert can be designed to write into each B-tree node independently, without owning a lock on the node's parent.

This algorithm requires that each node N have a link to its right sibling, denoted link(N). That is, link(N) points to the child of N's parent, P, that follows N, as in Fig. 3–15. If N is P's rightmost child, then link(N) points to the first child of P's right sibling (or, if P has no right sibling, then link(N) points to the first grandchild of the right sibling of P's parent, etc.). Thus, all of the nodes in each level are linked in key order through link(N). Only the rightmost node on each level has a null link.

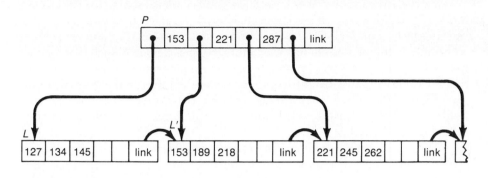

FIGURE 3–16
The B-tree of Fig. 3–15 after Inserting Key 153

Insert keeps these links up-to-date by adjusting them when it splits a node. Suppose Insert obtains a lock on node N, is ready to insert a value into N, but discovers that N is full. Then it splits N by moving the rightmost half of its contents to a newly allocated node N'. It sets $\text{link}(N') := \text{link}(N)$ and $\text{link}(N) := N'$, and then releases its lock on N (see Fig. 3–16, where $N = L$ and $N' = L'$). Notice that at this point, Insert owns no locks at all. Yet it now can obtain a lock on N's parent, P, and add a pointer to N' in P. If it can't add this pointer because P is full, it repeats the splitting process just described. Otherwise, it can simply insert the pointer and release the lock on P.

A Search proceeds down the tree as before, but without lock coupling. That is, after it reads an internal node N to obtain the pointer that directs it to the appropriate child C of N, it can release its read lock on N *before* obtaining its read lock on C. This obviously creates a window during which an Insert can come along and update both N and C, thereby appearing to both precede the Search (with respect to C) and follow it (with respect to N). Normally, this would be considered non-SR. However, by exploiting the semantics of B-trees and the link fields, we can modify the Search procedure slightly to avoid this apparent nonserializability.

The only way that Insert can upset Search's activity is to modify N in a way that would have caused Search to follow a different path than the one it is about to take to C. Any other update to N is irrelevant to Search's behavior. This can only happen if Insert splits C, thereby moving some of C's contents to a new right neighbor C' of C, and updating N to include a pointer to C'. If this occurred, then when Search looks in C, it may not find what it was looking for. However, in that case Search can look at C' by following $\text{link}(C)$. For example, suppose a Search is searching for key 189 in Fig. 3–15. It reads P, and releases its locks. Now an Insert inserts 153, producing the B-tree in Fig. 3–16. Key 189 is now no longer in the node L where Search will look for it, based on the state of P that it read.

We therefore modify Search as follows. If Search is looking for value v in a node N and discovers that v is larger than any value in N, then it reads link(N), releases its lock on N, locks the node N' pointed to by link(N), and reads N'. It continues to follow links in this way until it reaches a node N such that it either finds in N the value v it is looking for or determines that v is smaller than the largest value in N and therefore is not present in the tree. In the example of the preceding paragraph, Search will discover that the largest key in L is 145, so it will follow link(L), just in case L split after Search read P. It will thereby find 189 in L' as desired.

Notice that since Search and Insert each requests a lock only when it owns no locks, it cannot be a party to a deadlock.

BIBLIOGRAPHIC NOTES

Two phase locking was introduced in [Eswaran et al.76]. Proofs of correctness have appeared in [Bernstein, Shipman, Wong 79], [Eswaran et al. 76], and [Papadimitriou 79]. Our proof in Section 3.3 is based on one in [Ullman 82]. Treating deadlock detection as cycle detection in a digraph is from [Holt 72]. Other work on centralized deadlock detection includes [Coffman, Elphick, Shoshani 71], [King, Collmeyer 74], and [Macri 76]. The implementation issues presented in Section 3.6 are largely from Gray's classic work on transaction management implementation [Gray 78], and from many discussions with implementors; see also [Weinberger 82]. The phantom problem was introduced in [Eswaran et al, 76], which suggested predicate locks to solve it. Predicate locks were later developed in [Wong, Edelberg 77] and [Hunt, Rosenkrantz 79]. Versions of the hot spot technique of Section 3.8 appeared in [Reuter 82] and [Gawlick, Kinkade 85]. Multigranularity locking was introduced in [Gray et al. 75] and [Gray, Lori, Putzolu 75]; further work appeared in [Korth 82]. Path pushing deadlock detection is described in [Gligor, Shattuck 80] and [Obermarck 82]. Timestamp-based prevention appears in [Rosenkrantz, Stearns, Lewis 78] and [Stearns, Lewis, Rosenkrantz 76]. Other distributed deadlock techniques are described in [Beeri, Obermarck 81], [Chandy, Misra 82], [Chandy, Misra, Haas 83], [Isloor, Marsland 80], [Kawazu et al. 79], [Korth et al. 83], [Lomet 79], [Lomet 80a], [Lomet 80b], [Marsland, Isloor 80], [Menasce, Muntz 79], [Obermarck 82], [Stonebraker 79b], and [Tirri 83].

The performance effect of transaction characteristics and locking protocols other than those mentioned in Section 3.12 has mostly been studied in the literature through simulations. Locking performance in a distributed system was examined in [Ries, Stonebraker 77] [Ries, Stonebraker 79] [Thanos, Carlesi, Bertino 81], and [Garcia-Molina 79] for replicated data. Ries and Stonebraker also considered hierarchical locking, as did [Carey, Stonebraker 84]. Multiversion systems were studied in [Carey, Stonebraker 84], [Kiessling, Landherr 83], and [Peinl, Reuter 83] (see Chapter 5). Mixtures of queries and updaters were studied in [Lin, Nolte 82a].

The results we have presented about locking performance can be found in [Tay, Goodman, Suri 85], but most of them can be found elsewhere too. Some were previously known to other researchers, and some were corroborated by later work. (See [Tay,

Goodman, Suri 84] for an account of the agreements and contradictions among the papers.) For instance, thrashing caused by locking was observed in [Balter, Berard, Decitre 82], [Franaszek, Robinson 85], [Lin, Nolte 82b], and [Ryu, Thomasian 86]; blocking was identified as the main cause of this thrashing in the first and fourth papers. That most deadlock cycles have only two transactions was pointed out in [Devor, Carlson 82] and [Gray et al. 81b]. The former, as well as [Beeri, Obermarck 81], also observed that deadlocks are rare in System R and IMS/VS. A pure restart policy was first studied in [Shum, Spirakis 81]; it is also a special case of the protocol in [Chesnais, Gelenbe, Mitrani 83], and was compared to a blocking policy under various levels of resource contention in [Agrawal, Carey, Livny 85]. But the locking protocol that has received the most attention is conservative 2PL [Galler, Bos 83], [Mitra, Weinberger 84], [Morris, Wong 85], [Potier, Leblanc 80], and [Thomasian, Ryu 83]. The problem of choosing the appropriate granularity was addressed in [Carey, Stonebraker 84], [Ries, Stonebraker 77], [Ries, Stonebraker 79], and [Ryu, Thomasian 86]. The effect of shared locks was evaluated in [Lavenberg 84] and [Mitra 85]. The model of nonuniform access we have described was introduced in [Munz, Krenz 77], and used in [Lin, Nolte 82].

Lock coupling protocols for tree locking appeared in [Bayer, Schkolnick 77], [Kedem, Silberschatz 81], [Samadi 76], and [Silberschatz, Kedem 76]. The linking method appeared in [Kung, Lehman 80] for binary trees, and was extended for B-trees in [Lehman, Yao 81]. Other work on locking protocols for dynamic search structures includes [Buckley, Silberschatz 84], [Ellis 82], [Ford, Schultz, Jipping 84], [Goodman, Shasha 85], [Kedem 83], [Kwong, Wood 82], and [Manber, Ladner 84].

EXERCISES

3.1   Give an example of a serializable history that could not have been produced by a 2PL scheduler.

3.2   Give an example of a non-SR execution that is two phased locked, except for one transaction that converts a write lock to a read lock.

3.3   Suppose all transactions that write into the database are two phase locked, but read-only transactions may violate the two phase rule. In what sense will the database be kept in a consistent state? Is there any sense in which it will be inconsistent? If we dropped all read-only transactions from a history, would the resulting history be SR? Do queries read consistent data?

3.4*   Prove that every 2PL history H has the following property: There exists a serial history H_s such that for every two transactions T_i and T_j in H, if T_i and T_j are not interleaved (see Exercise 2.12) in H and T_i precedes T_j in H, then T_i precedes T_j in H_s.

3.5*   Give a serializability theoretic proof that if each transaction is two phase locked, releases its read locks before it terminates, and releases its write locks after it commits, then the resulting execution is strict.

3.6* Define a *locked point* of a transaction to be any moment at which it owns all of its locks; that is, it is a moment after it has performed its last lock operation and before it has released any lock. Using serializability theory, prove that for every history H produced by a 2PL scheduler there is an equivalent serial history in which transactions are in the order of their locked points in H.

3.7 Design an efficient algorithm that finds and lists all cycles in a WFG. (The algorithm should be efficient in the sense that its running time is polynomial in the size of the graph and in the number of cycles in the graph.)

3.8 Suppose T_j is waiting for a lock on x held by T_i. Now suppose T_k requests that lock on x and it too must wait. In general, is it better to add $T_k \rightarrow T_j$, $T_k \rightarrow T_i$, or both to the WFG? Discuss the effect of this decision on the algorithm that schedules waiting requests after a lock is released.

3.9 Consider a centralized DBS that uses 2PL and in which all transactions are sequential programs. Thus, no transaction can have more than one outstanding Read or Write request that is blocked. Could a transaction be involved in more than one deadlock? Prove your answer.

3.10 Suppose that if a lock request for x cannot be granted immediately, edges are added to the WFG from the blocked transaction to every transaction that owns a conflicting lock on x. Deadlock detection is then performed. If no deadlock is detected, then the request is added to the end of x's lock queue. The queue is serviced in a first-come-first-served manner. Show that this method does not detect all deadlocks. Propose a modified method that does.

3.11 Let $T_1 \rightarrow \ldots \rightarrow T_n \rightarrow T_1$ be a cycle in a WFG. An edge $T_i \rightarrow T_j$ is a *chord* of the cycle if T_i and T_j are nodes of the cycle and $T_i \rightarrow T_j$ is not an edge of the cycle. A cycle is *elementary* if it has no chords. Suppose we use a deadlock detector that finds all of the elementary cycles in a WFG, and breaks each such deadlock by aborting a victim in the cycle. Prove that this breaks *all* cycles in the WFG.

3.12 In our description of Conservative 2PL, we assumed that a transaction predeclares the set of data items it reads or writes. Describe a 2PL scheduler that does *not* predeclare its readset and writeset, yet is not subject to deadlocks.

3.13 Write a program that implements a Strict 2PL scheduler. Prove that your program satisfies all of the conditions in Propositions 3.1–3.3.

3.14* To prove the correctness of 2PL, in Propositions 3.1–3-3 stated conditions that every 2PL history must satisfy. State the additional conditions that must be satisfied by every 2PL history that represents an execution of a Strict 2PL scheduler and of a Conservative 2PL scheduler.

3.15 Suppose we partition the lock table, and we assign a distinct semaphore to each partition to ensure it is accessed atomically. Suppose each lock is assigned to a partition based on its data item name, so each transaction may own locks in multiple partitions. To release a transaction's locks, the LM must access more than one partition. Since the LM may acquire more than one semaphore to do this, it may deadlock if two transactions release their locks concurrently. Give an example of the problem, and propose a solution to it.

3.16 Instead of using an end-of-file marker as in Section 3.7, suppose we use fixed length records and maintain a *count* of the number of records in a file F. Give an example of a non-SR execution where transaction T_1 scans F, T_2 inserts a record into F, T_1 reads some other data item x, T_2 writes x, both transactions are two phase locked, and neither transaction locks count. Explain why this is an example of the phantom problem.

3.17 Consider a database consisting of one file, F. Each transaction begins by issuing a command "getlock where Q," where Q is a qualification (i.e., a Boolean formula) that's true for some records and false for others. The scheduler processes the Getlock command by write locking the set of all records in F that satisfy Q. The transaction can only read and modify records that were locked by its Getlock command. The transaction can insert a new record, which the scheduler write locks just before it inserts it. The scheduler holds a transaction's locks until it commits. Does this locking algorithm prevent phantoms? If so, prove it correct. If not, show a non-SR execution.

3.18 Suppose we modify the MGL protocol for dags so that T_i can set $iwl_i[x]$ as long as it owns an iw lock on some parent (rather than all parents) of x. Prove or disprove that the resulting protocol is correct.

3.19 Suppose we reverse the MGL protocol for dags: to set $rl_i[x]$ or $irl_i[x]$, T_i must have an ir or iw lock on *all* parents of x, and to set $wl_i[x]$ or $iwl_i[x]$, T_i must have an iw lock on *some* parent of x. Prove that the resulting protocol is correct. Under what conditions would you expect this protocol to outperform the MGL protocol for dags in Section 3.9?

3.20 The MGL protocol for lock instance graphs that are trees is limited to read and write locks. Generalize the protocol so that it will work for arbitrary lock types (e.g., Increment and Decrement).

3.21 Rule (2) of the MGL protocol requires that if a transaction has a w lock or iw lock on a data item x, then it must have an iw lock on x's parent. Is it correct for it to hold a w lock on x's parent instead? Is there a case in which it would be useful to set such a w lock if the lock instance graph is a tree? What about dags?

3.22 In the dag lock type graph in Fig. 3–7, a lock on an index entry locks all fields of all records that the entry points to. Suppose we distinguish indexed fields from non-indexed fields. A lock on an index entry should only lock the indexed field of the records it points to. Other fields of these records can be concurrently locked. Design a lock instance dag that implements this approach and argue that it has the intended effect, assuming the dag MGL protocol.

3.23   Prove that the MGL protocol for dag lock instance graphs is correct in the sense of Theorem 3.7.

3.24   In the MGL protocol for lock instance graphs that are trees, suppose we allow a transaction to release a lock on a data item x before it releases its lock on some child of x. Assuming the scheduler uses Basic 2PL, give an example of an incorrect execution that can result from this.

3.25   In Section 3.11, we argued that if no transaction spontaneously aborts and every lock obtained by a transaction corresponds to a database operation (i.e., no intention locks), then there are no phantom deadlocks. Are phantom deadlocks possible if we allow intention locks? Prove your answer.

3.26   Consider a distributed DBS. Give an example execution of two transactions which is not SR and satisfies the 2PL rules locally (i.e., at each site, considered individually) though not globally (i.e., considering all sites together). In your example, be sure to give the precise sequence in which locks are set and released by the schedulers as well as the sequence in which Reads and Writes are executed.

3.27   In this problem, we will simplify the path pushing algorithm for distributed deadlock detection. Assume that each transaction is a sequential process; thus, it is only active (unblocked) at one site at a time. Suppose we augment the WFG at each site, say A, with an additional node labelled EX for "external." For each transaction T_i, if T_i was formerly executing at site A and now is stopped waiting for a response from some other site, then add an edge $T_i \rightarrow EX$. If T_i is executing at A and was formerly executing at any other site, then add an edge $EX \rightarrow T_i$.

We now modify the algorithm as follows. Site A periodically detects cycles in its WFG. If a cycle does not contain the node EX, then a transaction is aborted. For each cycle $EX \rightarrow T_i \rightarrow \cdots \rightarrow T_j \rightarrow EX$, site A sends the path $T_i \rightarrow \cdots \rightarrow T_j$ to the site from which T_j is waiting for a response. When a site receives a list of paths from another site, it adds those edges to its WFG and performs the above steps. Prove that this algorithm detects all deadlock cycles.

3.28   Design an approach to deleting edges from each site's WFG in the path pushing deadlock detection algorithm of Section 3.11.

3.29   In timestamp-based deadlock detection, we assigned each transaction a unique timestamp. Suppose we do not require transactions' timestamps to be unique. Do the Wait-Die and Wound-Wait methods still prevent deadlock? Do they prevent cyclic restart?

3.30 Suppose we alter the definition of Wait-Die as follows:

if $\text{ts}(T_i) > \text{ts}(T_j)$ **then** T_i waits **else** abort T_i.

Does this method prevent deadlock? Does it prevent cyclic restart? Back up your claims with proofs or counterexamples. Compare the dynamic behavior of this method with standard Wait-Die and Wound-Wait.

3.31 Suppose a transaction is assigned a new timestamp every time it is aborted and restarted. Using Wound-Wait for deadlock detection, give an example of two transactions T_i and T_j that cyclically restart each other using this method. If possible, design them so they "self-synchronize" in the sense that even with small variations in transaction execution time and communications delay, they still experience cyclic restart.

3.32 Design a hybrid deadlock detection and prevention algorithm that, to the extent possible, uses WFG cycle detection locally at each site, and uses timestamp-based prevention to avoid global deadlocks.

3.33 In Wound-Wait timestamp-based deadlock prevention, suppose that when T_i wounds T_j, T_j aborts only if it is waiting, or later tries to wait, for another lock. Does this version of Wound-Wait prevent deadlock? Prove your answer.

3.34 Suppose we partition the set of sites in a distributed DBS into regions. Each site has a local deadlock detector. Each region has a global deadlock detector to which its sites send their WFGs. There is also a system-wide deadlock detector to which all the regional deadlock detectors send their WFGs. This arrangement of deadlock detectors is called *hierarchical deadlock detection*. Under what circumstances would you expect hierarchical deadlock detection to perform better or worse than a single global deadlock detector? Is hierarchical deadlock detection subject to phantom deadlocks under different conditions than a single global deadlock detector?

3.35 Suppose we modify the hierarchical deadlock detector of the previous problem as follows. Define a transaction to be *local* if it only accesses data at one site. Each site constructs a *locally compressed* WFG by taking the transitive closure of its WFG and then deleting all nodes corresponding to local transactions (along with edges that are incident with those nodes). Each site periodically sends its locally compressed WFG (not its full WFG) to its regional deadlock detector. Each regional deadlock detector also does "local" compression, where in this case "local" means local to the set of sites in the region. Each regional deadlock detector periodically sends its locally compressed WFG to the system-wide deadlock detector. Does this deadlock detection scheme detect all deadlocks? Might it detect a phantom deadlock? Prove your answers.

3.36 Let k, N, and D be as defined in Section 3.12. If the deadlock rate is low, so that most transactions terminate without restarts, then a transaction has $k/2$ locks on average. Assume all locks are write locks, and lock requests are uniformly distributed over the database.

   a. What is the probability of conflict per request?
   b. What is the probability that a transaction will encounter a conflict?
   c. Suppose $k = 1$ if $D = 2$, and $k = 2$ if $D = 5$. Let $N = 2$. Compute the probabilities in (a) and (b) for $D = 2$ and $D = 5$. Note that one probability decreases while the other increases.
   d. Show that, if $kN/2D$ is small, then the probability in (b) is $k^2N/2D$ approximately. Note the relationship with the DC-workload.

3.37   Assume again the conditions in Exercise 3.37. Let R be the response time of a transaction. If we assume that when a transaction is blocked, there is no other transaction waiting for the same lock, then the waiting time for the lock is $R/2$ on average (since the deadlock rate is low). Now let T be the response time of a transaction if the concurrency control were switched off.

   a. Show that (with the concurrency control switched on)

$$R = T + \frac{R}{2} \sum_{r=1}^{k} r \binom{k}{r} p^r (1-p)^{k-r}$$

   where p is the probability of conflict per request, and $\binom{k}{r} = \frac{k!(k-r)!}{r!}$.

   b. Using the identity $\sum_{r=1}^{k} r \binom{k}{r} p^r (1-p)^{k-r} = kp$, and the probability of conflict from Problem 3.37, deduce that $R = T/\left(1 - \frac{k^2N}{4D}\right)$.

   c. Little's Law from elementary queueing theory now implies that the throughput is $\frac{N}{T}\left(1 - \frac{k^2N}{4D}\right)$. Does this formula predict DC-thrashing?

   d. How does resource contention affect the formulas in (b) and (c)?

3.38   Consider a DBS that uses a Strict 2PL scheduler. In the following, throughput (i.e., user demand) is the same before and after the change.

   a. The code of the transactions running on a particular system is changed, but the number of locks (all of which are write locks) required by a transaction is unaffected. The change results in an increase in response time. Give two possible reasons.
   b. A system is running a mixture of queries and updates. (Queries only set read locks, whereas updates set write locks.) Whenever the proportion of queries increases, overall response time becomes worse. Give three possible reasons.

    c. A certain portion of a database is identified as a high contention area, so the granularity for this portion was refined. However, response time becomes worse. Give three possible reasons.

3.39 Modify the TL protocol so that a transaction need not begin by locking the root of DT. Prove that the modified protocol is correct.

3.40 Extend the TL protocol to handle read locks and write locks. Prove the resulting protocol produces SR executions and is free of deadlocks.

3.41 Prove that the DL protocol produces SR executions and is free of deadlocks.

3.42 Do Exercise 3.41 for an arbitrary set of lock types with its associated compatibility matrix.

3.43 Extend the various versions of B-tree locking in Secion 3.13 to handle the deletion of nodes.

4

NON-LOCKING SCHEDULERS

4.1 INTRODUCTION

In this chapter we will examine two scheduling techniques that do not use locks, timestamp ordering (TO) and serialization graph testing (SGT). As with 2PL, we'll see aggressive and conservative as well as centralized and distributed versions of both techniques.

We will also look at a very aggressive variety of schedulers, called certifiers. A certifier never delays operations submitted by TMs. It always outputs them right away. When a transaction is ready to commit, the certifier runs a "certification test" to determine whether the transaction was involved in a non-SR execution. If the transaction fails this test, then the certifier aborts the transaction. Otherwise, it allows the transaction to commit. We will describe certifiers based on all three techniques: 2PL, TO, and SGT.

In the final section, we will show how to combine scheduling techniques into composite schedulers. For example, a composite scheduler could use 2PL for part of its synchronization activity and TO for another part. Using the composition rules, you can use the basic techniques we have discussed to construct hundreds of different types of schedulers, all of which produce SR executions.

Unlike 2PL, the techniques described in this chapter are not currently used in many commercial products. Moreover, their performance relative to 2PL is not well understood. Therefore, the material in this chapter is presented mostly at a conceptual level, with fewer performance comparisons and practical details than in Chapter 3.

4.2 TIMESTAMP ORDERING (TO)

Introduction

In timestamp ordering, the TM assigns a unique timestamp, $ts(T_i)$, to each transaction, T_i. It generates timestamps using any of the techniques described in Section 3.11, in the context of timestamp-based deadlock prevention. The TM attaches a transaction's timestamp to each operation issued by the transaction. It will therefore be convenient to speak of the timestamp of an *operation* $o_i[x]$, which is simply the timestamp of the transaction that issued the operation. A TO scheduler orders conflicting operations according to their timestamps. More precisely, it enforces the following rule, called the TO rule.

TO Rule: If $p_i[x]$ and $q_j[x]$ are conflicting operations, then the DM processes $p_i[x]$ before $q_j[x]$ iff $ts(T_i) < ts(T_j)$.

The next theorem shows that the TO rule produces SR executions.

> **Theorem 4.1:** If H is a history representing an execution produced by a TO scheduler, then H is SR.
>
> *Proof:* Consider $SG(H)$. If $T_i \rightarrow T_j$ is an edge of $SG(H)$, then there must exist conflicting operations $p_i[x]$, $q_j[x]$ in H such that $p_i[x] < q_j[x]$. Hence by the TO rule, $ts(T_i) < ts(T_j)$. If a cycle $T_1 \rightarrow T_2 \rightarrow ... \rightarrow T_n \rightarrow T_1$ existed in $SG(H)$, then by induction $ts(T_1) < ts(T_1)$, a contradiction. So $SG(H)$ is acyclic, and by the Serializability Theorem, H is SR. $\square$

By enforcing the TO rule, we are ensuring that every pair of conflicting operations is executed in timestamp order. Thus, a TO execution has the same effect as a serial execution in which the transactions appear in timestamp order. In the rest of this section we will present ways of enforcing the TO rule.

Basic TO

Basic TO is a simple and aggressive implementation of the TO rule. It accepts operations from the TM and immediately outputs them to the DM in first-come-first-served order. To ensure that this order does not violate the TO rule, the scheduler rejects operations that it receives too late. An operation $p_i[x]$ is *too late* if it arrives after the scheduler has already output some conflicting operation $q_j[x]$ with $ts(T_j) > ts(T_i)$. If $p_i[x]$ is too late, then it cannot be scheduled without violating the TO rule. Since the scheduler has already output $q_j[x]$, it can only solve the problem by rejecting $p_i[x]$.

If $p_i[x]$ is rejected, then T_i must abort. When T_i is resubmitted, it must be assigned a larger timestamp — large enough that its operations are less likely to be rejected during its second execution. Notice the difference with timestamp-based deadlock prevention, where an aborted transaction is resubmitted with the *same* timestamp to avoid cyclic restart. Here it is resubmitted with a *new* and *larger* timestamp to avoid certain rejection.

To determine if an operation has arrived too late, the Basic TO scheduler maintains for every data item x the maximum timestamps of Reads and Writes on x that it has sent to the DM, denoted max-r-scheduled[x] and max-w-scheduled[x] (respectively). When the scheduler receives $p_i[x]$, it compares ts(T_i) to max-q-scheduled[x] for all operation types q that conflict with p. If ts(T_i) < max-q-scheduled[x], then the scheduler rejects $p_i[x]$, since it has already scheduled a conflicting operation with a larger timestamp. Otherwise, it schedules $p_i[x]$ and, if ts(T_i) > max-p-scheduled[x], it updates max-p-scheduled[x] to ts(T_i).

The scheduler must handshake with the DM to guarantee that operations are processed by the DM in the order that the scheduler sent them. Even if the scheduler decides that $p_i[x]$ can be scheduled, it must not send it to the DM until every conflicting $q_j[x]$ that it previously sent has been acknowledged by the DM. Notice that 2PL automatically takes care of this problem. 2PL does not schedule an operation until all conflicting operations previously scheduled have released their locks, which does not happen until after the DM acknowledges those operations.

To enforce this handshake, the Basic TO scheduler also maintains, for each data item x, the number of Reads and Writes that have been sent to, but not yet acknowledged by, the DM. These are denoted r-in-transit[x] and w-in-transit[x] (respectively). For each data item x the scheduler also maintains a queue, queue[x], of operations that *can* be scheduled insofar as the TO rule is concerned, but are waiting for acknowledgments from the DM to previously sent conflicting operations. Conflicting operations are in the queue in timestamp order.

Let us consider a simple scenario to see how the scheduler uses these data structures to enforce the TO Rule. For simplicity, assume that the timestamp of each transaction (or operation) is equal to its subscript (i.e., ts(T_i) = i). We use ack($o_i[x]$) to denote the acknowledgment that the DM sends to the scheduler indicating that $o_i[x]$ has been processed. Suppose initially max-r-scheduled[x] = 0, r-in-transit[x] = 0, and queue[x] is empty.

1. *$r_1[x]$* arrives and the scheduler dispatches it to the DM. It sets max-r-scheduled[x] to 1 and r-in-transit[x] to 1.

2. *$w_2[x]$* arrives. Although the TO rule says $w_2[x]$ can be scheduled, since r-in-transit[x] = 1 the scheduler must wait until it receives ack($r_1[x]$). It therefore appends $w_2[x]$ to queue[x]. (w-in-transit[x] is unaffected.)

3. $r_4[x]$ arrives and although the TO rule says $r_4[x]$ can be scheduled, the scheduler must wait until it receives $ack(w_2[x])$. It therefore appends $r_4[x]$ to queue[x] (after $w_2[x]$). (r-in-transit[x] is unaffected.)

4. $r_3[x]$ arrives. Just like $r_4[x]$, it must wait for $w_2[x]$. So, the scheduler appends it to queue[x] (after $r_4[x]$).

5. $ack(r_1[x])$ arrives from the DM. The scheduler decrements r-in-transit[x] to 0. It can now dispatch $w_2[x]$, so it removes $w_2[x]$ from queue[x], sends it to the DM, and sets max-w-scheduled to 2 and w-in-transit[x] to 1. It cannot yet dispatch $r_4[x]$ and $r_3[x]$ because w-in-transit[x] > 0, indicating that the DM has not yet acknowledged some conflicting Write.

6. $ack(w_2[x])$ arrives from the DM. The scheduler decrements w-in-transit[x] to 0. Now it can send both $r_4[x]$ and $r_3[x]$ to the DM simultaneously. So, it sets max-r-scheduled to 4 and r-in-transit[x] to 2, and queue[x] becomes empty again.

The principles of operation of a Basic TO scheduler should now be clear. When it receives an operation $p_i[x]$, it accepts it for scheduling if $ts(T_i) \geq$ max-q-scheduled[x] for all operation types q that conflict with p. Otherwise, it rejects $p_i[x]$ and T_i must be aborted. Once $p_i[x]$ is accepted for scheduling, the scheduler dispatches it to the DM immediately, if for all operation types q that conflict with p, q-in-transit[x] $= 0$ and there are no q operations in queue[x]. Otherwise a conflicting operation $q_j[x]$ is in transit between the scheduler and the DM, or is waiting in queue[x], and so $p_i[x]$ must be delayed; it is therefore inserted in queue[x]. Finally, when it receives $ack(p_i[x])$, the scheduler updates p-in-transit[x] accordingly, and removes all the operations in (the head of) queue[x] that can now be dispatched and sends them to the DM.

Strict TO

Although the TO rule enforces serializability, it does not necessarily ensure recoverability. For example, suppose that $ts(T_1) = 1$ and $ts(T_2) = 2$, and consider the following history: $w_1[x]\ r_2[x]\ w_2[y]\ c_2$. Conflicting operations appear in timestamp order. Thus this history could be produced by Basic TO. Yet it is not recoverable: T_2 reads x from T_1, T_2 is committed, but T_1 is not.

As we discussed in Chapters 1 and 2, we usually want the scheduler to enforce an even stronger condition than recoverability, namely, strictness. Here is how Basic TO can be modified to that end.

Recall that w-in-transit[x] denotes the number of $w[x]$ operations that the scheduler has sent to the DM but that the DM has not yet acknowledged. Since two conflicting operations cannot be "in transit" at any time and Writes on the same data item conflict, w-in-transit[x] at any time is either 0 or 1.

The Strict TO scheduler works like Basic TO in every respect, except that it does *not* set w-in-transit[x] to 0 when it receives the DM's acknowledgment of a $w_i[x]$. Instead it waits until it has received acknowledgment of a_i or c_i. It then sets w-in-transit[x] to zero for every x for which it had sent $w_i[x]$ to the DM. This delays all $r_j[x]$ and $w_j[x]$ operations with ts(T_j) > ts(T_i) until after T_i has committed or aborted. This means that the execution output by the scheduler to the DM is strict. Notice that since T_j waits for T_i only if ts(T_j) > ts(T_i), these waiting situations cannot lead to deadlock.

Note that w-in-transit[x] acts like a lock. It excludes access to x by other transactions until the transaction that owns this "lock" — the transaction that issued the Write that is "in transit" — commits or aborts. This may lead one to believe that we, in effect, turned our TO scheduler into a 2PL scheduler. The following history shows that this is not so:

$$H_1 = r_2[x]\ w_3[x]\ c_3\ w_1[y]\ c_1\ r_2[y]\ w_2[z]\ c_2.$$

H_1 is equivalent to the serial history $T_1\ T_2\ T_3$, and thus is SR. Moreover, it is strict. The only potentially troublesome conflict is $w_1[y] < r_2[y]$, but $c_1 < r_2[y]$, as required for strictness. If ts(T_1) < ts(T_2) < ts(T_3), this history could be produced by the Strict TO scheduler we described. However, H_1 could not possibly have been produced by 2PL. In 2PL, T_2 must release its read lock on x before $w_3[x]$ but may not set its read lock on y until after $w_1[y]$. Since $w_3[x] < w_1[y]$, T_2 would release a lock before obtaining another lock, violating the two phase rule.

It is possible to modify Basic TO to enforce only the weaker conditions of recoverability or cascadelessness (see Exercise 4.2).

Timestamp Management

Suppose we store timestamps in a table, where each entry is of the form [x, max-r-scheduled[x], max-w-scheduled[x]]. This table could consume a lot of space. Indeed, if data items are small, this timestamp information (and o-in-transit) could occupy as much space as the database itself. This is a potentially serious problem.

We can solve the problem by exploiting the following observation. Suppose TMs use relatively accurate real time clocks to generate timestamps, and suppose transactions execute for relatively short periods of time. Then at any given time t, the scheduler can be pretty sure it won't receive any more operations with timestamps smaller than $t - \delta$, where δ is large compared to transaction execution time. The only reason the scheduler needs the timestamps in max-r-scheduled[x] and max-w-scheduled[x], say ts_r and ts_w, is to reject Reads and Writes with even smaller timestamps than ts_r and ts_w. So, once ts_r and ts_w are smaller than $t - \delta$, ts_r and ts_w are of little value to the scheduler, because it is unlikely to receive any operation with a timestamp smaller than ts_r or ts_w.

Using this observation, we can periodically purge from the timestamp table entries that have uselessly small timestamps. Each Purge operation uses a timestamp ts_{min}, which is the $t - \delta$ value in the previous paragraph. Purge(ts_{min}) removes every entry $[x, \text{max-r-scheduled}[x], \text{max-w-scheduled}[x]]$ from the timestamp table where max-r-scheduled$[x] < ts_{min}$ and max-w-scheduled$[x] < ts_{min}$. In addition, it tags the table with ts_{min}, indicating that a Purge with that timestamp value has taken place.

Once the timestamp table has been purged, the scheduler must use a modified test to determine whether an operation $o_i[x]$ is too late. First, it looks for an entry for x in the timestamp table. If it finds one, it compares ts(T_i) to max-r-scheduled$[x]$ and/or max-w-scheduled$[x]$ in the usual manner. However, if there is no entry for x, then it must compare ts(T_i) with the ts_{min} that tags the table. If ts(T_i) $\geq ts_{min}$, then if an entry for x was purged from the table, it was irrelevant, and thus $o_i[x]$ is not too late. But if ts(T_i) $< ts_{min}$, then the last Purge might have deleted an entry for x, where either ts(T_i) $<$ max-r-scheduled$[x]$ or ts(T_i) $<$ max-w-scheduled$[x]$. If that entry still existed, it might tell the scheduler to reject $o_i[x]$. To be safe, the scheduler must therefore reject $o_i[x]$.

If ts_{min} is sufficiently small, it will be rare to reject an $o_i[x]$ with ts(T_i) $< ts_{min}$. However, the smaller the value of ts_{min}, the smaller the number of entries that Purge will delete, and hence the larger the size of the timestamp table. Therefore, selecting ts_{min} entails a tradeoff between decreasing the number of rejections and minimizing the size of the timestamp table.

Distributed TO schedulers

TO schedulers are especially easy to distribute. Each site can have its own TO scheduler which schedules operations that access the data stored at that site. The decision to schedule, delay, or reject an operation $o_i[x]$ depends only on other operations accessing x. Each scheduler can maintain all the information about the operations accessing the data items it manages. It can therefore go about its decisions independently of the other schedulers. Unlike distributed 2PL, where coordination among distributed schedulers is usually needed to handle distributed deadlocks, distributed TO requires no inter-scheduler communication whatsoever.

Conservative TO

If a Basic TO scheduler receives operations in an order widely different from their timestamp order, then it may reject too many operations, thereby causing too many transactions to abort. This is due to its aggressive nature. We can remedy this problem by designing more conservative schedulers based on the TO rule.

One approach is to require the scheduler to artificially delay each operation it receives for some period of time. To see why this helps avoid rejections, consider some operation $o_i[x]$. The danger in scheduling $o_i[x]$ right away is that the scheduler may later receive a conflicting operation with a smaller timestamp, which it will therefore have to reject. However, if it holds $o_i[x]$ for a while before scheduling it, then there is a better chance that any conflicting operations with smaller timestamps will arrive in time to be scheduled. The longer the scheduler holds each operation before scheduling it, the fewer rejections it will be forced to make. Like other conservative schedulers, conservative TO delays operations to avoid rejections.

Of course, delaying operations for too long also has its problems, since the delays slow down the processing of transactions. When designing a conservative TO scheduler, one has to strike a balance by adding enough delay to avoid too many rejections without slowing down transactions too much.

An "ultimate conservative" TO scheduler *never* rejects operations and thus never causes transactions to abort. Such a scheduler can be built if we make certain assumptions about the system. As with Conservative 2PL, one such assumption is that transactions predeclare their readset and writeset and the TM conveys this information to the scheduler. We leave the construction of a conservative TO scheduler based on this assumption as an exercise (Exercise 4.11).

In this section we'll concentrate on an ultimate conservative TO scheduler based on a different assumption, namely, that each TM submits its operations to each DM in timestamp order. One way to satisfy this assumption is to adopt the following architecture. At any given time, each TM supervises *exactly* one transaction (e.g., there is one TM associated with each terminal from which users can initiate transactions). Each TM's timestamp generator returns increasing timestamps every time it's called. Thus, each TM runs transactions serially, and each transaction gets a larger timestamp than previous ones supervised by that TM. Of course, since many TMs may be submitting operations to the scheduler in parallel, the scheduler does not necessarily receive operations serially.

Under these assumptions we can build an ultimate conservative TO scheduler as follows. The scheduler maintains a queue, called unsched-queue, containing operations it has received from the TMs but has not yet scheduled. The operations in unsched-queue are kept in timestamp order, the operations with the smallest timestamp being at the head of the queue. Operations with the same timestamp are placed according to the order received, the earlier ones being closer to the head.

When the scheduler receives $p_i[x]$ from a TM, it inserts $p_i[x]$ at the appropriate place in unsched-queue to maintain the order properties just given. The scheduler then checks if the operation at the head of unsched-queue is ready to be dispatched to the DM. The head of unsched-queue, say $q_j[x]$, is said to be *ready* if

1. unsched-queue contains at least one operation from *every* TM, and
2. all operations conflicting with $q_j[x]$ previously sent to the DM have been acknowledged by the DM.

If the head of unsched-queue is in fact ready, the scheduler removes it from unsched-queue and sends it to the DM. The scheduler repeats this activity until the head of unsched-queue is no longer ready.

Ready rule (1) requires that we know if there are operations from all TMs in unsched-queue. One way of doing this efficiently is to maintain, for each TM_v, the count of operations in unsched-queue received from TM_v, denoted op-count[v]. To enable the scheduler to decrement the appropriate op-count when it removes an operation from unsched-queue, unsched-queue should actually store pairs of the form $(v, o_i[x])$, meaning that operation $o_i[x]$ was submitted by TM_v. Each scheduler needs this information anyway, so it knows which TM should receive the acknowledgment for each operation.

Ready rule (2) is a handshake between the scheduler and the DM. This can be implemented as in Basic TO, by keeping for each x a count of the Reads and Writes that are in transit between the scheduler and the DM.

It is easy to see that the ultimate conservative TO scheduler described previously enforces the TO rule. This follows from the fact that the operations in unsched-queue are maintained in timestamp order, and it is always the head of the queue that is sent to the DM. Thus, not only conflicting operations but *all* operations are scheduled in timestamp order. Moreover, the handshake mechanism guarantees that the DM will process conflicting operations in timestamp order.

One problem with this scheduler is that it may get stuck if a TM stops sending operations for a while. To send *any* operation to the DM, the scheduler must have at least one unscheduled operation from *all* TMs. If some TM has no operations to send, then the scheduler is blocked. To avoid this problem, if a TM has no operations to send to the scheduler, it sends a *Null* operation. A Null must carry a timestamp consistent with the requirement that each TM submits operations to the scheduler in timestamp order. When a TM sends a Null to the scheduler, it is promising that every operation it sends in the future will have a timestamp greater than ts(Null). The scheduler treats Nulls just like other operations, except that when a Null becomes the head of the queue, the scheduler simply removes it, and decrements the appropriate op-count, but does *not* send it to the DM.

Particular care must be exercised if a TM fails and is therefore unable to send any operations, whether Null or not, to the scheduler. In this case, the scheduler must somehow be informed of the failure, so that it does not expect operations from that TM. After the TM is repaired and before it starts submitting operations to the scheduler, the latter must be made aware of that fact. Indeed, the TM should not be allowed to submit operations to the scheduler before it is explicitly directed that it may do so.

A second, and maybe more serious, problem with conservative TO schedulers is that they are, true to their name, extremely restrictive. The executions they produce are serial! There are several methods for enhancing the degree of concurrency afforded by conservative TO schedulers.

One way to improve conservative TO is to avoid the serialization of nonconflicting operations by using transaction classes. A *transaction class* is defined by a readset and a writeset. A transaction is *a member of a transaction class* if its readset and writeset are subsets of the class's readset and writeset (respectively). Transaction classes need not be mutually exclusive. That is, they may have overlapping readsets and writesets, so a transaction can be a member of many classes.

We associate each TM with exactly one class and require that each transaction be a member of the class of the TM that supervises it. Conservative TO exploits the association of TMs with transaction classes by weakening ready rule (1). Instead of requiring that operations are received from *all* TMs, the scheduler only needs to have received operations from the TMs associated with transaction classes that contain x in their writeset, if the head of unsched-queue is $r_i[x]$, or x in either their readset or writeset, if the head of the queue is $w_i[x]$. By relaxing the condition under which a queued operation may be sent to the DM, we potentially reduce the time for which operations will be delayed.

Each transaction must predeclare its readset and writeset, so the system can direct it to an appropriate TM. Alternatively, a preprocessor or compiler could determine these sets and thereby the class(es) to which a transaction belongs. The scheduler must know which TMs are associated with which classes. Class definitions and their associations with TMs must remain static during normal operation of the DBS. Changing this information can be done, but usually must be done off-line so that various system components can be simultaneously informed of such changes and modified appropriately.

A more careful analysis of transaction classes can lead to conditions for sending operations to the DM that are even weaker than the one just described. Such an analysis can be conveniently carried out in terms of a graph structure called a *conflict graph*. However, we shall not discuss this technique in this book. Relevant references appear in the Bibliographic Notes.

4.3 SERIALIZATION GRAPH TESTING (SGT)

Introduction

So far, we have seen schedulers that use locks or timestamps. In this section we shall discuss a third type of scheduler, called *serialization graph testing* (*SGT*) schedulers. An SGT scheduler maintains the SG of the history that represents the execution it controls. As the scheduler sends new operations to the DM, the execution changes, and so does the SG maintained by the scheduler. An SGT scheduler attains SR executions by ensuring the SG it maintains always remains acyclic.

According to the definition in Chapter 2, an SG contains nodes for all committed transactions and for no others. Such an SG differs from the one that is usually maintained by an SGT scheduler, in two ways. First, the SGT scheduler's SG may not include nodes corresponding to all committed transactions, especially those that committed long ago. Second, it usually includes nodes for all active transactions, which by definition are not yet committed. Due to these differences, we use a different term, *Stored SG* (*SSG*), to denote the SG maintained by an SGT scheduler.

Basic SGT

When an SGT scheduler receives an operation $p_i[x]$ from the TM, it first adds a node for T_i in its SSG, if one doesn't already exist. Then it adds an edge from T_j to T_i for every previously scheduled operation $q_j[x]$ that conflicts with $p_i[x]$. We have two cases:

1. The resulting SSG contains a cycle. This means that if $p_i[x]$ were to be scheduled now (or at any point in the future), the resulting execution would be non-SR. Thus the scheduler rejects $p_i[x]$. It sends a_i to the DM and, when a_i is acknowledged, it deletes from the SSG T_i and all edges incident with T_i. Deleting T_i makes the SSG acyclic again, since all cycles that existed involved T_i. Since the SSG is acyclic, the execution produced by the scheduler now — with T_i aborted — is SR.

2. The resulting SSG is still acyclic. In this case, the scheduler can accept $p_i[x]$. It can schedule $p_i[x]$ immediately, if all conflicting operations previously scheduled have been acknowledged by the DM; otherwise, it must delay $p_i[x]$ until the DM acknowledges all conflicting operations. This handshake can be implemented as in Basic TO. Namely, for each data item x the scheduler maintains queue[x] where delayed operations are inserted in first-in-first-out order, and two counts, r-in-transit[x] and w-in-transit[x], for keeping track of unacknowledged Reads and Writes for each x sent to the DM.

To determine if an operation conflicts with a previously scheduled one, the scheduler can maintain, for each transaction T_i that has a node in SSG, the sets of data items for which Reads and Writes have been scheduled. These sets will be denoted r-scheduled[T_i] and w-scheduled[T_i], respectively. Then, $p_i[x]$ conflicts with a previously scheduled operation of transaction T_j iff $x \in q$-scheduled[T_j], for q conflicting with p.

A significant practical consideration is when the scheduler may discard the information it has collected about a transaction. To detect conflicts, we have to maintain the readset and writeset of every transaction, which could consume a lot of space. It is therefore important to discard this information as soon as possible.

One may naively assume that the scheduler can delete information about a transaction as soon as it commits. Unfortunately, this is not so. For example, consider the (partial) history

$$H_2 = r_{k+1}[x] \, w_1[x] \, w_1[y_1] \, c_1 \, w_2[x] \, w_2[y_2] \, c_2 \, ... \, w_k[x] \, w_k[y_k]c_k.$$

Since $SSG(H_2)$ is acyclic, the execution represented by H_2 could have been produced by an SGT scheduler. Now, suppose that the scheduler receives $w_{k+1}[z]$. According to the SGT policy, the operation can be scheduled iff $z \notin \{x, y_1, ... y_k\}$. But for the scheduler to be able to test that, it must remember that x, $y_1, ..., y_k$ were the data items accessed by transactions $T_1, T_2, ..., T_k$ even *though these transactions have committed.*

The scheduler can delete information about a terminated transaction T_i iff T_i could not, at any time in the future, be involved in a cycle of the SSG. For a node to participate in a cycle it must have at least one incoming and one outgoing edge. As in H_2, new edges *out* of a transaction T_i may arise in the SSG even after T_i terminates. However, once T_i terminates no new edges directed *to* it may subsequently arise. Therefore, once a terminated transaction has no incoming edges in the SSG, it cannot possibly become involved in a cycle in the future. So a safe rule for deleting nodes is that *information about a transaction may be discarded as soon as that transaction has terminated and is a source* (i.e., a node with no incoming edges) *in the SSG.* If it is not a source at the time it terminates, then it must wait until all transactions that precede it have terminated and therefore have been deleted from the SSG.

By explicitly checking whether the SSG is acyclic, an SGT scheduler allows any interleaving of Reads and Writes that is SR. In this sense, it is more lenient than TO (which only allows timestamp ordered executions of Reads and Writes) and 2PL (which doesn't allow certain interleavings of Reads and Writes, such as history H_1 in Section 4.2). However, it attains this flexibility at the expense of extra overhead in maintaining the SG and checking for cycles. Moreover, it is currently unknown under what conditions the extra leniency of SGT leads to improved throughput or response time.

Conservative SGT

A conservative SGT scheduler never rejects operations but may delay them. As with 2PL and TO, we can achieve this if each transaction T_i predeclares its readset and writeset, denoted r-set$[T_i]$ and w-set$[T_i]$, by attaching them to its Start operation.

When the scheduler receives T_i's Start, it saves r-set$[T_i]$ and w-set$[T_i]$. It then creates a node for T_i in the SSG and adds edges $T_j \rightarrow T_i$ for every T_j in the SSG such that p-set$[T_i] \cap$ q-set$[T_j] \neq \{\}$[1] for all pairs of conflicting operation types p and q.

For each data item x the scheduler maintains the usual queue$[x]$ of delayed operations that access x. Conflicting operations in queue$[x]$, say $p_i[x]$ and

---

[1] We use "$\{\}$" to denote the empty set.

$q_j[x]$, are kept in an order consistent with SSG edges. That is, if $T_j \rightarrow T_i$ is in the SSG, then $q_j[x]$ is closer to the head of queue[x] than $p_i[x]$; thus, $q_j[x]$ will be dequeued before $p_i[x]$. The order of nonconflicting operations in queue[x] (i.e., Reads) is immaterial; for specificity, let's say they are kept in order of arrival. When the scheduler receives operation $o_i[x]$ from the TM, it inserts $o_i[x]$ in queue[x] in accordance with the ordering just specified.

The scheduler may send the operation at the head of some queue to the DM iff the operation is "ready." An operation $p_i[x]$ is *ready* if

1. all operations that conflict with $p_i[x]$ and were previously sent to the DM have been acknowledged; and

2. for every T_j that directly precedes T_i in the SSG (i.e., $T_j \rightarrow T_i$ is in the SSG) and for every operation type q that conflicts with p, either $x \notin q$-set$[T_j]$ or $q_j[x]$ has already been received by the scheduler (i.e., $x \in q$-scheduled$[T_j]$).

Condition (1) amounts to the usual handshake that makes sure the DM processes conflicting operations in the order they are scheduled. Condition (2) is what makes this scheduler avoid aborts. The rationale for it is this. Suppose T_j precedes T_i in the SSG. If the SSG is acyclic, then the execution is equivalent to a serial one in which T_j executes before T_i. Thus if $p_i[x]$ and $q_j[x]$ conflict, $q_j[x]$ must be scheduled before $p_i[x]$. So if $p_i[x]$ is received before $q_j[x]$, it must be delayed. Otherwise, when $q_j[x]$ is eventually received it will have to be rejected, as its acceptance would create a cycle involving T_i and T_j in the SSG. Note that to evaluate condition (2), the Conservative SGT scheduler must, in addition to o-set$[T_j]$, maintain the sets o-scheduled$[T_j]$, as discussed in Basic SGT.

One final remark about condition (2). You may wonder why we have limited it only to transactions that *directly* precede T_i. The reason is that the condition is necessarily satisfied by transactions T_j that indirectly precede T_i; that is, the shortest path from T_j to T_i has more than one edge. Then T_i and T_j do not issue conflicting operations. In particular, $x \in p$-set$[T_i]$ implies $x \notin q$-set$[T_j]$ for all conflicting operation types p, q.

Every time it receives $p_i[x]$ from the TM or an acknowledgment of some $q_j[x]$ from the DM, the scheduler checks if the head of queue[x] is ready. If so, it dequeues the operation and sends it to the DM. The scheduler then repeats the same process with the new head of queue[x] until the queue is empty or its head is not ready. The policy for discarding information about terminated transactions is the same as for Basic SGT.

Recoverability Considerations

Basic and Conservative SGT produce SR histories, but not necessarily recoverable — much less cascadeless or strict — ones.

Both types of SGT schedulers can be modified to produce only strict (and SR) histories by using the same technique as Strict TO. The scheduler sets w-in-transit[x] to 1 when it sends $w_i[x]$ to the DM. But rather than decrementing it back to zero when the DM acknowledges $w_i[x]$, the scheduler does so when it receives an acknowledgment that the DM processed a_i or c_i. Recall that w-in-transit[x] is used to delay sending $r_j[x]$ and $w_j[x]$ operations until a previously sent $w_i[x]$ is processed. By postponing the setting of w-in-transit[x] to zero, the scheduler delays $r_j[x]$ and $w_j[x]$ until the transaction that last wrote into x has terminated, thereby ensuring the execution is strict.

It's also easy to modify Basic or Conservative SGT to enforce only the weaker condition of avoiding cascading abort. For this, it is only necessary to make sure that before scheduling $r_i[x]$, the transaction from which T_i will read x has committed. To do this, every time the scheduler receives an acknowledgment of a Commit operation, c_j, it marks node T_j in the SSG as "committed." Now suppose the scheduler receives $r_i[x]$ from the TM and accepts it. Let T_j be a transaction that satisfies:

1. $x \in$ w-scheduled[T_j]; and

2. for any $T_k \neq T_j$ such that $x \in$ w-scheduled[T_k], $T_k \rightarrow T_j$ is in the SSG.

At most one T_j can satisfy both of these conditions. (It is possible that no transaction does, for instance, if all transactions that have ever written into x have been deleted from the SSG by now.) The scheduler can send $r_i[x]$ to the DM only if T_j is marked "committed" or no such T_j exists.

The same idea can be used to enforce only the weaker condition of recoverability. The difference is that instead of delaying individual Reads, the scheduler now delays T_i's Commit until all transactions T_j from which T_i has read either are marked "committed" or have been deleted from the SSG. Also, since in this case cascading aborts are possible, when the scheduler either receives T_i's Abort from the TM or causes T_i to abort to break a cycle in the SSG, it also aborts any transaction T_j that read from T_i. An SGT scheduler can detect if T_j has read from T_i by checking if

1. $T_i \rightarrow T_j$ is in the SSG, and

2. there is some $x \in$ r-scheduled[T_j] $\cap$ w-scheduled[T_i] such that for every T_k where $T_i \rightarrow T_k$ and $T_k \rightarrow T_j$ are in the SSG, $x \notin$ w-scheduled[T_k].

Distributed SGT Schedulers

SGT schedulers present problems in distribution of control since their decisions are based on the SSG, an inherently global structure. The problems are reminiscent of distributed deadlocks. If each scheduler maintains a local SSG reflecting only the conflicts on the data items that it manages, then it is possible to construct executions in which all such local SSGs are acyclic, yet the global SSG contains a cycle.

For example, consider

$$H_3 = w_1[x_1] \; r_2[x_1] \; w_2[x_2] \; r_3[x_2] \; w_3[x_3] \; r_4[x_3] \; w_4[x_4] \; ... \; r_k[x_{k-1}] \; w_k[x_k].$$

Suppose that there are k sites, and x_i is stored at site i, for $1 \le i \le k$. At each site $i < k$, the local SSG contains the edge $T_i \to T_{i+1}$. Now, if T_1 issues $w_1[x_k]$, the local SSG at site k contains the edge $T_k \to T_1$. Thus, globally we have a cycle $T_1 \to T_2 \to ... \to T_k \to T_1$, yet all local SSGs are acyclic (each consists of a single edge).

This is essentially the same problem we had with global deadlock detection in 2PL (Section 3.11). There is an important difference, however, that makes our new problem more severe. In global deadlock detection any transactions involved in a cycle in the WFG are just waiting for each other and thus none can proceed; in particular, none can commit. So we may take our time in checking for global cycles, merely at the risk of delaying the discovery of a deadlock. On the other hand, transactions that lie along an SSG cycle do *not* wait for each other. Since a transaction should not commit until the scheduler has checked that the transaction is not in an SSG cycle, global cycle detection must take place *at least* at the same rate as transactions are processed. In typical applications, the cost of this is prohibitive.

*Space-Efficient SGT Schedulers

The implementations of SGT just described have the unpleasant property of potentially requiring an unbounded amount of space. History

$$H_2 = r_{k+1}[x] \; w_1[x] \; w_1[y_1] \; c_1 \; w_2[x] \; w_2[y_2] \; c_2 \; ... \; w_k[x] \; w_k[y_k] \; c_k$$

is a model for histories with an arbitrary number of committed transactions about which the scheduler must keep readset and writeset information. Recall that in the implementation we discussed, each transaction T_i that appears in the SSG requires space for representing T_i and, more substantially, for storing r-scheduled$[T_i]$ and w-scheduled$[T_i]$. If t is the total number of transactions appearing in an execution such as H_2, and D is the set of data items, then the scheduler may require space proportional to t^2 for storing the SSG and space proportional to $t \cdot |D|$ for other information maintained by the scheduler. Since there is no bound on the number of transactions in the execution, the scheduler's space requirements can grow indefinitely.

In all of the other schedulers we have studied, the space required is proportional to $a \cdot |D|$, where a is the number of *active* transactions (i.e., those that have not yet committed or aborted). We can make SGT's space requirements comparable to those schedulers by using a different implementation, which requires space proportional to the maximum of a^2 (for the SSG) and $a \cdot |D|$ (for the conflict information). Since at any given time a is generally much smaller than the total number of transactions that have appeared in that execution and is a number under system control, this is a significant improvement over Basic SGT.

In outline, here is the space-efficient implementation for Basic SGT. The scheduler maintains an SSG which is transitively closed and only contains nodes for active transactions. For each node T_i of SSG, the scheduler also maintains four sets: o-scheduled$[T_i]$ and o-conflict$[T_i]$, for $o \in \{r, w\}$. As before, r-scheduled$[T_i]$ (or w-scheduled$[T_i]$) is the set of data items for which Reads (or Writes) have been scheduled. r-conflict$[T_i]$ (or w-conflict$[T_i]$) is the set of data items read (or written) by terminated transactions that must follow T_i in any execution equivalent to the present one. More precisely, at the end of an execution represented by history H, o-conflict$[T_i] = \{x \mid o_j[x] \in H, T_j$ is committed in H, and $T_i \rightarrow T_j \in SG^+(H)\}$, where $SG^+(H)$ is the transitive closure of $SG(H)$.[2]

When a transaction T_i begins, the scheduler adds a new node to the SSG, and initializes o-scheduled$[T_i]$ and o-conflict$[T_i]$ to the empty set, for $o \in \{r, w\}$. When the scheduler receives an operation $p_i[x]$, it tests whether x is in q-conflict$[T_i]$ for some q conflicting with p. If so, it rejects $p_i[x]$. Otherwise, it adds edges $T_j \rightarrow T_i$ to the SSG for every transaction T_j with $x \in q$-scheduled$[T_j]$ $\cup$ q-conflict$[T_j]$ for all operation types q conflicting with p. If the resulting SSG contains a cycle, the scheduler rejects $p_i[x]$. Otherwise, it schedules $p_i[x]$ after all conflicting operations previously sent to the DM have been acknowledged.

When the scheduler receives the acknowledgment of c_i from the DM, it computes SG^+. For each T_j with $T_j \rightarrow T_i$ in SSG^+, it sets o-conflict$[T_j]$ to o-conflict$[T_j]$ $\cup$ o-scheduled$[T_i]$ $\cup$ o-conflict$[T_i]$, $o \in \{r, w\}$. Note that at this point, r-scheduled$[T_i]$ (or w-scheduled$[T_i]$) is precisely the readset (or writeset) of T_i. Then the scheduler deletes T_i from SSG^+ along with all its incoming and outgoing edges. The resulting graph becomes the new SSG.

To see why this method is correct, first consider the scheduler's response to receiving $p_i[x]$. Let history H represent the execution at the time the scheduler receives $p_i[x]$. If x is in q-conflict$[T_i]$ for some q conflicting with p, then for some committed transaction T_j, some operation $q_j[x]$ has been scheduled and $T_i \rightarrow T_j \in SG^+(H)$. If $p_i[x]$ were to be scheduled, we would also have that $T_j \rightarrow T_i$ (because of $q_j[x]$ and $p_i[x]$) and thus a cyclic SG would result. To avoid this, $p_i[x]$ is rejected.

Next, consider the scheduler's response to c_i, and let history H represent the execution at this time. Consider any active transaction T_j such that $T_j \rightarrow T_i$ is in $SG^+(H)$ (which implies $T_j \rightarrow T_i$ is in SSG^+). Before discarding T_i we must record the fact that the scheduler must not subsequently schedule any of T_j's operations that conflict with T_i's operations or with operations of committed transactions that follow T_i in SG^+. Otherwise, a cyclic SG will subsequently arise. This is why we must, at this point, update r-conflict$[T_j]$ (or w-conflict$[T_j]$) by adding r-scheduled$[T_i]$ $\cup$ r-conflict$[T_i]$ (or w-scheduled$[T_i]$ $\cup$ w-conflict$[T_i]$) to it.

---

[2]See Section A.3 of the Appendix for the definition of transitive closure of a directed graph.

We compute SSG^+ before deleting the node corresponding to T_i, the transaction that committed, to avoid losing indirect precedence information (represented as paths in the SSG). For example, suppose that there is a path from T_j to T_k in the SSG and that *all* such paths pass through node T_i. Then, deleting T_i will produce a graph that doesn't represent the fact that T_j must precede T_k. SSG^+ contains an edge $T_j \rightarrow T_k$ iff the SSG has a *path* from T_j to T_k. Thus SSG^+ represents exactly the same precedence information as SSG. Moreover, the *only* precedence information lost by deleting T_i from the SSG^+ pertains to T_i itself (in which we are no longer interested since it has terminated) and to no other active transactions.

The scheduler as described produces SR executions. By using the techniques of the previous subsection we can further restrict its output to be recoverable, cascadeless, or strict (see Exercise 4.19).

4.4 CERTIFIERS

Introduction

So far we have been assuming that *every* time it receives an operation, a scheduler must decide whether to accept, reject, or delay it. A different approach is to have the scheduler immediately schedule each operation it receives. From time to time, it checks to see what it has done. If it thinks all is well, it continues scheduling. On the other hand, if it discovers that in its hurry to process operations it has inappropriately scheduled conflicting operations, then it must abort certain transactions.

When it's about to schedule a transaction T_i's Commit, the scheduler checks whether the execution that includes c_i is SR. If not, it rejects the Commit, thereby forcing T_i to abort. (It cannot check less often than on every Commit, as it would otherwise risk committing a transaction involved in a non-SR execution.) Such schedulers are called *certifiers*. The process of checking whether a transaction's Commit can be safely scheduled or must be rejected is called *certification*. Certifiers are sometimes called *optimistic schedulers*, because they aggressively schedule operations, hoping nothing bad, such as a non-SR execution, will happen.

There are certifiers based on all three types of schedulers — 2PL, TO, and SGT — with either centralized or distributed control. We will explore all of these possibilities in this section.

2PL Certification

When a 2PL certifier receives an operation from the TM, it notes the data item accessed by the operation and immediately submits it to the DM. When it receives a Commit, c_i, the certifier checks if there is any operation $p_i[x]$ of T_i that conflicts with some operation $q_j[x]$ of some other active transaction, T_j. If so, the certifier rejects c_i and aborts T_i.[3] Otherwise it *certifies* T_i by passing c_i to the DM, thereby allowing T_i to terminate successfully.

The 2PL certifier uses several data structures: a set containing the names of active transactions, and two sets, r-scheduled[T_i] and w-scheduled[T_i], for each active transaction T_i, which contain the data items read and written, respectively, by T_i so far.

When the 2PL certifier receives $r_i[x]$ (or $w_i[x]$), it adds x to r-scheduled[T_i] (or w-scheduled[T_i]). When the scheduler receives c_i, T_i has finished executing, so r-scheduled[T_i] and w-scheduled[T_i] contain T_i's readset and writeset, respectively. Thus, testing for conflicts can be done by looking at intersections of the r-scheduled and w-scheduled sets. To process c_i, the certifier checks every other active transaction, T_j, to determine if any one of r-scheduled[T_i] ∩ w-scheduled[T_j], w-scheduled[T_i] ∩ r-scheduled[T_j], or w-scheduled[T_i] ∩ w-scheduled[T_j] is nonempty. If so, it rejects c_i. Otherwise, it certifies T_i and removes T_i from the set of active transactions.

To prove that the 2PL certifier only produces SR executions, we will follow the usual procedure of proving that every history it allows must have an acyclic SG.

Theorem 4.2: The 2PL certifier produces SR histories.

Proof: Let H be a history representing an execution produced by the 2PL certifier. Suppose $T_j \rightarrow T_i$ is an edge of SG(H). Then T_i and T_j are committed in H and there are conflicting operations $q_j[x]$ and $p_i[x]$ such that $q_j[x] < p_i[x]$. We claim that the certification of T_j preceded the certification of T_i. For suppose T_i was certified first. At the time T_i is certified, $p_i[x]$ must have been processed by the scheduler; hence x is in p-scheduled[T_i]. Moreover, since $q_j[x] < p_i[x]$, x is in q-scheduled[T_j]. Thus p-scheduled[T_i] ∩ q-scheduled[T_j] $\neq \{\}$. T_j, not having been certified yet, is active. But then the scheduler would not certify T_i, contrary to our assumption that T_i is committed in H. We have therefore shown that if $T_j \rightarrow T_i$ is in SG(H), T_j must be certified before T_i in H. By induction, if a cycle existed in SG(H), every transaction on that cycle would have to be certified before itself, an absurdity. Therefore SG(H) is acyclic. By the Serializability Theorem, H is SR. □

We called this certifier a 2PL certifier, yet there was no mention of locks anywhere! The name is justified if one thinks of an imaginary read (or write) lock being obtained by T_i on x when x is added to r-scheduled[T_i] (or w-scheduled[T_i]). If there is ever a lock conflict between two active transactions,

---

[3]A transaction is committed *only* when the scheduler acknowledges to the TM the processing of Commit, *not* when the TM sends the Commit to the scheduler. So, it is perfectly legitimate for the scheduler to reject c_i and abort T_i at this point.

the first of them to attempt certification will be aborted. This is very similar to a 2PL scheduler that never allows a conflicting operation to wait, but rather always rejects it. In fact, the committed projection of every history produced by a 2PL certifier could also have been produced by a 2PL scheduler.

To enforce recoverability, when a 2PL certifier aborts a transaction T_i, it must also abort any other active transaction T_j such that w-scheduled$[T_i]$ $\cap$ r-scheduled$[T_j] \neq \{\}$. Note that this may cause T_j to be aborted unnecessarily if, for example, there are data items in w-scheduled$[T_i]$ $\cap$ r-scheduled$[T_j]$ but T_j actually read them *before* T_i wrote them. However, the 2PL certifier does not keep track of the order in which conflicting operations were processed; it can't distinguish, at certification time, the case just described from the case in which T_j read some of the items in w-scheduled$[T_i]$ $\cap$ r-scheduled$[T_j]$ *after* T_i wrote them. For safety, then, it must abort T_j.

One can modify the 2PL certifier to enforce the stronger conditions of cascadelessness or strictness, although this involves delaying operations and therefore runs counter to the optimistic philosophy of certifiers (see Exercise 4.25).

To understand the performance of 2PL certification, let's compare it to its on-line counterpart, Basic 2PL. Both types of scheduler check for conflicts between transactions. Thus, the overhead for checking conflicts in the two methods is about the same. If transactions rarely conflict, then Basic 2PL doesn't delay many transactions and neither Basic 2PL nor 2PL certification aborts many. Thus, in this case throughput for the two methods is about the same.

At higher conflict rates, 2PL certification performs more poorly. To see why, suppose T_i issues an operation that conflicts with that of some other active transaction T_j. In 2PL certification, T_i and T_j would execute to completion, even though at least one of them is doomed to be aborted. The execution effort in completing that doomed transaction is wasted. By contrast, in 2PL T_i would be delayed. This ensures that at most one of T_i and T_j will be aborted due to the conflict. Even if delaying T_i causes a deadlock, the victim is aborted before it executes completely, so less of its execution effort is wasted than in 2PL certification.

Quantitative studies are consistent with this intuition. In simulation and analytic modelling of the methods, 2PL certification has lower throughput than 2PL for most application parameters. The difference in throughput increases with increasing conflict rate.

SGT Certification

SGT lends itself very naturally to a certifier. The certifier dynamically maintains an SSG of the execution it has produced so far, exactly as in Basic SGT. Every time it receives an operation $p_i[x]$, it adds the edge $T_j \rightarrow T_i$ to the SSG for every transaction T_j such that the certifier has already sent to the DM an operation $q_j[x]$ conflicting with $p_i[x]$. After this is done, it immediately dispatches $p_i[x]$ to the DM (without worrying whether the SSG is acyclic). Of course, handshaking is still necessary to ensure that the DM processes conflicting operations in the order scheduled.

When the scheduler receives c_i, it checks whether T_i lies on a cycle of the SSG. If so, it rejects c_i and T_i is aborted. Otherwise it certifies T_i and T_i commits normally.

The implementation issues are essentially those that we discussed for Basic SGT. The same data structures can be used to maintain the SSG and to enforce handshaking between the certifier and DM. The problem of space inefficiency is of concern here also, and the same remedies apply.

Finally, the SGT certifier is modified to enforce recoverability in essentially the same way as SGT schedulers. The rule is that if T_i aborts, the certifier also aborts any active transaction T_j such that, for some data item x, $x \in$ w-scheduled$[T_i] \cap$ r-scheduled$[T_j]$, $T_i \rightarrow T_j$ is in the SSG, and for every T_k such that $T_i \rightarrow T_k$ and $T_k \rightarrow T_j$ are in the SSG, $x \notin$ w-scheduled$[T_k]$.

TO Certification

A TO certifier schedules Reads and Writes without delay, except for reasons related to handshaking between the certifier and the DM. When the certifier receives c_i, it certifies T_i if all conflicts involving operations of T_i are in timestamp order. Otherwise, it rejects c_i and T_i is aborted. Thus, T_i is certified iff the execution so far satisfies the TO rule. That is, in the execution produced thus far, if some operation $p_i[x]$ precedes some conflicting operation $q_j[x]$ of transaction T_j, then ts$(T_i) <$ ts(T_j). This is the very same condition that Basic TO checks when it receives each operation. However, when Basic TO finds a violation of the TO rule, it immediately rejects the operation, whereas the TO certifier delays this rejection until it receives the transaction's Commit. Since allowing such a transaction to complete involves extra work, with no hope that it will ultimately commit, Basic TO is preferable to a TO certifier.

Distributed Certifiers

A distributed certifier consists of a collection of certifier processes, one for each site. As with distributed schedulers, we assume that the certifier at a site is responsible for regulating access to exactly those data items stored at that site.

Although each certifier sends operations to its respective DM independently of other certifiers, the activity of transaction certification must be carried out in a coordinated manner. To certify a transaction, a decision must be reached involving all of the certifiers that received an operation of that transaction. In SGT certification, the certifiers must exchange their local SSGs to ensure that the global SSG does not have a cycle involving the transaction being certified. If no such cycle exists, then the transaction is certified (by all certifiers involved); otherwise it is aborted.

In 2PL or TO certification, each certifier can make a local decision whether or not to certify a transaction, based on conflict information for the data items it manages. A global decision must then be reached by consensus. If the local decision of *all* certifiers involved in the certification of a transaction is to certify the transaction, then the global decision is to certify. If even one certifier's local decision is to abort the transaction, then the global decision is to abort. The fate of a transaction is decided only after this global decision has been reached. A certifier *cannot* proceed to certify a transaction on the basis of its local decision only.

This kind of consensus can be reached by using the following communication protocol between the TM that is supervising T_i and the certifiers that processed T_i's operations. The TM distributes T_i's Commit to all certifiers that participated in the execution of T_i. When a certifier receives c_i, it makes a local decision, called its *vote*, on whether to certify T_i or not, and sends its vote to the TM. After receiving the votes from all the certifiers that participate in T_i's certification, the TM makes the global decision accordingly. It then sends the global decision to all participating certifiers, which carry it out as soon as they receive it.[4]

Using this method for reaching a unanimous decision, a certifier may vote to certify a transaction, yet end up having to abort it because some other certifier voted not to certify. Thus, a certifier that votes to certify experiences a period of uncertainty on the fate of the transaction, namely, the period between the moment it sends its vote and the moment it receives the global decision from the TM. Of course, a certifier that votes to abort is not uncertain about the transaction. It knows it will eventually be aborted by all certifiers.

4.5 INTEGRATED SCHEDULERS

Introduction

The schedulers we have seen so far synchronize conflicting operations by one of three mechanisms: 2PL, TO, or SGT. There are other schedulers that use combinations of these techniques to ensure that transactions are processed in an SR manner. Such schedulers are best understood by decomposing the problem of concurrency control into certain subproblems. Each subproblem is solved by one of our familiar three techniques. Then we have to make sure that these solutions fit together consistently to yield a correct solution to the entire problem of scheduling.

---

[4]We'll study this type of protocol in much greater detail in Chapter 7.

We decompose the problem by separating the issue of scheduling Reads against conflicting Writes (and, symmetrically, of Writes against conflicting Reads) from that of scheduling Writes against conflicting Writes. We'll call the first subproblem *rw synchronization* and the second, *ww synchronization*. We will call an algorithm used for rw synchronization an *rw synchronizer*, and one for ww synchronization a *ww synchronizer*. A complete scheduler consists of an rw and a ww synchronizer. In a correct scheduler, the two synchronizers must resolve read-write and write-write conflicts in a consistent way. Schedulers obtained in this manner are called *integrated schedulers*. Integrated schedulers that use (possibly different versions of) the same mechanism (2PL, TO, or SGT) for both the rw and the ww synchronizer are called *pure schedulers*. All of the schedulers we have seen so far are pure schedulers. Schedulers combining different mechanisms for rw and ww synchronization are called *mixed schedulers*.

To use any of the variations of the three concurrency control techniques that we have seen to solve each of these two subproblems, all we need to do is change the definition of "conflicting operations" to reflect the type of synchronization we are trying to achieve. Specifically, in rw synchronization, two operations accessing the same data item conflict if one of them is a Read and the other is a Write. Two Writes accessing the same data item are *not* considered to conflict in this case. Similarly, in ww synchronization two operations on the same data item conflict if *both* are Writes.

For example, if a scheduler uses 2PL for rw synchronization only, $w_i[x]$ is delayed (on account of the 2PL rw synchronizer) *only* if some other transaction T_j is holding a *read* lock on x. That is, several transactions *may* be sharing a write lock on x, as long as no transaction is concurrently holding a read lock on x. This may sound wrong, but remember that there is another part to the scheduler, the ww synchronizer, which will somehow ensure that write-write conflicts are resolved consistently with the way the 2PL rw synchronizer resolves read-write conflicts. Similarly, in a scheduler using 2PL for ww synchronization only, Reads are never delayed by the 2PL ww synchronizer, although they may be delayed by the rw synchronizer.

A TO rw synchronizer only guarantees that Reads and Writes accessing the same data item are processed in timestamp order. It will *not* force two Writes $w_i[x]$ and $w_j[x]$ to be processed in timestamp order, unless there is some operation $r_k[x]$ such that $ts(T_i) < ts(T_k) < ts(T_j)$ or $ts(T_j) < ts(T_k) < ts(T_i)$. Similarly, a TO ww synchronizer ensures that $w_i[x]$ is processed before $w_j[x]$ only if $ts(T_i) < ts(T_j)$, but imposes no such order on $r_i[x]$ and $w_j[x]$; of course, the rw synchronizer will impose such an order.

In SGT, the SG maintained by the scheduler contains only those edges that reflect the kind of conflicts being resolved. An SGT rw (or ww) synchronizer adds edges corresponding to read-write (or write-write) conflicts, every time it receives an operation.

The *rw serialization graph of history H*, denoted $SG_{rw}(H)$, consists of nodes corresponding to the committed transactions appearing in H and edges $T_i \to T_j$ iff $r_i[x] < w_j[x]$ or $w_i[x] < r_j[x]$ for some x. Similarly, the *ww serialization graph of H*, denoted $SG_{ww}(H)$, consists of nodes corresponding to the committed transactions appearing in H and edges $T_i \to T_j$ iff $w_i[x] < w_j[x]$ for some x.

It is easy to show that if a history H represents some execution produced by a scheduler using an rw (or ww) synchronizer based on 2PL, TO, or SGT, then $SG_{rw}(H)$ (or $SG_{ww}(H)$) is acyclic. The arguments are similar to those used in earlier sections to prove that $SG(H)$ is acyclic if H represents an execution produced by a 2PL, TO, or SGT scheduler. Therefore for a scheduler using any combination of 2PL, TO, and SGT for rw or ww synchronization, we know that if H is produced by the scheduler, then $SG_{rw}(H)$ and $SG_{ww}(H)$ are both acyclic.

To ensure that H is SR, we need the complete graph $SG(H)$ to be acyclic. It is not enough for each of $SG_{rw}(H)$ and $SG_{ww}(H)$ to be acyclic. In addition, we need the two graphs to represent *compatible* partial orders. That is, the *union* of the two graphs must be acyclic. Ensuring the compatibility of these two graphs is the hardest part of designing correct integrated schedulers, as we'll see later in this section.

Thomas' Write Rule (TWR)

Suppose a TO scheduler receives $w_i[x]$ after it has already sent $w_j[x]$ to the DM, but $ts(T_i) < ts(T_j)$. The TO rule requires that $w_i[x]$ be rejected. But if the scheduler is only concerned with ww synchronization, then this rejection is unnecessary. For if the scheduler had processed $w_i[x]$ when it was "supposed to," namely, before it had processed $w_j[x]$, then x would have the same value as it has now, when it is faced with $w_i[x]$'s having arrived too late. Said differently, processing a sequence of Writes in timestamp order produces the same result as processing the single Write with maximum timestamp; thus, late operations can be ignored.

This observation leads to a ww synchronization rule, called *Thomas' Write Rule (TWR)*, that never delays or rejects any operation. When a TWR ww synchronizer receives a Write that has arrived too late insofar as the TO rule is concerned, it simply *ignores* the Write (i.e., doesn't send it to the DM) but reports its successful completion to the TM.

More precisely, Thomas' Write Rule states: Let T_j be the transaction with maximum timestamp that wrote into x before the scheduler receives $w_i[x]$. If $ts(T_i) > ts(T_j)$, process $w_i[x]$ as usual (submit it to the DM, wait for the DM's $ack(w_i[x])$, and then acknowledge it to the TM). Otherwise, process $w_i[x]$ by simply acknowledging it to the TM.

But what about Reads? Surely Reads care about the order in which Writes are processed. For example, suppose we have four transactions T_1, T_2, T_3, and

T_4 where $ts(T_1) < ts(T_2) < ts(T_3) < ts(T_4)$; T_1, T_2, and T_4 just write x; and T_3 reads x. Now, suppose the scheduler schedules $w_1[x]$, $r_3[x]$, $w_4[x]$ in that order, and then receives $w_2[x]$. TWR says that it's safe for the ww synchronizer to accept $w_2[x]$ but not process it. But this seems wrong, since T_2 should have written x before $r_3[x]$ read the value written by $w_1[x]$. This is true. But the problem is one of synchronizing Reads against Writes and therefore none of the ww synchronizer's business. The rw synchronizer must somehow prevent this situation.

This example drives home the division of labor between rw and ww synchronizers. And it emphasizes once more that care must be taken in integrating rw and ww synchronizers to obtain a correct scheduler.

We will examine two integrated schedulers, one using Basic TO for rw synchronization and TWR for ww synchronization, and another using 2PL for rw synchronization and TWR for ww synchronization. The first is a pure integrated scheduler because both rw and ww synchronization are achieved by the same mechanism, TO. The second is a mixed integrated scheduler because it combines a 2PL rw synchronizer with a TWR ww synchronizer.

A Pure Integrated Scheduler

Our first integrated scheduler can be viewed as a simple optimization over Basic TO, in the sense that it sometimes avoids rejecting Writes that Basic TO would reject.

Recall that a Basic TO scheduler schedules an operation if all conflicting operations that it has previously scheduled have smaller timestamps. Otherwise it rejects the operation. Our new scheduler uses this principle for rw synchronization only. For ww synchronization it uses TWR instead. That is, it behaves as follows:

1. It schedules $r_i[x]$ provided that for all $w_j[x]$ that have already been scheduled, $ts(T_i) > ts(T_j)$. Otherwise, it rejects $r_i[x]$.

2. It rejects $w_i[x]$ if it has already scheduled some $r_j[x]$ with $ts(T_j) > ts(T_i)$. Otherwise, if it has scheduled some $w_j[x]$ with $ts(T_j) > ts(T_i)$, it ignores $w_i[x]$ (i.e., acknowledges the processing of $w_i[x]$ to the TM but does not send the operation to the DM). Otherwise, it processes $w_i[x]$ normally.

Thus, the difference from Basic TO is that a late Write is only rejected if a conflicting *Read* with a greater timestamp has already been processed. If the only conflicting operations with greater timestamps that have been processed are Writes, the late Write is simply ignored. The implementation details and recoverability considerations of this scheduler are similar to those of Basic TO (see Exercise 4.33).

A Mixed Integrated Scheduler

Now let's construct an integrated scheduler that uses Strict 2PL for rw synchronization and TWR for ww synchronization. Suppose that H is a history representing some execution of such a scheduler. We know that $SG_{rw}(H)$ and $SG_{ww}(H)$ are each acyclic. To ensure that $SG(H) = SG_{rw}(H) \cup SG_{ww}(H)$ is acyclic, we will also require that

1. if $T_i \rightarrow T_j$ is an edge of $SG_{rw}(H)$, then $ts(T_i) < ts(T_j)$.

We know that TO synchronizes all conflicts in timestamp order, so if $T_i \rightarrow T_j$ is in $SG_{ww}(H)$ then $ts(T_i) < ts(T_j)$. By (1), the same holds in $SG_{rw}(H)$. Since every edge $T_i \rightarrow T_j$ in $SG_{rw}(H)$ and $SG_{ww}(H)$ has $ts(T_i) < ts(T_j)$, $SG(H)$ must be acyclic. The reasoning is identical to that of Theorem 4.1, which proved that TO is correct. In the remainder of this section we describe a technique for making condition (1) hold.

If $T_i \rightarrow T_j$ is in $SG_{rw}(H)$, then T_j cannot terminate until T_i releases some lock that T_j needs. In Strict 2PL, a transaction holds its locks until it commits. Therefore, if $T_i \rightarrow T_j$, then T_i commits before T_j terminates, which implies that T_i commits before T_j commits. Thus, we can obtain (1) by ensuring that

2. if T_i commits before T_j, then $ts(T_i) < ts(T_j)$.

The scheduler can't ensure (2) unless it delays assigning a timestamp to a transaction T_i until it receives T_i's Commit. But the scheduler cannot process any of T_i's Writes using TWR until it knows T_i's timestamp. These last two observations imply that the scheduler must delay processing all of the Writes it receives from each transaction T_i until it receives T_i's Commit.

This delaying of Writes creates a problem if, for some x, T_i issues $r_i[x]$ after having issued $w_i[x]$. Since $w_i[x]$ is still delayed in the scheduler when the scheduler receives $r_i[x]$, the scheduler can't send $r_i[x]$ to the DM; if it did, then $r_i[x]$ would not (as it should) read the value produced by $w_i[x]$.

The scheduler can deal with this problem by checking a transaction's queue of delayed Writes every time it receives a Read to process. If the transaction previously wrote the data item, the scheduler can service the Read internally, without going to the DM. Since the scheduler has to get a read lock before processing the Read, it will see the transaction's write lock at that time, and will therefore know to process the Read internally. If there is no write lock owned by the same transaction, then the scheduler processes the Read normally.

In a centralized DBS, the scheduler can enforce (2) simply by assigning each transaction a larger timestamp than the previous one that committed. In a distributed DBS, this is difficult to do, because different schedulers (and TMs) are involved in committing different transactions. Therefore, for distributed DBSs we need a way to assign timestamps to different transactions independently at different sites. The following is one method for accomplishing this.

Each scheduler maintains the usual information used by 2PL and TO schedulers. Each transaction has a timestamp, which its TM assigns according to a rule that we will describe later on. For each data item x (that it manages), a scheduler maintains read locks and write locks (used for 2PL rw synchronization), and a variable max-w-scheduled[x] containing the largest timestamp of all transactions that have written into x (used for the TWR ww synchronization). (Since TO is not used for rw synchronization, max-r-scheduled[x] is unnecessary.) To coordinate handshaking with the DM, the scheduler also keeps the usual queue of delayed operations on x, queue[x], and two counts, r-in-transit[x] and w-in-transit[x], of the Reads and Writes sent to, but not yet acknowledged by, the DM. The scheduler also maintains a variable to help in generating transaction timestamps; for each data item x, max-ts[x] contains the largest timestamp of all transactions that have ever obtained a lock on x (be it a read or a write lock). And for each active transaction T_i, the TM keeps a variable max-lock-set[T_i], which it initializes to 0 when T_i begins executing.

Each scheduler uses 2PL for rw synchronization. To process $r_i[x]$, the scheduler obtains $rl_i[x]$. To process $w_i[x]$, it sets $wl_i[x]$, after which it inserts $w_i[x]$ into w-queue[T_i], a buffer that contains T_i's Writes. After processing $o_i[x]$ ($o \in \{r, w\}$), the scheduler sends the TM an acknowledgment that includes max-ts[x]. The TM processes the acknowledgment by setting max-lock-set[T_i] := max(max-lock-set[T_i], max-ts[x]).

When the TM receives c_i, it generates a unique timestamp for T_i greater than max-lock-set[T_i]. It then sends c_i and ts(T_i) to each scheduler that processed operations on behalf of T_i. To process c_i, a scheduler sets max-ts[x] := max(ts(T_i), max-ts[x]) for each x that T_i has locked (at that scheduler). Then, the scheduler processes T_i's Writes. For every $w_i[x]$ buffered in w-queue[T_i], if ts(T_i) > max-w-scheduled[x], then the scheduler sends $w_i[x]$ to the DM and sets max-w-scheduled[x] to ts(T_i); otherwise it discards $w_i[x]$ without processing it. Notice that it's crucial that no $w_i[x]$ was sent to the DM before the scheduler receives c_i and ts(T_i), because the latter is needed for processing $w_i[x]$ according to TWR. After a DM acknowledges all of the Writes that were sent to it, its scheduler sends c_i to the DM. After it receives ack(c_i), the scheduler can release T_i's locks (that were set by that scheduler) and acknowledge T_i's commitment (by that scheduler) to the TM.

We want to show that the implementation sketched here achieves condition (1), which is sufficient for proving that Strict 2PL rw synchronization and TWR ww synchronization are integrated correctly. Let H be a history representing an execution of the DBS just outlined and suppose that $T_i \rightarrow T_j$ is in $SG_{rw}(H)$. This means that $p_i[x] < q_j[x]$ for some x where p is r or w and q is w or r, respectively. Because we are using Strict 2PL for rw synchronization, T_i committed before T_j did. Consider the time at which T_j is ready to commit. At that time max-lock-set[T_j] $\geq$ max-ts[x], since T_j is holding a q lock on x, and after it obtained that lock, the TM set max-lock-set[T_j] to at least max-ts[x]. But before T_i released its p lock on x, the scheduler set max-ts[x] to at least ts(T_i). Since max-ts[x] never decreases with time, max-lock-set[T_j] $\geq$ ts(T_i). By the rule for generating timestamps, ts(T_j) > max-lock-set[T_j] and therefore ts(T_j) > ts(T_i). Thus, timestamps assigned by the TM are consistent with the order of Commits, which is the condition we needed to show that Strict

2PL rw synchronization and TWR ww synchronization are correctly integrated.

BIBLIOGRAPHIC NOTES

Early TO based algorithms appear in [Shapiro, Millstein 77a], [Shapiro, Millstein 77b], and [Thomas 79]. The latter paper, first published in 1976 as a technical report, also introduced certification and TWR, and was the first to apply voting to replicated data (see Chapter 8). An elaborate TO algorithm using TWR, classes, and conflict graphs was built in the SDD-1 distributed DBS [Bernstein et al. 78], [Bernstein, Shipman 80], [Bernstein, Shipman, Rothnie 80], and [McLean 81]. Other TO algorithms include [Cheng, Belford 80] and [Kaneko et al. 79]. Multigranularity locking ideas are applied to TO in [Carey 83].

Serialization graph testing has been studied in [Badal 79], [Casanova 81], [Hadzilacos, Yannakakis 86], and [Schlageter 78]. [Casanova 81] contains the space-efficient SGT scheduler in Section 4.3.

The term "optimistic" scheduler was coined in [Kung, Robinson 81], who developed the concept of certifier independently of [Thomas 79]. Other work on certifiers includes [Haerder 84], [Kersten, Tebra 84], and [Robinson 82]. [Lai, Wilkinson 84] studies the atomicity of the certification activity. The performance of certifiers is analyzed in [Menasce, Nakanishi 82a], [Morris, Wong 84], [Morris, Wong 85], and [Robinson 82].

The rw and ww synchronization paradigm of Section 4.5 is from [Bernstein, Goodman 81] and [Bernstein, Goodman 81]. The 2PL and TWR mixed integrated scheduler is from [Bernstein, Goodman, Lai 83].

EXERCISES

4.1   In Basic TO, suppose the scheduler adjusts max-q-scheduled[x] when it sends $p_i[x]$ to the DM, instead of when it adds $p_i[x]$ to queue[x]. What effect does this have on the rate at which the scheduler rejects operations? What are the benefits of this modification to Basic TO?

4.2   Modify Basic TO to avoid cascading aborts. Modify it to enforce the weaker condition of recoverability. Explain why your modified schedulers satisfy the required conditions.

4.3   In Basic TO, under what conditions (if any) is it necessary to insert an operation $p_i[x]$ to queue[x] other than at the end?

4.4   Generalize the Basic TO scheduler to handle arbitrary operations (e.g., Increment and Decrement).

4.5   Modify the Basic TO scheduler of the previous problem to avoid cascading aborts. Does the compatibility matrix contain enough information to make this modification? If not, explain what additional information is needed. Prove that the resulting scheduler produces histories that are cascadeless.

4.6   Compare the behavior of distributed 2PL with Wait-Die deadlock prevention to that of distributed Basic TO.

4.7   Prove that the Strict TO scheduler of Section 4.2 produces strict histories.

4.8   Design a conservative TO scheduler that uses knowledge of process speeds and message delays to avoid rejecting operations.

4.9   Prove that the ultimate conservative TO scheduler in Section 4.2 produces SR histories.

4.10   Modify the ultimate conservative TO scheduler in Section 4.2 so that each TM can manage more than one transaction concurrently.

4.11   Design an ultimate conservative TO scheduler that avoids rejections by exploiting predeclaration. (Do not use the TM architecture of Section 4.2, where each TM submits operations to the DM in timestamp order.) Prove that your scheduler produces SR executions.

4.12   Design a way of changing class definitions on-line in conservative TO.

4.13   Design a TO scheduler that guarantees the following property: For any history H produced by the scheduler, there is an equivalent serial history H_s such that if T_i is committed before T_j in H, then T_i precedes T_j in H_s. (T_i and T_j may not have operations that conflict with each other.) Prove that it has the property.

4.14   A *conflict graph* for a set of classes is an undirected graph whose nodes include R_I and W_I, for each class I, and whose edges include

□ (R_I, W_I) for all I,

□ (R_I, W_J) if the readset of class I intersects the writeset of class J, and

□ (W_I, W_J) if the writeset of class I intersects the writeset of class J $(I \neq J)$.

Suppose each class is managed by one TM, and that each TM executes transactions serially. A transaction can only be executed by a TM if it is a member of the TM's class.

  a. Suppose the conflict graph has no cycles. What additional constraints, if any, must be imposed by the scheduler to ensure SR executions? Prove that the scheduler produces SR executions.

  b. Suppose the scheduler uses TWR for ww synchronization, and the conflict graph has no cycles containing an (R_I, W_J) edge (i.e., all cycles only contain (W_I, W_J) edges). What additional constraints, if any, must be imposed by the scheduler to ensure SR executions? Prove that the scheduler produces SR executions.

4.15   If the size of the timestamp table is too small, then too many recent timestamps will have to be deleted in order to make room for even more recent ones. This will cause a TO scheduler to reject some older operations that access data items whose timestamps were deleted from the table. An interesting project is to study this effect quantitatively, either by simulation or by mathematical analysis.

4.16 Prove that the conservative SGT scheduler described in Section 4.3 produces SR executions.

4.17 Show that for any history produced by an SGT scheduler, there exists an assignment of timestamps to transactions such that the same history could be produced by a TO scheduler.

4.18 Design an SGT scheduler that guarantees the following property: For any history H produced by the scheduler, there is an equivalent serial history H_s such that if T_i is committed before T_j in H, then T_i precedes T_j in H_s. Prove that it has the property.

4.19 Modify the space-efficient SGT scheduler described in Section 4.3 to produce recoverable, cascadeless, and strict executions. Explain why each of your modified schedulers satisfies the required condition.

4.20 Give a serializability theoretic correctness proof of the space-efficient `SGT scheduler described in Section 4.3.

4.21 Although the space requirements of both 2PL and space-efficient SGT are proportional to $a \cdot |D|$, where a is the number of active transactions and D is the size of the database, space-efficient SGT will usually require somewhat more space than 2PL. Explain why.

4.22 Since a certifier does not control the order in which Reads and Writes execute, a transaction may read arbitrarily inconsistent data. A correct certifier will eventually abort any transaction that reads inconsistent data, but this may not be enough to avoid bad results. In particular, a program may not check data that it reads from the database adequately enough to avoid malfunctioning in the event that it reads inconsistent data; for example, it may go into an infinite loop. Give a realistic example of a transaction that malfunctions in this way using 2PL certification, but never malfunctions using Basic 2PL.

4.23 Prove that the committed projection of every history produced by a 2PL certifier could have been produced by a 2PL scheduler.

4.24 Give an example of a complete history that could be produced by a 2PL certifier but not by a 2PL scheduler. (In view of the previous exercise, the history must include aborted transactions.)

4.25 Modify the 2PL certifier so that it avoids cascading aborts. What additional modifications are needed to ensure strictness? Explain why each modified certifier satisfies the required condition.

4.26 If a 2PL certifier is permitted to certify two (or more) transactions concurrently, is there a possibility that it will produce a non-SR execution? Suppose the 2PL certifier enforces recoverability. If it is permitted to certify two transactions concurrently, is there a possibility that it will reject more transactions than it would if it certified transactions one at a time?

4.27 A transaction is called *rw phased* if it waits until all of its Reads have been processed before it submits any of its Writes. Its *read* (or *write*) phase consists of the time the scheduler receives its first Read (or Write) through the time the scheduler acknowledges the processing of its last Read (or Write). Consider the following certifier for rw phased transactions in a centralized DBS. The scheduler assigns a timestamp to a transaction when it receives the transaction's first Write. Timestamps increase monotonically, so that $ts(T_i) < ts(T_j)$ iff T_i begins its write phase before T_j begins its write phase. To certify transaction T_j, the certifier checks that for all T_i with $ts(T_i) < ts(T_j)$, either (1) T_i completed its write phase before T_j started its read phase, or (2) T_i completed its write phase before T_j started its write phase and w-scheduled(T_i) $\cap$ r-scheduled(T_j) is empty. If neither condition is satisfied for some such T_i, then T_j is aborted; otherwise, it is certified.

   a. Prove that this certifier only produces serializable executions.
   b. Are there histories produced by this certifier that could not be produced by the 2PL certifier?
   c. Are there histories involving only rw phased transactions that could be produced by the 2PL certifier but not by this certifier?
   d. Design data structures and an algorithm whereby a certifier can efficiently check (1) and (2).

4.28 In the previous exercise, suppose that for each T_i with $ts(T_i) < ts(T_j)$, the certifier checks that (1) or (2) or the following condition (3) holds: T_i completed its read phase before T_j completed its read phase and w-scheduled(T_i) $\cap$ (r-scheduled(T_j) $\cup$ w-scheduled(T_j)) is empty. Answer (a) - (d) in the previous exercise for this new type of certifier.

4.29 Suppose the scheduler uses a *workspace model* of transaction execution, as in the mixed integrated scheduler of Section 4.5. That is, it delays processing the Writes of each transaction T_i until after it receives T_i's Commit. Suppose a scheduler uses the 2PL certification rule, but uses the workspace model for transaction execution. Does the scheduler still produce SR executions? If so, prove it. If not, modify the certification rule so that it does produce SR executions. Are the executions recoverable? Cascadeless? Strict?

4.30 Does the SGT certifier still produce SR executions using a workspace model of transaction execution (see Exercise 4.29)? If so, prove it. If not, modify the certification rule so that it does produce SR executions.

4.31 In the workspace model of transaction execution (see Exercise 4.29), the scheduler buffers a transaction T_i's Writes in w-queue[T_i]. Since the scheduler must scan w-queue[T_i] for every Read issued by T_i, the efficiency of that scan is quite important. Design a data structure and search algorithm for w-queue[T_i] and analyze its efficiency.

4.32 Describe an SGT certifier based on the space-efficient SGT scheduler of Section 4.3, and prove that it produces SR executions.

4.33 Modify the pure integrated scheduler of Section 4.5 (Basic TO for rw synchronization and TWR for ww synchronization) to produce cascade-less executions. Describe the algorithm using the actual data structures maintained by the scheduler, such as max-r-scheduled, max-w-scheduled, and w-in-transit.

4.34 Describe a pure integrated scheduler that uses ultimate conservative TO for rw synchronization and TWR for ww synchronization. Prove that it produces SR executions.

4.35 Describe a mixed integrated scheduler that uses conservative TO for rw synchronization and 2PL for ww synchronization. Prove that it produces SR executions.

5
MULTIVERSION CONCURRENCY CONTROL

5.1 INTRODUCTION

In a multiversion concurrency control algorithm, each Write on a data item x produces a new copy (or *version*) of x. The DM that manages x therefore keeps a list of versions of x, which is the history of values that the DM has assigned to x. For each Read(x), the scheduler not only decides when to send the Read to the DM, but it also tells the DM which one of the versions of x to read.

The benefit of multiple versions for concurrency control is to help the scheduler avoid rejecting operations that arrive too late. For example, the scheduler normally rejects a Read because the value it was supposed to read has already been overwritten. With multiversions, such old values are never overwritten and are therefore always available to tardy Reads. The scheduler can avoid rejecting the Read simply by having the Read read an old version.

Maintaining multiple versions may not add much to the cost of concurrency control, because the versions may be needed anyway by the recovery algorithm. As we'll see in the next chapter, many recovery algorithms have to maintain some before image information, at least of those data items that have been updated by active transactions; the recovery algorithm needs those before images in case any of the active transactions abort. The before images of a data item are exactly its list of old versions. It is a small step for the DM to make those versions explicitly available to the scheduler.

An obvious cost of maintaining multiple versions is storage space. To control this storage requirement, versions must periodically be purged or archived. Since certain versions may be needed by active transactions, purging versions must be synchronized with respect to active transactions. This purging activity is another cost of multiversion concurrency control.

We assume that if a transaction is aborted, any versions it created are destroyed. In our subsequent discussion, the term "version" will refer to the value of a data item produced by a transaction that's either active or committed. Thus, when the scheduler decides to assign a particular version of x to Read(x), the value returned is not one produced by an aborted transaction. If the version read is one produced by an active transaction, recoverability requires that the reader's commitment be delayed until the transaction that produced the version has committed. If that transaction actually aborts (thereby invalidating its version), the reader must also be aborted.

The existence of multiple versions is only visible to the scheduler and DM, not to user transactions. Transactions still reference data items, such as x and y. Users therefore expect the DBS to behave as if there were only one version of each data item, namely, the last one that was written from that user's perspective. The scheduler may use multiple versions to improve performance by rejecting operations less frequently. But it must not change the system's functionality over a single version view of the database.

There are many applications of databases in which users *do* want to explicitly access each of the multiple versions of a data item. For example, a user may wish to maintain several versions of a design database: the last design released for manufacturing, the last design checked for correctness, and the most recent working design. The user may update each version of the design independently. Since the existence of these multiple versions is not transparent to the user, such applications are not appropriate for the multiversion concurrency control algorithms described in this chapter.

Analyzing Correctness

To analyze the correctness of multiversion concurrency control algorithms, we need to extend serializability theory. This extension requires two types of histories: multiversion (MV) histories that represent the DM's execution of operations on a multiversion database, and single version (1V) histories that represent the interpretation of MV histories in the users' single version view of the database. Serial 1V histories are the histories that the user regards as correct. But the system actually produces MV histories. So, to prove that a concurrency control algorithm is correct, we must prove that each of the MV histories that it can produce is equivalent to a serial 1V history.

What does it mean for an MV history to be equivalent to a 1V history? Let's try to answer this by extending the definition of equivalence of 1V histories that we used in Chapters 2–4. To attempt this extension, we need a little notation. For each data item x, we denote the versions of x by $x_i, x_j, \ldots$, where the subscript is the index of the transaction that wrote the version. Thus, each Write in an MV history is always of the form $w_i[x_i]$, where the version subscript equals the transaction subscript. Reads are denoted in the usual way, such as $r_i[x_j]$.

Suppose we adopt a definition of equivalence that says an MV history H_{MV} is equivalent to a 1V history H_{1V} if every pair of conflicting operations in H_{MV} is in the same order in H_{1V}. Consider the MV history

$$H_1 = w_0[x_0] \; c_0 \; w_1[x_1] \; c_1 \; r_2[x_0] \; w_2[y_2] \; c_2.$$

The only two operations in H_1 that conflict are $w_0[x_0]$ and $r_2[x_0]$. The operation $w_1[x_1]$ does not conflict with either $w_0[x_0]$ or $r_2[x_0]$, because it operates on a different version of x than those operations, namely x_1. Now consider the 1V history

$$H_2 = w_0[x] \; c_0 \; w_1[x] \; c_1 \; r_2[x] \; w_2[y] \; c_2.$$

We constructed H_2 by mapping each operation on versions x_0, x_1, and y_2 in H_1 into the same operation on the corresponding data items x and y. Notice that the two operations in H_1 that conflict, $w_0[x_0]$ and $r_2[x_0]$, are in the same order in H_2 as in H_1. So, according to the definition of equivalence just given, H_1 is equivalent to H_2. But this is not reasonable. In H_2, T_2 reads x from T_1, whereas in H_1, T_2 reads x from T_0.[1] Since T_2 reads a different value of x in H_1 and H_2, it may write a different value in y.

This definition of equivalence based on conflicts runs into trouble because MV and 1V histories have slightly different operations — version operations versus data item operations. These operations have different conflict properties. For example, $w_1[x_1]$ does not conflict with $r_2[x_0]$, but their corresponding 1V operations $w_1[x]$ and $r_2[x]$ *do* conflict. Therefore, a definition of equivalence based on conflicts is inappropriate.

To solve this problem, we need to return to first principles by adopting the more fundamental definition of view equivalence developed in Section 2.6. Recall that two histories are *view equivalent* if they have the same reads-from relationships and the same final writes. Comparing histories H_1 and H_2, we see that T_2 reads x from T_0 in H_1, but T_2 reads x from T_1 in H_2. Thus, H_1 is not view equivalent to H_2.

Now that we have a satisfactory definition of equivalence, we need a way of showing that every MV history H produced by a given multiversion concurrency control algorithm is equivalent to a serial 1V history. One way would be to show that $SG(H)$ is acyclic, so H is equivalent to a serial MV history. Unfortunately, this doesn't help much, because not every serial MV history is equivalent to a serial 1V history. For example, consider the serial MV history

---

[1] Recall from Section 2.4 that T_i reads x from T_j in H if (1) $w_j[x] < r_i[x]$, (2) $a_j \not< r_i[x]$, and (3) if there is some $w_k[x]$ such that $w_j[x] < w_k[x] < w_i[x]$, then $a_k < r_i[x]$.

$$H_3 = w_0[x_0] \, w_0[y_0] \, c_0 \, r_1[x_0] \, r_1[y_0] \, w_1[x_1] \, w_1[y_1] \, c_1 \, r_2[x_0] \, r_2[y_1] \, c_2.$$

If we treat the versions of x and y as independent data items, then we get

$$SG(H_3) = T_0 \rightarrow T_1 \rightarrow T_2.$$

Although H_3 is serial and $SG(H_3)$ is acyclic, H_3 is not equivalent to a serial 1V history. For example, consider the 1V history

$$H_4 = w_0[x] \, w_0[y] \, c_0 \, r_1[x] \, r_1[y] \, w_1[x] \, w_1[y] \, c_1 \, r_2[x] \, r_2[y] \, c_2.$$

We can show that H_3 is not view equivalent to H_4 by showing that they do not have the same reads-from relationships. In H_4, T_2 reads x and y from T_1. But in H_3, T_2 reads x from T_0 and reads y from T_1. Since T_2 reads different values in H_3 and H_4, the two histories are not equivalent. Similarly, H_3 is not equivalent to the 1V history

$$H_5 = w_0[x] \, w_0[y] \, c_0 \, r_2[x] \, r_2[y] \, c_2 \, r_1[x] \, r_1[y] \, w_1[x] \, w_1[y] \, c_1.$$

Clearly, H_3 is not equivalent to any 1V serial history over the same set of transactions.

Only a subset of serial MV histories, called 1-serial MV histories, are equivalent to serial 1V histories. Intuitively, a serial MV history is *1-serial* if for each reads-from relationship, say T_i reads x from T_j, T_j is the last transaction preceding T_i that writes *any* version of x. Notice that H_3 is not 1-serial because T_2 reads x from T_0, not T_1, which is the last transaction preceding T_2 that writes x.

All 1-serial MV histories are equivalent to serial 1V histories, so we can define 1-serial histories to be correct. To prove that a multiversion concurrency control algorithm is correct, we must show that its MV histories are equivalent to 1-serial MV histories. We will do this by defining a new graph structure called a multiversion serialization graph (MVSG). An MV history is equivalent to a 1-serial MV history iff it has an acyclic MVSG. Now proving multiversion concurrency control algorithms correct is just like standard serializability theory. We simply prove that its histories have acyclic MVSGs. We now proceed with a formal development of this line of proof.

5.2 *MULTIVERSION SERIALIZABILITY THEORY[2]

Let $T = \{T_0, \ldots T_n\}$ be a set of transactions, where the operations of T_i are ordered by $<_i$ for $0 \le i \le n$. To process operations from T, a multiversion scheduler must translate T's operations on (single version) data items into operations on specific versions of those data items. We formalize this transla-

---

[2]This section requires reading Section 2.6 as a prerequisite. We recommend skipping this and other starred sections of this chapter on the first reading, to gain some intuition for multiversion algorithms before studying their serializability theory.

tion by a function h that maps each $w_i[x]$ into $w_i[x_i]$, each $r_i[x]$ into $r_i[x_j]$ for some j, each c_i into c_i, and each a_i into a_i.

A *complete multiversion (MV) history* H over T is a partial order with ordering relation $<$ where

1. $H = h(\cup_{i=0}^{n} T_i)$ for some translation function h;

2. for each T_i and all operations p_i, q_i in T_i, if $p_i <_i q_i$, then $h(p_i) < h(q_i)$;

3. if $h(r_j[x]) = r_j[x_i]$, then $w_i[x_i] < r_j[x_i]$;

4. if $w_i[x] <_i r_i[x]$, then $h(r_i[x]) = r_i[x_i]$; and

5. if $h(r_j[x]) = r_j[x_i]$, $i \neq j$, and $c_j \in H$, then $c_i < c_j$.

Condition (1) states that the scheduler translates each operation submitted by a transaction into an appropriate multiversion operation. Condition (2) states that the MV history preserves all orderings stipulated by transactions. Condition (3) states that a transaction may not read a version until it has been produced.[3] Condition (4) states that if a transaction writes into a data item x before it reads x, then it must read the version of x that it previously created. This ensures that H is consistent with the implied semantics of the transactions over which it is defined. If H satisfies condition (4), we say that it *preserves reflexive reads-from relationships*. Condition (5) says that before a transaction commits, all the transactions that produced versions it read must have already committed. If H satisfies this condition we say it is *recoverable*.

An *MV history* H is a prefix of a complete MV history. We say that an MV history *preserves reflexive reads-from relationships* (or is *recoverable*) if it is the prefix of a complete MV history that does so. As in 1V histories, a transaction T_i is *committed* (respectively *aborted*) in an MV history H if c_i (respectively a_i) is in H. Also, the *committed projection* of an MV history H, denoted $C(H)$, is defined as for 1V histories; that is, $C(H)$ is obtained by removing from H the operations of all but the committed transactions. It is easy to check that if H is an MV history then $C(H)$ is a complete MV history, i.e., $C(H)$ satisfies conditions (1) – (5) (see Exercise 5.2).

For example, given transactions $\{T_0, T_1, T_2, T_3, T_4\}$,

$$T_0 = \begin{array}{l} w_0[x] \\ w_0[y] \\ w_0[z] \end{array} \rightarrow c_0 \qquad T_3 = r_3[z] \begin{array}{l} w_3[y] \\ w_3[z] \end{array} \rightarrow c_3$$

$$T_1 = r_1[x] \longrightarrow w_1[y] \longrightarrow c_1 \qquad T_4 = r_4[y] \begin{array}{l} r_4[x] \\ r_4[z] \end{array} \rightarrow c_4$$

$$T_2 = \begin{array}{l} r_2[x] \\ r_2[z] \end{array} \rightarrow w_2[x] \longrightarrow c_2$$

---

[3] To ensure condition (3), we will normally include in our examples an initializing transaction, T_0, that creates the initial version of each data item.

the following history, H_6, is a complete MV history over $\{T_0, T_1, T_2, T_3, T_4\}$.

$$H_6 = \begin{array}{c} w_0[x_0] \\ w_0[y_0] \\ w_0[z_0] \end{array} \quad c_0 \quad \begin{array}{c} r_1[x_0] \longrightarrow w_1[y_1] \longrightarrow c_1 \\ r_2[x_0] \rightrightarrows w_2[x_2] \longrightarrow c_2 \longrightarrow r_4[x_2] \\ r_2[z_0] \\ r_3[z_0] \longrightarrow w_3[y_3] \rightrightarrows c_3 \longrightarrow r_4[y_3] \rightarrow c_4 \\ w_3[z_3] \quad r_4[z_3] \end{array}$$

All complete MV histories over a set of transactions must have the same Writes, but they need not have the same Reads. For example, H_7 has $r_4[y_1]$ instead of $r_4[y_3]$.

$$H_7 = \begin{array}{c} w_0[x_0] \\ w_0[y_0] \\ w_0[z_0] \end{array} \quad c_0 \quad \begin{array}{c} r_1[x_0] \longrightarrow w_1[y_1] \longrightarrow c_1 \longrightarrow r_4[y_1] \\ r_2[x_0] \rightrightarrows w_2[x_2] \longrightarrow c_2 \longrightarrow r_4[x_2] \\ r_2[z_0] \quad\quad\quad\quad\quad\quad\quad\quad\quad\quad c_4 \\ w_3[y_3] \\ r_3[z_0] \longrightarrow w_3[z_3] \longrightarrow c_3 \longrightarrow r_4[z_3] \end{array}$$

MV History Equivalence

Two 1V histories over the same transactions are *view* equivalent if they contain the same operations, have the same reads-from relationships, and the same final writes. However, for MV histories, we can safely drop "and the same final writes" from the definition. If two histories are over the same transactions, then they have the same Writes. Since no versions are overwritten, all Writes are effectively final writes. Thus, if two MV histories over the same transactions have the same operations and the same reads-from relationships, then they have the same final writes and are therefore view equivalent.

To formalize the definition of equivalence, we must formalize the notion of reads-from in MV histories. To do this, we replace the notion of *data item* by *version* in the ordinary definition of reads-from for 1V histories. Transaction T_j *reads x from* T_i in MV history H if T_j reads the version of x produced by T_i. Since the version of x produced by T_i is x_i, T_j reads x from T_i in H iff T_j reads x_i, that is, iff $r_j[x_i] \in H$.

Two MV histories over a set of transactions T are *equivalent*, denoted $\equiv$, if they have the same operations and the same reads-from relationships. In view of the preceding discussion, having the same reads-from relationships amounts to having the same Read operations. Therefore, equivalence of MV histories reduces to a trivial condition, as stated in the following proposition.

Proposition 5.1: Two MV histories over a set of transactions are equivalent iff the histories have the same operations. $\square$

Next we want to define the equivalence of an MV history H_{MV} to a 1V history H_{1V}. We will only be interested in such an equivalence if H_{1V} is a valid one version view of H_{MV}. That is, H_{1V} and H_{MV} must be over the same set of transactions and their operations must be in one-to-one correspondence. More precisely, there must be a bijective (one-to-one and onto) function from the operations of H_{1V} to those of H_{MV}, mapping c_i to c_i, a_i to a_i, $r_i[x]$ to $r_i[x_j]$ for some version x_j of x and $w_i[x]$ to $w_i[x_i]$.

Given that the operations of H_{MV} and H_{1V} are in one-to-one correspondence, we can talk about their reads-from relationships being the same. We need not worry about final writes; all of the final writes in H_{1V} must be part of the state produced by H_{MV}, because H_{MV} retains all versions written in it. So, just like MV histories, an MV history and 1V history are *equivalent* if they have the same reads-from relationships.[4]

Serialization Graphs

Two operations in an MV history *conflict* if they operate on the same version and one is a Write. Only one pattern of conflict is possible in an MV history: if $p_i < q_j$ and these operations conflict, then p_i is $w_i[x_i]$ and q_j is $r_j[x_i]$ for some data item x. Conflicts of the form $w_i[x_i] < w_j[x_i]$ are impossible, because each Write produces a unique new version. Conflicts of the form $r_j[x_i] < w_i[x_i]$ are impossible, because T_j cannot read x_i until it has been produced. Thus, all conflicts in an MV history correspond to reads-from relationships.

The serialization graph for an MV history is defined as for a 1V history. But since only one kind of conflict is possible in an MV history, SGs are quite simple. Let H be an MV history. $SG(H)$ has nodes for the committed transaction in H and edges $T_i \rightarrow T_j$ $(i \neq j)$ whenever for some x, T_j reads x from T_i. That is, $T_i \rightarrow T_j$ is present iff for some x, $r_j[x_i]$ $(i \neq j)$ is an operation of $C(H)$. This gives us the following proposition.

Proposition 5.2: Let H and H' be MV histories. If $H \equiv H'$, then $SG(H)$ = $SG(H')$. ☐

The serialization graphs of H_6 and H_7 follow.

$$SG(H_6) = \quad T_0 \rightrightarrows \begin{matrix} T_2 \\ T_3 \rightarrow T_4 \\ T_1 \end{matrix} \qquad SG(H_7) = \quad T_0 \rightrightarrows \begin{matrix} T_2 \\ T_3 \rightrightarrows T_4 \\ T_1 \end{matrix}$$

---

[4] Two 1V histories can be equivalent in this sense without being view equivalent to each other, because they don't have the same final writes.

One Copy Serializability

A complete MV history is *serial* if for every two transactions T_i and T_j that appear in H, either all of T_i's operations precede all of T_j's or vice versa. Not all serial MV histories behave like ordinary serial 1V histories, for example,

$$H_3 = w_0[x_0]\, w_0[y_0]\, c_0\, r_1[x_0]\, r_1[y_0]\, w_1[x_1]\, w_1[y_1]\, c_1\, r_2[x_0]\, r_2[y_1]\, c_2.$$

The subset of serial MV histories that are equivalent to serial 1V histories is defined as follows.

A serial MV history H is *one-copy serial* (or *1-serial*) if for all i, j, and x, if T_i reads x from T_j, then $i = j$, or T_j is the last transaction preceding T_i that writes into *any* version of x. Since H is serial, the word *last* in this definition is well defined. History H_3 is not 1-serial because T_2 reads x from T_0 but $w_0[x_0] < w_1[x_1] < r_2[x_0]$. History H_8, which follows, *is* 1-serial.

$$H_8 = w_0[x_0]\, w_0[y_0]\, w_0[z_0]\, c_0\, r_1[x_0]\, w_1[y_1]\, c_1\, r_2[x_0]\, r_2[z_0]\, w_2[x_2]\, c_2\, r_3[z_0]\, w_3[y_3]$$
$$w_3[z_3]\, c_3\, r_4[x_2]\, r_4[y_3]\, r_4[z_3]\, c_4$$

An MV history is *one-copy serializable* (or *1SR*) if its committed projection is equivalent to a 1-serial MV history.[5] For example, H_6 is 1SR because $C(H_6) = H_6$ is equivalent to H_8, which you can verify by Proposition 5.1. $C(H_7) = H_7$ is equivalent to no 1-serial history, and thus H_7 is not 1SR.

A serial history can be 1SR even though it is not 1-serial. For example,

$$H_9 = w_0[x_0]\, c_0\, r_1[x_0]\, w_1[x_1]\, c_1\, r_2[x_0]\, c_2$$

is not 1-serial since T_2 reads x from T_0 instead T_1. But it *is* 1SR, because it is equivalent to

$$H_{10} = w_0[x_0]\, c_0\, r_2[x_0]\, c_2\, r_1[x_0]\, w_1[x_1]\, c_1.$$

To justify the value of one-copy serializability as a correctness criterion, we need to show that the committed projection of every 1SR history is equivalent to a serial 1V history.

Theorem 5.3: Let H be an MV history over T. $C(H)$ is equivalent to a serial, 1V history over T iff H is 1SR.

Proof: (If) Since H is 1SR, $C(H)$ is equivalent to a 1-serial MV history H_s. Translate H_s into a serial 1V history H_s', by translating each $w_i[x_i]$ into $w_i[x]$ and $r_j[x_i]$ into $r_j[x]$. To show $H_s \equiv H_s'$, consider any reads-from relationship in H_s, say T_j reads x from T_i. Since H_s is 1-serial, no $w_k[x_k]$ lies between $w_i[x_i]$ and $r_j[x_i]$. Hence no $w_k[x]$ lies between $w_i[x]$ and $r_j[x]$ in H_s'.

---

[5]It turns out that this is a prefix commit-closed property. Unlike view serializability, we need not require that the committed projection of *every prefix* of an MV history be equivalent to a 1-serial MV history. This follows from the fact that the committed projection of the history itself is equivalent to a 1-serial MV history (see Exercise 5.4).

Thus T_j reads x from T_i in H'_s. Now consider a reads-from relationship in H'_s, T_j reads x from T_i. If $r_j[x]$ was translated from $r_j[x_i]$ in H_s, then T_j reads x from T_i in H_s and we're done. So assume instead that $r_j[x]$ was translated from $r_j[x_k]$, $k \neq i$. If $i = j$, then $k = i$ by condition (4) in the definition of MV history and we're done. If $i \neq j$, then since H_s is 1-serial, either $w_i[x_i] < w_k[x_k]$ or $r_j[x_k] < w_i[x_i]$. But then, translating these operations into H'_s implies that T_j does not read x from T_i in H'_s, a contradiction. Thus T_j reads x from T_i in H_s. This establishes $H'_s, \equiv H_s$. Since $H_s \equiv C(H)$, $C(H) \equiv H'_s$ follows by transitivity of equivalence.

(Only if) Let H'_s be the hypothesized serial 1V history equivalent to $C(H)$. Translate H'_s into a serial MV history H_s by translating each c_i into c_i, $w_i[x]$ into $w_i[x_i]$, and $r_j[x]$ into $r_j[x_i]$ such that T_j reads x from T_i in H'_s. We must show that H_s is indeed a complete MV history. It is immediate that it satisfies conditions (1) and (2) of the complete MV history definition. For condition (3), it is enough to show that each $r_j[x]$ is preceded by some $w_i[x]$ in H'_s. Since H is an MV history, each $r_j[x_k]$ in $C(H)$ is preceded by $w_k[x_k]$. Since H'_s has the same reads-from relationships as the MV history $C(H)$, every Read in H'_s, must be preceded by a Write on the same data item, as desired. To show H_s satisfies condition (4), note that if $w_j[x] < r_j[x]$ in H'_s, then since H'_s is serial, T_j reads x from T_j in H'_s and $r_j[x]$ is translated into $r_j[x_j]$ in H_s. Finally, for condition (5) we must show that if $r_j[x_i]$ $(i \neq j)$ is in H_s then $c_i < c_j$. If $r_j[x_i]$ is in H_s then T_j reads x from T_i in H'_s. Since H'_s is serial and T_i, T_j are committed in it, we have $c_i < c_j$ in H'_s. By the translation then, it follows that $c_i < c_j$ in H_s, as wanted. This concludes the proof that H_s is indeed an MV history. Since the translation preserves reads-from relationships, so $H_s \equiv H'_s$. By transitivity, $C(H) \equiv H_s$.

It remains to prove that H_s is 1-serial. So consider any reads-from relationship in H_s, say T_j reads x from T_i, where $i \neq j$. Since H'_s is a 1V history, no $w_k[x]$ lies between $w_i[x]$ and $r_j[x]$. Hence no $w_k[x_k]$ lies between $w_i[x_i]$ and $r_j[x_i]$ in H_s. Thus, H_s is 1-serial, as desired. $\qquad\square$

The 1-Serializability Theorem

To determine if a multiversion concurrency control algorithm is correct, we must determine if all of its histories are 1SR. To do this, we use a modified SG. The modification is motivated by the fact that all known multiversion concurrency control algorithms sort the versions of each data item into a total order. We use this total order of versions to define an appropriately modified SG.

Given an MV history H and a data item x, a *version order*, $\ll$, for x in H is a total order of versions of x in H. A *version order* for H is the union of the version orders for all data items. For example, a possible version order for H_6 is $x_0 \ll x_2$, $y_0 \ll y_1 \ll y_3$, and $z_0 \ll z_3$.

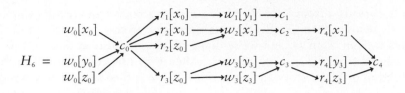

Given an MV history H and a version order $\ll$, the *multiversion serialization graph for H and $\ll$*, MVSG(H, $\ll$), is SG(H) with the following *version order edges* added: for each $r_k[x_j]$ and $w_i[x_i]$ in C(H) where i, j, and k are distinct, if $x_i \ll x_j$ then include $T_i \rightarrow T_j$, otherwise include $T_k \rightarrow T_i$.[6] (Note that there is no version order edge if $j = k$, that is, if a transaction reads from itself.) For example, given the preceding version order for H_6,

$$\text{MVSG}(H_6, \ll) = \qquad T_0 \rightarrow \begin{array}{c} T_1 \\ T_3 \\ T_2 \end{array} \rightarrow T_4$$

The version order edges that are in MVSG(H_6, $\ll$) but not in SG(H) are $T_1 \rightarrow T_2$, $T_1 \rightarrow T_3$, and $T_2 \rightarrow T_3$. Except for $T_0 \rightarrow T_1$, all edges in SG(H) are also version order edges.

Given an MV history H, suppose SG(H) is acyclic. We know that a serial MV history H_s obtained by topologically sorting SG(H) may not be equivalent to any serial 1V history. The reason is that some of H_s's reads-from relationships may be changed by mapping version operations into data item operations. The purpose of version order edges is to detect when this happens. If $r_k[x_j]$ and $w_i[x_i]$ are in C(H), then the version order edge forces $w_i[x_i]$ to either precede $w_j[x_j]$ or follow $r_k[x_j]$ in H_s. That way, when operations on x_i and x_j are mapped to operations on x when changing H_s to a 1V history, the reads-from relationship is undisturbed. This ensures that we can map H_s into an equivalent 1V history. Of course, all of this is possible only if SG(H) is still acyclic after adding version order edges. This observation leads us to the following theorem, which is our main tool for analyzing multiversion concurrency control algorithms.

Theorem 5.4: An MV history H is 1SR iff there exists a version order $\ll$ such that MVSG(H, $\ll$) is acyclic.

Proof: (If) Let H_s be a serial MV history $T_{i_1} T_{i_2} \ldots T_{i_n}$, where $T_{i_1}, T_{i_2}, \ldots T_{i_n}$ is a topological sort of MVSG(H, $\ll$). Since C(H) is an MV history, it follows that H_s is as well. Since H_s has the same operations as C(H), by Proposition 5.1, $H_s \equiv$ C(H).

---

[6]Recall that the nodes of SG(H) and, therefore, of MVSG(H, $\ll$) are the *committed* transactions in H.

It remains to prove that H_s is 1-serial. Consider any reads-from relationship in H_s, say T_k reads x from T_j, $k \neq j$. Let $w_i[x_i]$ ($i \neq j$ and $i \neq k$) be any other Write on x. If $x_i \ll x_j$, then MVSG(H, $\ll$) includes the version order edge $T_i \rightarrow T_j$, which forces T_j to follow T_i in H_s. If $x_j \ll x_i$, then MVSG(H, $\ll$) includes the version order edge $T_k \rightarrow T_i$, which forces T_k to precede T_i in H_s. Therefore, no transaction that writes x falls in between T_j and T_k in H_s. Thus, H_s is 1-serial.

(Only if) Given H and $\ll$, let MV(H, $\ll$) be the graph containing *only* version order edges. Version order edges depend only on the operations in H and $\ll$; they do *not* depend on the *order* of operations in H. Thus, if H and H' are MV histories with the same operations, then MV(H, $\ll$) = MV(H', $\ll$) for all version orders $\ll$.

Let H_s be a 1-serial MV history equivalent to C(H). All edges in SG(H_s) go "left-to-right;" that is, if $T_i \rightarrow T_j$ then T_i precedes T_j in H_s. Define $\ll$ as follows: $x_i \ll x_j$ only if T_i precedes T_j in H_s. All edges in MV(H_s, $\ll$) are also left-to-right. Therefore all edges in MVSG(H_s, $\ll$) = SG(H_s) $\cup$ MV(H_s, $\ll$) are left-to-right. This implies MVSG(H_s, $\ll$) is acyclic.

By Proposition 5.1, C(H) and H_s have the same operations. Hence MV(C(H), $\ll$) = MV(H_s, $\ll$). By Proposition 5.1 and 5.2 SG(C(H)) = SG(H_s). Therefore MVSG(C(H), $\ll$) = MVSG(H_s, $\ll$). Since MVSG(H_s, $\ll$) is acyclic, so is MVSG(C(H), $\ll$), which is identical to MVSG(H, $\ll$). $\square$

5.3 MULTIVERSION TIMESTAMP ORDERING

We can define schedulers for multiversion concurrency control based on each of the three basic types of schedulers: 2PL, TO, and SGT. We begin with a multiversion scheduler based on TO because it is the easiest to prove correct.

As for all TO schedulers, each transaction has a unique timestamp, denoted ts(T_i). Each operation carries the timestamp of its corresponding transaction. Each version is labeled by the timestamp of the transaction that wrote it.

A *multiversion TO (MVTO)* scheduler processes operations first-come-first-served. It translates operations on data items into operations on versions to make it appear as if it processed these operations in timestamp order on a single version database. The scheduler processes $r_i[x]$ by first translating it into $r_i[x_k]$, where x_k is the version of x with the largest timestamp less than or equal to ts(T_i), and then sending $r_i[x_k]$ to the DM. It processes $w_i[x]$ by considering two cases. If it has already processed a Read $r_j[x_k]$ such that ts(T_k) < ts(T_i) < ts(T_j), then it rejects $w_i[x]$. Otherwise, it translates $w_i[x]$ into $w_i[x_i]$ and sends it to the DM. Finally, to ensure recoverability, the scheduler must delay the processing of c_i until it has processed c_j for all transactions T_j that wrote versions read by T_i.

To understand MVTO, it is helpful to compare its effect to an execution, say H_{1V}, on a single version database in which operations execute in timestamp order. In H_{1V}, each Read, $r_i[x]$, reads the value of x with the largest timestamp less than or equal to $ts(T_i)$. This is the value of the version that the MVTO scheduler selects when it processes $r_i[x]$.

Since MVTO need not process operations in timestamp order, a Write could arrive whose processing would invalidate a Read that the scheduler already processed. For example, suppose $w_0[x_0] < r_2[x_0]$ represents the execution so far, where $ts(T_i) = i$ for all transactions. Now if $w_1[x]$ arrives, the scheduler has a problem. If it translates $w_1[x]$ into $w_1[x_1]$ and sends it to the DM, then it produces a history that no longer has the same effect as a TO execution on a single version database. For in such an execution, $r_2[x]$ would have read the value of x written by T_1, but in the execution $w_0[x_0] \, r_2[x_0] \, w_1[x_1]$, it reads the value written by T_0. In this case, we say that $w_1[x]$ would have *invalidated* $r_2[x_0]$. To avoid this problem, the scheduler rejects $w_1[x]$ in this case. In general, it rejects $w_i[x]$ if it has already processed a Read $r_j[x_k]$ such that $ts(T_k) < ts(T_i) < ts(T_j)$. This is exactly the situation in which processing $w_i[x]$ would invalidate $r_j[x_k]$.

To select the appropriate version to read and to avoid invalidating Reads, the scheduler maintains some timestamp information about operations it has already processed. For each version, say x_i, it maintains a timestamp interval, denoted $interval(x_i) = [wts, rts]$, where wts is the timestamp of x_i and rts is the largest timestamp of any Read that read x_i; if no such Read exists, then rts = wts. Let $intervals(x) = \{interval(x_i) \mid x_i \text{ is a version of } x\}$.

To process $r_i[x]$, the scheduler examines $intervals(x)$ to find the version x_j whose interval, $interval(x_j) = [wts, rts]$, has the maximal wts less than or equal to $ts(T_i)$. If $ts(T_i) > rts$, then it sets rts to $ts(T_i)$.

To process $w_i[x]$, the scheduler again examines $intervals(x)$ to find the version x_j whose interval $[wts, rts]$ has the maximal wts less than $ts(T_i)$. If rts $> ts(T_i)$, then it rejects $w_i[x]$. Otherwise, it sends $w_i[x_i]$ to the DM and creates a new interval, $interval(x_i) = [wts, rts]$, where wts = rts = $ts(T_i)$.

Eventually, the scheduler will run out of space for storing intervals, or the DM will run out of space for storing versions. At this point, old versions and their corresponding intervals must be deleted. To avoid incorrect behavior, it is essential that versions be deleted from oldest to newest. To see why, consider the following history,

$$H_{11} = w_0[x_0] \, c_0 \, r_2[x_0] \, w_2[x_2] \, c_2 \, r_4[x_2] \, w_4[x_4] \, c_4,$$

where $ts(T_i) = i$ for $0 \le i \le 4$. Suppose the system deleted x_2 but not x_0. If $r_3[x]$ now arrives, the scheduler will incorrectly translate it into $r_3[x_0]$. Suppose instead that the system deleted x_0. If $r_1[x]$ now arrives, the scheduler will find no version whose interval has a wts $< ts(T_1)$. This condition indicates that the DBS has deleted the version that $r_1[x]$ has to read, so the scheduler must reject $r_1[x]$.

*Proof of Correctness

To prove MVTO correct, we must describe it in serializability theory. As usual, we do this by inferring properties that all histories produced by MVTO will satisfy. Using these properties as our formal specification of the algorithm, we prove that all histories produced by MVTO have an acyclic MVSG and hence are 1SR.

The following properties describe the essential characteristics of every MVTO history H over $\{T_0, \ldots T_n\}$.

$MVTO_1$. For each T_i, there is a unique timestamp $ts(T_i)$; that is, $ts(T_i) = ts(T_j)$ iff $i = j$.

$MVTO_2$. For every $r_k[x_j] \in H$, $w_j[x_j] < r_k[x_j]$ and $ts(T_j) \leq ts(T_k)$.

$MVTO_3$. For every $r_k[x_j]$ and $w_i[x_i] \in H$, $i \neq j$, either (a) $ts(T_i) < ts(T_j)$ or (b) $ts(T_k) < ts(T_i)$ or (c) $i = k$ and $r_k[x_j] < w_i[x_i]$.

$MVTO_4$. If $r_j[x_i] \in H$, $i \neq j$, and $c_j \in H$, then $c_i < c_j$.

Property $MVTO_1$ says that transactions have unique timestamps. Property $MVTO_2$ says that each transaction T_k only reads versions with timestamps smaller than $ts(T_k)$. Property $MVTO_3$ states that when the scheduler processes $r_k[x_j]$, x_j is the version of x with the largest timestamp less than or equal to $ts(T_k)$. Moreover, if the scheduler later receives $w_i[x_i]$, it will reject it if $ts(T_j) < ts(T_i) < ts(T_k)$. $MVTO_4$ states that H is recoverable.

These conditions ensure that H preserves reflexive reads-from relationships. To see this, suppose not, that is, $w_k[x_k] < r_k[x_j]$ and $j \neq k$. By $MVTO_2$ and $j \neq k$, $ts(T_j) < ts(T_k)$. By $MVTO_3$, either (a) $ts(T_k) < ts(T_j)$, (b) $ts(T_k) < ts(T_k)$, or (c) $r_k[x_j] < w_k[x_k]$. All three cases are impossible, a contradiction.

We now prove that any history satisfying these properties is 1SR. In other words, MVTO is a correct scheduler.

Theorem 5.5: Every history H produced by MVTO is 1SR.

Proof: Define a version order as follows: $x_i \ll x_j$ iff $ts(T_i) < ts(T_j)$. We now prove that $MVSG(H, \ll)$ is acyclic by showing that for every edge $T_i \to T_j$ in $MVSG(H, \ll)$, $ts(T_i) < ts(T_j)$.

Suppose $T_i \to T_j$ is an edge of $SG(H)$. This edge corresponds to a reads-from relationship. That is, for some x, T_j reads x from T_i. By $MVTO_2$, $ts(T_i) \leq ts(T_j)$. By $MVTO_1$, $ts(T_i) \neq ts(T_j)$. So, $ts(T_i) < ts(T_j)$ as desired.

Let $r_k[x_j]$ and $w_i[x_i]$ be in H where i, j, and k are distinct, and consider the version order edge that they generate. There are two cases: (1) $x_i \ll x_j$, which implies $T_i \to T_j$ is in $MVSG(H, \ll)$; and (2) $x_j \ll x_i$, which implies $T_k \to T_i$ is in $MVSG(H, \ll)$. In case (1), by definition of $\ll$, $ts(T_i) < ts(T_j)$. In case (2), by $MVTO_3$, either $ts(T_i) < ts(T_j)$ or $ts(T_k) < ts(T_i)$. The first option is impossible, because $x_j \ll x_i$ implies $ts(T_j) < ts(T_i)$. So, $ts(T_k) < ts(T_i)$ as desired.

Since all edges in MVSG(H, $\ll$) are in timestamp order, MVSG(H, $\ll$) is acyclic. By Theorem 5.4, H is 1SR. $\square$

5.4 MULTIVERSION TWO PHASE LOCKING

Two Version 2PL

In 2PL, a write lock on a data item x prevents transactions from obtaining read locks on x. We can avoid this locking conflict by using two versions of x. When a transaction T_i writes into x, it creates a new version x_i of x. It sets a lock on x that prevents other transactions from reading x_i or writing a new version of x. However, other transactions *are* allowed to read the previous version of x. Thus, Reads on x are not delayed by a concurrent writer of x. In the language of Section 4.5, we are using 2PL for ww synchronization and version selection for rw synchronization. As we will see, there is also certification activity involved.

To use this scheme, the DM must store one or two versions of each data item. If a data item has two versions, then only one of those versions was written by a committed transaction. Once a transaction T_i that wrote x commits, its version of x becomes the unique committed version of x, and the previous committed version of x becomes inaccessible.

The two versions of each data item could be the same two versions used by the DM's recovery algorithm. If T_i wrote x but has not yet committed, then the two versions of x are T_i's before image of x and the value of x it wrote. As we will see, T_i's before image can be deleted once T_i commits. So, an old version becomes dispensable for both concurrency control and recovery reasons at approximately the same time.[7]

A *two version 2PL (2V2PL)* scheduler uses three types of locks: read locks, write locks, and certify locks. These locks are governed by the compatibility matrix in Fig. 5–1. The scheduler sets read and write locks at the usual time, when it processes Reads and Writes. When it learns that a transaction has terminated and is about to commit, it converts all of the transaction's write locks into certify locks. We will explain the handling and significance of certify locks in a moment.

When a 2V2PL scheduler receives a Write, $w_i[x]$, it attempts to set $wl_i[x]$. Since write locks conflict with certify locks and with each other, the scheduler delays $w_i[x]$ if another transaction already has a write or certify lock on x. Otherwise, it sets $wl_i[x]$, translates $w_i[x]$ into $w_i[x_i]$, and sends $w_i[x_i]$ to the DM.

When the scheduler receives a Read, $r_i[x]$, it attempts to set $rl_i[x]$. Since read locks only conflict with certify locks, it can set this lock as long as no

---

[7]This fits especially well with the shadow page recovery techniques used, for example, in the no-undo/no-redo algorithm of Section 6.7.

	Read	Write	Certify
Read	y	y	n
Write	y	n	n
Certify	n	n	n

FIGURE 5-1
Compatibility Matrix for Two Version 2PL

transaction already owns a certify lock on x. If T_i already owns $wl_i[x]$ and has therefore written x_i, then the scheduler translates $r_i[x]$ into $r_i[x_i]$, which it sends to the DM. Otherwise, it waits until it can set a read lock, and then sets the lock, translates $r_i[x]$ into $r_i[x_j]$, where x_j is the most recently (and therefore only) committed version of x, and sends $r_i[x_j]$ to the DM. Note that since only committed versions may be read (except for versions produced by the reader itself), the scheduler avoids cascading aborts and, *a fortiori*, ensures that the MV histories it produces are recoverable.

When the scheduler receives a Commit, c_i, indicating that T_i has terminated, it attempts to convert T_i's write locks into certify locks. Since certify locks conflict with read locks, the scheduler can only do this lock conversion on those data items that have no read locks owned by other transactions. On those data items where such read locks exist, the lock conversion is delayed until all read locks are released. Thus, the effect of certify locks is to delay T_i's commitment until there are no active readers of data items it is about to overwrite.

Note that lock conversions can lead to deadlock just as in standard 2PL. For example, suppose T_i has a read lock on x and T_j has a write lock on x. If T_i tries to convert its read lock to a write lock and T_j tries to convert its write lock to a certify lock, then the transactions are deadlocked. We can use any deadlock detection or prevention technique: cycle detection in a WFG, timestamp-based prevention, etc.

Since a transaction may deadlock while trying to convert its write locks, it may be aborted during this activity. Therefore, it must not release its locks or be committed until it has obtained all of its certify locks.

Certify locks in 2V2PL behave much like write locks in ordinary 2PL. Since the time to certify a transaction is usually much less than the total time to execute it, 2V2PL's certify locks delay Reads for less time than 2PL's write locks delay Reads. However, since existing read locks delay a transaction's certification in 2V2PL, the improved concurrency of Reads comes at the expense of delaying the certification and therefore the commitment of update transactions.

Using More than Two Versions

The only purpose served by write locks is to ensure that only two versions of a data item exist at a time. They are not needed to attain 1-serializability. If we relax the conflict rules so that write locks do not conflict, then a data item may have many *uncertified* versions (i.e., versions written by uncommitted transactions). However, if we follow the remaining 2V2PL locking rules, then only the most recently certified version may be read.

If we are willing to cope with cascading aborts, then we can be a little more flexible by allowing a transaction to read any of the uncertified versions. (We could make the same allowance in 2V2PL, in which there is at most one uncertified version to read.) To get the same correct synchronization behavior as 2V2PL, we have to modify the scheduler in two ways. First, a transaction cannot be certified until all of the versions it read (except for ones it wrote itself) have been certified. And second, the scheduler can only convert a write lock on x into a certify lock if there are no read locks on *certified* versions of x.

Essentially, the scheduler is ignoring a read lock on an uncertified version until either that version is certified or the transaction that owns the read lock tries to become certified. This is just like delaying the granting of that read lock until after the version to be read is certified. The only difference is that cascading aborts are now possible. If the transaction that produced an uncertified version aborts, then transactions that read that version must also abort.

*Correctness of 2V2PL

To list the properties of histories produced by executions of 2V2PL, we need to include the operation f_i, denoting the certification of T_i.

Let H be a history over $\{T_0, \ldots T_n\}$ produced by 2V2PL. Then H must satisfy the following properties.

2V2PL$_1$. For every T_i, f_i follows all of T_i's Reads and Writes and precedes T_i's commitment.

2V2PL$_2$. For every $r_k[x_j]$ in H, if $j \neq k$, then $c_j < r_k[x_j]$; otherwise $w_k[x_k] < r_k[x_k]$.

2V2PL$_3$. For every $w_k[x_k]$ and $r_k[x_j]$ in H, if $w_k[x_k] < r_k[x_j]$, then $j = k$.

Property 2V2PL$_2$ says that every Read $r_k[x_j]$ either reads a certified version or reads a version written by itself (i.e., T_k). Property 2V2PL$_3$ says that if T_k wrote x before the scheduler received $r_k[x]$, then it translates $r_k[x]$ into $r_k[x_k]$.

2V2PL$_4$. If $r_k[x_j]$ and $w_i[x_i]$ are in H, then either $f_i < r_k[x_j]$ or $r_k[x_j] < f_i$.

Property 2V2PL$_4$ says that $r_k[x_j]$ is strictly ordered with respect to the certification operation of every transaction that writes x. This is because each transaction T_i that writes x must obtain a certify lock on x. For each transaction T_k that reads x, either T_i must delay its certification until T_k has been certified (if it has not already been so), or else T_k must wait for T_i to be certified before it can set its read lock on x and therefore read x.

$2V2PL_5$.   For every $r_k[x_j]$ and $w_i[x_i]$ (i, j, and k distinct), if $f_i < r_k[x_j]$, then $f_i < f_j$.

Property $2V2PL_5$, combined with $2V2PL_2$, says that each Read $r_k[x_j]$ either reads a version written by T_k or reads the most recently certified version of x.

$2V2PL_6$.   For every $r_k[x_j]$ and $w_i[x_i]$, $i \neq j$ and $i \neq k$, if $r_k[x_j] < f_i$, then $f_k < f_i$.

Property $2V2PL_6$ says that a transaction T_i that writes x cannot be certified until all transactions that previously read a version of x have already been certified. This follows from the fact that certify locks conflict with read locks.

$2V2PL_7$.   For every $w_i[x_i]$ and $w_j[x_j]$, either $f_i < f_j$ or $f_j < f_i$.

Property $2V2PL_7$ says that the certification of every two transactions that write the same data item are atomic with respect to each other.

Theorem 5.6: Every history H produced by a 2V2PL scheduler is 1SR.

Proof: By $2V2PL_1$, $2V2PL_2$ and $2V2PL_3$, H preserves reflexive reads-from relationships and is recoverable, and therefore is an MV history. Define a version order $\ll$ by $x_i \ll x_j$ only if $f_i < f_j$. By $2V2PL_7$, $\ll$ is indeed a version order. We will prove that all edges in $MVSG(H, \ll)$ are in certification order. That is, if $T_i \rightarrow T_j$ in $MVSG(H, \ll)$, then $f_i < f_j$.

Let $T_i \rightarrow T_j$ be in $SG(H)$. This edge corresponds to a reads-from relationship, such as T_j reads x from T_i. By $2V2PL_2$, $f_i < r_j[x_i]$. By $2V2PL_1$, $r_j[x_i] < f_j$. Hence, $f_i < f_j$.

Consider a version order edge induced by $w_i[x_i]$, $w_j[x_j]$, and $r_k[x_j]$ (i, j, and k distinct). There are two cases: $x_i \ll x_j$ and $x_j \ll x_i$. If $x_i \ll x_j$, then the version order edge is $T_i \rightarrow T_j$, and $f_i < f_j$ follows directly from the definition of $\ll$. If $x_j \ll x_i$, then the version order edge is $T_k \rightarrow T_i$. Since $x_j \ll x_i$, $f_j < f_i$. By $2V2PL_4$, either $f_i < r_k[x_j]$ or $r_k[x_j] < f_i$. In the former case, $2V2PL_5$ implies $f_i < f_j$, contradicting $f_j < f_i$. Thus $r_k[x_j] < f_i$, and by $2V2PL_6$, $f_k < f_i$ as desired.

This proves that all edges in $MVSG(H, \ll)$ are in certification order. Since the certification order is embedded in a history, which is acyclic by definition, $MVSG(H, \ll)$ is acyclic too. So, by Theorem 5.4, H is 1SR.   □

5.5 A MULTIVERSION MIXED METHOD

As we have seen, multiversions give the scheduler more flexibility in scheduling Reads. If the scheduler knows in advance which transactions will *only* issue Reads (and no Writes), then it can get even more concurrency among transactions. Recall from Section 1.1 that transactions that issue Reads but no Writes are called *queries*, while those that issue Writes (and possibly Reads as well) are called *updaters*. In this section we'll describe an algorithm that uses MVTO to synchronize queries and Strict 2PL to synchronize updaters.

When a transaction begins executing, it tells its TM whether it's an updater or a query. If it's an updater, then the TM simply passes that fact to the scheduler, which executes operations from that transaction using Strict 2PL. When the TM receives the updater's Commit, indicating that the updater has terminated, the TM assigns a timestamp to the updater, using the timestamp generation method of Section 4.5 for integrating Strict 2PL and TWR. This ensures that updaters have timestamps that are consistent with their order in the SG.

Unlike Basic 2PL, in this method each Write produces a new version. The scheduler tags each version with the timestamp of the transaction that wrote it. The scheduler uses these timestamped versions to synchronize Reads from queries using MVTO.

When a TM receives the first operation from a transaction that identified itself as a query, it assigns to that query a timestamp smaller than that of any committed or active updater (and therefore, of any future updater as well). When a scheduler receives an $r_i[x]$ from a query T_i, it finds the version of x with the largest timestamp less than ts(T_i). By the timestamp assignment rule, this version was written by a committed transaction. Moreover, by the same rule, assigning this version of x to $r_i[x]$ will not invalidate the Read at any time in the future (so future Writes need never be rejected).

Note that a query does not set any locks. It is therefore never forced to wait for updaters and never causes updaters to wait for it. The scheduler can always process a query's Read without delay.

In a centralized DBS, selecting the timestamp of a query is easy, because active updaters are not assigned timestamps until they terminate. In a distributed DBS, TMs can ensure that each query has a sufficiently small timestamp by deliberately selecting an *especially* small timestamp. Suppose that the local clocks at any two TMs are known to differ by at most δ. If a TM's clock reads t, then it is safe to assign a new query any timestamp less than $t - δ$. Any updater that terminates after this point in real time will be assigned a timestamp of at least $t - δ$, so the problem of the previous paragraph cannot arise.

We can argue the correctness of this by using MVSGs as follows.[8] Let H be a history produced by the method. Define the version order for H as in

---

[8]This paragraph requires an understanding of Section 5.2, on Multiversion Serializability Theory, a starred section.

MVTO: $x_i \ll x_j$ iff $ts(T_i) < ts(T_j)$. We show that $MVSG(H, \ll)$ is acyclic by showing that for each of its edges $T_i \rightarrow T_j$, $ts(T_i) < ts(T_j)$. First, consider an edge $T_i \rightarrow T_j$ in $SG(H)$. Each such edge is due to a reads-from relationship. If T_j is an updater, then by the way timestamps are assigned to updaters, $ts(T_i)$; $< ts(T_j)$ (cf. Section 4.5). If T_j is a query, then by MVTO version selection, $ts(T_i) < ts(T_j)$. Now consider a version order edge in $MVSG(H, \ll)$ that arises because T_j reads x from T_i and T_k writes x $(i, j, k$ distinct). If $x_k \ll x_i$, then we have the edge $T_k \rightarrow T_i$ in $MVSG(H, \ll)$ and $ts(T_k) < ts(T_i)$. Otherwise, we have the edge $T_j \rightarrow T_k$, so we must show $ts(T_j) < ts(T_k)$. If T_j is an updater, then T_j released $rl_j[x]$ before T_k obtained $wl_k[x]$, so by the timestamp assignment method, $ts(T_j) < ts(T_k)$. If T_j is a query, then it is assigned a timestamp smaller than all active or future updaters. So again $ts(T_j) < ts(T_k)$. Thus, all edges in $MVSG(H, \ll)$ are in timestamp order, and $MVSG(H, \ll)$ is acyclic. By Theorem 5.4, H is 1SR.

To avoid running out of space, the scheduler must have a way of deleting "old" versions. Any committed version may be eliminated as soon as the scheduler can be assured that no query will need to read that copy in the future. For this reason, the scheduler maintains a non-decreasing value *min*, which is the minimum timestamp that can be assigned to a query. Whenever the scheduler wants to release some space used by versions, it sets min to be the smallest timestamp assigned to any active query. It can then discard a committed version x_i if $ts(T_i) <$ min and there is another committed version x_j, such that $ts(T_i) < ts(T_j)$.

The main benefit of this method is that queries and updaters never delay each other. A query can always read the data it wants without delay. Although updaters may delay each other, queries set no locks and therefore never delay updaters. This is in sharp contrast to 2PL, where a query may set many locks and thereby delay many updaters. This delay is also inherent in multiversion 2PL and 2V2PL, since an updater T_i cannot commit until there are no read locks held by other transactions on T_i's writeset.

The main disadvantages of the method are that queries may read out-of-date data and that the tagging and interpretation of timestamps on versions may add significant scheduling overhead. Both problems can be mitigated by using the methods described next.

Replacing Timestamps by Commit Lists

Tagging versions with timestamps may be costly because when a scheduler processes $w_i[x]$ by creating a new version of x, it doesn't know T_i's timestamp. Only after T_i terminates can the scheduler learn T_i's timestamp. However, by this time, the version may already have been moved to disk; it needs to be reread in order to be tagged, and then subsequently rewritten to disk.

One can avoid timestamps altogether by using instead a list of identifiers of committed transactions, called the *commit list*. When a query begins executing, the TM makes a copy of the commit list and associates it with the query. It attaches the commit list to every Read that it sends to the scheduler, essentially treating the list like a timestamp. When the scheduler receives $r_i[x]$ for a query T_i, it finds the most recently committed version of x whose tag is in T_i's copy of the commit list. To do this efficiently, all versions of a data item are kept in a linked list, from newest to oldest. That is, whenever a new version is created, it is added to the *top* of the version list. Since updaters use Strict 2PL, two transactions may not concurrently create new versions of the same data item. Thus, the order of a data item's versions (and hence the version list) is well defined.

Given this organization for versions, to process $r_i[x]$ for a query T_i, the scheduler scans the version list of x until it finds a version written by a transaction that appears in the commit list associated with T_i. This is just like reading the most recently committed version of x whose timestamp is less than $ts(T_i)$ (if T_i had a timestamp). This technique is used in DBS products by Prime Computer, and in the Adaplex DBS by Computer Corporation of America.

The problem with this scheme is the size and structure of commit lists. First, each list must be small. In a centralized system, every query will have a copy of the list consuming main memory. In a distributed system, every Read sent to a DM will have a copy of the list, which consumes communication bandwidth. Second, since the scheduler must search the list on every Read from a query, the list should be structured to make it easy to determine whether a given transaction identifier is in the list.

A good way to accomplish these goals is to store the commit list as a bit map. That is, the commit list is an array, CL, where $CL[i] = 1$ if T_i is committed; otherwise $CL[i] = 0$. Using the bit map, the scheduler can easily tell whether a version's tag is in the list. It simply looks up the appropriate position in the array. However, as time goes on, the list grows without limit. So we need a way to keep the list small.

We can shorten the list by observing that old transaction identifiers eventually become useless. A transaction identifier is only needed as long as there is a version whose tag is that identifier. Suppose we know that all versions whose tags are less than n (where n is a transaction identifier) have either been committed or discarded before all active queries began. Then when the scheduler reads a version whose tag is less than n, it may assume that n is in the commit list. Only transactions whose identifiers are greater than or equal to n need to be kept in the list.

The commit list can be kept short as follows. When the list has exceeded a certain size, the scheduler asks the TM for a transaction identifier, n, that is smaller than that which has been assigned to any active query or updater, or will be assigned to any future query or updater. The scheduler can then discard the prefix of the commit list through transaction identifier n, thereby shortening the list. To process $r_i[x]$ of some query T_i, the scheduler returns the first version in the version list of x written by a transaction whose identifier is either in, or smaller than any identifier in, the commit list given to T_i when it started.

We are assuming here, as always, that when a transaction aborts, all versions it has produced are removed from the version lists.

When the scheduler receives n from the TM for the purpose of reducing the size of the commit list, it can also garbage collect versions. In particular, it can discard a committed version of x, provided there is a more recent committed version of x whose identifier is less than n.

Distributed Commit Lists

In a distributed DBS, using a commit list in place of timestamps requires special care, because the commit lists maintained at different sites may not be instantaneously identical. For example, suppose an updater T_1 commits at site A, where it updated x, and is added to CL_A, the commit list at site A; but suppose T_1 has not yet committed at site B, where it updated y. Next, suppose an updater T_2 starts executing at A, reads the version of x written by T_1, writes a new version of z at site B, and commits, thereby adding its transaction identifier to CL_A and CL_B. (T_1 still hasn't committed at site B). Now suppose a query starts executing at site B, reads CL_B (which contains T_2 but not T_1), and reads y and z at site B. It will read the version of z produced by T_2 (which read x from T_1) but not the version of y produced by T_1. The result is not 1SR.

We can avoid this problem by ensuring that whenever a commit list at a site contains a transaction T_i, then it also contains all transactions from which T_i read a data item (at the same site or any other site). To do this, before an updater transaction T_j commits, it reads the commit lists at all sites where it read data items and takes the union of those commit lists along with $\{T_j\}$, producing a temporary commit list CL_{temp}. Then, instead of merely adding T_j to the commit list at every site where it wrote, it unions CL_{temp} into those commit lists. Using this method in the example of the previous paragraph, T_2 would read CL_A, which includes T_1, and would union it into CL_B. The query that reads CL_B now reads T_1's version of y, as required to be 1SR.

Using this method, each query reads a database that was effectively produced by a serial execution of updaters. However, executions may not be 1SR in the sense that two different queries may see mutually inconsistent views. For example, suppose TM_1 and TM_2 supervise the execution of queries T_1 and T_2, respectively, both of which read data items x and y stored, respectively, at sites A and B. Consider now the following sequence of events:

1. TM_1 reads CL_A.
2. TM_2 reads CL_B.
3. T_3 writes x at site A and commits, thereby adding T_3 to CL_A.
4. T_4 writes y at site B and commits, thereby adding T_4 to CL_B.
5. TM_1 reads CL_B.
6. TM_2 reads CL_A.

Now, T_1 reads a database state that includes T_4's Write on y but not T_3's Write on x, while T_2 reads a database state that includes T_3's Write on x but not T_4's Write on y. Thus, from T_1's viewpoint, transactions executed in the order T_4 T_1 T_3, but from T_2's viewpoint, transactions executed in the order T_3 T_2 T_4. There is no serial 1V history including all four transactions that is equivalent to this execution. Yet, the execution consisting only of updaters is 1SR, and in a sense, each query reads consistent data. We leave the proof of these properties as an exercise (see Exercise 5.22).

BIBLIOGRAPHIC NOTES

The serializability theoretic model of multiversion concurrency control is from [Bernstein, Goodman 83]. Other theoretical aspects are explored in [Hadzilacos, Papadimitriou 85], [Ibaraki, Kameda 83], [Lausen 83], and [Papadimitriou, Kanellakis 84]. The two version 2PL algorithm in Section 5.3 is similar to that of [Stearns, Rosenkrantz 81], which uses timestamp-based deadlock prevention. A similar method that uses SGT certification for rw synchronization is described in [Bayer et al. 80] and [Bayer, Heller, Reiser 80]. A multiversion tree locking algorithm appears in [Silberschatz 82]. Multiversion TO was introduced in [Reed 78], [Reed 79], and [Reed 83]. Multiversion mixed methods like those in Section 5.5 are described in [Bernstein, Goodman 81], [Chan et al. 82], [Chan, Gray 85], [Dubourdieu 82], and [Weihl 85]. [Dubourdieu 82] describes a method used in a product of Prime Computer. [Lai, Wilkinson 84] describes a multiversion 2PL certifier, where queries are never delayed, and each updater T_i is certified by checking its readset and writeset against the writeset of all transactions that committed after T_i starts.

EXERCISES

5.1*   Consider the following history:

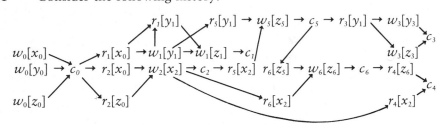

     a. Prove that this satisfies the definition of MV history.
     b. Is this history serializable?
     c. Is it one-copy serializable? If so, give a version order that produces an acyclic MVSG.
     d. Suppose we add the operation $r_4[y_3]$ (where $w_3[y_3] < r_4[y_3]$) to the history. Answer (c) for this new history.

5.2*   Give a careful proof of the fact that if H is an MV history then $C(H)$ is a complete MV history. Suppose in the definition of MV histories we required only conditions (1) – (4), but not recoverability. Prove that in that case, $C(H)$ would not necessarily be a complete MV history. (Incidentally, this is the reason for making recoverability part of the *definition* of MV histories, whereas in 1V serializability theory we treated recoverability as a property that some histories have and others do not.)

5.3*   Prove Proposition 5.2.

5.4*   Prove that if H is a 1SR MV history, then so is any prefix of H.

5.5*   Suppose no transaction ever reads a data item that it previously wrote. Then we can redefine MV history, such that it need not preserve reflexive reads-from relationships (since they cannot exist). Using this revised definition prove Theorem 5.3, making as many simplifications as possible.

5.6   MVTO can reject transactions whose Writes arrive too late. Design a conservative MVTO scheduler that never rejects Reads or Writes. Prove it correct. To show why your conservative MVTO is not worse than single version conservative TO, characterize those situations in which the latter will delay operations while the former will not. Are there situations where the opposite is true?

5.7   In MVTO, suppose that we store timestamp intervals in the data items themselves rather than in a separate table. For example, suppose the granularity of data items is a fixed size page and that each page has a header containing timestamp interval information. How does this organization affect the efficiency with which the MVTO scheduler processes operations? How does it affect the way the scheduler garbage collects old versions?

5.8   Since MVTO doesn't use locks, we need to add a mechanism for preventing transactions from reading uncommitted data and thereby avoiding cascading aborts. Propose such a mechanism. How much concurrency do you lose through this mechanism? Compare the amount of concurrency you get with the one you proposed for Exercise 5.6.

5.9   Show that there does or does not exist a sequence of Reads and Writes in which

   a. Basic TO rejects an operation and MVTO does not;
   b. Basic TO delays an operation and MVTO does not;
   c. MVTO rejects an operation and Basic TO does not; and
   d. MVTO delays an operation and Basic TO does not.

That is, for each situation, either give an example sequence with the desired property, or prove that such a sequence does not exist.

5.10   Modify MVTO so that it correctly handles transactions that write into a data item more than once.

5.11   Describe the precise conditions under which MVTO can safely discard a version without affecting any future transaction.

5.12 It is incorrect to use MVTO for rw synchronization and TWR for ww synchronization. Explain why.

5.13 Assume no transaction ever reads a data item that it previously wrote. Consider the following variation of standard 2PL, called *2PL with delayed writes*. Each TM holds all writes used by a transaction until the transaction terminates. It then sends all those held Writes to the appropriate DMs. DMs use standard 2PL. Compare the behavior of 2V2PL to 2PL with delayed writes.

5.14* Let H be the set of all 1V histories equivalent to the MV histories produced by 2V2PL. Is H identical to the set of histories produced by 2PL? Prove your answer.

5.15 Suppose we modify multiversion 2PL as follows. As in Section 5.5, we distinguish queries from updaters. Updaters set certify locks in the usual way. Queries set no (read) locks. To read a data item x, a query reads the most recently certified version of x. Does this algorithm produce 1SR executions? If so, prove it. If not, give a counterexample.

5.16 Suppose no transaction ever reads a data item that it previously wrote. Use this knowledge to simplify the 2V2PL algorithm. Does your simplification improve performance?

5.17 Show how to integrate timestamp-based deadlock prevention into 2V2PL. If most write locks will eventually be converted into certify locks (i.e., if very few transactions spontaneously abort), is it better to perform the deadlock prevention early using write locks or later using certify locks?

5.18* Prove the correctness of the extension to 2V2PL that uses more than two versions, described at the end of Section 5.4.

5.19 Compare the behavior of the multiple version extension to 2V2PL to standard 2V2PL. How would you expect them to differ in the number of delays and aborts they induce?

5.20* Prove that the mixed method of Strict 2PL and "MVTO" that uses commit lists for queries in a centralized DBS (in Section 5.5) is correct.

5.21 Consider the distributed Strict 2PL and "MVTO" mixed method in Section 5.5 that uses commit lists for queries. The method only guarantees that any execution of updaters is 1SR, and that each query reads consistent data. Propose a modification to the algorithm that ensures that queries do not read mutually inconsistent data; that is, any execution of updaters and queries is 1SR. Compare the cost of your method to the cost of the one in the chapter.

5.22* Prove that the distributed Strict 2PL and "MVTO" mixed method in Section 5.5 that uses commit lists for queries is correct, in the sense that any execution of updaters and one query is 1SR.

5.23 Design a multiversion concurrency control algorithm that uses SGT certification for rw synchronization and 2PL for ww synchronization. Prove that your algorithm is correct.

6
CENTRALIZED RECOVERY

6.1 FAILURES

Beginning with this chapter we turn to the question of how to process transactions in a fault-tolerant manner. In this chapter we will explore this issue for centralized DBSs. We treat failure handling for distributed DBSs in Chapter 7 and 8.

Our first task is to define the sorts of faults we are going to consider. Computer systems fail in many ways. It is not realistic to expect to build DBSs that can tolerate all possible faults. However, a good system must be capable of recovering from the most common types of failures automatically, that is, without human intervention.

Many failures are due to incorrectly programmed transactions and data entry errors (supplying incorrect parameters to transactions). Unfortunately, these failures undermine the assumption that a transaction's execution preserves the consistency of the database. They can be dealt with by applying software engineering techniques to the programming and testing of transactions, or by semantic integrity mechanisms built into the DBS. However they're dealt with, they are intrinsically outside the range of problems our recovery mechanisms can automatically solve. Thus, we assume that transactions indeed satisfy their defining characteristic, namely, that they halt for all inputs and their execution preserves database consistency.

Many failures are due to operator error. For example, an operator at the console may incorrectly type a command that damages portions of the database, or causes the computer to reboot. Similarly, a computer technician may damage a disk or tape during a computer maintenance procedure. The risk of such errors can be reduced by better human engineering of the system's interface to operators and by improved operator education. Preventing these errors is outside the scope of problems treated by DBS recovery. However, DBS recovery mechanisms *are* designed to deal with some of the consequences of these errors, namely, the loss of data due to such errors.

Given these assumptions, there are three types of failures that are most important in centralized DBSs, known as *transaction failures, system failures* and *media failures*. A *transaction failure* occurs when a transaction aborts. A *system failure* refers to the loss or corruption of the contents of *volatile* storage (i.e., main memory). For example, this can happen to semiconductor memory when the power fails. It also happens when the operating system fails. Although an operating system failure may not corrupt all of main memory, it is usually too difficult to determine which parts were actually corrupted by the failure. So one generally assumes the worst and reinitializes all of main memory. Because of system failures, the database itself must be kept on a stable storage medium, such as disk. (Of course other considerations, such as size, may also force us to store the database on stable mass storage media.) By definition, *stable* (or *nonvolatile*) storage withstands system failures. A *media failure* occurs when any part of the stable storage is destroyed. For instance, this happens if some sectors of a disk become damaged.

The techniques used to cope with media failures are conceptually similar to those used to cope with system failures. In each case, we consider a certain part of storage to be unreliable: volatile storage, in the case of system failures; a portion of stable storage, in the case of media failures. To safeguard against the loss of data in unreliable storage, we maintain another copy of the data, possibly in a different representation. This redundant copy is kept in another part of storage that we deem reliable: stable storage, in the case of system failures, or another piece of stable storage, such as a second disk, in the case of media failures. Of course, the different physical characteristics of storage in the two cases may require the use of different strategies. But the principles are the same.

For pedagogical simplicity, we will focus principally on the problem of system failures. We explain how to extend recovery techniques for system failure to those for media failure in the last section of the chapter.

We'll assume that all failures are detected. This is not an issue with transaction failures, because a transaction failure by definition results in the execution of an Abort operation. But it is conceivable that volatile or stable storage gets corrupted without this being detected. Usually, storage devices have error detecting codes, such as parity checks, to detect bit errors in hardware; software can use redundant pointer structures and the like to detect data structure inconsistencies. While these techniques make an undetected failure highly unlikely, it *is* possible. In general, the techniques described here will not handle the occurrence of such an undetected system or media failure.

6.2 DATA MANAGER ARCHITECTURE

As in our discussion of schedulers, we'll continue using the TM-scheduler-DM model of a DBS. Unlike Chapters 3–5, where we focused on the scheduler, our center of attention will now shift to the DM. It's the DM that manipulates storage, and it's storage that is corrupted by failures. We will principally be concerned with system failures that can destroy volatile but not stable storage. We must therefore incorporate the distinction between volatile and stable storage into the model, which we briefly discussed in Section 1.4.

Let's review our model of a DBS, focusing on the issues that will occupy us in this chapter (see Fig. 6–1). Transactions submit their operations to the TM, which passes them on to the scheduler. The scheduler receives Read, Write, Commit, and Abort operations from the TM. The scheduler can pass Aborts to the DM immediately. For Read, Write, or Commit operations, the scheduler must decide, possibly after some delay, whether to reject or accept the operation. If it rejects the operation, the scheduler sends a negative acknowledgment to the TM, which sends an Abort back to the scheduler, which in turn promptly passes the Abort to the DM. If the scheduler accepts the operation, it sends it to the DM, which processes it by manipulating storage. The exact details of this storage manipulation depend on the DM algorithm, and are the main subject of this chapter. When the DM has finished processing the operation, it acknowledges to the scheduler, which passes the acknowledgment to the TM. For a Read, the acknowledgment includes the value read.

In addition to Read, Write, Commit and Abort, the DM may also receive a Restart operation. This is sent by an external module, such as the operating system, upon recovery from a system failure. The task of Restart is to bring the database to a consistent state, removing effects of uncommitted transactions and applying missing effects of committed ones. To be more precise, define the *last committed value* of a data item x in some execution to be the value last written into x in that execution by a committed transaction. Define the *committed database state* with respect to a given execution to be the state in which each data item contains its last committed value. The goal of Restart is to restore the database into its committed state with respect to the execution up to the system failure.

To see why this is the right thing to do, let's use the tools of Chapter 2. Let H be the history representing the partial order of operations processed by the DM up to the time of the system failure. The committed projection of H, $C(H)$, is obtained by deleting from H all operations not belonging to the committed transactions. If H was produced by a correct scheduler, then it is recoverable. Consequently, the values read or written in $C(H)$ are identical to the values read or written by the corresponding operations in H. Therefore, by restoring the last committed value of each data item, Restart makes the database reflect the execution represented by the history $C(H)$, that is, the execution of precisely the transactions that were committed at the time of the system failure. Moreover, $C(H)$ is SR, because it was produced by a correct scheduler.

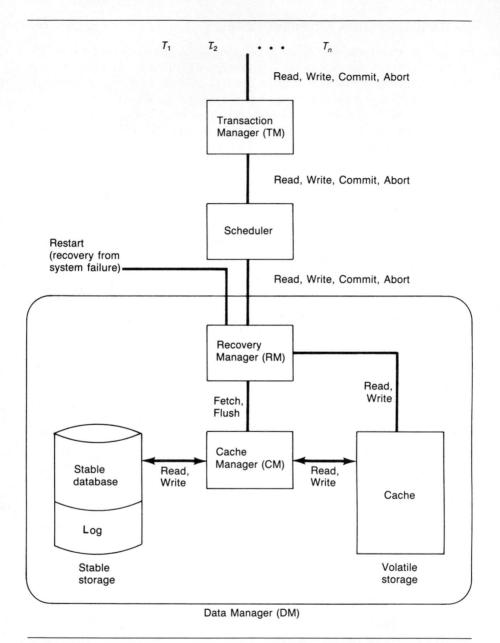

FIGURE 6–1
Model of a Centralized Database System

So when Restart terminates, the database is in a consistent state. A major goal of this chapter is to explain what data structures must be maintained by the DM so that Restart can do this using *only* information saved in stable storage.

Stable Storage

The DM is split into two components: a *cache manager* (*CM*), which manipulates storage, and a *recovery manager* (*RM*), which processes Read, Write, Commit, Abort, and Restart operations. The CM provides operations to *fetch* data from stable storage into volatile storage, and to *flush* data from volatile to stable storage. The RM partially controls the CM's flush operations, to ensure that stable storage always has the data that the RM needs to process a Restart correctly, should the need arise.

We assume that when the CM issues a Write operation to write a data item in stable storage, *the Write either executes in its entirety or not at all* and responds with a return code indicating which of the two outcomes occurred. This holds even if the system fails while the Write executes. Such Writes are called *atomic*. If a Write fails to be atomic (e.g., it modifies some but not all of a data item), then a media failure has occurred. For now, we assume that media failures do not occur. That is, all Writes are atomic. We treat media failures in Section 6.8.

For disks, currently the most popular form of stable storage, the granularity of data item that can be written is usually a fixed-sized *page* (or *block*). When a page is written to disk, there are two possible results: the old value of the page is correctly overwritten, and remains in the new state until it is overwritten again, or the new value of the page is corrupted somehow, in which case the error is detected when the page is subsequently read. That is, it either executes correctly or results in a media failure. Error detection is normally supported by the disk hardware. If a small number of bit errors alters the contents of a page, the disk hardware will detect the error through a checksum that is calculated when it reads the page. The checksum may also be a function of the page's disk address, *da*, thereby ensuring that the page that is read is one that was previously written to *da* (i.e., not one that was intended to be written to some other address but was incorrectly written to *da*). When these sorts of hardware error detection are unavailable, one can partially compensate for their absence using software error detection, with some degradation of performance (see Exercise 6.1).

The granularity of data items that are parameters to Writes issued to the DM may be different from that which can be atomically written to stable storage. That is, if stable storage supports atomic Writes to pages, the DM may receive Writes to short records (where each page may contain many such records) or to long records (which can span more than one page). This mismatch of data item granularity requires special attention when designing recovery algorithms, since individual data items cannot be written one by one (for short records) or atomically (for long records).

In this chapter, unless otherwise noted, we assume that the granularity of data items supported by the DM is identical to that supported by stable storage. With today's disk technology, this means a data item is a fixed-size page. We will also discuss some of the special problems that arise due to granularity mismatches. However, in these cases we will be careful to emphasize that we have abandoned the assumption of identical DM and stable storage granularities of data items (see also Exercise 6.2).

We distinguish between DMs that keep exactly one copy of each data item in stable storage and DMs that may keep more than one. If there is only one copy, then each time a data item is overwritten, the old value is destroyed. This is called *in-place updating*. If there is more than one copy, then the CM may write a data item to stable storage without destroying the older versions of that data item. The older versions are called *shadow copies*, and this technique is called *shadowing*.

With shadowing, the mapping of data items to stable storage locations changes over time. It is therefore convenient to implement this mapping using a *directory*, with one entry per data item, giving the name of the data item and its stable storage location. Such a directory defines a state of the database (see Fig. 6–2). With shadowing, there is usually more than one such directory, each directory identifying a different state of the database.

We define the *stable database* to be the state of the database in stable storage. With in-place updating, there is exactly one copy of each data item in stable storage, so the concept is well defined. With shadowing, we assume that there is a particular directory, D, in stable storage that defines the current state of the stable database. The copies of data items in stable storage that are referenced by directories other than D are shadow copies.

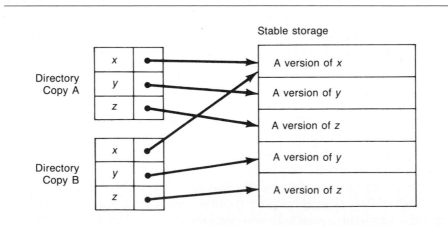

FIGURE 6–2
An Example of Shadowing
Using shadowing, directory copies A and B each define a database state.

The Cache Manager

To avoid accessing stable storage to process every Read and Write, we would like to keep a copy of the database in volatile storage. To read a data item we would simply obtain its value from the volatile storage copy. To write a data item we would record the new value in both the volatile and stable storage copies. The stable storage copy would be useful only for recovery from system failures. Since access to stable storage is slower than to volatile storage, this would improve performance in almost all cases. Unfortunately, keeping a copy of the entire database in volatile storage is usually too expensive due to the large size of databases and the relatively high cost of main memory. However, as main memory prices continue to drop, this approach may become more common in the future.

In any case, currently, we must cope with keeping less than the whole database in volatile storage. This can be done by using a technique called *caching* or *buffering*, similar to that of hardware caching and operating system virtual memory. A portion of volatile storage, called the *cache*, is reserved for holding portions of the database. The cache consists of a collection of *slots*, each of which can store the value of a data item (see Fig. 6–3). The granularity of data items stored in slots is that which can be atomically written to stable storage (i.e., a page). At any time a certain subset of data items occupies slots in the cache, in addition to occupying their more permanent locations in stable storage. A cache slot contains a value for the data item stored in that slot, and a *dirty bit* that is set if and only if the value of the data item stored in the cache slot is different from its value in stable storage (we'll see how this can arise momentarily). If the dirty bit is set, we say the slot is *dirty*. There is also a *cache directory* that gives the name of each data item in the cache and the number of its associated slot.

Cache				Cache Directory	
Slot Number	Dirty Bit	Data Item Value		Data Item Name	Slot Number
1	1	"October12"		x	2
2	0	3.1416		y	1
		.			.
		.			.
		.			.

FIGURE 6-3
Cache Structure

The traffic of data items into and out of the cache is controlled by the CM via two operations: Flush and Fetch. *Flush* takes a cache slot c as its parameter. If c is not dirty, then Flush does nothing. If c is dirty, it copies c's value into the stable storage location of the data item stored in c, and clears c's dirty bit. Flush does not return to its caller until the update of c on stable storage has completed.

Notice that Flush must map each data item to a stable storage location. If the CM uses shadowing, then the mapping is via a directory. The CM's choice and manipulation of directories depends on the recovery algorithm. If the CM uses in-place updating, then the mapping is unique. In this case, the method for performing the mapping is unimportant to our study.

Fetch takes a data item name x as its parameter. It causes the CM to perform the following actions:

1. It selects an empty cache slot, say c. If all cache slots are occupied, it selects some slot c, flushes c, and uses that as its empty slot.

2. It copies the value of x from its stable storage location into c.

3. It clears the dirty bit of c.

4. It updates the cache directory to indicate that x now occupies c.

If slot c was occupied in step (1), we say that x *replaces* the data item that occupied c. The criterion according to which the CM chooses c is called the *replacement strategy*. Some well known replacement strategies are *least recently used* (LRU) and *first-in–first-out* (FIFO), specifying, respectively, that the slot least recently accessed or least recently fetched be used for replacement.

To read a data item named x, the CM fetches the value of x if it is not already in the cache, and returns this value from the cache. To write x, the CM allocates a slot for x if it is not already in the cache, records the new value in the cache slot, and sets the dirty bit for the cache slot. Whether it flushes the new value of x to stable storage at this point or later on is a decision left to the RM. As we'll see, different RM algorithms use different strategies with respect to this issue.

There will be times when the RM must ensure that a cache slot is not flushed for some time period, for example, while it is updating the contents of the slot. For this reason, the CM offers two additional operations, *Pin* and *Unpin*. The operation Pin(c) tells the CM not to flush c, while Unpin(c) makes a previously pinned slot again available for flushing. Thus, the CM never flushes a slot while it is pinned.

6.3 THE RECOVERY MANAGER

The RM interface is defined by five procedures:

1. *RM-Read(T_i, x):* read the value of x for transaction T_i;

2. *RM-Write(T_i, x, v):* write v into x on behalf of transaction T_i;

3. *RM-Commit(T_i):* commit T_i;

4. *RM-Abort(T_i):* abort T_i; and

5. *Restart:* bring the stable database to the committed state following a system failure.

The RM should execute these operations atomically. That is, the RM's execution should be equivalent to a serial execution of these operations. This requirement is easily enforced if a 2PL, TO, or SGT scheduler is used. These schedulers never send two conflicting operations to the RM concurrently, so the RM can safely process any of its pending Reads and Writes concurrently. However, the RM may also access local data structures that are shared by the execution of two operations. For example, an RM-Commit and RM-Abort of two different transactions may both update local lists of active and terminated transactions. To ensure that these operations are atomic with respect to each other, the RM must synchronize access to these shared structures, for example by using semaphores or locks.

We assume that the scheduler invokes RM operations in an order that produces a serializable and strict execution. Since executions are strict, committed Writes will execute in the same order that their corresponding transactions commit. In particular, the last committed value of x will be written by the last committed transaction that wrote into x.

The RM algorithms become considerably more complicated under the weaker assumption that the scheduler produces an execution that is serializable and recoverable, the weakest possible requirements on the scheduler that will not compromise correctness.

Recall from Sections 1.2 and 2.4 that strict executions avoid cascading aborts. Thus, to erase the effects of an aborted transaction from the database, we merely have to restore in the database the before images of its Writes. To establish the terminology that we'll use later in the chapter, suppose T_i wrote into x: The *before image of x with respect to (wrt) T_i* is the value of x just before T_i wrote into it; the *after image of x wrt T_i* is the value written into x by T_i.

Logging

Suppose the RM uses in-place updating. Then, each data item has a unique location in stable storage. Ideally, the stable database would contain, for each x, the last value written into x by a committed transaction. Practically, two factors prevent this ideal state: the continual updating by transactions that take some time to terminate, and the buffering of data items in cache. Therefore, the stable database might contain values written by uncommitted transactions, or might not contain values written by committed ones.

In the event of a system failure, the RM's Restart operation must be able to transform the stable database state into the committed database state. In doing this, it can only rely on data in stable storage. For this reason, the RM usually stores information in stable storage in addition to the stable database itself. A *log* is one such type of information.

Conceptually, a log is a representation of the history of execution. A *physical log* is a type of log that contains information about the values of data items written by transactions. Like the stable database, the structure and contents of the log are highly dependent on the RM algorithm. Abstractly, however, we can think of a (physical) log as consisting of entries of the form $[T_i, x, v]$, identifying the value v that transaction T_i wrote into data item x.

The data structures used for the log must enable Restart to determine, for each x, which log entry contains x's last committed value. Thus, they must encode the *order* in which Writes occurred. An easy way to record this information is to require that the log be a sequential file and that the entries in the log be consistent with the order of their corresponding Writes. Thus, we assume that $[T_i, x, u]$ precedes $[T_j, x, v]$ in the log iff $w_i[x]$ executed before $w_j[x]$. Since we assume a strict execution, if $[T_i, x, u]$ precedes $[T_j, x, v]$ in the log and both T_i and T_j committed, then T_i committed before T_j.

Instead of containing values that were written into the database, a log may contain descriptions of higher level operations. This is called *logical logging*. For example, a log entry may say that "record r was inserted into file F, and F's indices were updated to reflect this insertion." Using logical logging, only this one log entry is recorded, instead of several log entries corresponding to the physical Writes of F and its indices. By recording higher level operations, fewer log entries are needed. Shortening the log in this way can improve the RM's performance, but sometimes at the expense of added complexity in interpreting log entries by the Restart algorithm. We will deal with the complexity of logical logging later in the chapter. Unless otherwise noted, when we use the term "log," we mean a physical log.

In addition to the stable database and the log, the RM may also keep in stable storage one or more of the *active*, *commit* and *abort* lists. These lists contain the identifiers of the set of transactions that are active, committed or aborted (respectively). These lists are often stored as part of the log.

In most RM algorithms, it is the act of adding a transaction identifier to the commit list that causes the transaction to become committed. Thus, after a system failure, the RM regards a transaction as having been committed iff its transaction identifier is in the commit list.

Undo and Redo

Whatever replacement strategy the CM uses, there are times when the RM must *insist* that the CM flush certain data items to stable storage. These flushes coordinate writing the stable database and the log, so that Restart will always find the information it needs in stable storage, be it in the stable database or the log. In this section we will investigate flushing requirements that all RMs must satisfy. This will lead to a natural categorization of RM algorithms that will carry us through the rest of the chapter.

We say that an RM *requires undo* if it allows an uncommitted transaction to record *in the stable database* values it wrote. Should a system failure occur at this point, on recovery the stable database will contain effects of the uncommitted transaction. These effects must be *undone* by Restart in order to restore the stable database to its committed state with respect to the execution up to the failure.

We say that an RM *requires redo* if it allows a transaction to commit before all the values it wrote have been recorded *in the stable database.* If a system failure occurs at this point, on recovery the stable database will be missing some of the effects of the committed transaction. These must be *redone* by Restart to restore the stable database to its committed state.

Notice that we use the terms "requires undo" and "requires redo" only relative to system failures, not media failures. That is, when we say that "an RM requires redo," we really mean that "the RM's Restart procedure requires redo for handling system failures." We treat the undo and redo requirements for media failures in Section 6.8.[1]

By regulating the order of a transaction's commitment relative to writing its values in the stable database, an RM can control whether it requires undo or redo. Thus, we can classify RM algorithms into four categories: (1) those that require both undo and redo; (2) those that require undo but not redo; (3) those that require redo but not undo; and (4) those that require neither undo nor redo.[2] Implementations of all four types have been proposed and we'll examine them later in this chapter.

The prospect that an RM may require undo or redo should raise some concern in view of our desire to be able to recover from system failures. In particular, since the stable database may contain inappropriate updates or be missing appropriate ones, the RM had better keep sufficient information in the log for Restart to undo the former and redo the latter. The requirements implied by this can be conveniently stated as two design rules that all RM implementations must observe.

Undo Rule:[3] If x's location in the stable database presently contains the last committed value of x, then that value must be saved in stable storage *before* being overwritten in the stable database by an uncommitted value.

---

[1] Recovery mechanisms for media failure generally require redo. Most such mechanisms keep a stable copy of the database, called the *archive*, which is almost surely out-of-date. So the RM must redo committed updates that occurred after the archive was created.

[2] In the paradigm of [Haerder, Reuter 83], these categories correspond to (1) Steal/No-Force, (2) Steal/Force, (3) No-Steal/No-Force, and (4) No-Steal/Force.

[3] This is often called the write ahead log protocol, because it requires that the before image of a Write be logged ahead of the Write being installed in the stable database.

Redo Rule: Before a transaction can commit, the value it wrote for each data item must be in stable storage (e.g., in the stable database or the log).

The Undo and Redo Rules ensure that the last committed value of each data item is always available in stable storage. The Undo Rule ensures that the last committed value of x is saved in stable storage (e.g., in the log) before being overwritten by an uncommitted value. And the Redo Rule ensures that a value is in stable storage at the moment it becomes committed. Observe that an RM that does *not* require undo (or redo) necessarily satisfies the Undo (or Redo) Rule.

Garbage Collection

Even though stable storage is usually abundant, it has bounded capacity. It is therefore necessary to restrict the amount of information the RM keeps in stable storage. Clearly, the size of the stable database is bounded by the number of data items it stores. To satisfy the Undo and Redo Rules, the RM has to keep inserting information into the log. To bound the growth of the log, the RM must free up and recycle any space used to store information that it can be certain will never be needed by Restart. Recycling space occupied by unnecessary information is called *garbage collection*.

Restart's requirement for log information is: for each data item x, if the stable database copy of x does not contain the last committed value of x, then Restart must be able to find that value in the log. To restate this requirement in terms of log entries requires a knowledge of the detailed structure of log entries. In terms of our abstract log entries of the form $[T_i, x, v]$, the following rule tells precisely what information can be dispensed with at any given time, insofar as Restart is concerned.

Garbage Collection Rule: The entry $[T_i, x, v]$ can be removed from the log iff (1) T_i has aborted or (2) T_i has committed but some other committed transaction wrote into x after T_i did (hence v is not the last committed value of x).

In case (1), once T_i has aborted we no longer care about what it wrote, since all of its Writes will be undone. In case (2), once a newly committed value is written into x, older committed values can be disposed of, because only the last committed value is needed for recovery. In both cases, deleting $[T_i, x, v]$ never affects Restart's ability to determine which Write on x is the last committed one, as long as the order of committed Writes is recorded in the log.

Notice that even if v is the last committed value of x and is stored in the stable database copy of x, $[T_i, x, v]$ cannot be deleted from the log. If a transaction T_j subsequently wrote into x in the stable database and then aborted, then $[T_i, x, v]$ would be needed to undo T_j's Write. However, if the RM does not require undo, then T_j's Write cannot be flushed to the stable database before T_j commits, so this scenario cannot occur. Therefore, we can augment the Garbage Collection Rule with a third case: (3) $[T_i, x, v]$ can be removed from the log if the RM does not require undo, v is the last committed value of x, v is the value of x in the stable database, and $[T_i, x, v]$ is the only log entry for x. The last condition ensures that Restart does not misinterpret some earlier log entry for x to be x's last committed value, after $[T_i, x, v]$ is deleted.

The Garbage Collection Rule defines the *earliest* time that a log entry can be deleted. Some Restart algorithms require keeping the log entries longer than required by the Garbage Collection Rule. This rule may also be overruled by the requirements of media recovery (see Section 6.8).[4]

As we mentioned before, the RM may also keep in stable storage one or more of the active, abort, or commit lists. The size of the active list is bounded by the number of transactions that are in progress at any given time, presumably a manageable number. The RM somehow has to bound the size of the abort and commit lists, since it would be impractical to keep a record of all transactions that have committed or aborted since the genesis of the system. In practice, the RM only needs to know about recently committed or aborted transactions. Exactly what "recently" means depends on the details of the RM algorithm.

Idempotence of Restart

Although Read, Write, Commit, and Abort execute atomically with respect to each other, Restart can interrupt any of them, because a system failure can happen at any time. Indeed, Restart can even interrupt its own execution, should a system failure occur while Restart is recovering from an earlier failure. That Restart can interrupt itself leads to another important requirement: Restart must be *idempotent*. This means that if Restart stops executing at any moment and starts executing again from the beginning, it produces the same result in the stable database as if the first execution had run to completion. Said more abstractly, it means that any sequence of incomplete executions of Restart followed by a complete execution of Restart has the same effect as just one complete execution of Restart.

If an execution of Restart is interrupted by a system failure, then a second execution of Restart will begin by reinitializing volatile storage, since it assumes that this storage was corrupted by the failure. However, it will accept the state of stable storage as is, including updates produced by the first execution of Restart. Thus, the pragmatic implication of idempotence is that Restart should ensure that stable storage is always in a state that a new execution of

---

[4]For media recovery, the Garbage Collection Rule applies, but with respect to the archive database. That is, case (2) applies iff some other transaction wrote into x in *the archive database* after T_i did.

Restart can properly interpret. This amounts to being careful about the values Restart writes to stable storage and the order in which it writes them. In this sense, idempotence is similar to the Undo and Redo Rules, in that it also restricts the order of certain updates to stable storage so that Restart can do its job.

Preview

In the following sections, we'll describe the four different types of RMs mentioned previously: undo/redo, undo/no-redo, no-undo/redo, and no-undo/no-redo. For convenience of exposition, we present an RM as a collection of five procedures representing the RM's five operations: RM-Read, RM-Write, RM-Commit, RM-Abort, and Restart. In each of the four RM algorithms presented, we first describe the five procedures at a fairly abstract level. The purpose is to state *what* the RM has to do, rather than *how* it does it. The "how" issues are taken up later, when we examine various implementation strategies.

6.4 THE UNDO/REDO ALGORITHM

In this section we describe an RM algorithm that requires both undo and redo. This is the most complicated of the four types of RMs. However, it has the significant advantage of being very flexible about deciding when to flush dirty cache slots into the stable database. It leaves the decision to flush almost entirely to the CM. This is desirable for two reasons. First, an RM that uses undo/redo avoids forcing the CM to flush unnecessarily, thereby minimizing I/O. By contrast, a no-redo algorithm generally flushes more frequently, since it must ensure that all of a transaction's updated items are in the stable database before the transaction commits. Second, it allows a CM that uses in-place updating to replace a dirty slot last written by an uncommitted transaction. A no-undo algorithm cannot flush the slot in this case, since it would be writing an uncommitted update into the stable database. In general, the undo/redo algorithm is geared to maximize efficiency during normal operation, at the expense of less efficient processing of failures than is possible with other algorithms.

Suppose transaction T_i writes value v into data item x. In this algorithm, the RM fetches x if it isn't already in cache, records v in the log and in x's cache slot, c, but does not ask the CM to flush c. The CM only flushes c when it needs to replace x to free up c for another fetch. Thus, recording an update in the stable database is in the hands of the CM, not the RM. If the CM replaces c and either T_i aborts or the system fails before T_i commits, then undo will be required. On the other hand, if T_i commits and the system fails before the CM replaces c, then redo will be required.

We assume the granularity of data items on which RM procedures operate is the same as the unit of atomic transfer to stable storage. We assume a physical log that is an ordered list of records of the form $[T_i, x, v]$, and that is recycled according to the Garbage Collection Rule. We assume that the initial value of each data item is written in the log before any transactions are processed. (Alternatively, the first Write to each data item can store the initial value of the data item in the log.) Each update of the log and the commit list goes directly to the stable storage device and must be acknowledged by that device before proceeding to the next step.

We now outline the five RM procedures for this algorithm.

RM-Write(T_i, x, v)

1. Add T_i to the active list, if it's not already there.

2. If x is not in the cache, fetch it.

3. Append $[T_i, x, v]$ to the log.

4. Write v into the cache slot occupied by x.[(A) 5]

5. Acknowledge the processing of RM-Write(T_i, x, v) to the scheduler.

RM-Read(T_i, x)

1. If x is not in the cache, fetch it.

2. Return the value in x's cache slot to the scheduler.

RM-Commit(T_i)

1. Add T_i to the commit list.[(B)]

2. Acknowledge the commitment of T_i to the scheduler.

3. Delete T_i from the active list.[(C)]

RM-Abort(T_i)

1. For each data item x updated by T_i:

  ■ if x is not in the cache, allocate a slot for it;

  ■ copy the before image of x wrt T_i into x's cache slot.[(D)]

2. Add T_i to the abort list.

3. Acknowledge the abortion of T_i to the scheduler.

4. Delete T_i from the active list.

Restart

1. Discard all cache slots.[(E)]

---

[5]All comments are listed after the descriptions of the operations and are cross-referenced with superscripted capital letters.

2. Let $redone := \{\}$ and $undone := \{\}.^{(F)}$

3. Start with the last entry in the log and scan backwards toward the beginning. Repeat the following steps until either $redone \cup undone$ equals the set of all data items in the database, or there are no more log entries to examine. For each log entry $[T_i, x, v]$, if $x \notin redone \cup undone$, then

   - if x is not in the cache, allocate a slot for it;
   - if T_i is in the commit list, copy v into x's cache slot$^{(G)}$ and set $redone := redone \cup \{x\}$;
   - otherwise (i.e., T_i is in the abort list or in the active but not the commit list), copy the before image of x wrt $T_i^{(H)}$ into x's cache slot and set $undone := undone \cup \{x\}$.

4. For each T_i in the commit list, if T_i is in the active list, remove it from there.

5. Acknowledge the completion of Restart to the scheduler.$^{(I)}$

Comments

A. [Step (4) of RM-Write] To avoid repetitive comments, we assume here, and through the rest of the chapter, that when a cache slot is written into (thus making its value different from the value of the corresponding location in the stable database), the RM sets the slot's dirty bit. We also assume that the RM pins a cache slot before reading or writing it, and unpins it afterwards, thereby ensuring that RM-Reads and RM-Writes are atomic wrt flushes.

B. [Step (1) of RM-Commit(T_i)] It is the act of adding T_i to the commit list (in stable storage) that declares T_i committed. Should a system failure occur before this step completes, T_i will be considered uncommitted. Otherwise it will be considered committed even if Step (2) of RM-Commit(T_i) was not completed.

C. [Step (3) of RM-Commit] The significance of the active and abort lists will be discussed in a later subsection, on checkpointing.

D. [Step (1) of RM-Abort] At this point, the before image is only restored in the cache. The CM will restore it in the stable database when it replaces x's cache slot.

E. [Step (1) of Restart] A system failure destroys the contents of volatile storage, and hence the cache. Thus when Restart is invoked, the values in the cache cannot be trusted.

F. [Step (2) of Restart] $redone$ and $undone$ are variables local to Restart that keep track of which data items have been restored to their last committed value by a redo or undo action (respectively).

G. [Step (3) of Restart] At this point, x's last committed value is only restored in the cache. The CM will restore it in the stable database when it replaces x's cache slot.

H. [Step (3) of Restart] The before image of x wrt T_i can be found in the log.

I. [Step (4) of Restart] Upon recovery from a system failure, the scheduler must wait for the acknowledgment that Restart has been completed by the RM. It may then start sending operations to the RM again.

Undo and Redo Rules

This algorithm satisfies the Undo Rule. Suppose the location of x in the stable database contains the last committed value of x, say v, written by transaction T_i. When T_i wrote into x, the RM inserted $[T_i, x, v]$ in the log (see step (2) of RM-Write). By the Garbage Collection Rule, since v is the last committed value of x, this record cannot have been removed. In particular, it will still be in the log when the CM overwrites v in the stable database, as desired for the Undo Rule.

The Redo Rule is likewise satisfied. All of a transaction's updates are recorded in the log before the transaction commits, whether or not they were also recorded in the stable database. By the Garbage Collection Rule they must still be there when the transaction commits.

Since the algorithm satisfies the Undo and Redo Rules, Restart can always find in stable storage the information that it needs for restoring the last committed value of each data item in the stable database. In step (3), Restart redoes an update to x by a committed transaction, or undoes an update to x by an active or aborted transaction, only if no other committed transaction subsequently updated x. Thus, when Restart terminates, each data item will contain its last committed value. Moreover, Restart is idempotent. If it is interrupted by a system failure and reexecutes from the beginning, the updates it redoes and undoes in step (3) are the same as those it would have done if its first execution had not been interrupted.

Checkpointing

The Restart procedure just sketched may have to examine every record ever written in the log — except, of course, those that have been garbage collected. This is still a very large number of records, since garbage collection is an expensive activity and is carried out fairly infrequently. Moreover, since most data items in the database probably contain their last committed values at the time of the failure, Restart is doing much more work than necessary. This inefficiency of Restart is an important issue, because after a system failure, the DBS is unavailable to users until Restart has finished its job.

This problem is solved by the use of checkpointing methods. In general, *checkpointing* is an activity that writes information to stable storage during normal operation in order to reduce the amount of work Restart has to do after a failure.

Checkpointing performs its work by a combination of two types of updates to stable storage: (1) marking the log, commit list, and abort list to indicate which updates are already written or undone in the stable database, and (2) writing the after images of committed updates or before images of aborted updates in the stable database. Technique (1) tells Restart *which* updates don't have to be undone or redone again. Technique (2) reduces the amount of work that Restart has to do by doing that work during checkpointing. Technique (1) is essential to any checkpointing activity. Technique (2) is optional.

One simple checkpointing scheme is periodically to stop processing transactions, wait for all active transactions to commit or abort, flush all dirty cache slots, and then mark the end of the log to indicate that the checkpointing activity took place. This is called *commit consistent checkpointing*, because the stable database now contains the last committed value of each data item relative to the transactions whose activity is recorded in the log. With commit consistent checkpointing, Restart scans the log backward, beginning at the end, undoing and redoing updates corresponding to log records, until it reaches the last checkpoint marker. It may have to examine log records that precede the marker in order to find certain before images: namely, the before images of each data item that was updated after the last checkpoint marker, but not by any committed transaction.

The activity of checkpointing and the stable database created by checkpointing are both sometimes called *checkpoints*; we will use the word *Checkpoint* (capital "C") as the name of the procedure that performs the checkpointing activity.

The main problem with this Checkpoint procedure is performance. Users may suffer a long delay waiting for active transactions to complete and the cache to be flushed. We can eliminate the first of these two delays by using the following Checkpoint procedure, called *cache consistent checkpointing*, which ensures that all Writes written to cache are also in the stable database.

Periodically, Checkpoint causes the RM to stop processing other operations (temporarily leaving active transactions in a blocked state), flushes all dirty cache slots, and places markers at the end of the log and abort list to indicate that the flushes took place. Consider now what Restart must do after a system failure assuming that this Checkpoint procedure is used. All updates of committed transactions that happened before the last Checkpoint were installed in the stable database during that Checkpoint and need not be redone. Similarly, all updates of transactions that aborted prior to the last Checkpoint were undone during that Checkpoint, and need not be undone again. Therefore Restart need only redo those updates of transactions in the commit list that appear after the last checkpoint marker in the log. And it need only undo updates of those transactions that are in the active (but not the commit) list, or are in the abort list and appear after the last checkpoint marker in that list.

This checkpointing scheme still delays transactions while the cache is being flushed. We can reduce this delay by using the following technique, called *fuzzy checkpointing*. Instead of flushing *all* dirty cache slots, the Checkpoint procedure only flushes those dirty slots that have not been flushed since *before* the previous checkpoint. The hope is that the CM's normal replacement activity will flush most cache slots that were dirty since before the previous checkpoint. Thus Checkpoint won't have much flushing to do, and therefore won't delay active transactions for very long.

This Checkpoint procedure guarantees that, at any time, all updates of committed transactions that occurred before the *penultimate* (i.e., second to last) Checkpoint have been applied to the stable database — during the last Checkpoint, if not earlier. Similarly, all updates of transactions that had aborted before the penultimate Checkpoint have been undone.

As in cache consistent checkpointing, after flushing the relevant cache slots, the fuzzy Checkpoint procedure appends markers to the log and to the abort list. Thus, after a system failure, Restart redoes just those updates of transactions in the commit list that come after the penultimate checkpoint marker in the log, and it undoes just the updates of those transactions that are either in the active (but not the commit) list, or are in the abort list and follow the penultimate checkpoint marker in that list. Checkpoint and Restart algorithms that use this strategy are described in detail in the next subsection.

In reviewing the checkpointing schemes we have discussed, we see at work a fundamental parameter of checkpointing: the maximum length of time, t, that a cache slot can remain dirty before being flushed. Increasing t decreases the work of Checkpoint and increases the work of Restart. That is, it speeds up the system during normal operation at the expense of slowing down the recovery activity after a system failure. Hence t is a system parameter that should be tuned to optimize this trade-off.

An Implementation of Undo/Redo

A problem with the undo/redo algorithm is that after images of data items can consume a lot of space. If data items are pages of a file, then each update to a page generates a little over a page of log information, consisting of the page's address, its after image, and the identifier of the transaction that wrote the page. This produces a lot of disk I/O, which can seriously degrade performance. And it consumes a lot of log space, which makes garbage collection of the log a major factor.

These problems are especially annoying if most updates only modify a small portion of a data item. If data items are pages, then an update might only modify a few fields of one record stored on that page. In this case, it would be more efficient to log only *partial data items*, namely, the portion of each data item that was actually modified. A log record should now also include the offset and length of the portion of the data item that was modified.

The algorithm described next logs partial data items and uses fuzzy checkpointing. We will call it the *partial data item logging algorithm*.

The algorithm incorporates the active, commit, and abort lists into the log, which is stored as a sequential file. Each log entry may now be made smaller than a data item, which is the unit of transfer to stable storage. It is therefore inefficient to write each log entry to stable storage at the time it is created, as in step (2) of RM-Write. It is more efficient to write log entries into a log buffer in volatile storage. When the buffer fills up, the log buffer is appended to the stable copy of the log. This significantly reduces the number of Writes to the (stable) log, but jeopardizes the Undo and Redo Rules.

It jeopardizes the Redo Rule because it is possible to commit a transaction before the after images of all of its updates are in the log. This problem is avoided almost automatically. Recall that commit list entries are stored in the log. Therefore, to add T_i to the commit list in step (1) of RM-Commit, we simply add T_i's commit list entry to the log buffer and flush the log buffer to the (stable) log. Since T_i's commit list entry follows all of the log entries describing its Writes, this ensures that the after images of all of its Writes are in the log before it commits, thereby satisfying the Redo Rule. Of course, the log buffer may not be full at the time a transaction commits, thereby sending a partially full buffer to stable storage. This partially defeats the reason for using the log buffer in the first place. It may therefore be worthwhile to use the *delayed commit* (sometimes called *group commit*) heuristic, which deliberately delays a requested Commit operation if it arrives when the last log buffer is largely empty. This delay provides some extra time for other transactions to write log entries to the log buffer before the Commit flushes it.

Buffering the log jeopardizes the Undo Rule because it is illegal to write an uncommitted update to the stable database before its before image is in the (stable) log. To solve this problem, it is helpful to identify each log entry by its *log address* or *log sequence number* (*LSN*), and to add to each cache slot another field containing an LSN. After RM-Write(T_i, x, v) inserts a log entry for x in the log buffer and updates x's cache slot, and before it unpins that slot, it writes the LSN of that entry into the slot's LSN. Before the CM flushes a slot, it ensures that all log entries up to and including the one whose LSN equals the cache slot's LSN have been appended to the log. Only then may it flush the slot. Since the slot is flushed only after its log entries are written to stable storage, the Undo Rule is satisfied.

Notice that step (3) of RM-Write(T_i, x, v) writes the log record to stable storage before x's cache slot is updated. This is sooner than necessary. By using the LSN mechanism just described, or by simply keeping track of the order in which certain pages must be written, we can avoid forcing this log record to be written to stable storage until x's cache slot is flushed.

We now describe the contents of each of the four types of log records in detail.

1. *Update:* This type of record documents a Write operation of a transaction. It contains the following information:
   - the name of the transaction that issued the Write;
   - the name or stable database location of the data item written;
   - the offset and length of the portion of the data item that was updated;
   - the old value of the portion of the data item that was updated (its before image);[6]
   - the new value of the portion of the data item that was updated (its after image); and
   - a pointer to (i.e., the LSN of) the previous update record of the same transaction (Null if this is the first update of the transaction); this can be easily found by maintaining a pointer to the last update record of each active transaction.

   This record is inserted in the log by step (3) of RM-Write.

2. *Commit:* This type of record says that a transaction has committed, and simply contains the name of the transaction. It is appended to the log by step (1) of RM-Commit.

3. *Abort:* This record says that a transaction has aborted and contains the name of that transaction. It is appended to the log by step (2) of RM-Abort.

4. *Checkpoint:* This type of record documents the completion of a checkpoint. It contains the following information:
   - a list of the active transactions at the time of the checkpoint; and
   - a list of the data items that were in dirty cache slots, along with the "stable-LSNs" of these slots, at the time the checkpoint was taken.

The *stable-LSN* is an additional field of information that we associate with each cache slot. It is the LSN of the last record in the log buffer at the time the data item presently occupying the slot was last fetched or flushed. The stable-LSN of a cache slot storing x marks a point in the log where it is known that the value of the stable database copy of x reflects (at least) all of the log records up to that point.

---

[6]In the previous abstract description of logs, update records did *not* contain the before image of the updated data item. It turns out that keeping such information in these records greatly facilitates the processing of RM-Abort and Restart.

The checkpoint record is inserted in the log by the Checkpoint procedure, shown below.

Checkpoint

1. Stop the RM from processing any more Read, Write, Commit, and Abort operations, and wait until it finishes processing all such operations that are in progress.

2. Flush each dirty cache slot that has not been flushed since the previous checkpoint. To achieve this, scan the cache and flush any dirty slot whose stable-LSN is smaller than the LSN of the previous checkpoint record (which can be stored in a special location in main memory for convenience), and update the stable-LSN of the slot accordingly.

3. Create a checkpoint record containing the relevant information (see the previous description of checkpoint records) and append this record to the log.

4. Acknowledge the processing of Checkpoint, thereby allowing the RM to resume processing operations.

The Checkpoint procedure is invoked periodically by the RM itself. For example, the RM may invoke it whenever the number of update records inserted in the log since the previous checkpoint exceeds a certain amount. As we mentioned earlier, increasing the frequency of checkpoints decreases the work of Restart and therefore decreases the recovery time after a system failure.

Given this structure for the log, the implementation of RM-Read, RM-Write, RM-Commit, and RM-Abort follows the outline given earlier in the section. Note how efficiently RM-Abort can be carried out. Since all of a transaction's update records are linked together, only the relevant log records need to be considered. Because such links may have to be followed, it is much better to keep the log on disk or another direct access device, rather than on tape. And since before images are included in the update records, no additional searching of the log is needed.

Restart

Restart processes the log in two scans: a backwards scan during which it undoes updates of uncommitted transactions, followed by a forward scan during which it redoes updates of committed transactions. We will first describe a simple version of the algorithm, after which we will look at potential optimizations.

The backwards scan begins at the end of the log (see Exercise 6.11). During this scan, Restart builds lists of committed and aborted transactions, denoted CL and AL (respectively). When it reads a commit or abort record, it adds the transaction to the appropriate list. When it reads an update record of some transaction T_i for data item x, it performs the following steps:

1. If T_i is in CL, it ignores the update record.

2. If T_i is in neither CL nor AL, then T_i was active at the time of failure, so it adds T_i to AL.

3. If T_i is (now) in AL, then it fetches x if it is not already in cache, and restores the before image of the portion of x recorded in the update record. Moreover, if the update record has no predecessor (i.e., this is the first log record of T_i), then T_i is removed from AL (since there's nothing more of T_i to be undone).

Restart ignores the last checkpoint record. When it reads the penultimate checkpoint record, Restart examines the list of active transactions stored in that record and adds to AL any of those transactions that are not in AL or CL. These are transactions that were active at the time of the penultimate Checkpoint and didn't commit or abort (or perform any updates) ever since. Thus, they were active at the time of the failure and should be aborted.

From the penultimate checkpoint record, Restart continues its backward scan of the log, ignoring all records except update records of transactions in AL. These are processed as in step (3) just given. The backward scan terminates when AL is left empty (recall that when the first update record of some transaction T_i in AL is processed, T_i is removed from AL).

To understand the effect of the backward scan, consider a single byte b of some data item. Let U be the last update record in the log that reflects an update to b, and whose transaction committed before the failure. By definition, U's after image defines b's last committed value relative to the execution at the time of the failure. We claim that if U precedes the penultimate checkpoint record, then b's value is contained in U's after image at the conclusion of the backward scan. To see this, first observe that since U precedes the penultimate checkpoint record, its after image must have been written to the stable database before the failure. Let V be any update record that reflects an update to b and follows U in the log. Let T_V be the transaction corresponding to V. By definition of U, T_V did not commit before the failure. If its abort record precedes the penultimate checkpoint record, then V must have been undone in the stable database. If not, then Restart's backward scan of the log undid V's update. In either case, b contains its after image in U as claimed.

By the preceding argument, all that remains after the backward scan is to install the correct value in those bytes whose last committed value is defined by an update record that follows the penultimate checkpoint record. This is done by a forward scan of the log beginning at the penultimate checkpoint record. For each update record U whose transaction is in CL, the corresponding data item is fetched if it is not already in cache, and U's after image is written into the cache slot. Update records of transactions not in CL are ignored. The scan terminates when it reaches the end of the log, at which time the database (some of which is still dirty in cache) is in the committed state with respect to the log.

This Restart algorithm is idempotent. It makes no assumptions about the stable database state other than those implied by the checkpoint records. Thus, if it is interrupted by a system failure after having performed some of its undos and redos, it can still be reexecuted from the beginning after the failure.

With its two scans of the log and updates of many data items, Restart can be a time consuming process. If the system were to fail after Restart terminates but before a Checkpoint was executed, all of that work would have to be repeated after the second failure. Restart can protect itself against such a failure by performing two checkpoints after it terminates. In effect, this results in a commit consistent checkpoint.

Using the information in the last checkpoint record that tells which data items were in dirty cache slots, we can improve this Restart procedure and avoid undoing or redoing certain update records. More specifically, suppose that during the backward scan of the log, Restart reads an update record of transaction T_i for data item x, where T_i is in AL. Such an update record need not be undone if:

A1: T_i's abort record lies between the penultimate and last checkpoint records, but x is not among the data items occupying dirty slots at the time of the last checkpoint; or

A2: T_i's abort record lies between the penultimate and last checkpoint records, and x was in a dirty cache slot at the last checkpoint, but its stable-LSN (also stored in the checkpoint record) is greater than the LSN of T_i's abort record.

To see A1, observe that data item x's absence from a dirty cache slot at the last checkpoint means that x's cache slot was replaced after T_i aborted. Therefore the before image of T_i's update for x was restored in the stable database.

To see A2, recall that before T_i's abort record was written, RM-Abort restored in the cache the before image of T_i's update of x. The cache slot for x must have been replaced between this time and the last checkpoint. Otherwise the stable-LSN for x's cache slot at the last checkpoint would not have been greater than the LSN of T_i's abort record. Thus, the before image of T_i's update of x was restored in the stable database.

Similarly, suppose that during the forward scan of the log, Restart reads an update record of some transaction T_i in CL for data item x. Such a record need not be redone if:

C1: T_i's update record lies between the last two checkpoint records, but x is not in the list of data items that were in dirty cache slots at the time of the last checkpoint; or

C2: T_i's update record lies between the last two checkpoint records, x is in the list of data items in dirty cache slots at the last checkpoint, but its stable-LSN is greater than the LSN of the update record at hand.

The reasons why these conditions make it unnecessary to redo T_i's update of x are analogous to those of the corresponding conditions A1 and A2. However, there is a subtle difference: conditions C1 and C2 describe the position of an *update* record relative to other records, but the corresponding conditions A1 and A2 describe the position of an *abort* record relative to other records. The reason for the difference will become apparent if you attempt to carry out the arguments to justify C1 and C2.

Logical Logging

Even with partial data item logging, before and after images of data items may consume too much space. This will occur if each Write on a data item x modifies most of the contents of x. For example, suppose each data item is a page of a file. A user operation that inserts a new record, r, at the beginning of a page, p, may have to shift down the remaining contents of p to make room for r. From the RM's viewpoint, all of p is being written, so p's before and after image must be logged in an update record, even with partial data item logging.

Using logical logging, one could reduce the size of this two page update record by replacing it with a log record that says "insert record r on page p." This log record would be much smaller than one containing a before and after image of p. To interpret this log record after a failure, Restart can redo it by inserting r on p, or can undo it by deleting r from p, depending on whether the corresponding transaction committed or aborted.

To implement logical logging, we need to expand the RM's repertoire of update operations beyond the simple Write operation. The larger repertoire may include operations such as insert record, delete record, shift records within page, etc. For each update operation o, the RM must have a procedure that creates a log record for o, a procedure that redoes o based on what the log record says, and a procedure that undoes o based on what the log record says.

These procedures are then interpreted by Restart in much the same way that update records are interpreted. However, there is one important difference. When interpreting an update record in physical logging, we can restore a before or after image without worrying about the current state of the data item. With logical log records we must be more careful. Some undos or redos corresponding to logical log records may only be applicable to a data item when it is in exactly the same (logical) state as when the log record was created.

To see why this matters, consider the following example. Suppose that the logical log contains a record LR, "insert record r on page p." Suppose that p's cache slot that includes LR's insertion was not flushed to the stable database before the system failed, and that the transaction that issued the insertion is aborted by Restart. When scanning back through the log, Restart will undo LR. However, the procedure $undo(LR)$ is operating on a copy of p that does not have record r stored in it. Unfortunately, $undo(LR)$ may not be able to tell whether or not r is in p. If it tries to delete r anyway (i.e., undo the insertion), it may obliterate some other data in p, thereby corrupting p. Notice that this wouldn't be a problem if it were simply restoring a before image, since correctly restoring a before image does not depend on the current state of the data item.

One way to avoid this problem is to write undo and redo procedures that have no effect when applied to a data item that is already in the appropriate state. For example, $undo(LR)$ should have no effect if p does not include LR's update, and $redo(LR)$ should have no effect if p already does include LR's update.

A second way to avoid the problem is to keep a copy of the stable database state as of the last checkpoint. After a system failure, Restart works from the "checkpoint" copy instead of the current stable database. It undoes update records that precede the last checkpoint record and that were produced by transactions that were active at the last checkpoint and did not subsequently commit. Then it redoes update records that follow the last checkpoint and were produced by committed transactions. Given that the execution is strict, each undo and redo of a log record will be applied to the same database state as when the log record was created.

This technique is used in IBM's prototype database system, System R. In their algorithm, shadowing is used to define the stable database at each checkpoint. Two directories are maintained: D_{cur}, describing the current stable database state, and D_{ckpt}, describing the stable database state just after the execution of the Checkpoint procedure. To checkpoint, the cache slots are flushed and a copy of D_{cur} is saved as the new D_{ckpt}. Subsequent updates are written to new locations, pointed to by D_{cur}. The shadow copies pointed to by D_{ckpt} are not overwritten, and therefore are available to Restart in the event of a system failure.

A third way to avoid the problem is to store LSNs in *data items*. Each data item contains the LSN of the log record that describes the last update applied to that data item by an active or committed transaction. In practice, many databases are structured with header information attached to each data item (e.g., a page header). In such databases, the LSN would be a field of the header.

The LSN in a data item x is very helpful to Restart, because it tells exactly which updates in the log have been applied to x. All update records whose LSN is less than or equal to LSN(x) (i.e., the LSN stored in x) *have* been applied to x. All those with larger LSN have *not*. This information enables Restart to undo or redo an update record on x only if x is in the same state as when the update record was generated.

LSNs in data items also help Restart be more efficient. Since Restart can tell if an update has already been applied to the stable copy of a data item by examining that data item's LSN, it can avoid unnecessary undos and redos to that data item.

To help it maintain the correct value for the LSN in each data item, the RM uses a new field for each update record U for data item x. The field contains the LSN of the previous active or committed update record for x before U. This information is easy to obtain at the time U is produced, because it is simply the LSN in x just before U's update is performed. Thus, all of the updates to each data item are chained backward in the log through this field.

We will explain how the RM uses LSNs in data items by describing a modified version of the partial data item logging algorithm, presented earlier in the section. We call it the *LSN-based logging algorithm*. In this description, we assume logical logging where each update record describes an update to a single data item (where a data item is the unit of transfer to stable storage). We also assume that executions are strict and that fuzzy checkpointing is used, as described earlier in the Section.

To process an RM-Write on x, the RM creates an update record U. It stores the current $LSN(x)$ in U, updates x, and assigns $LSN(x)$ to be $LSN(U)$ (i.e., U's address in the log). When undoing U in the event of an Abort, it reassigns $LSN(x)$ to be the previous $LSN(x)$ stored in U.[7]

Restart does two scans of the log: a backward scan for undo, and a forward scan for redo. During the backward scan, suppose Restart encounters a log record U reflecting an update to x by a transaction T_i that subsequently aborted. It therefore fetches x and examines $LSN(x)$. There are three cases:

1. If $LSN(x) = LSN(U)$, then Restart undoes U, assigning to $LSN(x)$ the previous LSN, which is stored in U. Notice that $LSN(x) = LSN(U)$ implies that x is in the same state as it was after U was first applied, so it is safe to undo the logical log record.

2. If $LSN(x) < LSN(U)$, then x does not contain U's update. So Restart should not undo U. Notice that $LSN(x)$ helps us avoid incorrectly undoing U in this case.

3. If $LSN(x) > LSN(U)$, then x contains an update described in an update record V appearing after U in the log. Since V was already encountered in the backward scan and was not undone, the transaction that produced V must have committed. Since the execution is strict and U precedes V in the log, U was undone before V updated x. Thus, as in case (2), it would be incorrect for Restart to undo U, since x is not in the same state as when U was written.

The backward scan terminates after Restart has reached the penultimate checkpoint and has processed all update records from transactions that were active at the penultimate checkpoint and did not subsequently commit.

During the forward scan, Restart begins at the penultimate checkpoint and processes each update record U (on x, say) from a committed transaction.

---

[7]This requires that the execution is strict. See the later discussion on record level locking.

If $LSN(x) < LSN(U)$, then it must be that $LSN(x)$ is the LSN in of the previous update record for x, so Restart redoes U. If $LSN(x) \geq LSN(U)$, then Restart ignores U, because x either has the state originally produced by U (i.e., $LSN(x) = LSN(U)$) or x contains an update "later" than U's (i.e., $LSN(x) > LSN(U)$). The "later" update must have been done by a committed transaction, or else it would have been undone in the backward scan of the log.

This Restart algorithm not only uses LSNs in data items to ensure a data item is in the appropriate state before applying a logical log record, but it also avoids unnecessary undos and redos. For example, during Restart's undo scan of the log, in case (3) just given ($LSN(x) > LSN(U)$), x already contains a committed value that is "later" than the one that $undo(U)$ would have restored (had it been correct to do so). The Restart algorithm for partial data item *physical* logging would have undone U anyway, and then would redo V (the update record that produced the current value of x) during the forward scan. Using LSNs, we save the unnecessary work of $undo(U)$ and $redo(V)$. Thus, the use of LSNs in data items is valuable even with partial data item physical logging (see Exercise 6.26).

Logical logging may be especially useful for logical operations that update more than one data item. For example, in a dynamic search structure, such as a B-tree or dynamic hash table, an insertion of a single record may cause a page (i.e., data item) to be split, resulting in updates to three or more pages. One can save considerable log space by only logging the insertion, and leaving it to the undo and redo procedures to update all of the relevant pages.

However, a problem arises if the system fails when the database does not contain all of the updates performed by a single logical operation. For example, suppose operation o updates data items x, y, and z. (Operation o could be an insertion into a B-tree, which causes half of node x to be moved into a new node, z, and causes x's parent, y, to be updated to include a pointer to z.) After logging o in log record LR, the RM updates x and y, which are written to the stable database. But before the RM updates z, the system fails. Now, x and y contain LR's LSN, but z contains an earlier LSN. A straightforward implementation of $undo(LR)$ and $redo(LR)$ may not be able to properly interpret this mixed state of x, y, and z. To avoid this problem, a separate update record should be produced for each data item that is modified by the logical update.

Record Level Locking

Suppose we use a 2PL scheduler that locks records, where many records are stored on each page, and a page is the unit of atomic transfer to stable storage. To gain the benefit of record level locking, executions cannot be strict at the level of pages. If they were, then two active transactions could not concurrently update two different records on the same page, in which case they might as well lock pages instead of records. The next best alternative is to have executions be strict at the level of records. That is, a transaction can only write into a record r if all previous transactions that wrote into r have either committed or aborted.

Since the execution is strict, we can use the undo/redo algorithm for physical data item logging. Alternatively, we can use the logical logging algorithm, provided we make an adjustment for the way LSNs are handled during undo. To illustrate the problem, suppose records r_1 and r_2 are stored on the same page p. Consider the following history, which represents an execution of transactions T_i, T_j, and T_k: $w_i[r_1]\, c_i\, w_j[r_1]\, w_k[r_2]\, c_k\, a_j$. As the RM processes this execution, it produces a log. In fact, since there are no Reads in the execution, the log has exactly one record for each operation in the history. It will be convenient, for the moment, to use the history notation as representation for the log (e.g., the log record describing T_i's update of database record r_1 will be denoted "$w_i[r_1]$," etc.).

Using the previous approach on this log, to process a_j we would undo $w_j[r_1]$ and install $w_i[r_1]$'s LSN on p (which is the last update to p before $w_j[r_1]$). But this is the wrong LSN, because p contains $w_k[r_2]$, which has a larger LSN. In fact, there is no LSN that one can install in p to represent the precise state of p.

One good way around this problem is to write a log record for each undo that is performed. In the example, the log would now be $w_i[r_1]\, c_i\, w_j[r_1]\, w_k[r_2]\, c_k\, undo(w_j[r_1])$, where "$undo(w_j[r_1])$" is a log record that records the fact that $w_j[r_1]$ was undone. When performing the undo, the RM can install the LSN of $undo(w_j[r_1])$ in p, which correctly describes the state of p relative to the log. Since we can trust a data item's LSN to tell us the exact state of the data item relative to the log, we can use the Restart procedure that we just described for LSN-based logging (Exercise 6.23).

However, there are complications to consider. One is undoing and redoing log records that describe undos. For example, if the system fails after $undo(w_j[r_1])$ in the execution being discussed, then during the backward log scan Restart should undo the log record for $undo(w_j[r_1])$ and then undo the log record for $w_j[r_1]$. Another issue is the logging done by Restart itself. Suppose Restart logs the undos it performs during the backward scan. Then an execution of Restart that is interrupted by a system failure has lengthened the log, giving it more work to do when it is invoked again. In theory, it might never terminate, even if the intervals between successive failures grow monotonically (see Exercise 6.24).

A second approach is to store LSNs in records rather than pages. To undo $w_j[r_1]$ in the example under discussion now requires no special treatment; just assign to r_1's LSN the LSN of the previous update record reflecting a Write on r_1 (see Exercise 6.25). This method avoids the complications associated with logging undos, but incurs extra space overhead for an LSN per data item.

6.5 THE UNDO/NO-REDO ALGORITHM

In this section we present a DM algorithm that never requires redo. To achieve this, the algorithm records all of a transaction's updates in the stable database before that transaction commits. This can be achieved by a slight modification of the algorithm in Section 6.4. In fact, the RM-Write, RM-Read, and RM-Abort procedures are precisely the same. RM-Commit and Restart are outlined next.

RM-Commit(T_i)

1. For each data item x updated by T_i, if x is in the cache, flush the slot it occupies.
2. Add T_i to the commit list.[A]
3. Acknowledge the commitment of T_i to the scheduler.
4. Delete T_i from the active list.

Restart

1. Discard all cache slots.
2. Let $undone := \{\}$.
3. Start with the last entry in the log and scan backwards to the beginning. Repeat the following steps until either $undone$ equals the set of data items in the database, or there are no more log entries to examine. For each log entry $[T_i, x, v]$, if T_i is not in the commit list and $x \notin undone$, then:
   - allocate a slot for x in the cache;
   - copy the before image of x wrt T_i into x's cache slot;
   $undone := undone \cup \{x\}$.
4. For each T_i in the commit list, if T_i is in the active list, remove it from the active list.[B]
5. Acknowledge the completion of Restart to the scheduler.

Comments

A. [Step (2) of RM-Commit(T_i)] This is the action that declares a transaction committed. If the system fails before T_i is added to the commit list, Restart will consider T_i uncommitted and will abort it (see Restart).
B. [Step (2) of Restart] The system failure may have occurred after step (2) but before step (4) of RM-Commit(T_i). Thus it is possible for T_i to be found both in the active and the commit list. In this case, the transaction must be considered committed (see comment (A)).

This RM-Commit procedure is essentially the same as in the undo/redo algorithm of Section 6.4, with the addition of step (1) to ensure that all of a transaction's updates are in the stable database by the time the transaction commits. This means that redo is never required, resulting in a more efficient Restart procedure.

This algorithm satisfies the Undo Rule. The argument is the same as for the undo/redo algorithm. It also satisfies the Redo Rule for the trivial reason that it does not require redo, because all Writes are recorded in the stable database before the transaction that issued them can commit. Since the two rules are satisfied, Restart can always restore in the stable database the last committed value of each data item, using only information in stable storage. Also, Restart is idempotent. Since Restart does not alter the set of transactions it acts on, if it were interrupted by a system failure it would repeat exactly the same work.

Implementation

With minor modifications, the log structure that was described for partial data item logging can be used to implement the undo/no-redo algorithm. As before, the log is a sequential disk file consisting of update, commit, abort, and checkpoint records. The only difference is that update records need not include after images. Since this algorithm never requires redo, the information becomes useless.

To reflect the change in the RM-Commit procedure, all cache slots written by a transaction must be flushed before the commit record is appended to the log. One can view this as a limited kind of checkpoint. However, we still need checkpointing to ensure that restored before images of aborted transactions are eventually recorded in the stable database. It is possible to eliminate checkpoints altogether from this algorithm by appropriately modifying RM-Abort (see Exercise 6.27).

If transactions have random reference patterns, then few of the data items updated by a transaction are likely to be updated again before becoming candidates for replacement. Therefore, the work in flushing a data item at commit isn't wasted, although forcing it at commit may increase response time. However, for a hot spot data item, the required flush for every committed Write may create a heavy I/O load that would not be experienced using undo/redo.

Another way of implementing RM-Commit in this algorithm is to take a cache consistent checkpoint just before adding a transaction to the commit list (i.e., instead of step (1) of RM-Commit). This means checkpointing (by flushing *all* dirty cache slots) each time a transaction commits. This is a viable method if the cache is not too large and the database system is not designed to handle a very high rate of transactions.

The undo/no-redo algorithm can be integrated nicely with the multiversion concurrency control algorithm described in Section 5.4. All versions of a data item are chained together in a linked list in stable storage. The versions appear in the list in the order in which they were produced, from youngest to oldest. The RM-Abort procedure can arrange to exclude versions produced by aborted transactions from the chain. The head of the list is the most recently created version (possibly written by an active transaction). Since the multiple copies themselves contain the data item's before images, we do not need a log. Said differently, the multiple copies of all data items constitute the log, but they are not structured as a sequential file. To ensure no-redo, the RM must flush the cache slots containing versions produced by a transaction before that transaction commits. To undo versions written by active or aborted transactions that were flushed to stable storage before a system failure, Restart must be able to distinguish versions written by committed transactions from those written by aborted or active ones. This is accomplished by tagging each version by the (unique) transaction that produced it, as in Section 5.4, and by maintaining commit, abort, and active lists (see Exercise 6.28). This implementation is used in DBS products of Prime Computer.

An interesting variation of this scheme is to transfer the undo activity from Restart to RM-Read. That is, Restart does not perform any undos, leaving it with nothing to do at all. When RM-Read reads a data item, it checks whether the data item's tag is in the commit list. If so, it processes it normally. If not, then it discards (i.e., undoes) that version and tries reading the next older version instead. It continues reading older versions until it finds a committed one. This algorithm eliminates Restart activity at the cost of more expensive RM-Reads, a good trade-off if system failures are frequent.

6.6 THE NO-UNDO/REDO ALGORITHM

In this section we'll present another RM algorithm, one that may require redo but never requires undo. To avoid undo, we must avoid recording updates of uncommitted transactions in the stable database. For this reason, when a data item is written, the new value is not recorded in the cache at that time; this happens only after a transaction commits. Consequently, when a new value is recorded in the stable database as a result of a cache slot's being replaced or flushed, it is assuredly the value of a committed transaction and will never need to be undone.

The five RM procedures are outlined next.

RM-Write(T_i, x, v)

  1. Append a $[T_i, x, v]$ record to the log.
  2. Acknowledge to the scheduler the processing of RM-Write(T_i, x, v).

RM-Read(T_i, x)

  1. If T_i has previously written into x, then return to the scheduler the after image of x wrt T_i.$^{(A)}$

2. Otherwise,
   - if x is not in the cache, fetch it;
   - return to the scheduler the value in x's cache slot.

RM-Commit(T_i)

1. Add T_i to the commit list.[B]
2. For each x updated by T_i:
   - if x is not in the cache, fetch it;
   - copy the after image of x wrt T_i into x's cache slot.[A]
3. Acknowledge the processing of RM-Commit(T_i) to the scheduler.

RM-Abort(T_i)

1. Add T_i to the abort list.[C]
2. Acknowledge the processing of RM-Abort(T_i) to the scheduler.

Restart

1. Discard all cache slots.
2. Let $redone := \{\}$.
3. Start with the last entry in the log and scan backwards toward the beginning. Repeat the following steps until either $redone$ equals the set of data items in the database, or there are no more log entries to examine. For each log entry $[T_i, x, v]$, if T_i is in the commit list and $x \notin redone$, then
   - allocate a slot for x in the cache;
   - copy v into x's cache slot;
   - $redone := redone \cup \{x\}$.
4. Acknowledge the processing of Restart to the scheduler.

Comments

A. [Step (1) of RM-Read(T_i, x), step (2) of RM-Commit(T_i)] The after image of x wrt T_i can be found in the log. It is inserted there by RM-Write.

B. [Step (1) of RM-Commit(T_i)] This is the action that declares a transaction committed.

C. [Step (1) of RM-Abort(T_i)] At the level we are describing things, the abort list is not needed (it is only mentioned in this step). In practice, information in that list might be used by the garbage collector to recycle log space that contains information pertaining to aborted transactions.

This algorithm satisfies the Redo Rule: Each value written by a transaction is recorded in the log by RM-Write and, by the Garbage Collection Rule, it cannot have been deleted by the time the transaction commits. The Undo Rule is also satisfied for the trivial reason that the algorithm does not require undo. Since both rules are satisfied, Restart will always find in stable storage all of the information it needs to restore the stable database to its committed state. Since Restart does not affect the set of committed transactions, if it were interrupted by a system failure it would repeat exactly the same work and hence is idempotent.

Implementation

We can implement this algorithm using a log structure similar to that employed for the previous two algorithms. The elimination of undo simplifies matters in several ways. First, there is no need to bother with abort records. Second, since undo is never required, the update records need not contain before images. Since finding the before images to be included in the update record may require an additional access to the stable database, this feature could be important. As usual, checkpointing must be used to limit the amount of time an update can stay in the cache before it is flushed. Any of the techniques described in Section 6.4 can be used.

Various other structures for the log have been proposed for the no-undo/redo algorithm. A common one is *intentions lists*. In effect, the log is organized as a collection of lists, one per transaction, which are kept in stable storage. T_i's list contains the after images (wrt T_i) of all data items updated by T_i. These updates are not applied to the stable database before the transaction commits. Thus, we can think of the list as containing the transaction's "intentions." If a transaction aborts, its intentions list is simply discarded. If a transaction commits, its list is marked accordingly and flushed to stable storage, and the updates contained therein are applied to the stable database one at a time. When this is completed, the intentions list is discarded. On Restart, all intentions lists are inspected. Those not marked as committed are simply discarded. The rest have their updates applied to the stable database and are then discarded as in the commit process. Note that a particular update could be redone more than once if Restart is interrupted by a system failure, but this causes no harm.

Although Writes are not applied to the database until the transaction commits, they may need to be read sooner than that. If a transaction writes x and subsequently reads it, then the Read must return the previously written value.[8] Since the transaction is not yet committed, the value of x is not in the

---

[8]This is same problem we encountered in Section 5.5, where we delayed the application of a transaction's Writes until it terminates. Since that multiversion concurrency control algorithm requires this mechanism for reading from the intentions list, it fits especially neatly with no-undo/redo recovery.

database or cache. So the RM must find the value in the intentions list (i.e., step (1) of RM-Read). Doing this efficiently takes some care. One way is to index the intentions list by data item name. On each RM-Read(T_i, x), the RM checks the index for an entry for x. If there is one, it returns the last intentions list value for x. Otherwise, it finds x in the database (i.e., step (2) of RM-Read).

Another way to solve the problem is by using shadowing; see Exercise 6.30.

6.7 THE NO-UNDO/NO-REDO ALGORITHM

To avoid redo, all of a transaction T_i's updates must be in the stable database by the time T_i is committed. To avoid undo, none of T_i's updates can be in the stable database before T_i is committed. Hence, to eliminate both undo and redo, all of T_i's updates must be recorded in the stable database in a single atomic operation, at the time T_i commits. The RM-Commit(T_i) procedure would have to be something like the following:

RM-Commit(T_i)

1. In a single atomic action:
- For each data item x updated by T_i, write the after image of x wrt T_i in the stable database.
- Insert T_i into the commit list.

2. Acknowledge to the scheduler the processing of RM-Commit(T_i).

Incredible as it may sound, such a procedure is realizable! The difficulty, of course, is to organize the data structures so that an atomic action — a single atomic Write to stable storage — has the entire effect of step (1) in RM-Commit. That is, it must indivisibly install all of a transaction's updates in the stable database and insert T_i into the commit list. It should do this without placing an unreasonable upper bound on the number of updates each transaction may perform.

We can attain these goals by using a form of shadowing. The location of each data item's last committed value is recorded in a directory, stored in stable storage, and possibly cached for fast access. There are also working directories that point to uncommitted versions of some data items. Together, these directories point to all of the before and after images that would ordinarily be stored in a log. We therefore do not maintain a log as a separate sequential file.

When a transaction T_i writes a data item x, a new version of x is created in stable storage. The working directory that defines the database state used by T_i is updated to point to this version. Conceptually, this new version is part of the log until T_i commits. When T_i commits, the directory that defines the committed database state is updated to point to the versions that T_i wrote. This makes the results of T_i's Writes become part of the committed database state, thereby committing T_i.

With this structure, an RM-Commit procedure with the desired properties requires atomically changing the directory entries for *all* data items written by the transaction that is being committed. If the directory fits in a single data item, then the problem is solved. Otherwise, it seems we have simply moved our problem to a different structure. Instead of atomically installing updates in the stable database, we now have to atomically install updates in the directory.

The critical difference is that since the directory is much smaller than the database, it is feasible to keep two copies of it in stable storage: a *current* directory, pointing to the committed database, and a *scratch* copy. To commit a transaction T_i, the RM updates the scratch directory to represent the stable database state that includes T_i's updates. That is, for each data item x that T_i updates, the RM makes the scratch directory's entry for x point to T_i's new version of x. For data items that T_i did not update, it makes the scratch directory's entries identical to the current directory's entries. Then it swaps the current and scratch directories in an atomic action. This atomic swap action is implemented through a *master record* in stable storage, which has a bit indicating which of the two directory copies is the current one. To swap the directories, the RM simply complements the bit in the master record, which is surely an atomic action! Writing that bit is the operation that commits the transaction. Notice that the RM can only process one Commit at a time. That is, the activity of updating the scratch directory followed by complementing the master record bit is a critical section.

Figure 6–4 illustrates the structures used in the algorithm to commit transaction T_i which updated data items x and y. In Fig. 6–4(a) the transaction has created two new versions, leaving the old versions intact as shadows (appropriately shaded). In Fig. 6–4(b) T_i has set up the scratch directory to reflect the stable database as it should be after its commitment. In Fig. 6–4(c) the master record's bit is flipped, thereby committing T_i and installing its updates in the stable database. Note that there are two levels of indirection to obtain the current value of a data item. First the master record indicates the appropriate directory, and then the directory gives the data item's address in the stable database.

Before describing the five RM procedures, let us define some notation for the stable storage organization used in this algorithm. We have a master record, M, that stores a single bit. We have two directories D^0 and D^1. At any time D^b is the current directory, where b is the present value of M. $D^b[x]$ denotes the entry for data item x in directory D^b. It contains x's address in the stable database. We use $-b$ to denote the complement of b, so D^{-b} is the scratch directory. There may be one or two versions of a data item at any given time: one in the stable database (pointed to by D^b and possibly a new version. All this information — the stable database, the new versions, the two directories, and the master record — must be kept in stable storage. The master record and the directories can also be cached for efficient access.

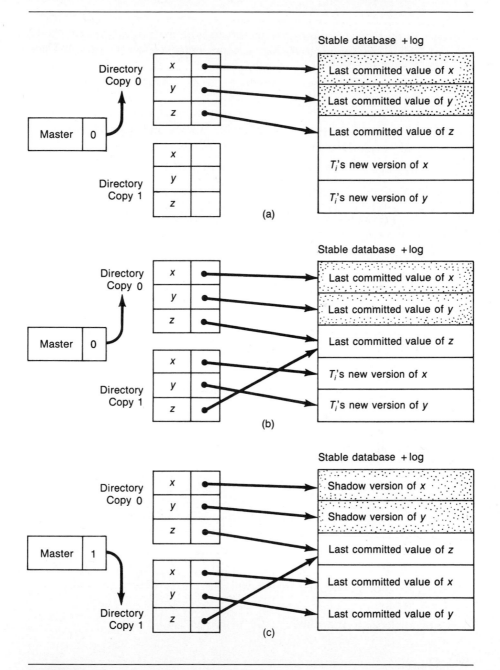

FIGURE 6–4
An Example of the No-Undo/No-Redo Algorithm
(a) Database state after creating new versions for T_i (b) Database state after preparing
directory for T_i's commitment (c) Database state after committing T_i

In addition, for each active transaction T_i there is a directory D_i with the addresses of the new versions of the data items written by T_i. $D_i[x]$ denotes the entry of D_i that corresponds to data item x (presumably T_i wrote into x). These directories need not be stored in stable storage. Given this organization of data, the RM procedures are as follows.

RM-Write(T_i, x, v)

1. Write v into an unused location in stable storage and record this location's address in $D_i[x]$.(A)

2. Acknowledge to the scheduler the processing of RM-Write(T_i, x, v).

RM-Read(T_i, x)

1. If T_i has previously written into x, return to the scheduler the value stored in the location pointed to by $D_i[x]$.

2. Otherwise, return to the scheduler the value stored in the location pointed to by $D^b[x]$, where b is the present value of the bit in the master record M.(B)

RM-Commit(T_i)

1. For each x updated by T_i: $D^{-b}[x] := D_i[x]$, where b is the value of M.(C)

2. $M := -b$.(D)

3. For each x updated by T_i: $D^{-b}[x] := D_i[x]$, where b is the (new) value of M.(E)

4. Discard D_i (free any storage used by it).

5. Acknowledge to the scheduler the processing of RM-Commit(T_i).

RM-Abort(T_i)

1. Discard D_i.

2. Acknowledge to the scheduler the processing of RM-Abort(T_i).

Restart

1. Copy D^b into D^{-b}.

2. Free any storage reserved for active transactions' directories and their new versions.

3. Acknowledge to the scheduler the processing of Restart.

Comments

A. [Step (1) of RM-Write] This step creates the new version of x, leaving the shadow version in the stable database untouched.

B. [Step (2) of RM-Read] If T_i has written into x it reads the new version of x that it created when it wrote into x (see step (1) of RM-Write); otherwise it reads the version of x in the stable database.

C. [Step (1) of RM-Commit] This step sets up the scratch directory to reflect the updates of T_i.

D. [Step (2) of RM-Commit] This step complements the bit in the master record, thereby making the scratch directory into the current one (and what used to be the current into the scratch). It is the atomic action that makes T_i committed. Failure before this step will result in T_i's abortion.

E. [Step (3) of RM-Commit] This step records T_i's changes in D^{-b}, which has now become the scratch directory. This ensures that when that directory again becomes the current one, T_i's updates will be properly reflected in the stable database.

The algorithm satisfies the Undo Rule since the stable database never has values written by uncommitted transactions. It also satisfies the Redo Rule because at the time of commitment all of a transaction's updates are in the stable database. In fact, under this algorithm the stable database *always* contains the last committed database state. As a result, virtually no work is needed to abort a transaction or restart the system following a failure.

While Restart is efficient, this algorithm does have three important costs during normal operation. First, accesses to stable storage are indirect and therefore more expensive. However, this cost may be small if the directory is small enough to be stored in cache. Second, finding uncommitted versions and reclaiming their space may be difficult to do efficiently, given the absence of a log. Third, and most importantly, the movement of data to new versions destroys the original layout of the stable database. That is, when a data item is updated, there may not be space for the new copy close to the original data item's (i.e., its shadow's) location. When the update is committed, the data item has changed location from the shadow to the new version. Thus, if the database is designed so that related data items are stored in nearby stable storage locations, that design will be compromised over time as some of those data items are updated. For example, if records of a file are originally stored contiguously on disk for efficient sequential access, they will eventually be spread into other locations thereby slowing down sequential access. This problem is common to many implementations of shadowing.

Because of the organization of the log, this algorithm is also known as the *shadow version algorithm*. And because of the way in which it commits a transaction, by atomically recording all of a transaction's updates in the stable database, it has also been called the *careful replacement algorithm*.

6.8 MEDIA FAILURES

As with recovery from system failures, the goal of recovery from media failures is to ensure the system's ability to reconstruct the last committed value of each data item. The difference is in the availability of memory we can rely on. In a system failure, we could rely on the availability of all the information the DM had been wise enough to save in stable storage. In a media failure, recovery cannot proceed on this assumption, since by definition such failures destroy part of stable storage — perhaps exactly the part needed by Restart.

Our only recourse is to maintain redundant copies of every data item's last committed value. This provides protection to the extent it can be assured that one of the redundant copies will survive a media failure. Thus the recovery mechanism for media failures must be designed with a probabilistic goal in mind: minimize the probability that all copies of a data item's last committed value are destroyed. By contrast, the recovery mechanism for system failures is designed with an absolute goal: guarantee the availability of the last committed value of each data item *in stable storage*. Of course, this only provides absolute protection against *system* failures, in which stable storage survives by definition.

Resiliency to media failure can be increased by increasing the number of copies kept. But at least as important as the *number* of copies is *where* these copies are stored. We want the copies to be kept on devices with *independent failure modes*. This means that no single failure event can destroy more than one copy. To achieve, or rather to approximate, independence of failures requires a detailed knowledge of the kinds of events that are likely to cause media failures in a particular system. Thus, keeping two copies on different disk drives is better than two copies on the same drive; since disk drives tend to fail independently, copies on two different drives may survive a single failure while copies on the same drive may not. Using disk drives with different controllers helps tolerate a controller's failure. Keeping the disk drives in separate rooms enhances the probability of the drives' surviving a fire. The perceived probability of such failures and the cost of minimizing their impact will determine how far the designer cares to go in protecting different media from common failure modes.

In practice, keeping two copies of the last committed value of each data item on two different devices is deemed to be sufficient protection for most applications. One approach, called *mirroring*, is to keep a duplicate copy of each disk on-line, in the form of a second disk. That is, the contents of each disk have an identical copy on another disk, its *mirror*. Since every data item is now stored on two disks, every Write must now be applied to two disks. Moreover, to ensure that the two disks are kept identical, Writes must be applied to both disks in the same order. To protect against the simultaneous failure of both disks, e.g., due to a power failure, it is safer to perform each pair of Writes in sequence: First write to one disk, wait for the acknowledgment, then write to the other disk. A Read can be sent to either disk that holds the desired data. So, mirrored disks increase the disks' capacity for Reads but not for Writes.

If a disk fails, then its mirror automatically handles all of the Reads that were formerly split between them. When the failed disk recovers or is replaced, it must be brought up-to-date by copying the contents of its up-to-date mirror. This can be done efficiently using the techniques for initializing a replicated database described in Chapter 8.[9]

Another approach to keeping duplicate copies is *archiving*. Periodically, the value of each data item is written (or *dumped*) to an *archive database*. The log contains (at least) all of the updates applied to the database since the last dump. Moreover, the log itself is mirrored. If a media failure destroys one of the log copies, the other one can be used. If a media failure destroys the contents of the stable database, then we execute a Restart algorithm using the log and archive database to bring the archive to the committed state with respect to the log.

This approach to media failures surely requires redo to bring the archive database to the committed state. Therefore, after images of Writes must be in the log. These after images are needed for media failures, even if we are using a no-redo algorithm for system failures (which ordinarily doesn't need after images). If the archive database contains uncommitted updates, then media failure recovery requires undo as well.

Producing an archive database is essentially the same as checkpointing the stable database. To distinguish them, we call the former *archive checkpointing* and the latter *stable checkpointing*. In each case, we are trying to avoid too much redo activity by making a copy of the database more up-to-date: the archive database for media failures, and the stable copy for system failures. For stable checkpointing, we (1) update the log to indicate which logged updates are in the stable database, and possibly (2) update the stable database to include updates that are only in cache. For archive checkpointing, we (1) update the log to indicate which logged updates are in the archive database, and possibly (2) update the archive database to include updates that are only in the stable database and cache. Thus, to modify a stable Checkpoint procedure to become an archive Checkpoint procedure, we simply substitute "the archive database" for "the stable database" and substitute "the stable database and the cache" for "the cache" in the definition of the procedure. Let's revisit the stable checkpointing algorithms of Section 6.4 with this correspondence in mind.

In commit consistent stable checkpointing, we complete the execution of all active transactions, flush the cache, and mark the log to indicate that the checkpoint has occurred. To modify this for archive checkpointing, we replace

---

[9]Briefly speaking, we can bring the mirror up-to-date by running "copier transactions." Copiers are synchronized like any user transaction (e.g., using 2PL). As soon as the recovering mirror is operational (i.e., before it is up-to-date), user transactions write into both disks. A data item copy in the recovering mirror cannot be read until it has been written at least once. See Sections 8.5 and 8.6.

"flush the cache" by "write to the archive all data items that were updated (in the stable database or cache) since the last archive checkpoint." To do this, for each data item in stable storage there must be a dirty bit that tells whether the data item has been updated in stable storage since it was last written to the archive database. (It needn't tell whether the data item has been updated in cache, since the cache slots' dirty bits give this information.) Checkpoint clears this bit after the data item is written to the archive (i.e., after the archive storage device has acknowledged the Write). After a media failure, Restart brings the archive to the committed state by redoing updates of transactions that committed after the last *archive checkpoint record* (i.e., the last checkpoint record written by archive checkpointing).

In cache consistent stable checkpointing, we complete the execution of all RM operations, flush the cache, and mark the log to indicate that the checkpoint has occurred. We modify this for archive checkpointing in exactly the same way we modified commit consistent checkpointing. The archive checkpoint record in the log should include a list of transactions that were active at the last checkpoint. After a media failure, Restart brings the archive to the committed state by redoing the update records that followed the last archive checkpoint record and were issued by committed transactions, and undoing transactions that were active at the last archive checkpoint and did not subsequently commit.

Cache consistent archive checkpointing is an improvement over commit consistent archive checkpointing in that the RM does not need to wait for all active transactions to terminate before initiating the checkpointing activity. However, commit consistent archive checkpointing provides a second line of defense if the stable database and both copies of the log are destroyed. We can at least restore a database state that reflects a consistent point in the past, merely by loading the archive database as the stable database. In some applications, this is an acceptable compromise.

The problem with both of these algorithms is the delay involved in bringing the archive up-to-date during the checkpoint procedure. This is a much bigger performance problem than flushing the cache in stable checkpointing, for two reasons. First, there is more data to write to the archive — all data items that were written since the previous archive checkpoint, even if they are in the stable database. And second, much of the data to be written to the archive database must first be read from the stable database. This delay is intolerable for many applications.

One way to avoid the delay is to use shadowing. When archive checkpointing begins, an *archive shadow directory* is created, which defines the state of the database at the time checkpointing began. An archive checkpoint record is written to the log to indicate that Checkpointing has begun. Now the RM can resume normal operation in parallel with checkpointing. When the RM processes an update to the stable database, it leaves intact the shadow page which is still referenced by the archive shadow directory. When the checkpointing procedure terminates, it writes another archive checkpoint record in the log, which says that all of the log updates up to the *previous* archive checkpoint record are now in the archive database.

Another way to avoid the delay is to use a variation of fuzzy checkpointing. When archive checkpointing begins, it writes a begin-archive-checkpoint record that includes a list of transactions that are active at this time. It then reads from the stable database those data items that have been written since the previous begin-archive-checkpoint record and copies them to the archive database. The RM can process operations concurrently with this activity. When Checkpoint terminates, it writes an end-archive-checkpoint record, indicating that all log updates up to the previous begin-archive-checkpoint record are now in the archive database, and possibly some later ones as well. Restart for media failures can now function like the Restart algorithm described in Section 6.4 for partial data item physical logging. The only difference is in the interpretation of checkpoint records; the last matched pair of begin-archive-checkpoint/end-archive-checkpoint records should be regarded as the penultimate and last checkpoint records, respectively. Notice that the backward scan of the log for undo is only needed beginning with the second (i.e., the one closer to the end of the log) of the last pair of archive checkpoint records, because later update records in the log could not have been written to the archive during the last checkpointing activity.

Media failures frequently only corrupt a small portion of the database, such as a few cylinders of a disk, or only one of many disk packs. The Restart procedures we just described are designed to restore the *entire* archive database to its committed state. The performance of Restart for partial media failures can be improved substantially by designing it to restore a defined set of data items (see Exercise 6.34).

To reduce the software complexity of the RM, it is valuable to design archive and stable checkpointing so that exactly the same Restart procedure can be used for system and media failures, the only difference being the choice of stable or archive database and stable or archive log. The algorithms we described for commit consistent checkpointing and cache consistent checkpointing (with and without shadowing) have this property. The one we described for fuzzy checkpointing requires some modification to attain this property (see Exercise 6.35).

BIBLIOGRAPHIC NOTES

The undo-redo paradigm for understanding centralized DBS recovery grew from the early work of [Bjork 73], [Bjork, Davies 72], and [Davies 73], and from work on fault tolerant computing (e.g., see [Anderson, Lee 81], [Shrivastava 85], and [Siewiorek, Swarz 82]). The categorization of algorithms by their undo and redo characteristics was developed independently in the survey papers [Bernstein, Goodman, Hadzilacos 83] and [Haerder, Reuter 83]. Shadowing is discussed in [Lorie 77], [Reuter 80], [Verhofstad 77], and [Verhofstad 78]. The undo/redo model and its connection to recoverability is formalized in [Hadzilacos 83] and [Hadzilacos 86]. Strategies for cache management are described in [Effelsberg, Haerder 84].

In this chapter, we assumed strict executions throughout. Some aspects of cascading aborts are discussed in [Briatico, Ciuffoletti, Simoncini 84] and [Hadzilacos 82].

The undo/redo algorithm for partial data item physical logging is from [Gray 78]. A discussion of the many subtleties of logging algorithms appears in [Traiger 82]. Using LSNs in pages is described in [Lindsay 80]. Logging algorithms for particular DBSs are described in [Crus 84] (IBM's DB2), [Gray et al. 81a] (IBM's System R), [Ong 84] (Synapse), and [Peterson, Strickland 83] (IBM's IMS).

Undo/no-redo algorithms are described in [Chan et al. 82] (CCA's Adaplex), [Dubourdieu 82] (Prime's DBSs), and [Rappaport 75] (where undo is performed by Reads, as described at the end of Section 6.5). Redo/no-undo algorithms are described in [Bayer 83], [Elhardt, Bayer 84], [Lampson, Sturgis 76], [Menasce, Landes 80], and [Stonebraker 79b] (the university version of INGRES). The no-undo/no-redo algorithm in Section 6.7 is from [Lorie 77].

The performance of recovery algorithms has been analyzed in [Garcia-Molina, Kent, Chung 85], [Griffeth, Miller 84], and [Reuter 84]. Recovery algorithms for database machines are discussed in [Agrawal, DeWitt 85a].

EXERCISES

6.1   Consider disk hardware that provides no checksum protection. We can partially compensate for this missing functionality by the following technique: Put a serial number in the first and last word of the block; put the disk address of the block in the second word of the block; and increment the serial number every time the block is written. What types of errors can we detect using this method? What types of errors are not detected? What types of CM and RM algorithms would best compensate for the weak error detection functionality?

6.2   Suppose that the disk hardware provides checksum protection on the address and data of each *sector* (i.e., each fixed length segment of a track). Suppose that the operating system offers Read and Write commands on pages, each page consisting of two sectors. What additional behavior of the disk hardware and operating system would you require (if any) so that the RM can view each Write of a page as an atomic operation? Suppose the operating system can report errors on a sector-by-sector basis. How might this information be used by the CM or RM to improve its performance?

6.3   Suppose each Write is either atomic or causes a media failure. Is it still useful for a Write to respond with a return code indicating whether it executed in its entirety or not at all, assuming that the return code is not reliable in the event of a media failure? Why?

6.4   Sketch the design of a cache manager for in-place updating, assuming page level granularity. In addition to supporting Fetch and Flush, your CM should give the RM the ability to specify the order in which any pair of pages is written to disk (e.g., to satisfy the undo and redo rules). You may assume that the CM will be used by an RM that does undo/redo logging. Remember that the RM will use the interface to read and write log pages as well as data item pages. Treat the replacement strategy as an uninterpreted procedure, but do define the interface to that procedure. What measures of performance did you use in selecting your design? What assumptions about application behavior did you make when deciding among alternative approaches? What alternatives did you reject for performance reasons?

6.5 Suppose the scheduler produces SR executions that avoid cascading aborts but are not strict. Suppose that the order of log records is consistent with the order in which the RM executed Writes. If $[T_i, x, u]$ precedes $[T_j, x, v]$ in the log, then what can you say about the order of Write, Commit, and Abort operations in the history that produced that log? What else can you say about the order of operations if you are given that T_j read x before writing it?

6.6 Since many transactions are writing entries to the end of the log concurrently, the RM must synchronize those log updates. This becomes a hot spot when the transaction rate becomes too high. Propose two mechanisms to minimize the effect of this hot spot. Describe the effects that each of the mechanisms has on Restart, if any.

6.7 Suppose we use an archive database and log to handle media recovery. Restate the Undo, Redo, and Garbage Collection Rules to properly reflect the combined requirements of system failures and media failures.

6.8 In cache consistent or fuzzy checkpointing, it is possible that a long running transaction prevents the RM from garbage collecting the log. How can this happen? One solution is to rewrite the log records of long running transactions at the end of the log. Suppose we take this approach in the partial data item logging algorithm. Checkpoint should find all log records that precede the penultimate checkpoint record and that are needed to handle transactions that are still active at the last checkpoint, and it should rewrite them at the end of the log. Restart should make appropriate use of these rewritten log records. Sketch the modifications needed for Checkpoint and Restart to perform these activities. Compare the cost and benefit of this algorithm with the approach in which Checkpoint aborts any transactions that are active at two consecutive checkpoints.

6.9 Consider the following variation on fuzzy checkpointing. Each execution of Checkpoint *initiates* flushes of all those cache slots that have not been flushed since before the previous checkpoint. Before writing its checkpoint record and allowing the RM to resume normal operation, it waits until all flushes initiated by the *previous* invocation of Checkpoint have completed. However, it does not wait until the flushes that *it* initiated have completed. Compare the performance of this fuzzy Checkpoint procedure with Restart algorithm described in the chapter. How does this new Checkpoint procedure affect the behavior of Restart for the partial data item logging algorithm?

6.10 Suppose that we allow the RM to continue to process operations while a cache consistent checkpointing procedure is in progress. Checkpoint must pin (or otherwise lock) each data item x while it is writing it to the stable database, to avoid interfering with RM-Writes to x. Under what conditions can Checkpoint write a checkpoint record in the log and terminate? Is Checkpoint in any danger of becoming involved in a deadlock or of being indefinitely postponed? If so, give a method for circumventing the problem.

6.11 When Restart begins executing after a system failure, it must find the end of the log. Propose a method for doing this. Remember that your method can only use information in stable storage for this purpose. What control information regarding the log is kept on stable storage? How often is it updated? Estimate the average time required for Restart to find the end of the log, e.g., measured in number of stable storage accesses.

6.12 Rewrite the Restart procedure for the partial data item logging algorithm in pseudo-code. Include the optimizations A1, A2, C1, and C2. Write a procedure to garbage collect the log, assuming that the log is not needed for media recovery. Explain why the algorithm produces the committed database state.

6.13 In the partial data item logging algorithm, it is unnecessary to undo any of T_i's updates if the LSN of T_i's abort record is less than the minimum stable-LSN over all dirty cache slots at the time of the last checkpoint. Similarly, it it is unnecessary to redo any update record with LSN less than the minimum stable-LSN over those cache slots. Explain why. Modify your solution to Exercise 6.12 to incorporate these optimizations.

6.14 Ordinarily, the Restart procedure for the partial data item logging algorithm would have to reexecute from the beginning if it were interrupted by a system failure. Propose a method for checkpointing the Restart procedure, to reduce the amount of work Restart has to repeat after a system failure. To reduce the chances of damaging the existing log, Restart should only append records to the log; it should not modify any previously existing log records.

6.15 Is the Restart procedure for the partial data item logging algorithm still correct under the assumption that the scheduler avoids cascading abort but is not strict? If so, explain why. If not, propose a way of circumventing the problem without strengthening the scheduling guarantees beyond ACA and SR.

6.16 Design a garbage collection procedure for the partial data item logging algorithm. The procedure should run concurrently with ordinary RM processing, and should not affect Restart's ability to recover from a system failure. How would you lay out the log on disk to avoid head contention between RM logging and the garbage collection algorithm?

6.17 The last step of the Restart procedure for the partial data item logging algorithm was to execute Checkpoint twice. Why is one checkpoint not enough? What is the benefit of doing only one checkpoint? Under what conditions, if any, might this be a good compromise?

6.18 In a tightly-coupled multiprocessor computer, the sequential Restart procedure for the partial data item logging algorithm is limited to execute on only one processor. Propose a modification to the algorithm and/or log structure to exploit the inherent parallelism of the computer.

6.19 Suppose we use an undo/redo algorithm that logs complete data items, where data items *don't* contain the LSN of the update record that last modified it. Given the large amount of log space that update records will consume, it is undesirable to log both the before and after image of each Write. Suppose we avoid this problem by logging just the after image, since the before image must be somewhere earlier in the log. Suppose we use commit consistent checkpointing.

Define a data structure for the log (update records, checkpoint records, etc.). Describe algorithms that use that data structure to implement the five RM procedures and Checkpoint. What problems would you have to solve to extend your algorithm to handle cache consistent checkpointing?

6.20 Suppose we use an undo/redo algorithm that logs complete data items, and uses fuzzy checkpointing. Suppose each update record in the log contains the (complete) before and after image of the data item updated, and a pointer to the previous update record of the same transaction. Assume that each checkpoint record contains lists of transactions that committed and aborted since the previous checkpoint, in addition to a list of active transactions at the time of the checkpoint and the stable-LSNs of dirty cache slots.

Write a Restart procedure that recovers from a system failure by doing a single backward scan of the log. Compare the working storage requirements of this algorithm with those of Restart in the partial data item logging algorithm. What modifications would you need to make to handle partial data item logging and still be able to perform Restart with a single log scan?

6.21 In logical logging, suppose each update record describes an operation that is applied to at most one data item. Suppose we implement undo and redo procedures for all operations so that for each log record LR on data item x, $undo(LR)$ has no effect if x does not include LR's update, and

$redo(LR)$ has no effect if x already includes LR's update. Does Restart in the partial data item logging algorithm work correctly on a log with this structure? That is, assuming fuzzy checkpointing, is it correct to undo all uncommitted updates during a backward scan of the log, and then redo all committed updates during a forward scan? If so, argue the correctness of the algorithm. If not, explain why.

6.22   System R allows a single logical update record to cause an update to more than one data item. Work out the details of the System R RM algorithm described in Section 6.4 so that such multi-data-item updates are properly handled.

6.23   Revise the LSN-based logical logging algorithm for record locking so that it logs undos.

6.24   Suppose we use LSN-based logging and record locking, with logging of undos (see Exercise 6.23). If Restart logs undos during its backward scan of the log, and it is interrupted by a system failure, then it has more work to do on its next execution. It might not terminate, even if the inter-failure time grows with each execution. One approach is to have Restart periodically checkpoint its activity. Using this approach, or one of your own, sketch a method for ensuring that Restart always terminates, assuming that Restart logs undos and the interval between some two system failures is greater than some minimum value.

6.25   Revise the LSN-based logging algorithm so that it stores an LSN in every record rather than in every page (i.e., data item), and does not log undos.

6.26   The Restart procedure for the LSN-based logging algorithm saves unnecessary work by only undoing or redoing update records whose effect is not already in the stable copy of the data item. Characterize the set of data items that are read and written by Restart in the partial data item logging algorithm *without* LSNs in data items but are not read or written *with* LSNs in data items. What application and system parameters affect the size of this set (e.g., the number of dirty data items in cache at the time of failure, the number of log pages in between each pair of checkpoint records)? Derive a formula that estimates the size of this set as a function of these parameters.

6.27   In the undo/no-redo algorithm, checkpointing is needed because a data item containing an undone update may sit in cache for a long time without being flushed. Propose a modification to RM-Abort that avoids this problem, and therefore eliminates the need for checkpointing.

6.28   Describe the RM procedures for the undo/no-redo algorithm using multiversion concurrency control, as sketched in Section 6.5.

6.29   Suppose the entire database can fit in volatile storage. Design a no-undo/redo algorithm that logs partial data items and protects against system failures (i.e., no media recovery). Assume that the database is updated frequently, so that keeping the log small is important. Assume also that there is limited bandwidth to stable storage, so that a relatively small number of data items can be flushed per unit time. Notice that the only reason to flush data items is for checkpointing purposes. Propose a strategy for checkpointing that minimizes the time to recover from a system failure.

6.30   In the no-undo/redo algorithm, shadowing can be used to facilitate a transaction's reading data items that it previously wrote. When a transaction T_i first writes a data item x, a new version of x is created in stable storage and is written into a cache slot. The previous (i.e., shadow) version of x is not overwritten. Using this approach, each RM-Read from T_i can be processed normally on the database state that includes T_i's updates. Work out the details of this approach by providing algorithms for the five RM procedures.

6.31   Is it possible to modify the no-undo/no-redo algorithm to use record locking? If so, explain how. What are the performance implications? If not, explain why.

6.32   To compress the archive log, it is helpful to use a checkpointing method that allows most before images and abort records to be dropped from the log. Design such an archive checkpointing strategy for the partial data item logging algorithm. Propose an efficient algorithm for compressing the stable log before moving it to the archive.

6.33   Explain why each of the archive recovery methods proposed in Section 6.8 is idempotent.

6.34   Since only a small portion of the database may be affected by a media failure, it is helpful if the archive Restart procedure is able to recover a given set of data items, rather than the whole database. Suppose we use LSN-based logging and fuzzy archive checkpointing. Design an efficient algorithm that can recover individual data items independently. Notice the problem with redo; update records on the same data item do not normally have forward pointers, so it is hard to avoid a complete scan of the log. Consider the possibility of using an extra forward pointer field in each update record, which is filled in by Restart during the backward scan of the log, in order to speed up the redo scan by following those pointers.

6.35   Explain why the procedure outlined in Section 6.8 for fuzzy archive checkpointing leads to a different Restart procedure than the one we used for fuzzy stable checkpointing in the partial data item logging algorithm. Propose modifications to the checkpointing algorithms so that their Restart algorithms can be identical (except for the choice of stable or archive database and log as input).

The problem is more subtle than it may appear at first. Merely having the TM of a distributed transaction's home site send Commit operations to all other sites is not enough. This is because a transaction is not committed by virtue of the TM's sending a Commit, but rather by virtue of the DM's executing the Commit. It is possible that the TM sends Commit to the scheduler but the scheduler rejects it and aborts the transaction. In this case, if the transaction is distributed, it should abort at all other sites where it accessed data items.

Another significant difference between transaction processing in a centralized and a distributed DBS concerns the nature of failures. In a centralized system, a failure is an all-or-nothing affair. Either the system is working and transactions are processed routinely, or the system has failed and no transaction can be processed at all. In a distributed system, however, we can have partial failures. Some sites may be working while others have failed.

The fact that failures in distributed systems do not necessarily have the crippling effect they do in centralized ones creates opportunities for greater reliability. This is one of the most widely advertised features of distribution. Less widely advertised is the fact that the partial failures that make this possible are often the source of non-trivial problems that must be solved before the "opportunities for greater reliability" can be realized.

In transaction processing (and in the absence of data replication), the only such non-trivial problem is that of consistent termination. As we saw, the Commit or Abort operation of a distributed transaction must be processed at all sites where the transaction accessed data items. Ensuring that a single logical action (Commit or Abort) is consistently carried out at multiple sites is complicated considerably by the prospect of partial failures.

An algorithm that ensures this consistency is called an *atomic commitment protocol (ACP)*. Our main goal in this chapter is to present ACPs that are as resilient to failures as possible. Before we do so, we must examine in more detail the nature of failures that the protocol must worry about.

7.2 FAILURES IN A DISTRIBUTED SYSTEM

A distributed system consists of two kinds of components: sites, which process information, and communication links, which transmit information from site to site. A distributed system is commonly depicted as a graph where nodes are sites and undirected edges are bidirectional communication links (see Fig. 7–1).

We assume that this graph is connected, meaning that there is a path from every site to every other. Thus, every two sites can communicate either directly via a link joining them, or indirectly via a chain of links. The combination of hardware and software that is responsible for moving messages between sites is called a *computer network*. We won't worry about how to route messages

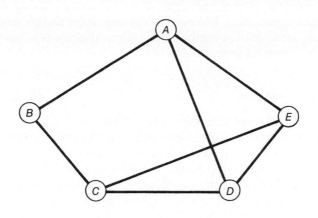

FIGURE 7-1
A Computer Network

from one site to another, since routing is a computer network service normally available to the distributed database system.

Site Failures

When a site experiences a system failure, processing stops abruptly and the contents of volatile storage are destroyed. In this case, we'll say the site has *failed*. When the site recovers from a failure it first executes a *recovery procedure* (called *Restart* in Chapter 6), which brings the site to a consistent state so it can resume normal processing.

In this model of failure, a site is always either working correctly (is *operational*) or not working at all (is *down*). It never performs incorrect actions. This type of behavior is called *fail-stop*, because sites fail only by stopping.

Surely this is an idealization of a site's possible faulty behavior. Computers can occasionally act incorrectly due to software or hardware bugs. By using extensive testing during implementation and manufacturing, and built-in redundancy in hardware and software, one can build systems that approximate fail-stop behavior. But we will not discuss these techniques in this book. We'll simply assume that sites are fail-stop. The correctness of the protocols we'll discuss in this chapter depends on this assumption.

Even though each site either is functioning properly or has failed, different sites may be in different states. A *partial failure* is a situation where some sites are operational while others are down. A *total failure* occurs when all sites are down.

Partial failures are tricky to deal with. Fundamentally, this is because operational sites may be uncertain about the state of failed ones. As we'll see, operational sites may become blocked, unable to commit or abort a transaction, until such uncertainty is resolved. An important design goal of atomic commitment protocols is to minimize the effect of one site's failure on other sites' ability to continue processing.

Communication Failures

Communication links are also subject to failures. Such failures may prevent processes at different sites from communicating. A variety of communication failures are possible: A message may be corrupted due to noise in a link; a link may malfunction temporarily, causing a message to be completely lost; or a link may be broken for a while, causing all messages sent through it to be lost.

Message corruption can be effectively handled by using error detecting codes, and by retransmitting a message in which the receiver detects an error. Loss of messages due to transient link failures can be handled by retransmitting lost messages. Also, the probability of losing messages due to broken links can be reduced by rerouting. If a message is sent from site A to site B, but the network is unable to deliver the message due to a broken link, it may attempt to find another path from A to B whose intermediate links and sites are functioning properly. Error correcting codes, message retransmission, and rerouting are usually provided by computer network protocols. We'll take them for granted.

Unfortunately, even with automatic rerouting, a combination of site and link failures can disable the communication between sites. This will happen if *all* paths between two sites A and B contain a failed site or a broken link. This phenomenon is called a *network partition*. In general, a network partition divides up the operational sites into two or more *components*, where every two sites within a component can communicate with each other, but sites in different components cannot. For example, Fig. 7–2 shows a partition of the system of Fig. 7–1. The partition consists of two components, $\{B, C\}$ and $\{D, E\}$, and is caused by the failure of site A and links (C, D) and (C, E).

As sites recover and broken links are repaired, communication is reestablished between sites that could not previously exchange messages, thereby merging components. For example, in Fig. 7–2, if site A recovers or if either link (C, D) or (C, E) is repaired, the two components merge and every pair of operational sites can communicate.

We can reduce the probability of a network partition by designing a highly connected network, that is, a network where the failure of a few sites and links will not disrupt all paths between any pair of sites. However, making a network highly connected requires the use of more components and therefore entails more expense. Moreover, the network's topology is often constrained by other factors, such as geography or the communication medium. Thus, our ability to avoid partitions is limited.

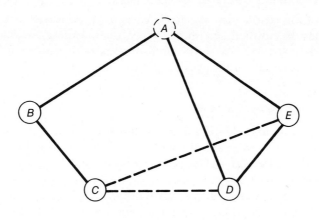

FIGURE 7–2
A Network Partition
Components shown in broken lines are faulty.

To sum up, a *communication failure* occurs when a site A is unable to communicate with site B, even though neither site is down. Network partitions are one cause of communication failures. (We'll see another one shortly.) If two sites can communicate, messages are delivered correctly (uncorrupted).

Undeliverable Messages

Site and communication failures require us to deal with undeliverable messages. A message may be undeliverable because its recipient is down when the message arrives, or because its sender and recipient are in different components of a network partition. There are two options:

1. The message *persists*. The computer network stores the message, and delivers it to its destination when that becomes possible.

2. The message is *dropped*. The computer network makes no further attempt to deliver it.

We'll adopt option (2) — as, alas, many postal services do. Option (1) is *not* routinely supported by computer networks. It requires fairly elaborate protocols, quite similar to ACPs, and therefore merely moves the atomic commitment problem to a different part of the system (see Exercise 7.1).

Some computer networks that adopt option (2) attempt to notify the sender of an undeliverable message that the message was dropped. But this is inherently unreliable. If a site fails to acknowledge the receipt of a message, the network cannot tell whether the site did not receive the message or it received the message but failed before acknowledging it. Even if it could make this distinction, notifying the sender of nondelivery may lead to unbounded recursion. If a notification message itself cannot be delivered, its sender (the notifier) must be notified and so on. Thus, such notifications of nondelivery can*not* be relied upon. We will therefore assume they don't exist. For our purposes, undeliverable messages simply vanish.

Detecting Failures by Timeouts

Both site failures and communication failures manifest themselves as the inability of one site to exchange messages with another. That is, if site A cannot communicate with site B, it is either because B has failed or because A and B belong to different components of a partition. In general, A cannot distinguish these two cases. It just knows that it can't communicate with B.

How can A find out that it can't communicate with B? Usually this is done by using *timeouts*. A sends a message to B and waits for a reply within a predetermined period of time δ called the *timeout period*. If a reply arrives, clearly A and B can communicate, as evidenced by the pair of messages just exchanged. If the period δ elapses and A has not yet received a reply, A concludes that it cannot communicate with B. δ must be chosen to be the maximum possible time it can take for the message to travel from A to B, for B to process the message and generate the reply, and for the reply to travel back to A. Computing a value for the timeout period is not a simple matter. It depends on many hard-to-quantify variables: the physical characteristics of the sites and communication lines, the system load, message routing algorithms, and accuracy of clocks, among others. Pragmatically, it is usually possible to select a timeout period that works well most of the time. When we use the timeout mechanism, we assume that an appropriate value for δ has been determined.

If the timeout period is underestimated, a site may think it cannot communicate with another when, in fact, it can. This can also happen because the clock that's measuring the timeout period is too fast. Such errors are called *timeout failures* or *performance failures*. Timeout failures are, in effect, communication failures. However, unlike network partitions, they can give rise to very peculiar situations, such as A thinking that it can communicate with B but B thinking it can't communicate with A; or A thinking it can communicate with B and B with C, but A thinking it cannot communicate with C.

In Chapters 7 and 8, we'll be careful to indicate whether each algorithm under consideration can tolerate site failures only, or both site and communication failures.

7.3 ATOMIC COMMITMENT

Consider a distributed transaction T whose execution involves sites $S_1, S_2, \ldots, S_n$. Suppose the TM at site S_1 supervises T's execution. Before the TM at S_1 can send Commit operations for T to S_1, S_2, ..., S_n, it must make sure that the scheduler and DM at each of these sites is ready and willing to process that Commit. Otherwise, T might wind up committing at some sites and aborting at others, thereby terminating inconsistently. Let's look at the conditions that a scheduler or DM must satisfy to be "ready and willing" to commit a transaction.

The scheduler at a site may agree to process Commit(T) as long as T satisfies the recoverability condition at that site. That is, every value read by T at that site was written by a transaction that has committed. Note that if the scheduler produces executions that avoid cascading aborts (or *a fortiori*, are strict), then this is true at all times. In this case, since the scheduler is always able to process Commit(T), S_1's TM need not get the scheduler's approval to send a Commit.

The DM at a site may agree to process Commit(T) as long as T satisfies the Redo Rule at that site. That is, all values written by T at that site are in stable storage — the stable database or the log, depending on the DM's recovery algorithm. If T has submitted only Reads to some site, it need *not* request the consent of that site's DM.

The TM at S_1 can issue Commit(T) to the schedulers and DMs of S_1, S_2, ..., S_n only after having received the schedulers' and DMs' consent from *all* these sites. In essence, this is the *two phase commit* (*2PC*) protocol that we'll study in detail in the next section. Why must we devote a separate section to what seems like such a simple idea? The reason is that the preceding discussion does not address site or communication failures. What if one or more sites fail during this process? What if one or more messages are lost? The real difficulty of atomic commitment is to design protocols that provide maximum resistance to such failures.

As an aside, we have already encountered a protocol analogous to 2PC in our discussion of distributed certifiers (cf. Section 4.4). To certify a distributed transaction T, the local certifiers of all sites where T executed had to agree. If even one site did not certify T, the transaction had to be aborted at *all* sites. In our discussion of distributed certification, we evaded the issue of site and communication failures. Our discussion of how to handle failures in 2PC will apply to the distributed certification protocol as well. In practice, the two protocols would be combined.

To simplify the discussion and concentrate on the essentials of atomic commitment, it is convenient to deviate from the TM-scheduler-DM model. To separate atomic commitment from the other aspects of transaction processing, we'll assume that for each distributed transaction T, there is a process at every site where T executed. These processes carry out the atomic commitment protocol for T. The process at T's home site is called T's *coordinator*. The remaining processes are T's *participants*. The coordinator knows the names of all the participants, so it can send them messages. The participants know the name of the coordinator, but they don't necessarily know each other.

attractive, because it makes recovery cheaper and simpler. Moreover, lack of independent recovery in conjunction with *total failures* (when all processes fail) gives rise to blocking. To see this, suppose that p in Scenario II is the first process to recover from a total failure. Since p is uncertain, it must communicate with other processes before it can reach a decision. But it can't communicate with them, since they all are down. Thus p is blocked.

These two scenarios show that failures while a process is uncertain can cause serious problems. Can we design an ACP that eliminates uncertainty periods? Unfortunately, not. Doing so would essentially require that a process cast its vote *and* learn the votes of *all* other processes all at once. In general, this is impossible. Thus, we have the following important observations.

> **Proposition 7.1:** If communication failures or total failures are possible, then every ACP may cause processes to become blocked.   □

> **Proposition 7.2:** No ACP can guarantee independent recovery of failed processes.   □

Proposition 7.1 does not preclude the existence of a non-blocking ACP if only site failures, but not *total* site failures, can occur. In fact, such a protocol exists, as we'll see in Section 7.5.

Propositions 7.1 and 7.2 can be formulated as theorems. Unfortunately, we lack a precise enough model of distributed computation to carry out rigorous proofs, the keys to which are Scenarios I and II. Developing such a model would lead us astray. The Bibliographic Notes cite proofs of these propositions.

7.4 THE TWO PHASE COMMIT PROTOCOL

The simplest and most popular ACP is the *two phase commit (2PC)* protocol. Assuming no failures, it goes roughly as follows:

1. The coordinator sends a VOTE-REQ[1] (i.e., vote request) message to all participants.

2. When a participant receives a VOTE-REQ, it responds by sending to the coordinator a message containing that participant's vote: YES or NO. If the participant votes No, it decides Abort and stops.

3. The coordinator collects the vote messages from all participants. If all of them were YES and the coordinator's vote is also Yes, then the coordinator decides Commit and sends COMMIT messages to all participants. Otherwise, the coordinator decides Abort and sends ABORT messages to

---

[1] We use all small capital letters to indicate messages.

all participants that voted Yes (those that voted No already decided Abort in step (2)). In either case, the coordinator then stops.

4. Each participant that voted Yes waits for a COMMIT or ABORT message from the coordinator. When it receives the message, it decides accordingly and stops.

The two phases of 2PC are the voting phase (steps (1) and (2)) and the decision phase (steps (3) and (4)). A participant's uncertainty period starts when it sends a YES to the coordinator (step (2)) and ends when it receives a COMMIT or ABORT (step (4)). The coordinator has no uncertainty period since it decides as soon as it votes — with the knowledge, of course, of the participants' votes (step (3)).

It is easy to see that 2PC satisfies conditions AC1 – AC4. Unfortunately, as presented so far, it does not satisfy AC5 for two reasons. First, at various points of the protocol, processes must wait for messages before proceeding. However, such messages may not arrive due to failures. Thus, processes may be waiting forever. To avoid this, timeouts are used. When a process' waiting is interrupted by a timeout, the process must take special action, called a *timeout action*. Thus, to satisfy AC5, we must supply suitable timeout actions for each protocol step in which a process is waiting for a message.

Second, when a process recovers from a failure, AC5 requires that the process attempt to reach a decision consistent with the decision other processes may have reached in the meanwhile. (It *may* be that such a decision can't be made until after some other failures have been repaired as well.) Therefore, a process must keep some information in stable storage, specifically in the DT log. To satisfy AC5 we must indicate what information to keep in the DT log and how to use it upon recovery.

We consider these two issues in turn.

Timeout Actions

There are three places in 2PC where a process is waiting for a message: in the beginning of steps (2), (3) and (4). In step (2), a participant waits for a VOTE-REQ from the coordinator. This happens before the participant has voted. Since any process can unilaterally decide Abort before it votes Yes, if a participant times out waiting for a VOTE-REQ, it can simply decide Abort and stop.

In step (3) the coordinator is waiting for YES or NO messages from all the participants. At this stage, the coordinator has not yet reached any decision. In addition, no participant can have decided Commit. Therefore, the coordinator can decide Abort but must send ABORT to every participant from which it received a YES.

In step (4), a participant p that voted Yes is waiting for a COMMIT or ABORT from the coordinator. At this point p is uncertain. Therefore, unlike the previous two cases where a process can unilaterally decide, in this case the participant must consult with other processes to find out what to decide. This consultation is carried out in a *termination protocol* (for 2PC).[2]

The simplest termination protocol is the following: p remains blocked until it can re-establish communication with the coordinator. Then, the coordinator can tell p the appropriate decision. The coordinator can surely do so, since it has no uncertainty period. This termination protocol satisfies condition AC5, because if all failures are repaired, p will be able to communicate with the coordinator and thereby reach a decision.

The drawback of this simple termination protocol is that p may be blocked unnecessarily. For example, suppose there are two participants p and q. The coordinator might send a COMMIT or ABORT to q but fail just before sending it to p. Thus, even though p is uncertain, q is not. If p can communicate with q, it can find out the decision from q. It need not block waiting for the coordinator's recovery.

This suggests the need for participants to know each other, so they can exchange messages directly (without the mediation of the coordinator). Recall that our description of the atomic commitment problem states that the coordinator knows the participants and the participants know the coordinator, but that the participants do not initially know each other. This does not present any great difficulty. We can assume that the coordinator attaches the list of the participants' identities to the VOTE-REQ message it sends to each of them. Thus, participants get to know each other when they receive that message. The fact that they do not know each other earlier is of no consequence for our purposes, since a participant that times out before receiving VOTE-REQ will unilaterally decide Abort.

This example leads us to the *cooperative termination protocol*: A participant p that times out while in its uncertainty period sends a DECISION-REQ message to every other process, q, to inquire whether q either knows the decision or can unilaterally reach one. In this scenario, p is the *initiator* and q a *responder* in the termination protocol. There are three cases:

1. q has already decided Commit (or Abort): q simply sends a COMMIT (or ABORT) to p, and p decides accordingly.

2. q has not voted yet: q can unilaterally decide Abort. It then sends an ABORT to p, and p therefore decides Abort.

3. q has voted Yes but has not yet reached a decision: q is also uncertain and therefore cannot help p reach a decision.

With this protocol, if p can communicate with *some* q for which either (1) or (2) holds, then p can reach a decision without blocking. On the other hand,

---

[2]In general, a termination protocol is invoked by a process when it fails to receive an anticipated message while in its uncertainty period. Different ACPs have different termination protocols associated with them.

if (3) holds for all processes with which p can communicate, then p is blocked. This predicament will persist until enough failures are repaired to enable p to communicate with a process q for which either (1) or (2) applies. At least one such process exists, namely, the coordinator. Thus this termination protocol satisfies AC5.

In summary, even though the cooperative termination protocol reduces the probability of blocking, it does not eliminate it. In view of Proposition 7.1, this is hardly surprising. However, even with the cooperative termination protocol, 2PC is subject to blocking *even if only site failures occur* (see Exercise 7.3).

Recovery

Consider a process p recovering from a failure. To satisfy AC5, p must reach a decision consistent with that reached by the other processes — if not immediately upon recovery, then some time after all other failures are also repaired.

Suppose that when p recovers it remembers its state at the time it failed — we'll discuss later how this is done. If p failed before having sent YES to the coordinator (step (2) of 2PC), then p can unilaterally decide Abort. Also, if p failed after having received a COMMIT or ABORT from the coordinator or after having unilaterally decided Abort, then it has already decided. In these cases, p can recover independently.

However, if p failed while in its uncertainty period, then it cannot decide on its own when it recovers. Since it had voted Yes, it is possible that all other processes did too, and they decided Commit while p is down. But it is also possible that some processes either voted No or didn't vote at all and Abort was decided. p can't distinguish these two possibilities based on information available locally and must therefore consult with other processes to make a decision. This is a reflection of the inability to have independent recovery (Proposition 7.2).

In this case, p is in exactly the same state as if it had timed out waiting for a COMMIT or ABORT from the coordinator. (Think of p as having used an extraordinarily long timeout period, lasting for the duration of its failure.) Thus, p can reach a decision by using the termination protocol. Note that p may be blocked, since it may be able to communicate only with processes that are themselves uncertain.

To remember its state at the time it failed, each process must keep some information in its site's DT log, which survives failures. Of course, each process has access only to its local DT log. Assuming that the cooperative termination protocol is used, here is how the DT log is managed.

1. When the coordinator sends VOTE-REQS, it writes a **start-2PC** record in the DT log. This record contains the identities of the participants, and may be written before or after sending the messages.

2. If a participant votes Yes, it writes a **yes** record in the DT log, *before* sending YES to the coordinator. This record contains the name of the coordinator and a list of the other participants (which is provided by the coordinator in VOTE-REQ). If the participant votes No, it writes an **abort** record either before or after the participant sends NO to the coordinator.

3. *Before* the coordinator sends COMMIT to the participants, it writes a **commit** record in the DT log.

4. When the coordinator sends ABORT to the participants, it writes an **abort** record in the DT log. The record may be written before or after sending the messages.

5. After receiving COMMIT (or ABORT), a participant writes a **commit** (or **abort**) record in the DT log.

In this discussion, writing a **commit** or **abort** record in the DT log is the act by which a process decides Commit or Abort.

At this point it is appropriate to comment briefly on the interaction between the commitment process and the rest of the transaction processing activity. Once the **commit** (or **abort**) record has been written in the DT log, the DM can execute the Commit (or Abort) operation. There are a number of details regarding how writing **commit** or **abort** records to the DT log relates to the processing of the commit or abort operations by the DM. For example, if the DT log is implemented as part of the DM log, the writing of the **commit** or **abort** record in the DT log may be carried out via a call to the Commit or Abort procedure of the local DM. In general, such details depend on which of the algorithms we discussed in Chapter 6 is used by the local DM (see Exercise 7.4).

When a site S recovers from a failure, the fate of a distributed transaction executing at S can be determined by examining its DT log:

☐ If the DT log contains a **start-2PC** record, then S was the host of the coordinator. If it also contains a **commit** or **abort** record, then the coordinator had decided before the failure. If neither record is found, the coordinator can now unilaterally decide Abort by inserting an **abort** record in the DT log. For this to work, it is crucial that the coordinator *first* insert the **commit** record in the DT log and *then* send COMMITs (point (3) in the preceding list).

☐ If the DT log doesn't contain a **start-2PC** record, then S was the host of a participant. There are three cases to consider:

1. The DT log contains a **commit** or **abort** record. Then the participant had reached its decision before the failure.

2. The DT log does not contain a **yes** record. Then either the participant failed before voting or voted No (but did not write an **abort** record before failing). (This is why the **yes** record must be written

before YES is sent; see point (2) in the preceding list.) It can therefore unilaterally abort by inserting an **abort** record in the DT log.

3. The DT log contains a **yes** but no **commit** or **abort** record. Then the participant failed while in its uncertainty period. It can try to reach a decision using the termination protocol. Recall that a **yes** record includes the name of the coordinator and participants, which are needed for the termination protocol.

Figures 7–3 and 7–4 give the 2PC protocol and the cooperative termination protocol, incorporating the preceding discussion on timeout actions and DT logging activity. The algorithms employed by each process are expressed in an *ad hoc*, but hopefully straightforward, language. We use **send** and **wait for** statements for inter-process communication. The statement "**send** m **to** p," where m is a message and p is one or more processes, causes the executing process to send m to all processes in p. The statement "**wait for** m **from** p," where m is one or more messages and p is a process, causes the executing process to suspend until m is received from p. If messages from multiple destinations are expected, the statement takes one of two forms: "**wait for** m **from all** p," in which case the waiting persists until messages m have been received from all processes in p, and "**wait for** m **from any** p," in which case waiting ends when m is received from *some* process in p. To avoid indefinite waiting, a **wait for** statement can be followed by a clause of the form "**on timeout** S," where S is some statement. This means that if the messages expected in the preceding **wait for** statement do not arrive within a predetermined timeout period, waiting is discontinued, statement S is executed, and control flows normally to the statement after the interrupted **wait for,** unless otherwise specified by S. If the expected messages arrive within the timeout period, S is ignored. We assume the timeout period is magically set to an appropriate value.

Although we have been presenting ACPs for a single transaction's termination, it is clear that the DT log will contain records describing the status of different transactions relative to atomic commitment. Thus to avoid confusing records of different transactions, the **start-2PC, yes, commit,** and **abort** records must contain the name of the transaction to which they refer. In addition, it is important to garbage collect DT log space taken up by outdated information. There are two basic principles regarding this garbage collection:

GC1: A site cannot delete log records of a transaction T from its DT log until at least after its RM has processed RM-Commit(T) or RM-Abort(T).

GC2: At least one site must not delete the records of transaction T from its DT log until that site has received messages indicating that RM-Commit(T) or RM-Abort(T) has been processed at all other sites where T executed.

Coordinator's algorithm

send VOTE-REQ **to** all participants;
write start-2PC record in DT log;
wait for vote messages (YES or NO) **from all** participants
    on timeout begin
        let P_Y be the processes from which YES was received;
        write abort record in DT log;
        send ABORT **to** all processes in P_Y;
        return
    end;
if all votes were YES and coordinator votes Yes **then begin**
    write commit record in DT log;
    send COMMIT **to** all participants
end
else begin
    let P_Y be the processes from which YES was received;
    write abort record in DT log;
    send ABORT **to** all processes in P_Y
end;
return

Participant's algorithm

wait for VOTE-REQ **from** coordinator
    on timeout begin
        write abort record in DT log;
        return
     end;
if participant votes Yes **then begin**
    write a yes record in DT log;
    send YES **to** coordinator;
    wait for decision message (COMMIT or ABORT) **from** coordinator
        on timeout initiate termination protocol /* cf. Fig. 7-4 */
    if decision message is COMMIT **then write commit** record in DT log
    else write abort record in DT log
end
else /* participant's vote is No */ **begin**
    write abort record in DT log;
    send NO **to** coordinator
end;
return

FIGURE 7–3
Two Phase Commit Protocol

Initiator's algorithm

start: **send** DECISION-REQ **to** all processes;
    wait for decision message **from any** process
        on timeout goto start; /* blocked! */
    if decision message is COMMMIT **then**
        write commit record in DT log
    else /* decision message is ABORT */
        write abort record in DT log;
    return

Responder's algorithm

    wait for DECISION-REQ **from any** process p;
    if responder has not voted Yes or has decided to Abort (i.e., has an
        abort record in DT log) **then send** ABORT **to** p
    else if responder has decided to Commit (i.e., has a **commit**
        record in DT log) **then send** COMMIT **to** p
    else /* responder is in its uncertainty period */ **skip;**[3]
    return

FIGURE 7–4
Cooperative Termination Protocol for 2PC

GC1 states that a site involved in T's execution can't forget about T until after T's effects at that site have been carried out. GC2 says that *some* site involved in T's execution must remember T's fate until that site knows that T's effects have been carried out at *all* sites. If this were not true and a site recovered from a failure and found itself uncertain about T's fate, it would never be able to find out what to decide about T, thus violating AC5.

GC1 can be enforced using information available locally at each site. However, GC2 calls for communication between sites. In particular, site A involved in T's execution must acknowledge the processing of RM-Commit(T) or RM-Abort(T) at site A to each site for which GC2 must hold. There are two extremes in the spectrum of possible strategies for achieving GC2: GC2 is true for only one site, typically T's coordinator, or GC2 is true for all sites involved in T's execution (see Exercise 7.5).

Our study of ACPs from the viewpoint of a single transaction has also hidden the issue of site recovery. When a site recovers, it must complete the ACP for all transactions that might not have committed or aborted before the

---

[3]"Skip" is the "do-nothing" statement (no-op).

failure. At what point can the site resume normal transaction processing? After the recovery of a centralized DBS, transactions cannot be processed until Restart has terminated, thereby restoring the committed database state. A similar strategy for the recovery of a site in a distributed DBS is unattractive, in view of the possibility that some transactions are blocked. In this case, the DBS at the recovered site would remain inaccessible until *all* transactions blocked at that site were committed or aborted.

Methods to avoid this problem depend on the type of scheduler being used. Consider Strict 2PL. After a site's recovery procedure has made decisions for all unblocked transactions, it should ask its scheduler to reacquire the locks that blocked transactions owned before the failure. In fact, a blocked transaction T need only reacquire its write locks. Read locks may be left released because doing so does not violate either the two phase rule (T must have obtained all of its locks, or else it would have been aborted, instead of blocked) or the strictness condition (which requires that *write* locks be held until after Commit is processed). The problem is that lock tables are usually stored in main memory and are therefore lost in a system failure. To avoid losing this information, the process that manages T's atomic commitment at a site must record T's write locks at that site in the **yes** record it writes in the DT log. This is unnecessary if that information can be determined from the log maintained by the RM at that site. This is the case, for example, in the undo/redo algorithm described in Chapter 6, since before T votes Yes at a site all of its update records will be in the log (and therefore in stable storage). These records can be used to determine the set of T's write locks, which can then be set.

Evaluation of 2PC

One can evaluate an ACP according to many criteria:

- □ *Resiliency*: What failures can it tolerate?
- □ *Blocking*: Can processes be blocked? If so, under what conditions?
- □ *Time Complexity*: How long does it take to reach the decision?
- □ *Message Complexity*: How many messages are exchanged to reach a decision?

The first two criteria measure the protocol's *reliability*, and the other two its *efficiency*. Reliability and efficiency are conflicting goals; each can be achieved at the expense of the other. The choice of protocol depends largely on which goal is more important to a specific application. However, whatever protocol is chosen, we should usually optimize for the case of no failures — hopefully the system's normal operating state.

We'll measure an ACP's time complexity by counting the number of message exchange rounds needed for unblocked sites to reach a decision, in the worst case. A *round* is the maximum time for a message to reach its destination. The use of timeouts to detect failures is founded on the assumption that such a maximum message delay is known. Note that many messages can be sent in a single round — as many as there are sender-destination pairs. Two messages must belong to different rounds if and only if one cannot be sent until the other is received. For example, a COMMIT and a YES in 2PC belong to different rounds because the former cannot be sent until after the latter is received. On the other hand, all VOTE-REQ messages are assigned to the same round, because they can all be in transit to their destination concurrently. The same goes for all COMMIT messages. An easy way to count the number of rounds is to pretend that all messages in a round are sent at the same time and experience the same delay to all sites. Thus each round begins the moment the messages are sent, and ends at the moment the messages arrive.

Using rounds to measure time complexity neglects the time needed to *process* messages. This is a reasonable abstraction in the common case where message delays far exceed processing delays. However, two other factors might be taken into account to arrive at a more precise measure of time complexity.

First, as we have seen, a process must record the sending or receipt of certain messages in the DT log. In some cases, such as a file server in a local area network, accessing stable storage incurs a delay comparable to that of sending a message. The number of accesses to stable storage may then be a significant factor in the protocol's time complexity.

Second, in some rounds a process sends the same message to all other processes. For instance, in the first round the coordinator sends VOTE-REQs to all participants. This activity is called *broadcasting*. To broadcast a message, a process must place n copies of the message in the network,[4] where n is the number of receivers. Usually, the time to place a message in the network is negligible compared with the time needed to deliver that message. However, if n is sufficiently large, the time to prepare a broadcast may be significant and should be accounted for.

Thus, a more accurate measure of time complexity might be a weighted sum of the number of rounds, accesses to stable storage, and broadcast messages. However, we'll ignore the latter two factors and concern ourselves only with the number of rounds.

We'll measure message complexity by the number of messages used by the protocol. This is reasonable if individual messages are not too long. If they are, we should count the length of the messages, not merely their number. In all the protocols of this chapter messages are short, so we'll be content with counting the number of messages.

Let us now examine how 2PC fares with respect to resiliency, blocking, and time and message complexity.

---

[4]We are assuming, of course, that the communication medium is *not* a multiple access channel. In that case only one message needs to be placed in the channel; the receivers are all tapping the common channel and can "hear" the broadcast message.

Resiliency: 2PC is resilient to both site failures and communication failures, be they network partitions or timeout failures. To see this, observe that our justification for the timeout actions in the previous subsection did *not* depend on the timeout's cause. The timeout could be due to a site failure, a partition, or merely a false timeout.

Blocking: 2PC is subject to blocking. A process will become blocked if it times out while in its uncertainty period and can only communicate with processes that are also uncertain. In fact, 2PC may block even in the presence of only site failures. To calculate the probability of blocking precisely, one must know the probability of failures. This type of analysis is beyond the scope of this book (see the Bibliographic Notes).

Time Complexity: In the absence of failures, 2PC requires three rounds: (1) the coordinator broadcasts VOTE-REQS; (2) the participants reply with their votes; and (3) the coordinator broadcasts the decision. If failures happen, then the termination protocol may need two additional rounds: one for a participant that timed out to send a DECISION-REQ, and the second for a process that receives that message and is outside its uncertainty period to reply. Several participants may independently invoke the termination protocol. However, the two rounds of different invocations can overlap, so the combined effect of all invocations of the termination protocol is only two rounds.

Thus, in the presence of failures it will take up to five rounds for all processes that aren't blocked or failed to reach a decision. This is independent of the number of failures! The catch is that some processes may be blocked. By definition, a blocked process may remain blocked for an unbounded period of time. Therefore, to get meaningful results, we must exclude blocked processes from consideration in measuring time complexity.

Message Complexity: Let n be the number of participants (so the total number of processes is $n + 1$). In each round of 2PC, n messages are sent. Thus, in the absence of failures, the protocol uses $3n$ messages.

The cooperative termination protocol is invoked by all participants that voted Yes but didn't receive COMMIT or ABORT from the coordinator. Let there be m such participants, $\leq m \leq n$. Thus m processes will initiate the termination protocol, each sending n DECISION-REQ messages. At most $n - m + 1$ processes (the maximum that might not be in their uncertainty period) will respond to the first DECISION-REQ message. As a result of these responses, one more process may move outside its uncertainty period and thus respond to the DECISION-REQ message of another initiator of the termination protocol. Thus, in the worst case, the number of messages sent by the termination protocol (with m initiators) will be

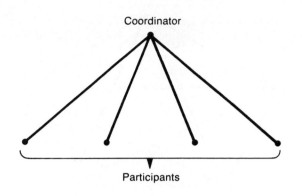

Coordinator

Participants

FIGURE 7–5
Communication Topology for 2PC with Five Processes

$$nm + \sum_{i=1}^{m} (n-m+i) = 2nm - m^2/2 + m/2.$$

Elementary calculus shows that this quantity is maximized when $n = m$ (recall that $0 \le m \le n$), that is, when all participants time out during their uncertainty period. Thus, the termination protocol contributes up to $n(3n+1)/2$ messages, for a total of $n(3n+7)/2$ for the entire 2PC protocol.

Alternative Communication Topologies for 2PC

The *communication topology* of a protocol is the specification of who sends messages to whom. For example, 2PC without the termination protocol has a communication topology in which the coordinator sends messages to the participants and *vice versa*. Participants do not send messages directly to each other. This communication topology is represented by a tree of height 1, with the coordinator as the root and the participants as the leaves (see Fig. 7–5.)

In an attempt to reduce the time and message complexity of 2PC, two other protocols have been proposed, the *decentralized 2PC protocol* and the *linear* (or *nested*) *2PC protocol*. Both have the same fundamental properties as *centralized 2PC*, the 2PC protocol we have studied so far. But they use different communication topologies than centralized 2PC.

Decentralized 2PC is designed to improve time complexity. Instead of funneling messages through the coordinator, processes may communicate directly with one another. Thus, the communication topology is represented as a *complete graph*, one that has an edge between every pair of nodes (see Fig. 7–6.)

Decentralized 2PC works as follows. Depending on its vote, the coordinator sends YES or NO to the participants. This message has a dual role: It

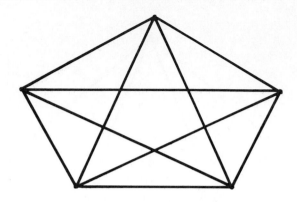

FIGURE 7–6
Communication Topology for Decentralized 2PC with Five Processes

informs the participants that it is time to vote (recall VOTE-REQ in centralized 2PC) and also tells them the coordinator's vote. If the message is NO, each participant simply decides Abort and stops. Otherwise, it responds by sending its own vote to *all* other processes. After receiving all the votes, each process makes a decision: If all were Yes and its own vote was Yes, the process decides Commit; otherwise it decides Abort. Timeout actions can be supplied just as in centralized 2PC (see Exercise 7.6).

In the absence of failures, decentralized 2PC requires only two rounds: one for the coordinator's YES or NO and another in which the participants broadcast their own votes. By not funneling the votes through the coordinator, we reduce the round complexity. Unfortunately, we also increase the message complexity. Let n be the number of participants. We now need n messages for the coordinator's vote and n^2 messages for the participants' votes, because each participant must send its vote to every other process, for a total of $n^2 + n$ messages. We need these messages even in the absence of failures, a case that centralized 2PC handles with only $3n$ messages.

Linear 2PC, on the other hand, is designed to reduce the number of messages. The processes are linearly ordered as shown in Fig. 7–7. Each process can communicate with its left and right neighbors. The protocol is initiated by the coordinator, which is the leftmost process in the linear order (numbered 1 in Fig. 7–7). The coordinator sends a message to its right neighbor (process 2) containing its vote, Yes or No. This message informs process 2 of the coordinator's vote and tells *it* to vote too. In general, a process p waits for a message from its left neighbor. If p receives a YES and its own vote is Yes, it forwards a YES to its right neighbor. If p receives a YES and its own vote is No, or if it receives a NO, then p forwards a NO to its right neighbor. If these rules are observed, then the rightmost process will have all the information it

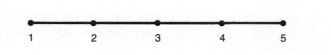

FIGURE 7–7
Communication Topology for Linear 2PC with Five Processes

needs to make a decision: If it receives a YES and its own vote is Yes, then the decision is Commit; otherwise the decision is Abort. Having made the decision, the rightmost process sends a COMMIT or ABORT to its left neighbor informing it of the decision. Each process that receives the decision message decides accordingly and then forwards that message to its left neighbor. Eventually the message reaches the leftmost process, at which time the protocol ends. It is possible to define timeout actions in this protocol similar to those we discussed for centralized 2PC (see Exercise 7.7). The timeout period for each process should depend on its position in the linear order because this influences the amount of time it will take for a message to arrive (see Exercise 7.8).

This protocol requires $2n$ messages (where n is the number of participants): n traveling left to right conveying votes, and n traveling right to left conveying the decision. Unfortunately, the economizing in messages is achieved at the expense of rounds. Linear 2PC requires as many rounds as messages because no two messages are sent concurrently. Thus linear 2PC uses $2n$ rounds, as compared with 3 for centralized 2PC and 2 for decentralized 2PC.

There are various ways to improve linear 2PC. The decision messages could all be sent concurrently by the rightmost process. That is, we could have a hybrid protocol that uses the communication topology of Fig. 7–7 for the voting phase of 2PC and that of Fig. 7–5 for the decision distribution phase (where the rightmost process is the tree's root). The resulting protocol still has message complexity $2n$ but uses $n+1$, rather than $2n$ rounds. Another improvement is suggested in Exercise 7.9.

Figure 7–8 summarizes the message and time complexities of the three variants of 2PC in the absence of failures for $n+1$ processes (n participants and the coordinator). If messages are too expensive, linear 2PC may be most appropriate. If end-to-end delays must be minimized, decentralized 2PC could be used. Centralized 2PC is a good middle ground. The choice of protocol might also be influenced by the physical characteristics of the network. A linear bus or ring network may be well suited for linear 2PC while a (nearly) completely connected network may be appropriate for decentralized 2PC.

	Messages	Rounds
Centralized 2PC	$3n$	3
Decentralized 2PC	$n^2 + n$	2
Linear 2PC	$2n$	$2n$

FIGURE 7–8
Comparison of 2PC Variants (No-Failures Case)

7.5 THE THREE PHASE COMMIT PROTOCOL

By Proposition 7.1, we cannot hope to devise a non-blocking protocol that tolerates communication failures or total site failures. Unfortunately, 2PC may cause blocking even if only non-total site failures[5] take place. In this section we study the *three phase commit* (*3PC*) protocol. In particular, we'll examine two variations of 3PC. The first, to which we devote most of the section, is designed to tolerate *only* site failures. The protocol is non-blocking in the absence of total site failures. In the event of a total failure, blocking may occur but correctness is still assured. Unfortunately, this protocol may cause inconsistent decisions to be reached in the event of communication failures.

The second variation of 3PC, discussed in the last subsection, can tolerate both communication and site failures. However, it is prone to blocking. Indeed, blocking may occur even if only processes have failed. This is unavoidable, in view of Proposition 7.1 and the fact that communication and site failures manifest themselves in the same manner, namely, as the inability to exchange messages within a pre-determined timeout period.

Both variations are more involved and have greater message and round complexity than 2PC. For systems built to tolerate only site failures, the first variation of 3PC has the advantage over 2PC that it completely eliminates blocking (except, unavoidably, in the event of total failures).

The second variation of 3PC can be used in systems designed to tolerate both site and communication failures. It does not completely eliminate blocking but causes blocking less frequently than 2PC. For instance, in 2PC processes may be blocked even if just one process — the coordinator — fails; in the second variation of 3PC no process will be blocked (in the absence of communication failures), as long as a majority of the processes are still operational.

---

[5]Henceforth, in this section, "site failures" means "non-total site failures" unless otherwise specified.

In most practical applications, the circumstances under which 2PC causes blocking are sufficiently rare that blocking is usually not considered a big problem. Consequently, almost all systems we know of that employ atomic commitment protocols use some version of 2PC.[6] Even though 3PC is not used in practice, it is an interesting protocol both in its own right and also because it illustrates a number of important techniques used in the design of fault-tolerant communication protocols. For these reasons, we feel that its study is a worthwhile endeavor. However, the rest of this section can be skipped without loss of continuity.

Basic Structure of 3PC

The first version of 3PC we'll describe is designed to handle site but not communication failures. Consequently, *we assume that only site failures occur.* Communication failures do not happen. There is a subtlety in this assumption. Depending on the network topology, site failures may cause communication failures as a side effect. For instance, in Fig. 7–1 if sites A and C fail, then sites B and E cannot communicate even though both are operational. Such site failures count as communication failures, too.

There are two major implications of assuming that only site failures happen. First, all operational processes can communicate with each other. Second, a process that times out waiting for a message from process q knows that q is down and therefore that no processing can be taking place there. In particular, no other process can be communicating with q. Neither of these statements is true if communication failures are possible.

In 2PC, if all operational processes are uncertain, they are blocked. They can't decide Abort, even if they know that processes they cannot communicate with have failed, because some failed process could have decided Commit before failing.

Suppose we've managed to design an ACP with the following "non-blocking property":

NB: If any operational process is uncertain then no process (whether operational or failed) can have decided to Commit.

If the operational sites discover they are all uncertain, they can decide Abort, safe in their knowledge that the failed processes had *not* decided Commit. When the failed processes recover they can be told to decide Abort too. This way blocking is prevented.

3PC is a protocol that satisfies NB. The idea is simple. Consider why 2PC violates NB. The coordinator sends COMMITs to the participants while the

---

[6]A notable exception is SDD-1, which uses a peculiar protocol that resembles 2PC in some respects and 3PC in others (see Exercise 7.13).

latter are uncertain. Thus if participant p receives a COMMIT before participant q, the former will decide Commit while the latter is still uncertain. 3PC avoids this as follows: After the coordinator has found that all votes were Yes, it sends PRE-COMMIT messages to the participants. When a participant p receives that message, it knows that all processes voted Yes and is thereby moved outside its uncertainty period. p does *not*, however, decide Commit yet. At this point p knows that it *will* decide Commit *provided it does not fail*.

Each participant acknowledges the receipt of PRE-COMMIT. When the coordinator has received all the acknowledgments to PRE-COMMITS, it knows that no participant is uncertain anymore. It then sends COMMITS to all participants. When a participant receives a COMMIT, it can decide Commit. This decision does not violate NB since no process is uncertain any longer.

If a process votes No, then 3PC behaves just like 2PC. The coordinator sends ABORTS to all processes. We now give the full description of the 3PC protocol.

1. The coordinator sends a VOTE-REQ to all participants.

2. When a participant receives a VOTE-REQ, it responds with a YES or NO message, depending on its vote. If a participant sends NO, it decides Abort and stops.

3. The coordinator collects the vote messages from all participants. If any of them was NO or if the coordinator voted No, then the coordinator decides Abort, sends ABORT to all participants that voted Yes, and stops. Otherwise, the coordinator sends PRE-COMMIT messages to all participants.

4. A participant that voted Yes waits for a PRE-COMMIT or ABORT message from the coordinator. If it receives an ABORT, the participant decides Abort and stops. If it receives a PRE-COMMIT, it responds with an ACK (i.e., acknowledgment) message to the coordinator.

5. The coordinator collects the ACKS. When they have all been received, it decides Commit, sends COMMITS to all participants, and stops.

6. A participant waits for a COMMIT from the coordinator. When it receives that message, it decides Commit and stops.

Messages received at steps (5) and (6) have the peculiar property of being known to their recipients even *before* they are received! In step (5) the coordinator knows it may only receive ACKS, and in step (6) a participant knows it can only receive a COMMIT. This casts some doubt on the utility of such messages. Their importance is that they inform their recipients of the occurrence of certain events. The receipt of ACK from participant p tells the coordinator that p is no longer uncertain. And since a COMMIT is sent only after all ACKS have been received, a participant that receives the COMMIT knows that *no* participant is uncertain. Thus it can decide Commit without violating NB.

This protocol works fine as long as there are no failures. To handle failures we must supply timeout actions describing what a process must do if an expected message does not arrive and must explain how a process can reach a decision after recovering from a failure. We address these issues in turn.

Timeout Actions

What a process should do when it times out depends on the message it was waiting for. There are five places in which a process waits for some message in 3PC:

1. In step (2) participants wait for VOTE-REQ.

2. In step (3) the coordinator waits for the votes.

3. In step (4) participants wait for a PRE-COMMIT or ABORT.

4. In step (5) the coordinator waits for ACKs.

5. In Step (6) participants wait for COMMIT.

Cases (1) and (2) are handled exactly as in 2PC. In both cases the process that times out knows that no process can have decided Commit. Thus, it can unilaterally decide Abort. In case (1) the participant can simply stop once it has decided Abort; in case (2) the coordinator should also send ABORTs to all participants that had voted Yes.

In case (4) the coordinator times out because one or more participants failed before sending an ACK. The coordinator does not know whether these participants failed before or after receiving a PRE-COMMIT. But it does know that these participants had voted Yes and were therefore prepared to decide Commit. Thus it ignores the failures and proceeds to send COMMIT to the operational participants as if it had received all ACKs. The failed participants, when they recover, are responsible for finding out that the decision was to Commit. With this timeout action, processes might decide Commit while some *failed* participant is uncertain. This will happen if some participant that did not send an ACK had actually failed before even receiving the PRE-COMMIT from the coordinator (cf. step (4) of 3PC). This does *not* violate NB, which requires only that no operational or failed process has decided Commit while some *operational* process is uncertain.

Cases (3) and (5) are more problematic. Here processes cannot act autonomously in response to the timeout. They must communicate with other processes to reach a consistent decision. It is clear why such communication is necessary in case (3); the timeout of an uncertain participant can't be handled unilaterally. But why does a participant p that times out in case (5) need to communicate with others? p has already received a PRE-COMMIT and is therefore not uncertain. After all, p knows that only COMMIT could possibly arrive from the coordinator. Why can't p ignore the timeout and simply decide Commit?

The reason is that by deciding Commit, p could be violating condition NB. To see this, suppose that the coordinator failed after having sent the PRE-COMMIT to p but before sending it to some other participant q. Thus p will time out in case (5) — outside its uncertainty period — while q will time out in case (3) — inside its uncertainty period. If p, on timeout, were to decide Commit while q (which is operational) is still uncertain, it would violate NB. This suggests that *before* deciding Commit, p should make sure that all operational participants have received a PRE-COMMIT, and have therefore moved outside their uncertainty periods. The termination protocol that a participant invokes if it times out in cases (3) and (5) does just that.

To explain how the termination protocol works, it is convenient to define the *state* of a process relative to the messages it has sent or received. There are four possible states:[7]

☐ *Aborted:* the process has not voted, has voted No, or has received an ABORT (i.e., it has either decided Abort or can unilaterally decide so).

☐ *Uncertain:* the process is in its uncertainty period.

☐ *Committable:* the process has received a PRE-COMMIT but has not yet received a COMMIT.

☐ *Committed:* the process has received a COMMIT (i.e., it has decided Commit).

First, note that any process is in precisely one state at any time. Second, some pairs of states cannot coexist, that is, cannot be occupied at the same time by two operational processes. Figure 7–9 shows which states can coexist and which cannot: A "Y" entry means that the states in the corresponding row and column can coexist, while an "N" means they cannot (see Exercise 7.14).

The termination protocol works as follows. when a participant times out in case (3) or (5), it initiates an *election protocol*. This protocol involves all processes that are operational and results in the "election" of a new coordinator. (The old one must have failed; otherwise no participant would have timed out!) We'll describe an election protocol later. For now let's just assume we have one. Once the new coordinator has been elected, the termination protocol proceeds as follows: The coordinator sends a STATE-REQ message to all processes that participated in the election. (By our assumption about failures, all operational sites will participate.) A participant in the termination protocol (i.e., any operational process other than the new coordinator) responds to this message by sending its state to the coordinator. The coordinator collects these states and proceeds according to the following *termination rule*:

TR1: If some process is Aborted, the coordinator decides Abort, sends ABORT messages to all participants, and stops.

---

[7]We capitalize the first letter of these four process states in the rest of the chapter.

	Aborted	Uncertain	Committable	Committed
Aborted	Y	Y	N	N
Uncertain	Y	Y	Y	N
Committable	N	Y	Y	Y
Committed	N	N	Y	Y

FIGURE 7–9
Coexistence of States

TR2: If some process is Committed, the coordinator decides Commit, sends COMMIT messages to all participants, and stops.

TR3: If all processes that reported their state are Uncertain, the coordinator decides Abort, sends ABORT messages to all participants, and stops.

TR4: If some process is Committable but none is Committed, the coordinator first sends PRE-COMMIT messages to all processes that reported Uncertain, and waits for acknowledgments from these processes. After having received these acknowledgments the coordinator decides Commit, sends COMMIT messages to all processes, and stops.

A participant that receives a COMMIT (or ABORT) message, decides Commit (or Abort), and stops.

Of course, processes can fail during the termination protocol. Thus we must supply timeout actions for all places in which a process is waiting in *this* protocol! It seems as though we are chasing our tail, but that's not so. Once elected, the coordinator will ignore any participants that fail before reporting their state. It will base its decision on the states of the participants that do report their state, in accordance with the termination rule. So, participant failures during the termination protocol are easily handled.

If the coodinator fails during the termination protocol, one of the participants waiting for the decision will time out. That participant will initiate a new election protocol, resulting in the election of a new coordinator. The termination protocol will then be started all over again. All processes will report their states to the new coordinator, which will proceed according to TR1–TR4. Before all operational processes reach a decision, several invocations of the termination protocol may be required, one for each coordinator failure. Eventually either some coordinator will finish the protocol or all processes will fail, resulting in total failure. We'll discuss total failures shortly.

It should be emphasized that processes that fail and then recover while the termination protocol is in progress are not allowed to participate in that protocol. Such processes will reach a decision using the recovery procedure that will be presented soon.

Correctness of 3PC and Its Termination Protocol

We now show that in the presence of only site failures, 3PC (with its termination protocol) is non-blocking and correct. Correctness amounts to proving that the five conditions of ACPs are satisfied. The only one that's non-trivial to show is AC1, i.e., that all processes that reach a decision reach the same one. AC2, AC3, and AC4 can be easily verified and we won't discuss them. To show that AC5 is satisfied we must consider failure recovery, which is the topic of the next subsection. Here we'll concentrate on proving the consistency of the decision reached by the processes. Although the argument is lengthy, it's worth studying carefully, because it elucidates how 3PC works in the case of failures.

Lemma 7.3: For any set of states received by the coordinator in the termination protocol, *exactly one* of the four cases of the termination rule (TR1-TR4) applies.

Proof: The reported states must coexist. Using Fig. 7–9 it is easy to verify that for any set of states that pairwise coexist, one and only one of TR1–TR4 must apply. □

Theorem 7.4: In the absence of total failures, 3PC and its termination protocol never cause processes to block.

Proof: If the coordinator does not fail then all operational processes will reach a decision, so in this case they do not block. If the coordinator fails, any processes that have not reached a decision will initiate the termination protocol and elect a new coordinator. By Lemma 7.3 at least one of the termination rule cases will apply. Moreover, in each case of the termination rule a decision is reached. Thus if the coordinator of the termination protocol does not fail, all remaining processes will reach a decision; again there is no blocking. If the coordinator fails, a new invocation of the termination protocol will be initiated. This will be repeated until either all remaining processes reach a decision or all processes fail (a total failure). Therefore, in the absence of total failures, all operational processes will reach a decision without blocking. □

Lemma 7.5: All processes that reach a decision on the same invocation of the termination protocol reach the same one.

Proof: By Lemma 7.3, at most one case of the termination rule applies and therefore the rule is unambiguous. This means that the coordinator sends the same decision to all processes (to which it sends anything at all). □

Lemma 7.6: If NB holds before the termination protocol starts, it will hold after *even a partial execution of that protocol.*

Proof: A (possibly partial) execution of the termination protocol can violate NB only if some process decides Commit while an operational process is Uncertain. A Commit decision is reached only in cases TR2 or TR4. By Fig. 7–9, in case TR2 all operational processes are Committable or Committed and thus are not Uncertain. In case TR4 all processes that are Uncertain and do not, in the meanwhile, fail are explicitly moved out of their uncertainty periods by receiving PRE-COMMITs and acknowledging them. Thus in all cases NB is preserved. □

Lemma 7.7: Consider the i-th invocation of the termination protocol, that is, the invocation after i coordinators have failed. If a process p that is operational during at least part of this invocation is Committable, then some process q that was operational in (at least part of) the $(i-1)$st invocation was Committable then.[8]

Proof: If p itself was Committable in the $(i-1)$st invocation we are done. If p became Committable on the i-th invocation (see case TR4 of the termination rule), some process q must have reported its state as being Committable. But q must have been Committable in the previous invocation, because no process changes its state in an invocation until after the coordinator has received all the state reports. □

Theorem 7.8: Under 3PC and its termination protocol, all operational processes reach the same decision.

Proof: We'll prove that all processes that have reached a decision by the i-th invocation of the termination protocol have reached consistent decisions. The proof is by induction on i.

BASIS: $i = 0$. Consider the "0-th invocation" of the termination protocol, i.e., the execution of the basic 3PC protocol. In this case a process decides according to the COMMIT OR ABORT it receives from the coordinator. Since the coordinator sends the same message to all processes (to which it sends anything at all), all processes that reach a decision during this invocation reach a consistent one.

---

[8]The "0-th invocation" of the termination protocol is taken to be the execution of the basic 3PC protocol (as described at the beginning of this section).

INDUCTION STEP: Suppose all processes that have reached a decision through the $(i-1)$st invocation of the termination protocol $(i > 0)$ have reached a consistent one. Consider now the processes that reach a decision during the i-th invocation of the termination protocol. By Lemma 7.5 all these processes must reach the same decision (among themselves). Thus it remains to show that this decision is consistent with earlier ones. We do this by considering each case of the termination rule, according to which the decision was reached in the i-th invocation of the termination protocol.

TR1: If this case applies, all processes that decide in this invocation will decide Abort. So we must show that no processes that had reached a decision earlier could have decided Commit. For TR1 to apply, some operational process p must have been Aborted, meaning that (1) p has not voted; or (2) p has voted No; or (3) p had received an ABORT before this invocation of the termination protocol. In cases (1) or (2) no process could have decided Commit in a previous invocation. In case (3), p had already decided Abort in an earlier invocation and, by induction hypothesis, all processes that had decided in earlier invocations must have decided Abort.

TR2: In this case there must be an operational process p in the Committed state. Thus, p had received a COMMIT and had therefore decided Commit in some previous invocation. By induction hypothesis, all processes that had decided in previous invocations must have decided Commit, which is the decision reached by processes when TR2 applies.

TR3: In this case all processes that decide in the i-th invocation will decide Abort. So we must show that no process could have previously decided Commit. For TR3 to apply, all operational processes must be Uncertain. By Lemma 7.6 (and induction) NB is satisfied through all invocations of the termination protocol. Since some operational process is Uncertain (indeed all of them are!), NB implies that no process could have previously decided Commit.

TR4: In this case, all processes that reach a decision in this invocation decide Commit. Suppose, by way of contradiction, that some process q had decided Abort in the j-th invocation of the termination protocol, for some $j < i$. At that time q was in the Aborted state. By Fig. 7–9, no operational process could have been Committable in the j-th invocation. By Lemma 7.7 (and induction) then, no process that's operational during the i-th invocation can be Committable, contradicting the fact that for TR4 to apply some operational process must be Committable.

This completes our proof that under 3PC and its termination protocol all processes reach a consistent decision. □

Recovering from Failures

We now explore how processes that recover from failures can reach a decision consistent with that reached by the operational sites. Let us assume that when a process recovers, it knows its state at the time it failed. A process extracts this knowledge from information it has kept in the DT log. We'll discuss the participants' recovery actions. Those for the coordinator are similar.

If a recovering participant had failed before having sent a YES to the coordinator, it can unilaterally decide Abort. Also, if p failed after having received a COMMIT or ABORT from the coordinator, then it has already decided. As in 2PC, these are the two cases in which a process can independently recover.

The remaining case is that p had failed after voting Yes but before receiving a COMMIT or ABORT. Thus, p needs help from other processes. It sends messages asking them what the decision was. Under our failure assumptions 3PC is non-blocking, so a decision either has already been made or is in the process of being made by the operational sites.[9] So p will eventually receive a message with the decision and adopt it.

Note that p must ask other processes about the decision even if, before failing, it had received a PRE-COMMIT and thereby left its uncertainty period. In this case, p cannot unilaterally decide Commit, because process failures could have occurred so that the termination protocol caused the operational processes to decide Abort (see Exercise 7.17).

To make recovery possible, each process must record in the DT log its progress towards commitment. By analyzing the DT log, the recovery procedure can determine how the recovering process can reach its decision. As in 2PC, each process writes records in the DT log that mark the sending or receipt of various messages. In fact, exactly the same messages are logged in 3PC as in 2PC. As we have seen, knowing that a participant has received a PRE-COMMIT doesn't help recovery, so such messages need not be logged. The same is true for ACKs. Since there is nothing new about logging in 3PC we won't discuss the issue any further. (The fine points of which messages are logged, and when, are described in Fig. 7–10.)

Total Failures

Suppose that a total failure has taken place and consider the first process p to recover. If p had failed after voting Yes but before having decided Commit or Abort, it cannot make a decision autonomously. Unless p was the last process to have failed it cannot proceed to terminate the transaction on its own. This is because the processes that failed after p could have decided either Commit or Abort, and p doesn't know the decision that was reached (see Exercise 7.18). Thus, after a total failure, the recovering processes must remain blocked until

---

[9]Unless, of course, p is recovering from a total failure, a situation we'll address momentarily.

a process q recovers such that either q can recover independently (i.e., can reach a decision without communicating with other processes) or q was the last process to have failed. In the former case, q simply communicates its decision to the other processes. In the latter case, q invokes the termination protocol.[10] All processes that have recovered will therefore reach a decision according to that protocol. We emphasize that processes recovering from a total site failure cannot use the termination protocol to reach a decision *unless they include the last process to have failed*. Otherwise, inconsistent decisions may be reached by these processes and the last process to have failed.

Coordinator's algorithm

send VOTE-REQ **to** all participants;
write start-3PC record in DT log;
wait for vote messages (YES or NO) **from all** participants
    on timeout begin
        let P_Y be the processes from which YES was received;
        write abort record in DT log;
        send ABORT **to** all processes in P_Y;
        return
    end;
if all messages were YES and coordinator voted Yes **then begin**
    send PRE-COMMIT **to** all participants;
    wait for ACK **from all** participants
        on timeout skip; /* ignore participant failures */
    write commit record in DT log;
    send COMMIT **to** all participants
end
else /* some process voted No */ **begin**
    let P_Y be the processes from which YES was received;
    write abort record in DT log;
    send ABORT **to** all processes in P_Y;
end;
return

FIGURE 7–10
The Three Phase Commit Protocol

---

[10]In our discussion of the termination protocol we said that processes that have failed do not participate in that protocol when they recover. This is only true if there has not been a total failure.

FIGURE 7–10
The Three Phase Commit Protocol (*continued*)

Participant's algorithm

```
wait for VOTE-REQ from coordinator
    on timeout begin
        write abort record in DT log;
        return
    end;
if participant's own vote is Yes then begin
    write yes record in DT log;
    send YES to coordinator;
    wait for message (PRE-COMMIT or ABORT) from coordinator
        on timeout begin
            initiate election protocol; /* See next subsection. */
            if elected then invoke coordinator's algorithm of
                termination protocol /* See Fig. 7-11. */
            else invoke participant's algorithm of termination protocol;
            return
        end;
    if message received is PRE-COMMIT then begin
        send ACK to coordinator;
        wait for COMMIT from coordinator
            on timeout begin
                initiate election protocol;
                if elected
                then invoke coordinator's algorithm of termination protocol
                else invoke participant's algorithm of termination protocol;
                return
            end;
        write commit record in DT log
    end
    else /* ABORT was received from coordinator */ write abort record in DT log;
end
else /* participant's vote is No */ begin
    send NO to coordinator;
    write abort record in DT log
end;
return
```

Apparently, correctly recovering from a total site failure requires that a set of processes be able to determine whether it includes the last process to have failed. They could wait until *all* processes have recovered. Certainly this set includes the last process to have failed! In the next subsection we'll describe a method in which processes don't wait that long.

The 3PC protocol and its termination protocol are shown in Figs. 7–10 and 7–11. In the pseudo-code, it is the writing of a **commit** (or **abort**) record in the DT log that corresponds to a process' deciding to Commit (or Abort).

(New) **Coordinator's algorithm**

send STATE-REQ **to** all participants (of the election protocol);
wait for state report messages **from all** participants
      on timeout skip; /* ignore participant failures */
if any state report message was Aborted or
    the coordinator is in the Aborted state **then begin** /* case TR1 */
      if the coordinator's DT log does not contain an **abort** record **then**
        write abort record in DT log;
    send ABORT **to** all participants
end
else if any state report message was Committed or
    the coordinator is in the Committed state **then begin** /* case TR2 */
      if the coordinator's DT log does not contain a **commit** record **then**
        write commit record in DT log;
    send COMMIT **to** all participants
end
else if all state report messages were Uncertain and
    the coordinator is also Uncertain **then begin** /* case TR3 */
    write abort record in DT log;
    send ABORT **to** all participants
end
else /* some processes are Committable - Case TR4 */ **begin**
    send PRE-COMMIT **to** all participants that reported Uncertain state;
    wait for ACK **from all** processes that reported Uncertain state
      on timeout skip; /* ignore participant failures */
    write commit record in DT log;
    send COMMIT **to** all participants
end;
return

FIGURE 7–11
The 3PC Termination Protocol

FIGURE 7–11
The 3PC Termination Protocol (*continued*)

Participant's algorithm

```
start: wait for STATE-REQ from coordinator
          on timeout begin
                initiate election protocol;
                if elected then begin execute coordinator's algorithm (above); return end
                else goto start
          end;
if this process had not voted in 3PC protocol or had voted No or
    has received an ABORT then state : = Aborted
else if this process has received a COMMIT then state : = Committed
else if this process has received a PRE-COMMIT then state : = Committable
else state : = Uncertain;
send state to coordinator;
wait for response from coordinator
    on timeout begin
          initiate election protocol;
          if elected then begin execute coordinator's algorithm (above); return end
          else goto start
    end;
if response was ABORT then begin
    if DT log does not contain an abort record for this process then
          write abort record in DT log
end
else if response was COMMIT then begin
    if DT log does not contain a commit record for this process then
          write commit record in DT log
end
else /* response was PRE-COMMIT */ begin
    send ACK to coordinator;
    wait for COMMIT from coordinator
          on timeout begin
                initiate election protocol;
                if elected then begin execute coordinator's algorithm (above); return end
                else goto start
          end;
    write commit record in DT log
end;
return
```

Election Protocol and Detecting the Last Process to Fail

For the purposes of the election protocol, the processes agree on a linear ordering among themselves using, for example, their unique identifiers. If p precedes (or follows) q in this ordering, we write $p < q$ (or $p > q$). The election rule is that if the present coordinator fails, the smallest of the operational processes will become the new coordinator.

Under our assumption that only site failures happen, this idea can be implemented simply and efficiently. Each process p maintains a set, UP_p, of all the processes it believes are operational. Initially, UP_p contains all processes.[11] Suppose a participant p detects the failure of the present coordinator c (by timing out while waiting for a message from c). Then it removes c from UP_p, and selects the smallest process q in UP_p. If $q = p$, then p considers itself elected and becomes the coordinator of the termination protocol; otherwise it sends a UR-ELECTED (you-are-elected) message to q and becomes a participant of the termination protocol. When q receives UR-ELECTED, it considers itself elected and becomes the termination protocol coordinator.

When the new coordinator q has been elected, some process p' may not yet have discovered the failure of c. When p' receives a STATE-REQ from q, it deduces that c has failed. p' will therefore remove c (and any other processes $q' < q$) from $UP_{p'}$ and will become a termination protocol participant with q as its coordinator.

Message delays can cause a process to receive a STATE-REQ from an old coordinator that failed before a new coordinator was elected. Thus, a termination protocol participant p that considers q to be the coordinator ignores STATE-REQ messages from any $q' < q$. On the other hand, if p receives a STATE-REQ from $q' > q$, then it deduces that q has failed and q' has been elected as the new coordinator. As before, p removes from UP_p all processes preceding q' and becomes a participant in a new invocation of the termination protocol, taking q' as its coordinator.

Maintaining the UP_p sets is also useful in recovering from total failures. It helps a set of processes R determine whether they contain, among them, the last process that failed.

Suppose that, when a process p recovers, it can retrieve the value of UP_p at the time it had failed. Thus, p knows that the last process to have failed must be in UP_p. Suppose a set of processes R have recovered from a total failure. The last process to have failed must be a process that each process in R believed to have been operational when it failed, that is, a process in the set $\cap_{p \in R} UP_p$. Thus, the processes in R know that the last process to have

---

[11]The coordinator, which by assumption knows all the processes, can send the set of all processes to each participant along with the VOTE-REQ messages, so that participant p can properly initialize UP_p. The fact that UP_p is not initialized until after the receipt of the VOTE-REQ is not a problem, since the election protocol is relevant only to a process after it has voted.

failed is in R if and only if they contain *all* potential candidates; that is, if $R \supseteq \cap_{p \in R} UP_p$ (*).

Therefore, when enough processes R recover after a total failure so that property (*) is satisfied, the processes in R can initiate the termination protocol to reach a decision as we discussed in the previous subsection.

For p to retrieve the value of UP_p when it recovers, it must have saved UP_p in stable storage — for example, in the DT log. Note that it is not necessary for p to save UP_p in stable storage every time UP_p's value changes. If p only periodically changes UP_p in stable storage, the value retrieved for UP_p when p recovers will be a superset of the actual value of UP_p at the time p failed. This is safe in that a set R satisfying (*) still contains the last process to have failed. However, a larger set R of processes may have to recover from a total failure before (*) is satisfied.

Evaluation of 3PC

Let's summarize the properties of 3PC with respect to resiliency, blocking, and time and message complexity.

Resiliency and Blocking: 3PC is resilient to site failures only. It is non-blocking except for a total site failure. By Propositions 7.1 and 7.2 this is the maximal level of fault tolerance a non-blocking ACP can attain.

Time Complexity: In the absence of failures, 3PC uses at most five rounds of messages: (1) to distribute VOTE-REQs; (2) to deliver votes; (3) to distribute PRE-COMMITs; (4) to acknowledge the PRE-COMMITs; and (5) to distribute COMMITs. (If the decision is Abort, only three rounds are needed.) Each invocation of the termination protocol contributes at most five more rounds, plus the election protocol, which requires only one round to send UR-ELECTEDs. Thus if f processes fail, at most $6f + 5$ rounds are needed. This may appear deceptively worse than the five rounds required, in the worst case, for 2PC (independent of the number of failures!). But recall that 2PC may cause blocking and the five round bound concerned only *non-blocked* processes.

Message Complexity: In each round of 3PC at most n messages are sent, where n is the number of participants. Thus, in the absence of failures, 3PC requires up to $5n$ messages. In each round of an invocation of the termination protocol the number of messages is the number of remaining participants. In the i-th invocation, there are at most $(n-i)$ operational participants left, so the number of messages is at most $6(n-i)$. Therefore, if there are f process failures, the number of messages is at most $5n + \Sigma_{i=1}^{f} 6(n-i) = 3(f+1)(2n-1) - n$.

3PC and Communication Failures

Up to this point in this section we have assumed that no communication failures occur. Let us now remove this assumption. Unfortunately, the termination protocol for 3PC we've presented may result in processes reaching inconsistent decisions. To see this, suppose that the processes are partitioned into two components A and B. It is possible that, at the time the partition occurred, all processes in A are Uncertain while all those in B are Committable (see Fig. 7–9). According to the termination protocol, the processes in A will decide Abort (case TR3), while those in B will decide Commit (case TR4).

In this subsection we'll describe a new termination protocol that avoids such inconsistencies and guarantees correctness even in the presence of communication failures. The new termination protocol may introduce blocking, but this is unavoidable in view of Proposition 7.1.

For now it is best to think of process failures as permanent. That is, a process that fails never recovers. Later we'll show how recoveries can be handled in a very simple manner.

The overall structure of the termination protocol is as before. That is, a coordinator is elected that collects the states of participants and decides how to proceed on the basis of the states it has received. The problem, illustrated in the example outlined previously, is that communication failures may result in the election of multiple coordinators (unable to communicate among themselves), each deciding on how to terminate the protocol on the basis of the states of disjoint sets of participants.

Seen in this light, the following remedy suggests itself. We will allow a coordinator to reach a decision only if it can communicate with a majority of processes. This ensures that decisions reached by two different coordinators will be based on the state of at least one process in common. The termination protocol will be designed in such a manner that the common process will prevent inconsistent decisions.

Here is how this is achieved. When a coordinator receives the states of (a majority of) processes, it determines its *intention*. The intention is (to decide) Commit, if at least one process has reported a Committable state; it is Abort, if all states the coordinator received were Uncertain.[12] *Intention* to decide Commit (or Abort), however, is not the same as *deciding* Commit (or Abort). In particular, before converting its intention to an actual decision, the coordinator must make sure that a majority of processes know its intention. This will prevent inconsistent decisions because a process that knows that some coordinator ever intended Commit (or Abort) will not allow another coordinator to decide Abort (or Commit).

---

[12]We are ignoring the situations where a Committed or Aborted state is received, since these can be handled in a straightforward manner; that is, the coordinator adopts the corresponding decision and relays it to every process whose state indicates it has not reached a decision.

To inform others of its intention to decide Commit, a coordinator sends PRE-COMMIT messages to all processes. A process that receives a PRE-COMMIT from its coordinator responds with a PRE-COMMIT-ACK. The coordinator can convert its intention to decide Commit to a Commit decision only when it has received PRE-COMMIT-ACKS from at least a majority of processes. After deciding Commit in this manner, the coordinator sends COMMIT messages to all processes. On receipt of such a message a process simply adopts the Commit decision.

The procedure for informing other processes of the intention to decide Abort is analogous. The coordinator sends PRE-ABORT messages and waits for PRE-ABORT-ACKS. It converts its intention to decide Abort to a decision upon receipt of such messages from at least a majority of processes. At that time it also sends ABORT messages to all processes.

Note that the PRE-ABORT message type is new; no such messages were used in the 3PC termination protocol we saw previously. By analogy to the Committable state, we'll say that a process that has received a PRE-ABORT, but not an ABORT, message is in the *Abortable* state (or simply is Abortable). Thus when a coordinator receives the states of other processes, it may receive Committable, Uncertain, or Abortable states.

If a coordinator receives an Abortable state it must not decide Commit. This is because an Abortable state is a signal that a coordinator had the intention to decide Abort. For all we know, it may have succeeded. Similarly, if a coordinator receives a Committable state it must not decide Abort.

Unfortunately, it is possible for one process to be Abortable and another to be Committable (see Exercise 7.24). Thus, unless there is a safe rule for convincing one to "convert" to the other state (at least when all failures are repaired), we risk perpetual indecision, which is a violation of the requirements for ACPs.

Fortunately, such a safe rule exists. If a coordinator has received a majority of non-Abortable states, including at least one Committable, then it can convince any Abortable processes to become Committable. The fact that there exists a majority of non-Abortable processes means that the coordinator that sent the PRE-ABORT messages to the Abortable ones did not, after all, succeed in forming a majority of Abortable processes. Consequently, it couldn't have decided to Abort. And the fact that there is a Committable state means that it is legitimate to decide Commit (i.e., all processes had originally voted Yes). By the same argument, it is easy to see that if there is a majority of non-Committable processes, any Committable ones can be "converted" to Abortable.

In summary, then, the termination protocol is this: After being elected (by a protocol to be described shortly), a coordinator sends STATE-REQ messages to all processes. A process that receives this message from its coordinator responds by sending its present state. The coordinator waits for a period of

ties that is needed here is that any two sets of processes that are majorities must intersect.

A quorum is a generalization of the concept of majority that also satisfies this intersection property. Suppose that each process p is assigned a non-negative weight $w(p)$. A set of processes A constitutes a *quorum* if the processes in A have a majority of the weight, that is, if $\Sigma_{p \in A}\, w(p) > (\Sigma_{p \in P}\, w(p))/2$, where P is the set of all processes. A majority is a special case of a quorum where all processes have equal weight. Since quorums have the intersection property (i.e., if A and B are quorums then $A \cap B \neq \{\}$), we can replace "majority" by "quorum" in the Majority Termination Rule.

It is sometimes useful to use this more general concept, because it allows us to assign weights to processes in a way that reflects their "importance." For instance, we may wish to assign more weight to the original coordinator than to other processes, to increase the chances that the group of processes that maintains communication with that coordinator will form a quorum. Or, we may assign greater weight to processes that run in sites that fail very infrequently, thereby maximizing the chance that a quorum will be formed and minimizing the chance that *all* processes will become blocked.

BIBLIOGRAPHIC NOTES

The two phase commit protocol is due to [Gray 78] and [Lampson, Sturgis 76]. Linear 2PC was devised independently by [Gray 78] and [Rosenkrantz, Stearns, Lewis 78]. Decentralized 2PC is from [Skeen 82a]. Variants of 2PC optimized to reduce the number of records written in the DT log for various types of transactions are described in [Mohan, Lindsay 83]. The cooperative 2PC termination protocol has been used in the Sirius-Delta system [LeLann 81], and in Prime's distributed database system [Dubourdieu 82].

The 3PC protocol was devised and analyzed by Skeen [Skeen 82a], [Skeen 82b], and [Skeen 82c]. The performance of several commitment protocols with respect to blocking is studied in [Cooper 82]. [Dwork, Skeen 83] and [Ramarao 85] derive upper and lower bounds for the complexity of non-blocking commitment protocols. Communication-failure-tolerant termination protocols for 3PC are proposed in [Cheung, Kameda 85], [Chin, Ramarao 83], and [Skeen 82c].

Election protocols are discussed in [Garcia-Molina 82]. [Skeen 85] addresses the issue of determining the last process to fail.

Answers to Exercises 7.15 and 7.16 can be found in [Skeen 82a]. An atomic commitment protocol that satisfies the properties stated in Exercise 7.13 is described in [Hammer, Shipman 80].

EXERCISES

7.1   Design protocols for implementing persistent messages, that is, protocols that ensure that any message sent by a process p to process q will eventually be received by q, even if failures make the delivery of the message to q impossible at the time it is sent. Your protocol should guarantee that messages are received by q in the order they were sent by p. It should also guarantee eventual delivery of all "pending" messages if all failures are repaired and no new failures take place for sufficiently long. Under your protocol a recovering process may have to wait for some failures to be repaired before it can be assured that it has received all the messages sent to it while it was down. This is a form of blocking. Investigate ways of reducing the chance that such blocking may occur and explore the trade-off between the probability of blocking and the overhead of the protocol.

7.2   Give an ACP that also satisfies the converse of condition AC3. That is, if all processes vote Yes, then the decision must be Commit. Why is it not a good idea to enforce this condition?

7.3   Consider 2PC with the cooperative termination protocol. Describe a scenario (a particular execution) involving site failures only, which causes operational sites to become blocked.

7.4   For each of the DM implementations described in Chapter 6, describe, in some detail, how the actions of the 2PC protocol relate to the actions of the DM in processing distributed transactions.

7.5   Explore and compare various techniques whereby sites can garbage collect DT records that will never be needed.

7.6   Write down the decentralized 2PC protocol in detail. For each step in which a process is waiting to receive a message, specify suitable timeout actions.

7.7   Write down the linear 2PC protocol in detail. For each step in which a process is waiting to receive a message, specify suitable timeout actions.

7.8   Consider linear 2PC. Assuming that the maximum delay for a message to go from a process to its left (or right) neighbor is the same for all processes, indicate the timeout period that each process should set when waiting for a message (as a function of the maximum delay, the position of the process in the linear chain and the type of message expected).

7.9   In the description of the linear 2PC protocol given in Section 7.4, we have a chain of left-to-right traveling messages (votes) and then a chain of right-to-left traveling messages (the decision). It is possible to speed the protocol up in the event a process' vote is No — namely, the process passes a NO message to the right and, at the same time, passes an ABORT message to the left. Develop this variation of the linear 2PC protocol.

7.10   Is there any process in linear 2PC which is never in an uncertainty period? If so, which one(s)? If not, describe the uncertainty period of each process.

7.11   In the 2PC protocol the coordinator *first* decides Commit (by writing a **commit** record to its site's DT log) and *then* sends COMMIT messages to the participants. Suppose the order of these two steps is reversed. Show that this variation of 2PC is non-blocking if

   a. there are no communication failures and at most one process can fail, or

   b. there are no communication failures and processes have the ability to broadcast messages atomically (i.e., so that either all recipients get it or no recipient does).

How does this variation of 2PC affect the recovery procedures? Give recovery procedures that work for the modified 2PC protocol.

7.12   In the 2PC termination protocol each process independently sends a DECISION-REQ message, and each process that knows the decision responds to all the DECISION-REQs it receives. An alternative approach would be to elect a new coordinator that will send the decision to all (if a decision can be reached, i.e., if not all operational processes are uncertain). Develop a termination protocol that uses this approach. The protocol should handle both site and communication failures. Analyze the worst case round and message complexity of the resulting protocol. How do these compare to the round and message complexity of the protocol given in Section 7.4? (Be sure to include the rounds and messages needed for election in your analysis.)

7.13   Design an ACP that guarantees that no process gets blocked if there are no communication failures and only up to k processes fail (for some specified number k). Describe the protocol in some detail, giving suitable timeout actions for each step in which a process is waiting for a message. First design the protocol that guarantees consistency only under site failures. Then modify the protocol (using ideas in the last subsection of the chapter) to obtain a protocol that works even in the event of communication failures (but is still non-blocking if there are no communication failures and no more than k processes fail).

7.14   Prove that the "co-existence table" for 3PC (Fig. 7–9) is correct. That is, two operational sites can occupy two states s and s' at the same time if and only if the entry whose row corresponds to s and whose column corresponds to s' contains a "Y."

7.15   In the 3PC termination protocol of Section 7.5 that guarantees consistency if only site failures happen, the elected coordinator first collects the votes of the remaining participants and on the basis of these it decides how to proceed (using termination rules TR1-TR4). It is actually possible to have the new coordinator proceed to terminate the transaction on the basis of its own state, without polling the participants. Develop such a termination protocol and prove that it ensures consistency. What are the advantages and disadvantages of your protocol relative to the one discussed in the text?

7.16 It is possible to do away with the need for elections in 3PC, by using a *decentralized termination protocol*. The basic idea is this: Participants, when they discover that the original coordinator has failed, send to each other their present state. Each participant collects the others' states and on that basis decides how to proceed. Design such a protocol and prove that it ensures that consistent decisions are reached. (Note that a participant may fail after having sent its state to one process but before sending it to another. It is this type of behavior that makes this protocol non-trivial.) First develop a non-blocking decentralized termination protocol that guarantees consistency under the assumption that only process failures happen. Then modify this (using ideas in the last subsection of the chapter) to obtain a decentralized termination protocol that may cause blocking, but that guarantees consistency under both process and communication failures.

7.17 Consider the 3PC version that guarantees consistent decisions when only site failures take place. Describe a scenario (involving site failures only) in which a process that failed was Committable at the time it failed, yet the other processes wound up deciding Abort.

7.18 Consider the 3PC version that guarantees consistent decisions when only site failures take place. Give two scenarios involving total site failures in both of which p fails (and therefore recovers) in the same state s but such that in one some process has decided Commit and in the other some process has decided Abort. (This implies that if p, on recovery, finds itself in state s, it cannot reach a decision *on its own* for, no matter what it decides, some other process may have decided the opposite!) For which state(s) s are such scenarios possible? Is it possible that p is the last process to have failed?

7.19 Complete Figures 7–10 and 7–11, by giving the pseudo-code for the election protocol.

7.20 Suppose we are using the 3PC protocol in conjunction with (distributed) strict two phase locking (i.e., locks are supposed to the held until the "end of transaction"). Can the locks held by a transaction be released at a site when the 3PC process supervising the termination of the transaction at that site receives the PRE-COMMIT message, or should locks be held until the COMMIT is actually received?

7.21 Investigate the possibility of alternative communication topologies for 3PC. In particular, develop a decentralized and a linear commitment protocol based on 3PC. Analyze the complexity of these protocols and compare them to the complexity of the 3PC protocol given in Section 7.5.

7.22 In 3PC, does the relative order of sending COMMIT messages and writing a **commit** record in the DT log matter? What about the relative order of sending ABORT messages and writing an **abort** record?

7.23 Write a pseudo-code specification for the 3PC version described in the last subsection of the chapter.

7.24 Consider the 3PC protocol described in the last subsection of this chapter. Describe a scenario in which some process is in the Committable and another in the Abortable state.

7.25 Give a careful proof of the fact that the 3PC version described in the last subsection of the chapter guarantees the consistency of the decisions reached, even in the presence of communication failures. (Hint: Your proof could be based on the following property of the protocol: If Commit is decided, then a majority of processes are either Committable or Committed; if Abort is decided, then either no process is Committable or Committed, or a majority of processes are Abortable or Aborted.)

7.26 In the 3PC version given in the last subsection of the chapter, it is possible (due to communication failures) for a process p to receive a STATE-REQ, PRE-COMMIT or PRE-ABORT message from a process that is not p's present coordinator. It is said in the text that p must ignore such messages. Give three scenarios (one for each message type) that illustrate what could go wrong if p did not ignore these messages. Also show that if p receives a STATE-REQ and p has decided, it is safe for it to respond as if the STATE-REQ had been received from its coordinator.

8

REPLICATED DATA

8.1 INTRODUCTION

A replicated database is a distributed database in which multiple copies of some data items are stored at multiple sites. The main reason for using replicated data is to increase DBS availability. By storing critical data at multiple sites, the DBS can operate even though some sites have failed. Another goal is improved performance. Since there are many copies of each data item, a transaction is more likely to find the data it needs close by, as compared to a single copy database. This benefit is mitigated by the need to update all copies of each data item. Thus, Reads may run faster at the expense of slower Writes.

Our goal is to design a DBS that hides all aspects of data replication from users' transactions. That is, transactions issue Reads and Writes on data items, and the DBS is responsible for translating those operations into Reads and Writes on one or more copies of those data items. Before looking at the architecture of a DBS that performs these functions, let's first determine what it means for such a system to behave correctly.

Correctness

We assume that a DBS managing a replicated database should behave like a DBS managing a one-copy (i.e., nonreplicated) database insofar as users can tell. In a one-copy database, users expect the interleaved execution of their

265

transactions to be equivalent to a serial execution of those transactions. Since replicated data should be transparent to them, they would like the interleaved execution of their transactions on a *replicated* database to be equivalent to a serial execution of those transactions on a *one-copy* database. Such executions are called *one-copy serializable* (or *1SR*). This is the goal of concurrency control for replicated data.

This concept of one-copy serializability is essentially the same as the one we used for multiversion data in Chapter 5. In both cases we are giving the user a one-copy view of a database that may have multiple copies (replicated copies or multiple versions) of each data item. The only difference is that here we are abstracting replicated copies, rather than multiple versions, from the users' view.

The Write-All Approach

In an ideal world where sites never fail, a DBS can easily manage replicated data. It translates each $Read(x)$ into $Read(x_A)$, where x_A is any copy of data item x (x_A denotes the copy of x at site A). It translates each $Write(x)$ into $\{Write(x_{A_1}), \ldots, Write(x_{A_m})\}$, where $\{x_{A_1}, \ldots, x_{A_m}\}$ are all copies of x. And it uses any serializable concurrency control algorithm to synchronize access to copies. We call this the *write-all approach* to replicated data.

To see why the write-all approach works, consider any execution produced by the DBS. Since the DBS is using a serializable concurrency control algorithm, this execution is equivalent to some serial execution. In that serial execution, each transaction that writes into a data item x writes into all copies of x. From the viewpoint of the next transaction in the serial execution, all copies of x were written simultaneously. So, no matter which copy of x the next transaction reads, it reads the same value, namely, the one written by the last transaction that wrote all copies of x. Thus, the execution behaves as though it were operating on a single copy database.

Unfortunately, the world is less than ideal — sites can fail and recover. This is a problem for the write-all approach, because it requires that the DBS process each $Write(x)$ by writing into *all* copies of x, even if some have failed. Since there will be times when some copies of x are down, the DBS will not always be able to write into all copies of x at the time it receives a $Write(x)$ operation. If the DBS were to adhere to the write-all approach in this situation, it would have to delay processing $Write(x)$ until it could write into all copies of x.

Such a delay is obviously bad for update transactions. If any copy of x fails, then no transaction that writes into x can execute to completion. The more copies of x that exist, the higher the probability that one of them is down. In this case, more replication of data actually makes the system less available to update transactions! For this reason, the write-all approach is unsatisfactory.

The Write-All-Available Approach

Suppose we adopt a more flexible approach. We still require the DBS to produce a serializable execution, but no longer require a transaction to write into all copies of each data item x in its writeset. It *should* write into all of the copies that it can, but it may ignore any copies that are down or not yet created. This is the *write-all-available approach*. It solves the availability problem, but may lead to problems of correctness.

Using the write-all-available approach, there will be times when some copies of x do not reflect the most up-to-date value of x. A transaction that reads an out-of-date copy of x can create an incorrect, i.e., non-1SR, execution. The following execution, H_1, shows how this can happen:

$$H_1 = w_0[x_A]\ w_0[x_B]\ w_0[y_C]\ c_0\ r_1[y_C]\ w_1[x_A]\ c_1\ r_2[x_B]\ w_2[y_C]\ c_2.$$

Notice that T_2 read copy x_B of x from T_0, even though T_1 was the last transaction before it that wrote into x. That is, T_2 read an out-of-date copy of x.

In a serial execution on a one-copy database, if a transaction reads a data item x, then it reads x from the last transaction before it that wrote into x. But this is not what happened in H_1. T_2 read x_B from T_0, which is *not* the last transaction before it that wrote into x. Thus H_1 is not equivalent to the serial execution $T_0\ T_1\ T_2$ on a one-copy database. We could still regard H_1 as correct if it were equivalent to another serial execution on a one-copy database. However, since $w_0[y_C] < r_1[y_C] < w_2[y_C]$, there are no other serial executions equivalent to H_1. Therefore, H_1 is not equivalent to any serial execution on a one-copy database. That is, H_1 is not 1SR.

T_1 seems to be the culprit here, because it did not write into *all* copies of x. Unfortunately, it may have had no choice. For example, suppose site B failed after T_0 but before T_1, and recovered after T_1 but before T_2, as in H_1':

$$H_1' = w_0[x_A]\ w_0[x_B]\ w_0[y_C]\ c_0\ B\text{-fails}\ r_1[y_C]\ w_1[x_A]\ c_1\ B\text{-recovers}\ r_2[x_B]\ w_2[y_C]\ c_2.$$

Rather than waiting for B to recover so it could write x_B, T_1 wrote into the one copy that it *could* write, namely, x_A. After B recovered, T_2 unwittingly read x_B, an out-of-date copy of x, and therefore produced an incorrect result. This particular problem could be easily solved by preventing transactions from reading copies from sites that have failed and recovered until these copies are brought up-to-date. Unfortunately, this isn't enough, as we'll see later (cf. Section 8.4.).

There are several algorithms, including some variations of the write-all-available approach, that correctly handle failures and recoveries and thereby avoid incorrect executions such as H_1. These algorithms are the main subject of this chapter. But before we delve deeply into this subject, let's first define a system architecture for DBSs that manage replicated data.

8.2 SYSTEM ARCHITECTURE

We will assume that the DBS is distributed. As usual, each site has a data manager (DM) and transaction manager (TM) that manage data and transactions at the site.

The Data Manager

The DM is a centralized DBS that processes Reads and Writes on local copies of data items. It has an associated local scheduler for concurrency control, based on one of the standard techniques (2PL, TO, or SGT). In addition, there may be some interaction between local schedulers, for example, to detect distributed deadlocks or SG cycles.

As in Chapter 7, we assume that the DM and scheduler at a site are able to commit a transaction's Writes that were executed at that site. By committing a transaction T, the scheduler guarantees that the recoverability condition holds for all of T's Reads at that site, and the DM guarantees that all of T's Writes at that site are in stable storage (i.e., it satisfies the Redo Rule).

The scheduler at a site is only sensitive to conflicts between operations on the same *copy* of a data item. For example, if the scheduler at site A receives an operation $r_i[x_A]$, it will synchronize $r_i[x_A]$ relative to Writes it has received on x_A. However, since it doesn't receive Writes on other copies of x, it cannot synchronize $r_i[x_A]$ relative to Writes on those other copies. The scheduler is really treating operations on copies as if they were operations on independent data items. In this sense, it is entirely oblivious to data replication.

The Transaction Manager

The TM is the interface between user transactions and the DBS. It translates users' Reads and Writes on data items into Reads and Writes on copies of those data items. It sends those Reads and Writes on copies to the appropriate sites, where they are processed by the local schedulers and DMs.

The TM also uses an atomic commitment protocol (ACP), so that it can consistently terminate a transaction that accessed data at more than one site. We assume that the DM and scheduler at each site are designed to participate in this ACP for any transaction that is active at that site.

To perform its functions, the TM must determine which sites have copies of which data items. It uses *directories* for this purpose.[1] There may be just one

---

[1]Note that the term *directory* has a different meaning here than in Chapter 6. In this chapter, a directory maps each data item x to the sites that have copies of x. In Chapter 6, it mapped each data item to its stable storage location.

directory that tells where all copies of all data items are stored. The directory can be stored at all sites or only at some of them. Alternatively, each directory may only give the location of copies of some of the data items. In this case, each directory is normally only stored at those sites that frequently access the information that it contains. To find the remaining directories, the TM needs a *master directory* that tells where copies of each directory are located.

To process a transaction, a TM must access the directories that tell it where to find the copies of data items that the transaction needs. If communication is expensive, then the directories should be designed so that each TM will usually be able to find a copy of those directories at its own site. Otherwise, the TM will have to send messages to other sites to find the directories it needs.

Failure Assumptions

We say that a copy x_A of a data item or directory at site A is *available to site B* if A correctly executes each Read and Write on x_A issued by B and B receives A's acknowledgment of that execution. Thus copy x_A may be unavailable to B for one of three reasons:

1. A does not receive Reads and Writes on x_A issued by B. In this case, by definition, a communications failure has occurred (see Section 7.2).

2. The communication network correctly delivers to A Reads and Writes on x_A issued by B, but A is unable to execute them, either because A is down or A has suffered a failure of the storage medium that contains x_A.

3. A receives and executes each Read and Write issued by B, but B does not receive A's acknowledgment of such executions (due to a communications failure).

We say a copy x_A is *available* (or *unavailable*) if it is available (or not available) to every site other than A.

As in Chapter 7, we assume that sites are fail-stop, and that site failures are detected by timeout. Thus, in the absence of communications failures, each site can determine whether any other site is failed simply by sending a message and waiting for a reply. That is, site failures are *detectable*.

If communications failures may occur, then a site A that is not responding to messages may still be functioning. This creates nasty problems for managing replicated data, because A may try to read or write its copies without being able to synchronize against Reads or Writes on copies of the same data item at other sites.

Distributing Writes

When a transaction issues Write(x), the DBS is responsible for eventually updating a set of copies of x (the exact set depends on the algorithm used for managing replicated data). It can distribute these Writes *immediately*, at the moment it receives Write(x) from the transaction. Or, it can *defer* the Writes on replicated copies until the transaction terminates.

With deferred writing, the DBS uses a nonreplicated view of the database while the transaction is executing. That is, for each data item that the transaction reads or writes, the DBS accesses one and only one copy of that data item. (Different transactions may use different copies.) The DBS delays the distribution of Writes to other copies until the transaction has terminated and is ready to commit. The DBS must therefore maintain an intentions list of deferred updates.[2] After the transaction terminates, it sends the appropriate portion of the intentions list to each site that contains replicated copies of the transaction's writeset, but that has not yet received those Writes. It can piggyback this message with the VOTE-REQ message of the first phase of the ACP.

Except for the copies it uses while executing the transaction, a DBS that uses deferred writing puts all replicated Writes destined for the same site in a single message. This tends to minimize the number of messages required to execute a transaction. By contrast, using immediate writing, the DBS sends Writes to replicated copies while the transaction executes. Although some piggybacking may be possible, it essentially uses one message for each Write. Thus, immediate writing tends to use more messages than deferred writing.

Another advantage of deferred writing is that Aborts often cost less than with immediate writing. In a DBS that uses immediate writing, when a transaction T_i aborts, the DBS is likely to have already distributed many of T_i's Writes to replicated copies. Not only are these Writes wasted, but they also must be undone. With deferred writing, the DBS delays the distribution of those Writes until after T_i has terminated. If T_i aborts before it terminates, then the abortion is less costly than with immediate writing.

A disadvantage of deferred writing is that it may delay the commitment of a transaction more than immediate writing. This is because the first phase of the ACP at each receiving site must process a potentially large number of Writes before it can respond to the VOTE-REQ message. With immediate writing, receiving sites can execute many of a transaction's Writes while the transaction is still executing, thereby avoiding the delay of executing them at commit time.

A second disadvantage of deferred writing is that it tends to delay the detection of conflicts between operations. For example, suppose transactions T_1 and T_2 execute concurrently and both write into x. Furthermore, suppose the DBS uses copy x_A while executing T_1 and uses x_B while executing T_2. Until the DBS distributes T_1's replicated Write on x_B or T_2's replicated Write on x_A, no scheduler will detect the conflicting Writes between T_1 and T_2. With deferred writing, this happens at the end of T_1's and T_2's execution. This may be less desirable than immediate writing, since it may cause a scheduler to

---

[2]Cf. the no-undo/redo centralized recovery algorithm in Section 6.6.

reject a Write later in a transaction's execution. The DBS ends up aborting the transaction after having paid for most of the transaction's execution. (This is similar to a disadvantage of 2PL certifiers described in Section 4.4.)

This disadvantage of deferred writing can be mitigated by requiring the DBS to use the same copy of each data item, called the *primary copy*, to execute every transaction. For example, the DBS would use the same (primary) copy of x, x_A, to execute both T_1 and T_2. The scheduler for x_A detects the conflict between T_1's and T_2's writes, thereby detecting it earlier than if T_1 and T_2 used different copies of x. In this case, deferred writing and immediate writing detect the conflict at about the same point in a transaction's execution.

8.3 SERIALIZABILITY THEORY FOR REPLICATED DATA

We will extend basic serializability theory by using two types of histories: *replicated data (RD)* histories and *one-copy (1C)* histories. RD histories represent the DBS's view of executions of operations on a replicated database. 1C histories represent the interpretation of RD histories in the users' single copy view of the database. (1C histories are quite similar to the 1V histories we used in Chapter 5.) As usual, we will characterize a concurrency control algorithm by the RD histories it produces. To prove an algorithm correct, we prove that its RD histories are equivalent to serial 1C histories, which are the histories that the user regards as correct.

The formal development of serializability theory for replicated databases is very similar to that for multiversion databases. The notations and the formal notions of correctness are analogous. You may find it helpful to think about these similarities while you're reading this section.

Replicated Data Histories

Let $T = \{T_0, \ldots, T_n\}$ be a set of transactions. To process operations from T, a DBS translates T's operations on data items into operations on the replicated copies of those data items. We formalize this translation by a function h that maps each $r_i[x]$ into $r_i[x_A]$, where x_A is a copy of x; each $w_i[x]$ into $w_i[x_{A_1}], \ldots, w_i[x_{A_m}]$ for some copies $x_{A_1}, \ldots, x_{A_m}$ of x ($m > 0$); each c_i into c_i and each a_i into a_i.

A *complete replicated data (RD)* history H over $T = \{T_0, \ldots, T_n\}$ is a partial order with ordering relation $<$ where

1. $H = h\left(\bigcup_{i=0}^{n} T_i\right)$ for some translation function h;
2. for each T_i and all operations p_i, q_i in T_i, if $p_i <_i q_i$, then every operation in $h(p_i)$ is related by $<$ to every operation in $h(q_i)$;
3. for every $r_j[x_A]$, there is at least one $w_i[x_A] < r_j[x_A]$;

4. all pairs of conflicting operations are related by $<$, where two operations *conflict* if they operate on the same *copy* and at least one of them is a Write; and

5. if $w_i[x] <_i r_i[x]$ and $h(r_i[x]) = r_i[x_A]$ then $w_i[x_A] \in h(w_i[x])$.

Condition (1) states that the DBS translates each operation submitted by a transaction into appropriate operations on copies. Condition (2) states that the RD history preserves all orderings stipulated by transactions. Condition (3) states that a transaction may not read a copy unless it has been previously initialized. Condition (4) states that the history records the execution order of noncommutative operations. Condition (5) states that if a transaction T_i writes into a data item x before it reads x, then it must write into the same copy x_A of x that it subsequently reads. (It may write into other copies of x as well.) By Condition (2), this implies $w_i[x_A] < r_i[x_A]$. We will revisit this issue in a moment.

Given transactions $\{T_0, T_1, T_2, T_3\}$:

$$T_0 = \begin{matrix} w_0[x] \searrow \\ w_0[y] \to c_0 \end{matrix} \qquad\qquad T_2 = \quad w_2[x] \to r_2[x] \to w_2[y] \to c_2$$

$$T_1 = \quad r_1[x] \to w_1[x] \to c_1 \qquad\qquad T_3 = \begin{matrix} r_3[x] \searrow \\ r_3[y] \to c_3 \end{matrix}$$

the following history, H_2, is an RD history over $\{T_0, \ldots, T_3\}$:

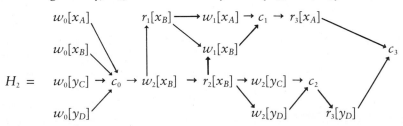

Let H be an RD history over T. Transaction T_j *reads-x-from* T_i in H if for some copy x_A T_j reads-x_A-from T_i, that is, if $w_i[x_A] < r_j[x_A]$ and no $w_k[x_A]$ $(k \neq i)$ falls between these operations. Since reads-from relationships on copies are unique by condition (4) of RD histories and since a transaction reads at most one copy of any given data item,[3] reads-from relationships on data items are unique as well.

In this chapter, *we will only consider histories that are complete and that only contain committed transactions* (i.e., histories that are committed projections of themselves). These restrictions are justified by requiring that we only

---

[3]This follows from the fact that $h(r_i[x]) = r_i[x_A]$ (i.e., $h(r_i[x])$ does not equal a set of Reads) and from the assumption that a transaction reads a data item at most once. As we mentioned in Chapter 2, the latter assumption is mainly a convenience that can be dispensed with at some cost in notational complexity.

use schedulers that produce recoverable executions. Recoverability for RD histories is defined as for 1C histories, but with respect to copies. That is, an RD history H is recoverable if whenever T_i reads (any copy) from T_j in H and $c_i \in H$, then $c_j < c_i$. We assume that all RD histories are recoverable.

The serialization graph for an RD history is defined as for a 1C history. That is, the nodes correspond to committed transactions in the history and there is an edge $T_i \to T_j$ if there are conflicting operations p_i in T_i and q_j in T_j such that $p_i < q_j$. Thus, the serialization graph for H_2 is

$$SG(H_2) = \begin{array}{ccc} T_0 & \longrightarrow & T_2 \\ \downarrow & \times & \downarrow \\ T_1 & \longrightarrow & T_3 \end{array}$$

If $SG(H)$ is acyclic, then conditions (2) and (5) in the definition of RD history ensure that H *preserves reflexive reads-from relationships*. More precisely, we have:

Lemma 8.1:   Let H be an RD history involving transaction T_i. If $SG(H)$ is acyclic and for some x $w_i[x] <_i r_i[x]$, then T_i reads-x-from T_i in H.

Proof: From conditions (2) and (5) on RD histories, $w_i[x] <_i r_i[x]$ implies that for some copy x_A of x, $w_i[x_A] < r_i[x_A]$. Suppose, by way of contradiction, T_i didn't read x from T_i in H. Then there must exist some $w_k[x_A]$ $(k \neq i)$ in H such that $w_i[x_A] < w_k[x_A] < r_i[x_A]$. But then $SG(H)$ contains edges $T_i \to T_k$ and $T_k \to T_i$ which contradicts the assumed acyclicity of $SG(H)$.   □

We would like to define an RD history H to be 1SR if it is equivalent to a serial 1C history H_{1C}. To determine if H is equivalent to H_{1C}, it would be unsatisfactory to use the notion of conflict equivalence, simply because H and H_{1C} have different operations.[4] However, reads-from relationships and final writes do behave the same way in both types of histories. Therefore, view equivalence provides a natural way to determine the equivalence of an RD history and 1C history (see Section 2.6 for a discussion of view equivalence in 1C histories).

Given RD history H, define $w_i[x_A]$ to be a *final write for x_A in H* if $a_i \notin H$ and for all $w_j[x_A]$ in H $(j \neq i)$, either $a_j \in H$ or $w_j[x_A] < w_i[x_A]$.

Two RD histories over T are *equivalent* (denoted $\equiv$) if they are view equivalent, that is, if they have the same reads-from relationships and final writes.

---

[4]That is, if we define H and H_{1C} to be equivalent if conflicting operations appear in the same order in both histories, then we must deal with the problem that some operations that conflict in H_{1C} may not have corresponding operations that conflict in H. For example, consider $H = w_2[x_B] \, w_1[x_A]$ and $H_{1C} = w_2[x] \, w_1[x]$.

This example illustrates the rather surprising fact that the write-all-available approach may lead to an incorrect execution, even if only failures, but no recoveries occur (i.e., failed copies never recover).

One explanation of the problem in H_4 relates to the fundamental technique that all concurrency control algorithms use to obtain correct executions, namely, controlling the order of conflicting operations on shared data. In H_4, even though T_1 and T_2 have conflicting accesses to data items x and y, they don't have conflicting accesses to *copies* of x and y. The copy of x and y that each of them read failed before the other transaction's conflicting Write into that copy could be issued. The copy that each of them wrote is a copy that the other transaction didn't read. Thus, the logical conflicts were never manifested as physical conflicts on copies, which is the only place that the DBS can control them.

In a sense, the problem is finding a way to ensure that any two transactions that have conflicting accesses to the same data item also have conflicting accesses to some copy of that data item. That way, the DBS will be able to synchronize the transactions. If the DBS can do this in all cases, then by attaining ordinary serializability it has also attained one-copy serializability.

*Replicated Data Serialization Graphs

To determine if an RD history is 1SR, we will use a modified SG. This graph models the observation that two transactions that have conflicting accesses to the same data item must be synchronized, even if they don't access the same copy of that data item. To define this graph, we need a little terminology. We say that node n_i *precedes* node n_j, denoted $n_i \ll n_j$, in a directed graph if there is a path from n_i to n_j.

Given an RD history H, a *replicated data serialization graph* (RDSG) for H is SG(H) with enough edges added (possibly none) such that the following two conditions hold: For all data items x,

1. if T_i and T_k write x, then either $T_i \ll T_k$ or $T_k \ll T_i$), and

2. if T_j reads-x-from T_i, T_k writes some copy of x $(k \neq i, k \neq j))$, and $T_i \ll T_k$, then $T_j \ll T_k$.

If a graph satisfies condition (1), we say it *induces a write order* for H. If it satisfies condition (2), we say it *induces a read order* for H. Thus RDSG(H) is an extension of SG(H) that induces a read order and a write order for H. Note that an RDSG for H isn't uniquely determined by H.

We explained that failures can lead to incorrect behavior because transactions that have conflicting accesses to the same data item may not have conflicting accesses to copies of that data item. An SG doesn't have enough edges (due to conflicting accesses to copies) to force an order on every pair of transactions with conflicting accesses to the same data item. An RDSG for H adds enough edges to SG(H) to make this so. The write order ensures that the

RDSG orders every pair of transactions that write into the same data item, even if they don't write into the same copy. If the RDSG induces a write order, then the read order ensures that the RDSG orders every pair of transactions (T_j and T_k) that (respectively) read and write the same data item.

$SG(H_4)$ is not an $RDSG(H_4)$. It induces a write order for H_4, but not a read order. We can make it into an $RDSG(H_4)$ by adding edges between T_1 and T_2.

$$G = \quad T_0 \xrightarrow{\quad\quad} T_1 \underset{\longleftarrow}{\overset{\longrightarrow}{}} T_2$$

Since T_1 reads-x-from T_0, T_2 writes x, and $T_0 \to T_2$, we added $T_1 \to T_2$. Since T_2 reads-y-from T_0, T_1 writes y, and $T_0 \to T_1$, we added $T_2 \to T_1$. Since these are the only two reads-from relationships in H_4, these two edges are enough to ensure that G induces a read order for H. Notice that G has a cycle. Since every RDSG for H_4 must contain the edges $T_1 \to T_2$ and $T_2 \to T_1$, every such RDSG has a cycle.

The following theorem is an important tool for analyzing the correctness of concurrency control algorithms for replicated data.

Theorem 8.4: Let H be an RD history. If H has an acyclic RDSG, then H is 1SR.

Proof: Let $H_s = T_{i_1} T_{i_2} \ldots T_{i_n}$ be a serial 1C history where $T_{i_1}, T_{i_2}, \ldots,$ T_{i_n} is a topological sort of $RDSG(H)$. Since $RDSG(H)$ contains $SG(H)$, by Theorem 8.3, we can prove that H is 1SR just by proving that H and H_s have the same reads-from relationships.

First, assume T_j reads-x-from T_i in H. Suppose, by way of contradiction, that T_j reads-x-from T_k in H_s, for some $k \neq i$. If $k = j$, Lemma 8.1 implies that T_j reads-x-from T_k in H, a contradiction (note that since H has an acyclic RDSG, $SG(H)$ is surely acyclic and therefore Lemma 8.1 applies). So, assume $k \neq j$. Since T_j reads-x-from T_i in H, $T_i \to T_j$ is in the RDSG of H, so T_i precedes T_j in H_s. Since the RDSG induces both a read and a write order, we have that either $T_k \ll T_i$ or $T_j \ll T_k$. Thus either T_k precedes T_i (which precedes T_j) or T_k follows T_j in H_s, both contradicting that T_j reads-x-from T_k in H_s.

Now assume T_j reads-x-from T_i in H_s. By conditions (3) and (4) in the definition of RD history and the definition of reads-from, T_j reads-x-from some transaction in H, say T_h. By the previous paragraph, T_j reads-x-from T_h in H_s. Since read-from relationships are unique, $T_h = T_i$. $\square$

8.5 ATOMICITY OF FAILURES AND RECOVERIES

Another characterization of 1SR histories is that they are RD histories in which failure and recovery events appear to be atomic. That is, in a 1SR history, all transactions have a consistent view of when copies fail and recover. In the next two subsections, we will explain this characterization by means of examples. Then we will describe a graph structure that captures this characterization.

Atomicity of Failures

Loosely speaking, a transaction learns about a failure when it tries to read or write a copy that turns out to be unavailable. Similarly, it knows that a copy could not have failed yet if it successfully accesses that copy. Depending on when each transaction learns about failures, different transactions might see failures occurring in different orders.

For example, reconsider history H_4.

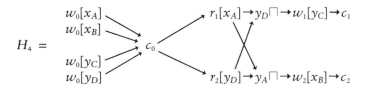

Since T_1 decided not to write y_D, it must have learned about y_D's failure before it committed; this means that in an equivalent serial execution, y_D failed before T_1 executed. And since it read x_A, it believes x_A failed after it executed. Thus, T_1 sees failures in the following order: $y_D\sqcap \rightarrow T_1 \rightarrow x_A\sqcap$. By contrast, T_2 sees the failures in the opposite order. It didn't write x_A, so it must have learned that x_A failed before it ran. But it read y_D, so it believes y_D failed after it ran. Thus, it sees $x_A\sqcap \rightarrow T_2 \rightarrow y_D\sqcap$.

Suppose we think of failures as atomic events that must be recorded in a serial execution. Given T_1's and T_2's view of these events, there is no serial execution of T_1 and T_2 in which we can place the failure events $x_A\sqcap$ and $y_D\sqcap$. For example, if the given execution were equivalent to the serial execution T_1T_2, then $T_1 \rightarrow x_A\sqcap \rightarrow T_2$ is consistent with T_1's and T_2's view. But T_1 thinks y_D failed before T_1, and T_2 thinks y_D failed after T_2. Both views cannot be true if $y_D\sqcap$ is an atomic event. Instead, if the given execution were equivalent to T_2T_1, then we have $T_2 \rightarrow y_D\sqcap \rightarrow T_1$, but now we have inconsistent views of $x_A\sqcap$ to contend with.

To ensure that failure events appear to be atomic, we need to synchronize failures with Reads and Writes. Unfortunately, failures are not controllable events. They happen whenever they want to. So, the best we can do is ensure that transactions *see* failures in a consistent order. This, as it turns out, is all we need.

Note that a transaction can see a failure by *not* issuing a Write on an unavailable copy. Therefore, the DBS must not only control the order in which transactions read and write copies, but must also control the transaction's decision whether or not to issue a Write on a copy. Thus, the TM's translation activity has an effect on one-copy serializability.

Atomicity of Recoveries

To create a new copy of x, or to recover a formerly failed copy of x, say x_B, the DBS must store an initial value in x_B. Any transaction that ordinarily writes into x can initialize x_B. Whenever it writes into other copies of x, it writes into x_B too. Rather than waiting for such a transaction to appear, the DBS can force the initialization of x_B by running a special transaction, called a *copier*. The copier simply reads an existing copy of the data item that is up-to-date and writes that value into the new copy. Whether the DBS uses an ordinary transaction or a copier to initialize x_B, it must ensure that no transaction reads x_B until it has been initialized.

The DBS must also make x_B known to all transactions that update x, so that they will write into x_B whenever they write into other copies of x. This latter activity requires some synchronization, as the following example illustrates.

Suppose the database has copies x_A and y_C at the time that the DBS is ready to create copy x_B. It runs a copier transaction, T_1, to initialize x_B at about the same time that two other transactions T_2 and T_3 execute. The resulting execution is as follows.

$$H_5 = \begin{array}{c} w_0[x_A] \\ \\ w_0[y_C] \end{array} \quad c_0 \quad \begin{array}{l} r_1[x_A] \to w_1[x_B] \to c_1 \to r_3[x_B] \to c_3 \\ r_2[x_A] \to w_2[x_A] \to c_2 \to r_3[y_C] \\ w_2[y_C] \end{array}$$

H_5 is incorrect. The only serial RD history equivalent to H_5 is

$$H_5' = w_0[x_A]\, w_0[y_C]\, c_0\, r_1[x_A]\, w_1[x_B]\, c_1\, r_2[x_A]\, w_2[x_A]\, w_2[y_C]\, c_2\, r_3[x_B]\, r_3[y_C]\, c_3$$

H_5' is not equivalent to the serial 1C history $T_0\, T_1\, T_2\, T_3$. In a one-copy database, T_2 would write x and y, and T_3 would read the values that T_2 wrote. But in this execution, T_3 read the value of x that T_1 wrote and the value of y that T_2 wrote. H_5 is not equivalent to any other serial 1C history either, and so is not 1SR.

The problem is that T_2 should have updated the new copy of x, x_B, but didn't. Since T_1 knows that x_B exists (it wrote x_B), and since T_1 effectively executes before T_2 (because $r_1[x_A] < w_2[x_A]$), T_2 should also know that x_B exists. Therefore, since T_2 writes into x, it should write all copies of x, including x_B. If it did, then $r_3[x_B]$ would have read the proper value.

We can also explain this in terms of the atomicity of recovery events. Let us denote the recovery (or initialization) of x_A as $x_A\sqcup$. Since T_1 wrote x_B, it believes x_B recovered before it executed. That is, $x_B\sqcup \to T_1$. Since T_2 wrote x_A but not x_B, it believes x_B recovered after it executed. That is, $T_2 \to x_B\sqcup$. But since $T_1 \to T_2$ is in $SG(H_5)$, these views of the recovery of x_B are inconsistent.[6]

---

[6]An alternative analysis is $x_B\sqcup \to T_1 \to x_B\sqcap \to T_2 \to x_B\sqcup \to T_3$. We have $x_B\sqcup \to T_3$ because T_3 read x_B. But now T_3 reads the recovered copy x_B before it has been initialized (with the value of x written by T_2), which is illegal.

*Failure-Recovery Serialization Graphs

As we have seen, another explanation why a serializable execution may not be 1SR is that different transactions observe failures and recoveries in different orders. We can formalize this reasoning by augmenting SGs to include nodes that represent the creation and failure of each copy. To keep the notation simple, we will assume that each copy is created once and sometime later fails. *Once it has failed, a copy never recovers.* This assumption is not a loss of generality because we can regard the recovery of a copy as the creation of a new copy. That is, a copy that fails and recovers several times is represented by a sequence of uniquely named incarnations, each of which is created, fails at most once, and never recovers. An alternative model for incarnations is suggested in Exercise 8.9.

Given an RD history H over transactions $\{T_0, \ldots, T_n\}$, a *failure-recovery serialization graph* (FRSG) for H is a directed graph with nodes N and edges E where:

$$N = \{T_0, \ldots, T_n\} \cup \{create[x_A] \mid x \text{ is a data item and } x_A \text{ is a copy of } x\}$$
$$\cup \{fail[x_A] \mid x \text{ is a data item and } x_A \text{ is a copy of } x\}$$
$$E = \{T_i \rightarrow T_j \mid T_i \rightarrow T_j \text{ is an edge of } SG(H)\} \cup E1 \cup E2 \cup E3$$

where

$E1 = \{create[x_A] \rightarrow T_i \mid T_i \text{ reads or writes } x_A\}$

$E2 = \{T_i \rightarrow fail[x_A] \mid T_i \text{ reads } x_A\}$

$E3 = \{T_i \rightarrow create[x_A] \text{ or } fail[x_A] \rightarrow T_i \mid T_i \text{ writes some copy of } x, \text{ but not } x_A\}$

The edges in $E1$ signify that if T_i read or wrote x_A, then x_A was created before T_i executed ($create[x_A] \rightarrow T_i$). $E2$ signifies that if T_i read x_A, then T_i executed before x_A failed ($T_i \rightarrow fail[x_A]$). Notice that this need not hold if T_i wrote (but did not read) x_A. $E3$ signifies that if T_i wrote some copies of x but did not write x_A, then it must have written those copies at a time when x_A did not exist, that is, either before it was created or after it failed. Thus, for each such situation, $E3$ must contain either $T_i \rightarrow create[x_A]$ or $fail[x_A] \rightarrow T_i$. As in RDSGs, H does not uniquely determine an FRSG.

For example, the following is an FRSG for H_4.

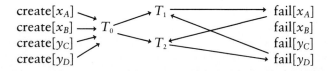

Since T_1 wrote y_C, but not y_D, we must include either $T_1 \rightarrow create[y_D]$ or $fail[y_D] \rightarrow T_1$; we chose the latter. Similarly, we added $fail[x_A] \rightarrow T_2$, because T_2 wrote x_B but not x_A. Notice that this FRSG has a cycle: $T_1 \rightarrow fail[x_A] \rightarrow T_2 \rightarrow fail[y_D] \rightarrow T_1$. In fact, *every* FRSG for H_4 has a cycle.

Given a history H, if there is an acyclic FRSG(H), then we can produce a serial history that is equivalent to H and which includes the creation and failure of copies as atomic events. That is, all transactions observe the creation and failure of each copy in the same order. This condition is enough to show that H is 1SR.

Theorem 8.5: Let H be an RD history. If H has an acyclic FRSG, then H is 1SR.

Proof: As in Theorem 8.4, let $H_s = T_{i_1} T_{i_2} \ldots T_{i_n}$ be a serial 1C history where $T_{i_1}, T_{i_2}, \ldots, T_{i_n}$ is a topological sort of FRSG(H). Since FRSG(H) contains SG(H), by Theorem 8.3 we can prove that H is 1SR just by proving that H and H_s have the same reads-from relationships.

First assume T_j reads-x_A-from T_i in H. Hence $T_i \rightarrow T_j$ is in the FRSG and T_i precedes T_j in H_s. Let T_k be any other transaction that writes x. If T_k writes x_A, then since T_j reads-x_A-from T_i, either $T_k \rightarrow T_i$ or $T_j \rightarrow T_k$ must be in the FRSG. If T_k does not write x_A, by definition of FRSG, either $T_k \rightarrow \text{create}[x_A]$ or $\text{fail}[x_A] \rightarrow T_k$. In the former case, since $\text{create}[x_A] \rightarrow T_i$, T_k precedes T_i in the FRSG. In the latter case, since $T_j \rightarrow \text{fail}[x_A]$, T_j precedes T_k in the FRSG. Hence, if T_k writes x, either T_k precedes T_i or follows T_j in the FRSG and in H_s, too. Thus, T_j reads-x-from T_i in H_s.

Now, suppose T_j reads-x-from T_i in H_s. By the definition of RD history, T_j reads-x-from some transaction in H, say T_h. By the previous paragraph, T_j reads-x-from T_h in H_s. Since reads-from relationships are unique, $T_h = T_i$. $\square$

8.6 AN AVAILABLE COPIES ALGORITHM

Available copies algorithms handle replicated data by using enhanced forms of the write-all-available approach. That is, every Read(x) is translated into a Read of *any* copy of x and every Write(x) is translated into Writes of all available copies of x. Simply doing this is not enough to guarantee one-copy serializability, as history H_4 showed. Available copy algorithms enforce special protocols that, in conjunction with this "read-any, write-all-available" discipline, ensure correctness.

These algorithms handle site failures but not communications failures. That is, they assume that every site is either operational or down, and that all operational sites can communicate with each other. Therefore, each operational site can independently determine which sites are down, simply by attempting to communicate with them. If a site doesn't respond to a message within the timeout period, then it must be down.

For available copies algorithms, we'll assume that *the scheduler uses strict two phase locking*. Thus, after transaction T_i has read or written a copy of x_A, no other transaction can access x_A in a conflicting mode until after T_i has committed or aborted.

In this section we'll describe a simple available copies algorithm. We assume that there is a fixed set of copies for each data item, known to every site. This set does not change dynamically. Moreover, to keep the description simple, we'll initially assume that each copy is created and fails at most once. Later we'll discuss how to accommodate repeated failures and recoveries of copies — no changes to the algorithm are needed for this extension! After a copy has been initialized and before it has failed, it is said to be *available*; otherwise, it is *unavailable*.

Processing Reads and Writes

When a transaction T_i issues a Read(x), the TM at T_i's home site[7] (henceforth simply "T_i's TM") will select some copy x_A of x and submit Read(x_A) on behalf of T_i to site A. Typically the selected copy will be the one "closest" to T_i's home site (ideally the home site itself), to minimize the communication cost incurred by the Read. The correctness of the algorithm, however, does not depend on which copy is read — any one will do.

Site A regards x_A as *initialized* if it has already processed a Write on x_A, even if the transaction that issued the Write has not yet committed. If site A is operational and x_A is initialized, Read(x_A) will be processed by the scheduler and DM at A. If x_A is initialized but the transaction T_j that initialized x_A has not yet committed, then by Strict 2PL the scheduler must delay Read(x_A) until T_j commits or aborts. If Read(x_A) is rejected, a negative acknowledgment will be returned and T_i will be aborted.[8] If Read(x_A) is accepted, the value read will be returned to T_i's TM and Read(x) will be done. However, if site A is down or if x_A hasn't been initialized, then T_i's TM will eventually time out while waiting for a response. In that event the TM could abort T_i or, better, it could submit Read(x_B) to another site B that contains a copy of x. As long as one of the copies of x can be read, Read(x) will be successful. If no copy of x can be read, T_i must abort.

When T_i issues a Write(x) operation, its TM sends Write(x_A) operations to every site A where a copy of x is supposed to be stored. If A is down, Write(x_A) will not be received and, of course, its processing will never be acknowledged. T_i's TM will eventually time out waiting for a response from A. If A is operational, the handling of Write(x_A) depends on whether or not x_A was previously initialized.

If x_A has been initialized, then Write(x_A) must be processed by A's scheduler and DM, and eventually a response is returned to T_i's TM indicating whether Write(x_A) was rejected or duly processed.

---

[7]Recall from Section 7.1 that T_i's "home site" is the site where it originated and whose TM supervises its execution.

[8]It is pointless to submit a Read(x_B) for a different copy x_B of x, as the conflict that caused the rejection of Read(x_A) will also cause the rejection of Read(x_B).

On the other hand, if x_A has not been initialized, the DBS at A has two options. It could use Write(x_A) to initialize x_A at this time (in which case the operation is processed as just described), or it may ignore Write(x_A), preferring to not initialize x_A yet. Ignoring the operation means that A doesn't send an acknowledgment to T_i's TM, that is, A acts as if it were down as far as x_A is concerned.[9]

After sending Writes to all of x's copies, T_i's TM waits for responses. It may receive rejections from some sites, positive responses from others (meaning the Write has been accepted and performed), and no responses from others (those that have failed or that have not initialized their copies of x). Writes for which no responses are received are called *missing writes*. If *any* rejection is received or if *all* Writes to x's copies are missing, then Write(x) is rejected and T_i must abort. Otherwise, Write(x) is successful.

Validation

So far we've described, in some detail, the "read-one, write-all-available" discipline. We know from history H_4 that this isn't enough to guarantee one-copy serializability. The available copies algorithm uses a *validation protocol* to ensure correctness. Transaction T_i's validation protocol starts after T_i's Reads and Writes on copies have been acknowledged or timed out. At that time T_i knows all its missing writes as well as all the copies it has actually accessed (read or written). The validation protocol consists of two steps:

1. *missing writes validation*, during which T_i makes sure that all copies it tried to, but couldn't, write are still unavailable, and

2. *access validation*, during which T_i makes sure that all copies it read or wrote are still available.

It is important that missing writes validation be performed before access validation (see Exercise 8.11).

To validate missing writes, T_i sends a message UNAVAILABLE(x_A) to site A, for each copy x_A that T_i found unavailable. A will acknowledge such a message only if it has, in the meanwhile, initialized x_A (i.e., received and processed a Write(x_A), even if the Write has not yet been committed).

After sending the UNAVAILABLE messages, T_i waits for responses. At the end of the timeout period, if it has *not* received *any* acknowledgments to these messages, it proceeds with access validation. Otherwise, some copy it hasn't updated has been initialized and T_i is aborted. At this point it is important to recall the assumption that there are no communication failures. It implies that if T_i has not received any acknowledgment to the UNAVAILABLE messages by

---

[9]Alternatively, A might send a message expressly indicating that x_A has not been initialized yet. This will prevent T_i's TM from waiting for the full timeout period before concluding that x_A is not available.

the end of the timeout period, then it must be that no such acknowledgment was sent and, therefore, that all copies T_i couldn't write are still unavailable.[10]

If the missing writes validation step succeeds, then T_i proceeds with access validation. To that end, T_i sends a message AVAILABLE(x_A) to site A, for each copy x_A that T_i read or wrote. A acknowledges this message if x_A is still available at the time A receives the message. If *all* AVAILABLE messages are acknowledged, then access validation succeeds and T_i is allowed to commit. Otherwise T_i must abort.

The validation protocol requires a significant amount of communication and is therefore expensive. We can reduce the number of messages sent by combining all UNAVAILABLE messages from T_i to some particular site into one message. Similarly for AVAILABLE messages and acknowledgments. Even so, we will have two steps (missing writes validation and access validation), each requiring two rounds of message exchanges (one for the UNAVAILABLE/ AVAILABLE messages and one for acknowledgments). Fortunately, things aren't as bad as this may suggest.

First, if a transaction has no missing writes, there is no need for missing writes validation! Thus, after all copies have been initialized and in the absence of (site) failures, the first step of the validation protocol is avoided.

Second, access validation can be combined with atomic commitment. Recall that when T_i terminates, its TM sends VOTE-REQ messages to all sites where T_i accessed copies. The VOTE-REQ message sent to a site can be used as an implicit AVAILABLE message. If a site responds YES, surely all copies accessed by T_i at that site are still available; thus a YES response can be used as an implicit acknowledgment for AVAILABLE. Therefore, access validation can ride for free on the coattails of atomic commitment.[11]

Some Examples

To develop some insight on how the validation protocol ensures one-copy serializability, we consider some examples of non-1SR executions and show how they are prevented from happening. In the next subsection we prove the correctness of the algorithm.

Let's start with history H_4. We reproduce it next, embellished with certain new symbols to represent events of interest. For transaction T_i, t_i represents the

---

[10]It is possible that a copy was initialized after T_i attempted to write it and failed before T_i started its missing writes validation step. The proof of the algorithm's correctness, which will be presented shortly, should quell any concern that such behavior could compromise one-copy serializability.

[11]Under certain circumstances the atomic commitment protocol needn't involve sites where a transaction only read but did not write (cf. Section 7.3). However, access validation requires that messages be sent to such sites, to verify that copies read are still available. Thus, some additional cost to atomic commitment may be incurred by access validation.

moment when T_i *begins* its access validation step. By the specification of the algorithm, t_i must follow all Read and Write operations of T_i as well as the missing writes validation step (if present), and must precede c_i. As usual, the symbol $x_A \sqcap$ stands for the failure of x_A.

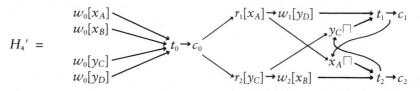

Consider the precedences involving the failure and access validation events. Since T_1 read x_A, the failure of x_A must have occurred after T_1 started its access validation. Otherwise T_1 would have found x_A to be unavailable and would therefore abort. Therefore, $t_1 < x_A \sqcap$ and, similarly, $t_2 < y_C \sqcap$.

Since T_1 wrote y_D but not y_C, it must have carried out missing writes validation and found that y_C is still unavailable. Since at that time y_C had already been initialized, it must be that y_C failed before the completion of T_1's missing writes validation and thus before the beginning of access validation. Hence, $y_C \sqcap < t_1$. The precedence $x_A \sqcap < t_2$ is justified on similar grounds.

Given these precedences we have a cycle in H_4': $t_1 < x_A \sqcap < t_2 < y_C \sqcap < t_1$. This is impossible since H_4', being a history, is supposed to be a partial order. This means that H_4' could not have happened.

In terms of the algorithm, the reason why H_4' couldn't have happened is this: If T_1's access validation succeeded we'd have $t_1 < x_A \sqcap < t_2$, so T_2's access validation started after T_1's. Since $y_C \sqcap < t_1$, we get $y_C \sqcap < t_2$. But then T_2's access validation would not have succeeded, so T_2 would have aborted. Similarly, if T_2's validation succeeded, T_1's would fail. (Of course, both transactions' validations could have failed.)

Note the pivotal role of validation in the justification of why H_4' couldn't occur. Without missing writes and access validation, we wouldn't be able to assert the existence of the precedences that yield the cycle in H_4'.

Our next example illustrates the significance of the assumption that the scheduler uses Strict 2PL. History H_6 is an execution of T_1, T_2 (the same transactions as in H_4) where there is only one copy of y, y_C. For the moment ignore the broken arrow from c_2 to $w_1[y_C]$.

$$H_6 = \begin{array}{c} w_0[x_A] \\ w_0[x_B] \rightarrow t_0 \longrightarrow c_0 \\ w_0[y_C] \end{array} \begin{array}{c} r_1[x_A] \rightarrow w_1[y_C] \rightarrow t_1 \longrightarrow c_1 \\ \\ r_2[y_C] \rightarrow w_2[x_B] \longrightarrow t_2 \longrightarrow c_2 \end{array}$$

Like H_4, H_6 is not 1SR; T_1 doesn't read the value of x written by T_2, and T_2 doesn't read the value of y written by T_1, one of which would have to hold in any serial one-copy execution over T_1, T_2. Unfortunately, the validation steps don't prevent either T_1 or T_2 from committing, as you can easily verify. What stops H_6 from happening is the scheduler's use of Strict 2PL. Since T_2 read y_C

before T_1 wrote into it, T_2 must have locked y_C before T_1 did. But then T_1 won't lock y_C until after T_2 has committed; i.e., we have $c_2 < w_1[y_C]$ (a stronger precedence than just $r_2[y_C] < w_1[y_C]$). Now we get a cycle in H_6, meaning that H_6 couldn't have occurred. Note that the precedence $r_2[y_C] < w_1[y_C]$ isn't enough to give rise to a cycle. It's important that T_2 keeps its locks until it commits.

*Proof of Correctness

We'll state seven properties that are satisfied by histories representing executions of the available copies algorithm. We'll justify why each property is satisfied and then show that any history satisfying them is 1SR, thereby proving that the available copies algorithm is correct.

In addition to the symbols we used in the previous examples, we'll use the symbol t_i' to denote the point at which T_i begins its missing writes validation step. Hence all Read and Write operations of T_i must precede t_i' and $t_i' < t_i$. We'll also use the symbol $x_A\sqcup$ to denote the creation (initialization) of copy x_A. x_A is created when the first transaction that writes it, say T_0, begins its access validation. Thus $x_A\sqcup$ is a "synonym" for t_0.

The properties that must be satisfied by any history H produced by the available copies algorithm are as follows

AC_1: For every T_i, $t_i' < t_i < c_i$. And for every Read or Write p_i of T_i, $p_i < t_i'$.

AC_2: SG(H) is acyclic.

AC_3: If $T_i \rightarrow T_j$ is in SG(H) then $t_i < t_j'$.

AC_1 defines the execution and validation phases of a transaction. AC_2 is satisfied because the scheduler that controls access to copies produces serializable executions. AC_3 is satisfied because the scheduler uses Strict 2PL. If $T_i \rightarrow T_j$ is an edge in SG(H), then there exist conflicting operations $p_i[x_A] < q_j[x_A]$ in H. By Strict 2PL, $c_i < q_j[x_A]$. Consequently, $t_i < t_j'$ (because, by AC_1, $t_i < c_i$ and $q_j[x_A] < t_j'$).[12]

AC_4: For any $r_i[x_A]$ in H, $x_A\sqcup < r_i[x_A]$.

AC_5: For any $w_i[x_A]$ in H, either $x_A\sqcup = t_i$ or $x_A\sqcup < w_i[x_A]$.

AC_4 and AC_5 say that a copy must be initialized before it may be read or written. This is obviously satisfied by the available copies algorithm (cf. the subsection on Processing Reads and Writes).

AC_6: If $r_i[x_A]$ or $w_i[x_A]$ is in H then $t_i < x_A\sqcap$.

---

[12]At the beginning of this section we said that available copies algorithms require a Strict 2PL scheduler. That's not quite true. The correct statement is that these algorithms require a scheduler that will guarantee AC_2 through AC_5.

AC_6 says that T_i's access validation begins before the failure of any copy read or written by T_i. This is satisfied because otherwise one of T_i's AVAILABLE messages would not be acknowledged and so T_i would be aborted.

AC_7:   If T_i writes into some copy of x but not x_A then either $x_A \sqcap < t_i$ or, for any $w_j[x_A]$ in H, $t_i' < w_j[x_A]$.

To understand AC_7, consider the missing writes validation step, in which T_i sent UNAVAILABLE(x_A) to site A. If A had responded to the message, then T_i would have aborted. So assume not. Thus, either x_A failed before A received the message (in which case $x_A \sqcap < t_i$) or x_A had not yet been initialized (in which case $t_i' < w_j[x_A]$ for all T_j that write x_A.

AC_7 is where we use the fact that missing writes validation completes before access validation begins. Without this handshake, the two validation steps would execute concurrently, so t_i and t_i' would not be distinguishable events. If x_A failed before A received UNAVAILABLE(x_A), we could conclude that $x_A \sqcap < c_i$, but not that $x_A \sqcap < t_i' = t_i$, which is needed in the correctness proof.

We begin the proof with a preliminary lemma that strengthens AC_7.

Lemma 8.6:   Let H be a history produced by the available copies algorithm. In H, if T_i writes some copy of x but not x_A, then either $x_A \sqcap < t_i$ or $t_i < x_A \sqcup$.

Proof: Suppose T_i writes into x_B but not x_A. By AC_7 either $x_A \sqcap < t_i$ or $t_i' < w_0[x_A]$, where T_0 is the transaction that initialized x_A. In the former case, H obviously satisfies the lemma. Therefore let us assume the latter and consider two cases, depending on whether or not T_0 wrote into x_B.

CASE 1:   Suppose $w_0[x_B]$ is in H. We claim that $w_i[x_B] < w_0[x_B]$. For, otherwise, we'd have $w_0[x_B] < w_i[x_B]$ and, by AC_3, $t_0 < t_i'$. By assumption, $t_i' < w_0[x_A]$. By AC_1, $w_0[x_A] < t_0$, so by transitivity $t_0 < t_0$, a contradiction. Therefore, $w_i[x_B] < w_0[x_B]$. By AC_3, $t_i < t_i'$. Since $t_0' < t_0$ by AC_1, and $t_0 = x_A \sqcup$ by assumption, we have $t_i < x_A \sqcup$, as desired.   □

CASE 2:   Suppose T_0 doesn't write x_B. By AC_7 either (a) $x_B \sqcap < t_0$ or (b) $t_0' < w_i[x_B]$. If (a), we have $t_i < x_B \sqcap$ (by AC_6), so $t_i < t_0 = x_A \sqcup$, and we get $t_i < x_A \sqcup$, as desired. If (b), we have $t_i' < w_0[x_A]$ by assumption, $w_0[x_A] < t_0'$ by AC_1, $t_0' < w_i[x_B]$ (this is (b)), and $w_i[x_B] < t_i'$ by AC_1. All these imply $t_i' < t_i'$, a contradiction.   □

Any history that satisfies AC_1 - AC_7 is an RD history. Conditions (1), (2), and (4) in the definition of RD history are immediate. Condition (3), which requires each $r_j[x_A]$ to be preceded by a $w_i[x_A]$, follows AC_4. Condition (5) says that if $w_i[x] <_i r_i[x]$ and $r_i[x_A] \in H$, then $w_i[x_A] \in H$. To see this, suppose $w_i[x_A] \notin H$. Then by Lemma 8.6, either (a) $x_A \sqcap < t_i$ or (b) $t_i < x_A \sqcup$. AC_6 contradicts (a). By AC_4 $x_A \sqcup < r_i[x_A]$, and by AC_1 $r_i[x_A] < t_i$; thus $x_A \sqcup < t_i$, which contradicts (b). Hence, $w_i[x_A] \in H$ as desired.

Theorem 8.7: The available copies algorithm produces only 1SR histories.

Proof: Let H be a history that satisfies AC_1 - AC_7. We claim H is 1SR. Since H is an RD history, by Theorem 8.5 it's enough to show that H has an acyclic FRSG. From H construct a graph G with nodes N and edges E, where:

$$N = \{T_i \mid T_i \text{ appears in } H\} \cup$$
$$\{\text{create}[x_A], \text{fail}[x_A] \mid x_A \text{ is a copy of some data item}\}$$
$$E = \{T_i \rightarrow T_j \mid T_i \rightarrow T_j \text{ is an edge of } SG(H)\} \cup F1 \cup F2 \cup F3 \cup F4$$
$$F1 = \{\text{create}[x_A] \rightarrow T_i \mid x_A \sqcup < t_i \text{ or } x_A \sqcup = t_i\}$$
$$F2 = \{T_i \rightarrow \text{fail}[x_A] \mid t_i < x_A \sqcap\}$$
$$F3 = \{\text{fail}[x_A] \rightarrow T_i \mid x_A \sqcap < t_i\}$$
$$F4 = \{T_i \rightarrow \text{create}[x_A] \mid t_i < x_A \sqcup\}$$

To show that G is an FRSG, we must show that it contains the edges E1–E3 in the definition of FRSG.

$$E1 = \{\text{create}[x_A] \rightarrow T_i \mid T_i \text{ reads or writes } x_A\}$$
$$E2 = \{T_i \rightarrow \text{fail}[x_A] \mid T_i \text{ reads } x_A\}$$
$$E3 = \{T_i \rightarrow \text{create}[x_A] \text{ or fail}[x_A] \rightarrow T_i \mid T_i \text{ writes some copy of } x$$
$$\text{but not } x_A\}$$

By AC_6, if T_i reads x_A, then $t_i < x_A \sqcap$, so E2 $\subseteq$ F2. By Lemma 8.6, if T_i writes x but not x_A, then either $x_A \sqcap < t_i$ or $t_i < x_A \sqcup$, so some E3 is contained in F3 $\cup$ F4.

To show G contains E1, suppose T_i reads x_A. By AC_4, $x_A \sqcup < r_i[x_A]$, and by AC_1, $r_i[x_A] < t_i$. Hence, $x_A \sqcup < t_i$. If T_i writes x_A, then by AC_5, either $x_A \sqcup = t_i$ or $x_A \sqcup < w_i[x_A]$. In the latter case, by AC_1 $w_i[x_A] < t_i$, so $x_A \sqcup < t_i$. Thus E1 $\subseteq$ F1, and G contains an FRSG for H.

We now show that G is acyclic. Define a mapping f by $f(\text{create}[x_A]) = x_A \sqcup$, $f(\text{fail}[x_A]) = x_A \sqcap$, and $f(T_i) = t_i$. If $n_j \rightarrow n_k$ is in G, then either $f(n_j) < f(n_k)$ in H or $f(n_j) = f(n_k) = x_A \sqcup$ for some x_A (i.e., $n_j = \text{create}[x_A]$ and $n_k = t_i = \text{create}[x_A]$; see F1). Thus, for any cycle $P = n_1, ..., n_m, n_1$ in G ($m > 1$), there is a corresponding sequence $P' = f(n_1) \leq ... \leq f(n_m) \leq f(n_1)$ in H. Clearly, P must contain at least one edge $n_j \rightarrow n_k$ not in F1. For each such edge, $f(n_j) < f(n_k)$, by definition of F2 - F4. Therefore, $f(n_1) < f(n_1)$ in P, contradicting that H is a partial order. Thus, G is acyclic.

Since G contains an FRSG for H, that FRSG is acyclic too. Thus, by Theorem 8.5, H is 1SR. $\square$

Repeated Failures and Recoveries

So far we have assumed that each copy is initialized and fails at most once. This assumption results in a notational simplification — that for each copy x_A, we have at most one $x_A \sqcup$ and one $x_A \sqcap$ symbol. The usual justification for this assumption is that one can view a single copy that's initialized and fails repeatedly as a sequence of copies, each of which is created and fails once.

This view might appear to contradict another basic assumption of the available copies algorithm, namely, that the set of copies is fixed. Fortunately, as long as *all* copies of a data item don't fail, the "contradiction" is a red herring (see Exercise 8.13). Though the set of copies is fixed, it does not have to be finite!

In particular, for each site A where there is a copy of x we can imagine we have an infinite supply of such copies, x_A^1, x_A^2, x_A^3, ... At any time at most one of these copies is available. If copy x_A^j is the one presently available, then copies x_A^1, ..., x_A^{j-1} have failed and copies x_A^{j+1}, x_A^{j+2}, ... are uninitialized. When (and if) x_A^j fails, x_A^{j+1} will be the next copy of x at site A to be initialized. Since there is a finite number of sites and at most one copy of x is available at any one of them, Write(x) results in the writing of a finite number of copies — a relief! Read(x) involves just one copy, so there is no problem here. Access validation involves the copies read or written — a finite number, as we just argued.

Missing writes validation, however, must ensure that an infinite number of copies is unavailable. Since these copies are stored at a finite number of sites, we can do this with a finite number of messages. The only problem is that now any transaction that writes some data item x will have missing writes (in fact an infinite number of them!), *even if it writes copies at all sites where x is stored*. Does this mean that every transaction must perform missing writes validation? If this were so, it would negate our earlier assertion that in the absence of failures the available copies algorithm incurs no validation cost at all. Fortunately, it isn't so. The reason is that access validation can now be used implicitly for missing writes validation. That is, if T_j writes copy x_A^j and during access validation it finds x_A^j is still available, it implicitly knows that copies x_A^1, ..., x_A^{j-1}, x_A^{j+1}, x_A^{j+2}, ... are still unavailable. Thus there is no need for separate missing writes validation in this case. Of course, missing writes validation is required, as before, if T_j couldn't write any copy of x at site A.

8.7 DIRECTORY-ORIENTED AVAILABLE COPIES

The static assignment of copies to sites in the available copies algorithm of the previous section is a serious disadvantage. It requires, among other things, that transactions attempt to update copies at down sites. If site failures persist for long periods, this is clearly inefficient. In addition, it is not possible to dynamically create or destroy copies at new sites.

In this section we study the *directory-oriented* available copies algorithm, which rectifies these problems. The algorithm uses directories to define the set of sites that currently stores the copies of an item. More precisely, for each data item x there is a directory $d(x)$ listing the set of x's copies. Like a data item, a directory may be replicated, that is, it may be implemented as a set of directory *copies*, stored at different sites.

The directory for x at site U, denoted $d_U(x)$, contains a list of the copies of x and a list of the directory copies for x that site U believes are available. For notational clarity, we will typically use $\{U, V\}$ for names of sites that store directories, and $\{A, B, C, D\}$ for those that store data item copies. These sets of sites need not be disjoint. Usually, a site will store both directory and data item copies. We assume that before we begin executing transactions, all copies of directories exist, but that no copies of data items exist. That is, we assume that new directory copies are never created. A method for creating directory copies appears in a later subsection.

Directories are treated like ordinary data items by the DBS. In particular, concurrent access to directory copies is controlled by the same scheduler that controls concurrent access to data item copies.[13] The only difference is that ordinary transactions can only read directories. Directories are updated by two special transactions, *Include* (or *IN*) for creating new data item copies and *Exclude* (or *EX*) for destroying data item copies.

Basic Algorithm

When a site A containing x recovers from failure, or when A wants to create a new copy of x, the DBS runs a transaction $IN(x_A)$. $IN(x_A)$ brings the value of x_A up-to-date by:

1. finding a directory copy $d_U(x)$, for example, by using a local copy that it knows exists, by reading a master directory that lists copies of $d(x)$, or by polling other sites;

2. reading $d_U(x)$ to find an available copy of x, say x_B;

3. reading x_B; and

4. copying x_B's value into x_A.

Thus, it performs the function of a copier. If $d_U(x)$ says that there are no copies of x and never were any, then A should provide an initial value for x_A, the first

---

[13]As for the simple available copies algorithm, we are assuming a Strict 2PL scheduler or, to be somewhat more general, that transactions that access a data item copy in conflicting modes start their validation protocols in the order in which they accessed that copy.

copy of x.[14] In any case, it declares x_A to be available by adding x_A to each available copy of $d(x)$.

When a site fails, some DBS that tries to access data at that site observes the failure. Based on directories it has read, the DBS believes that certain copies are stored at the failed site. Therefore, for each such copy, it runs an EX transaction for each copy stored there. $EX(x_A)$ declares x_A to be unavailable by removing x_A from every available copy of $d(x)$. That is, it

1. reads some directory copy $d_U(x)$,

2. removes x_A from the list of available copies it read from $d_U(x)$, and

3. writes that updated list into each directory copy listed in $d_U(x)$.

Notice that if a DBS incorrectly believes a copy x_A was at the failed site when in fact it wasn't, it does no harm by executing $EX(x_A)$.

Let NX be any IN or EX transaction. $NX(x_A)$ begins by reading a directory, say $d_U(x)$. It expects to be able to update all of $d(x)$'s copies listed in $d_U(x)$. However, some of these directory copies may have recently failed and are therefore unavailable. Not only is NX unable to update such directory copies, but it now knows that the list of available directories in the (remaining) available copies of $d(x)$ directories is wrong. NX corrects such errors as follows.

After reading $d_U(x)$, NX attempts to access the directory copies listed in $d_U(x)$. Let AD be the directory copies listed in $d_U(x)$ that it determines are available (including $d_U(x)$). NX then updates each directory copy in AD by modifying its list of available data item copies *and* updating its list of available directory copies to be AD. This distribution of directory updates can be overlapped with the first phase of its ACP, by sending the directory update and VOTE-REQ in the same message.

To process Read(x) on behalf of a user transaction, the DBS reads a copy of $d(x)$, say $d_U(x)$. If it tries to read a directory copy that is unavailable, then it simply ignores the attempt and keeps trying other copies until it finds one that *is* available. It then selects a copy x_A of x that $d_U(x)$ says is available and issues Read(x_A). Since a failure can happen at any time, it is possible that $d_U(x)$ says that x_A is available, but the DBS discovers that x_A is unavailable when it tries to read it. In this case, the DBS can take one of three actions: (1) it can select another copy that $d_U(x)$ says is available and try to read that copy; (2) it can read a different copy of $d(x)$, $d_V(x)$, and try to read a copy that $d_V(x)$ says is available; or (3) it can abort the transaction.

To process Write(x), the DBS reads a copy of $d(x)$, $d_U(x)$, and issues Write(x_A) for every copy x_A that $d_U(x)$ says is available. If the DBS discovers

---

[14]If $d_U(x)$ says that there are no copies of x but that there *were* some in the past, then x is recovering from a total failure. In this case, A can initialize x using its last committed value for x only if x_A was among the last copies of x to have failed. It can determine this fact using the technique of Section 7.5. For pedagogical clarity, we will not incorporate this complexity in the remainder of this section. See Exercise 8.13).

that any copy that $d_U(x)$ says is available is actually unavailable, it must abort the transaction T_i that issued the Write and run an $EX(x_A)$ transaction. When that commits, it can try running T_i again.[15]

After performing all its operations, transaction T_i must carry out its validation protocol. Since there are never missing writes, missing writes validation is unnecessary. The reason there are no missing writes is that the set of available copies for x is listed in $d(x)$ and, as we just saw, unless all these copies are actually written, T_i will abort. Thus only access validation is needed in the directory-oriented available copies algorithm (another advantage over the simpler algorithm of the preceding section). As we have seen, access validation can be done together with atomic commitment.

In fact, in the directory-oriented algorithm, access validation can be done merely by checking that the *directory* copies that T_i read still contain the data item copies T_i accessed (see Exercise 8.15). Thus, if directory copies are stored at all sites, access validation requires no communication at all.[16]

This is especially important if the DBS uses deferred Writes. The DBS cannot do Read validation until the transaction terminates, which doesn't occur until all Writes are distributed. If the DBS at site A can validate T_i only using directory copies stored at A, then it can do access validation locally. This avoids another round of communication after the distribution of T_i's Writes.

Correctness Argument

We can argue that this algorithm produces 1SR executions by using Theorem 8.5. The theorem says that if all transactions observe creations and failures in the same order, then the execution is 1SR. We can see that every execution of the algorithm satisfies this property by the following intuitive line of reasoning. We will show in a moment that user transactions behave as if the creation or failure of a copy occurred at the moment its IN or EX executed. All transactions, including INs and EXes, effectively execute in the serialization order. Thus, all user transactions see the same order of INs and EXes, and hence see the same order of creations and failures. This is the condition of Theorem 8.5, so the execution is 1SR.

A transaction T_i demonstrates its belief that a copy x_A is available by operating on x_A. If it operated on x_A then it must have read some directory copy $d_U(x)$ that said that x_A was available. $IN(x_A)$ must have written x_A into $d_U(x)$

---

[15] A fancier (and better) way to do this is to have T_i incorporate $EX(x_A)$'s actions before proceeding. More precisely, T_i will execute $EX(x_A)$ as a subtransaction and will commit only if $EX(x_A)$ commits. Since this gets us into nested transactions, a topic not discussed in this book, we'll stick with the brute force method of aborting T_i, running $EX(x_A)$, and then restarting T_i from scratch.

[16] Of course, the atomic commitment protocol must still be carried out. However, now it need not involve sites at which the transaction only read copies.

before T_i read $d_U(x)$. Thus, T_i executed after $IN(x_A)$. Furthermore, after T_i terminated it checked that x_A was still available. Since $EX(x_A)$ doesn't execute until after x_A fails, T_i executed before $EX(x_A)$. So T_i executed after $IN(x_A)$ and before $EX(x_A)$. This is consistent with the view that x_A was created when $IN(x_A)$ executed and failed when $EX(x_A)$ executed.

A transaction T_i demonstrates its belief that a copy x_A is *not* available by *not* operating on that copy when it should, namely when it writes into data item x. When T_i writes x, it decides which copies to write by reading one of x's directories, say $d_U(x)$, and writing into all of the copies listed there. If x_A wasn't in $d_U(x)$ at the time the transaction read it, then T_i does not write x_A, thereby observing the failure of x_A. One way this could occur is if T_i read $d_U(x)$ before $IN(x_A)$ wrote x_A into $d_U(x)$. The other possibility is that $EX(x_A)$ wrote $d_U(x)$ to delete x_A before T_i read $d_U(x)$. In the former case, T_i executed before $IN(x_A)$ and in the latter case it executed after $EX(x_A)$. This too is consistent with the view that the copy was created when IN executed and failed when EX executed. Thus, transactions behave as if each IN (or EX) executes at the moment the copy is created (or fails), so, by Theorem 8.5, the execution is 1SR. This argument can be formalized along the lines of the proof given in the previous section for the simpler AC algorithm (see Exercise 8.16).

Creating Directories

To create a directory copy $d_U(x)$, we must store the current list of copies of x and directory copies for x in $d_U(x)$. We must also add $d_U(x)$ to the list of directories in every other directory for x. Thus, a *Directory Include* (or *DIN*) transaction for $d_U(x)$ begins by reading an existing directory copy for x, $d_V(x)$. Like an IN or EX, it checks to see which directory copies, AD, in $d_V(x)$ are still available. Then it updates the directory copies. It sets the list of data item copies in $d_U(x)$ to be that of $d_V(x)$. And it writes AD into the list of directory copies in each directory copy in AD (including $d_U(x)$).

How does a DIN know where to look for an existing copy of $d(x)$? If there is a copy of $d(x)$ at the site that is executing the DIN, then it can easily find the copy. If not, then it could poll other sites, to find out which of them have a copy.

If it can't find a copy, then it should try to initialize the first copy of $d(x)$. Unfortunately, it can't assume that it is the only DIN that is trying to initialize $d(x)$. The reason is that some other DIN may have been polling sites at the same time and reached the same conclusion that $d(x)$ was uninitialized. If both DINs try to create the initial copy of $d(x)$, neither copy will include a reference to the other. This could ultimately lead to an inconsistent state of x. For example, each subsequent IN would include copies of x that were only listed in one directory copy or the other. Then a user transaction would update only some copies of x, namely, those listed in the directory copy it read. It is therefore essential that only one DIN initialize a first copy of $d(x)$.

Another bad outcome will occur if $d(x)$ doesn't currently exist because it has experienced a total failure. That is, there used to be copies of $d(x)$, but they have all failed. It would be incorrect to initialize a new copy of $d(x)$, because there may still be copies of x around that are listed in the last copies of $d(x)$ to have failed.

One way to ensure that a DIN can correctly initialize the first copy of a directory is to have a master directory that contains a list of all directories for which an initial directory has been created and initialized. A DIN that initializes a directory $d(x)$ must update the master directory. If two DINs try to initialize $d(x)$ concurrently, they will have conflicting accesses to the master directory, so one DIN will have to wait until the other terminates. The second DIN will therefore see that it is not really the initial DIN for $d(x)$, and will act accordingly. Moreover, a total failure of $d(x)$ will be detectable, because the master directory will say that $d(x)$ exists, but no available site will have a copy.

Clearly, if the master directory is unavailable, then no directories can be initialized. The master directory should therefore be replicated, and all copies updated by each initial DIN. To avoid unbounded recursion, some additional restrictions are needed, such as fixing the set of master directory copies for all time. We leave the algorithms for including and excluding copies of the master directory as an exercise (see Exercise 8.18).

8.8 COMMUNICATION FAILURES

The main problem with available copies algorithms is that they do not tolerate communication failures. That is, if two or more operational sites cannot communicate, they may produce executions that are not 1SR.

For example, suppose there are copies $\{x_A, x_B, x_C\}$ of x and $\{y_B, y_C, y_D\}$ of y, but a communication failure has partitioned the network into two independent components, $P_1 = \{A, B\}$ and $P_2 = \{C, D\}$. That is, component P_1 has copies $\{x_A, x_B, y_B\}$ and P_2 has copies $\{x_C, y_C, y_D\}$. Suppose transactions T_1 and T_2 execute in components P_1 and P_2 (respectively) using an available copies algorithm, producing history H_7.

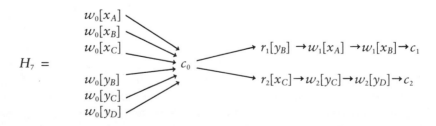

In P_1, T_1 reads the one and only available copy of y, namely y_B, and writes both available copies of x, x_A and x_B. Similarly for T_2 in P_2. Since each transaction can validate that the copies it accessed were still available at the time it terminated, each can commit. Yet the execution is clearly not 1SR, since neither transaction reads the output of the other.

The general problem is that transactions in different components may have conflicting accesses on different copies of the same data item, as in H_7 just shown. The serialization order of such transactions is essential to the one-copy serializability of their execution (cf. Section 8.4 and Theorem 8.4). But since DBSs executing in different components cannot communicate, they cannot synchronize transactions that execute in different components, and thus cannot ensure one-copy serializability. Therefore, nearly all techniques for handling communications failures focus on preventing transactions that access the same data item from executing in different components.[17]

Site Quorums

Surely one way to prevent conflicting transactions from executing in different components is to insist that only one component be allowed to process any transactions at all. Since the components can't communicate, each component must be able to independently decide whether *it* is the component that can process transactions. One way to accomplish this is to use *site quorums*.

In site quorums, we assign a non-negative weight to each site. Every site knows the weight of all sites in the network. A *quorum* is any set of sites with more than half the total weight of all sites (cf. Section 7.5). Only the one component that has a quorum of sites can process transactions.

Unfortunately, it is possible that *no* component has a quorum. This can occur if the network splits into more than two components, or if sites fail in the component that would have contained a quorum. If this happens, then no component can process transactions. The DBS fails totally.

One should assign weights to sites based on their relative importance to the enterprise that is using the DBS. A site with higher weight is more likely to be in the quorum component.

We can improve on the basic site quorum rule by allowing certain transactions to execute in components that don't have a quorum of sites. Since a nonreplicated data item can only be accessed in the component that has its one and only copy, there cannot be two transactions that access a nonreplicated data item but execute in different components. Therefore, a transaction can safely read and write nonreplicated data in any component. For the same reason, a transaction can read and write any replicated data item x in a component that has all of the replicated copies of x. Thus, the site quorum rule need only apply to transactions that access a replicated data item x in a component that is missing one or more copies of x.

---

[17]See Exercise 8.19 for an approach that allows certain conflicting transactions to execute in different components.

The major problem with site quorums is that if transactions have inconsistent views of the components, then they can produce incorrect results. For example, given a database containing $\{x_A, x_B, x_C\}$, suppose site A's TM executes T_1 believing that only A and B are accessible, while site C's TM executes T_2 believing that only B and C are accessible, thereby producing H_8.

$$H_8 = \begin{array}{l} w_0[x_A] \\ w_0[x_B] \\ w_0[x_C] \end{array} \Rightarrow c_0 \begin{array}{l} r_1[x_A] \to w_1[x_A] \to w_1[x_B] \longrightarrow c_1 \\ \\ r_2[x_C] \to w_2[x_B] \to w_2[x_C] \longrightarrow c_2 \end{array}$$

TM_A and TM_C both believed they had access to a majority of the sites. But due to a communication anomaly, A and C were each able to communicate with B without being able to communicate with each other. Alternatively, H_8 might have occurred due to the following sequence of events.

1. A disconnects from B and C.

2. TM_C executes T_2.

3. B disconnects from C and connects to A.

4. TM_A executes T_1.

We'll look at two solutions to this problem: the quorum consensus algorithm, which requires each transaction to access a quorum of *copies* of data items on which it operates (Section 8.9), and the virtual partition algorithm, in which each site synchronizes its view of its component with other sites in its component (Section 8.10). The quorum consensus algorithm has less overhead to handle failures and recoveries than the virtual partition algorithm, but has more overhead to process transactions during periods in which no failures or recoveries take place. Thus, the former is more suitable for environments where failures and recoveries are frequent, and the latter for those where they are relatively rare.

Queries

Since queries (i.e., read-only transactions) do not modify the database, it would seem to be safe to execute them in all components. After all, since each component uses a correct concurrency control algorithm, each query will read a database state produced by a serializable execution of the transactions in the same component. Curiously, however, the execution across two partitions may not be 1SR.

For example, consider the following history.

$$H_9 = \begin{array}{l} w_0[x_A] \\ w_0[y_A] \\ w_0[x_B] \\ w_0[y_B] \end{array} \Rightarrow c_0 \begin{array}{l} w_1[x_A] \longrightarrow c_1 \longrightarrow \begin{array}{l} r_2[x_A] \\ r_2[y_A] \end{array} \Rightarrow c_2 \\ \\ w_3[y_B] \longrightarrow c_3 \longrightarrow \begin{array}{l} r_4[x_B] \\ r_4[y_B] \end{array} \Rightarrow c_4 \end{array}$$

Sites A and B partition into different components after T_0 executes. In H_9, we allowed queries T_2 and T_4 to read x and y in both partitions. H_9 produces a consistent database state, in the sense that update transactions are 1SR. Moreover, each query reads a consistent database state. Yet there is no serial one-copy history equivalent to H_9, so H_9 is not 1SR.

Whether to allow queries to read all copies in all components is more of a policy issue than a technical one. For most applications the level of data consistency provided by this technique is probably satisfactory. Although anomalies like H_9 are disturbing, the increased data availability to queries will often be the overriding consideration.

Application-dependent Techniques

Site quorums, quorum consensus, and virtual partitions all have the disadvantage of possibly restricting access to copies that are not down. While this restriction is needed to attain one-copy serializability, it does have a cost in lost opportunities. That is, the DBS user is unable to execute certain transactions, and may thereby lose the opportunity to perform certain functions in the real world, resulting in lost revenue, unhappy customers, higher inventory costs, etc. One has to balance these opportunity costs against the value of database integrity. If these costs are high enough, some loss of correctness may be tolerable.

It may therefore be advisable to allow transactions to operate on any available data, even at the risk of non-1SR execution during a communications failure. After the failure is repaired, a special recovery process is invoked to fix database inconsistencies. To make this approach practical for even moderately sized databases, the recovery process needs to be automated.

For example, the recovery process could analyze the logs from sites in different components to find read-write conflicts between transactions in different components. To produce a correct database state, the recovery process could undo and reexecute those transactions as needed. This might entail reexecuting a transaction that committed before the partition (e.g., T_1 or T_2 in H_8), causing it to produce different results than its first execution, a violation of the definition of commitment. Alternatively, the recovery process might only find database inconsistencies by performing validation checks on the data items themselves. Once found, those inconsistencies could be repaired by human intervention, perhaps with the help of a rule-based system.

These approaches may be essential for attaining any appropriately high level of data availability. However, since they allow non-1SR executions to occur, the solutions are necessarily application dependent, and therefore require a highly trained application engineering staff. For users that lack such expertise, general purpose solutions that ensure 1SR executions are usually preferable.

8.9 THE QUORUM CONSENSUS ALGORITHM

In the *quorum consensus* (QC) algorithm, we assign a non-negative weight to each copy x_A of x. We then define a read threshold RT and write threshold WT for x, such that both $2 \cdot$ WT and (RT + WT) are greater than the total weight of all copies of x. A *read* (or *write*) *quorum* of x is any set of copies of x with a weight of at least RT (or WT). (Note that the quorums defined here are *copy* quorums, as opposed to the site quorums of the previous section.) The key observation is that each write quorum of x has at least one copy in common with every read quorum and every write quorum of x.

In QC, the TM is responsible for translating Reads and Writes on data items into Reads and Writes on copies. A TM translates each Write(x) into a set of Writes on each copy of some write quorum of x. It translates each Read(x) into a set of Reads on each copy of some read quorum of x, and it returns to the transaction the most up-to-date copy that it read.

To help the TM figure out which copy is most up-to-date, we tag each copy with a *version number*, which is initially 0. When the TM processes Write(x), it determines the maximum version number of any copy it is about to write, adds one to it, and tags all of the versions that it writes with that version number. Clearly, this requires reading all of the copies in the write quorum before writing any of them. This can be done by having Write(x_A) return its version number to the TM. The TM can send the new value and new version number piggybacked on the first round of messages of the atomic commitment protocol.

The version numbers measure how up-to-date each copy is. Each Read of a copy returns its version number along with its data value. The TM always selects a copy in the read quorum with the largest version number (there may be more than one such copy but they will all have the same value).

The purpose of quorums is to ensure that Reads and Writes that access the same data item also access at least one copy of that data item in common. This avoids the problems we saw in histories H_1, H_7, and H_8. Even if some copies are down and are therefore unavailable to Reads and Writes, as long as there are enough copies around to get a read quorum and write quorum, transactions can still continue to execute. Every pair of conflicting operations will always be synchronized by some scheduler, namely, one that controls access to a copy in the intersection of their quorums.

QC works with any correct concurrency control algorithm. As long as the algorithm produces serializable executions, QC will ensure that the effect is just like an execution on a single copy database. To see why, consider any serial execution equivalent to the actual interleaved execution. If a transaction T_j reads a copy of data item x, it reads it from the last transaction before it, T_i, that wrote any copy of x. This is because T_i wrote a write quorum of x, T_j read a read quorum of x, and every read and write quorum has a nonempty intersection. And since T_i is the last transaction that wrote x before T_j read it, T_i

placed a bigger version number on all of the copies of x it wrote than the version number written by any transaction that preceded it. This ensures that T_j will read the value written by T_i, and not by some earlier transaction.

A nice feature of QC is that recoveries of copies require no special treatment. A copy of x that was down and therefore missed some Writes will not have the largest version number in any write quorum of which it is a member. Thus, after it recovers, it will not be read until it has been written at least once. That is, transactions will automatically ignore its value until it has been brought up-to-date.

Unfortunately, QC has some not so nice features, too. Except in trivial cases, a transaction must access multiple copies of each data item it wants to read. Even if there is a copy of the data item in the DM at the site at which it is executing, the transaction still has to look elsewhere for other copies so it can build a read quorum. In many applications, transactions read more data items than they write. Such applications may not perform well using QC.

One might counter this argument by recommending that each read quorum of x contain only one copy of x. But then there can only be one write quorum for x, one that contains all copies of x. This would lead us to the write-all approach in Section 8.1, which we found was unsatisfactory.

A second problem with QC is that it needs a large number of copies to tolerate a given number of site failures. For example, suppose quorums are all majority sets. Then QC needs three copies to tolerate one failure, five copies to tolerate two failures, and so forth. In particular, two copies are no help at all. With two copies QC can't even tolerate one failure.

A third problem with quorum consensus is that all copies of each data item must be known in advance. A known copy of x can recover, but a new copy of x cannot be created because it could alter the definition of x's quorums. In principle, one can change the weights of the sites (and thereby the definition of quorums) while the DBS is running, but this requires special synchronization (see Exercise 8.20).

We will see other approaches to replicated data concurrency control that circumvent QC's weaknesses. Before moving on, though, let's define the histories that QC produces and prove that they are all 1SR.

*Correctness Proof for Quorum Consensus

A *QC history* is an RD history that models an execution of the QC algorithm. Every QC history H has the following properties.

QC_1: If T_i writes x, then H contains $w_i[x_{A_1}], ..., w_i[x_{A_n}]$ for some write quorum $wq(x) = \{x_{A_1}, ..., x_{A_n}\}$ of x.

QC_1 is simply the rule for using write quorums.

Let $last_i(x) = \{T_j \mid$ for some $x_A \in wq(x)$, $w_j[x_A]$ is the last Write on x_A that precedes $w_i[x_A]$ in $H\}$. Notice that $last_i(x) = \{\}$ if T_i is the first transaction in

H to write x. Define T_i's version number for x to be $VN_i(x) = 1 + \max\{VN_j(x) \mid T_j \in last_i(x)\}$, where $\max\{\} = 0$. Intuitively, $VN_i(x)$ is the version number that T_i assigns to the copies of x that it writes.

We have to distinguish between the Reads that a transaction applies to the database, and the real Read that is actually selected from among those Reads, that is, the one with the largest version number. We will use $rr_i[x]$, for "real Read," to represent the Read that is selected.

QC_2: If T_j reads x, then H contains $r_j[x_{A_1}], \ldots, r_j[x_{A_n}]$ for some read quorum $rq(x) = \{x_{A_1}, \ldots, x_{A_n}\}$ of x. For each x_B in $rq(x)$, let $VN(x_B) = VN_i(x)$ where $w_i[x_B]$ is the last Write on x_B that precedes $r_j[x_B]$ in H. Then H contains $rr_j[x_{A_k}]$ for some x_{A_k} in $rq(x)$ where $VN(x_{A_k}) = \max\{VN(x_B) \mid x_B \in rq(x)\}$. Moreover, $r_j[x_{A_i}] < rr_j[x_{A_k}]$ for each x_{A_i} in $rq(x)$.

QC_2 says that each transaction that reads x reads a read quorum of x and selects from that read quorum a copy with a maximal version number. Since the TM cannot determine the real Read until it knows the version numbers of all copies in $rq(x)$, all Reads of those copies must precede $rr_j[x_{A_k}]$.

QC_3: Every $r_j[x_A]$ follows at least one $w_i[x_A]$, $i \neq j$.

QC_4: $SG(H)$ is acyclic.

QC_3 requires that each copy be initialized before it can be read. QC_4 says that the schedulers use a correct concurrency control algorithm.

For example, consider a database with data items x and y, with copies x_A, x_B, x_C, y_D, y_E, and y_F. Let the read and write quorums be all majority sets. Consider transactions $\{T_0, T_1, T_2\}$:

$$T_0 = w_0[x] \searrow \atop \nearrow c_0 \atop w_0[y] \nearrow \qquad T_1 = r_1[x] \rightarrow w_1[y] \rightarrow c_1 \qquad T_2 = r_2[y] \rightarrow w_2[x] \rightarrow c_2$$

A possible QC history over these transactions is

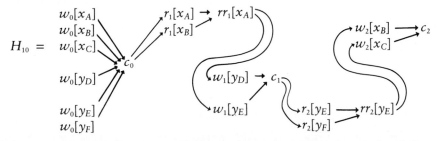

In H_{10}, $last_0(x) = last_0(y) = \{\}$, hence $VN_0(x) = VN_0(y) = 0$; $last_1(y) = last_2(x) = \{T_0\}$, hence $VN_1(y) = VN_2(x) = 1$. The copies of x that T_1 reads were both written by T_0, hence have identical VNs, and T_1 may use the value of either. The copies of y that T_2 reads were written by different transactions, hence have different VNs; T_2 uses the value of copy y_E, which has the larger

VN, as required. The inclusion of both $r_1[x_A]$ and $rr_1[x_A]$ does not signify that T_1 reads x_A twice; it merely means that x_A is determined to be the copy to be used by T_1 as the value of x.

We will prove that every QC history H is 1SR by proving that $SG(H)$ is an RDSG of H. Since $SG(H)$ is acyclic by QC_4, H is 1SR by Theorem 8.4.

Lemma 8.8: Let H be a QC history. $SG(H)$ induces a write order for H.

Proof: Let T_i and T_k write x. Since all write quorums of a data item intersect, there exists a copy x_A that T_i and T_k both write. These Writes on x_A conflict, so $SG(H)$ must have an edge connecting T_i and T_k. Thus, $T_i \rightarrow T_k$ or $T_k \rightarrow T_i$, so $SG(H)$ induces a write order. □

Lemma 8.9: Let H be a QC history. $SG(H)$ induces a read order for H.

Proof: Suppose T_j reads-x-from T_i, T_k writes x ($i \neq k$ and $j \neq k$), and $T_i \rightarrow T_k$. We need to prove $T_j \rightarrow T_k$. By QC_2, T_j reads a read quorum of x; by QC_1, T_k writes a write quorum of x. Since any two such quorums must intersect, there is a copy of x, say x_B, such that $r_j[x_B]$ and $w_k[x_B]$ are in H. Since these are conflicting operations, either $r_j[x_B] < w_k[x_B]$ or $w_k[x_B] < r_j[x_B]$. In the former case, $T_j \rightarrow T_k$ is in $SG(H)$ and we are done. We now prove that the latter case leads to contradiction.

Let $w_h[x_B]$ be the last Write on x_B preceding $r_j[x_B]$ (possibly $h = k$). Since T_j reads-x-from T_i, by QC_2 $VN_h(x) \leq VN_i(x)$.

We claim that $VN_k(x) \leq VN_h(x)$. If $h = k$, $VN_k(x) = VN_h(x)$. If $h \neq k$, let $w_k[x_B] < w_{h_n}[x_B] < \dots < w_{h_1}[x_B] < w_h[x_B]$ be the sequence of Writes on x_B between $w_k[x_B]$ and $w_h[x_B]$. For each pair of adjacent Writes in the sequence, say $w_f[x_B] < w_g[x_B]$, by the definition of VN we have $VN_f(x) < VN_g(x)$. So in this case $VN_k(x) < VN_h(x)$. Therefore, $VN_k(x) \leq VN_h(x)$ as claimed. Since $VN_h(x) \leq VN_i(x)$, we also have $VN_k(x) \leq VN_i(x)$.

Since T_i and T_k write x, by QC_1 they write some copy x_C in common. Since $T_i \rightarrow T_k$ and $SG(H)$ is acyclic (by QC_4), it must be that $w_i[x_C] < w_k[x_C]$. Applying the argument of the previous paragraph, we get $VN_i(x) < VN_k(x)$. But this contradicts $VN_k(x) \leq VN_i(x)$. □

Theorem 8.10: The quorum consensus algorithm is correct.

Proof: It is enough to show that any history H that satisfies $QC_1 - QC_4$ is 1SR. By Lemmas 8.8 and 8.9, $SG(H)$ is an RDSG of H. By QC_4, $SG(H)$ is acyclic. By Theorem 8.4, then, H is 1SR. □

The Missing Writes Algorithm

Quorum consensus pays for its resiliency to communications failures by increasing the cost of Reads and by increasing the required degree of replication. These costs are high if communications failures are infrequent. It would be preferable if the cost could be reduced during reliable periods of operation, possibly at the expense of higher overhead during unreliable periods.

The *missing writes* algorithm is one approach that exploits this trade-off. During a reliable period, the DBS processes Read(x) by reading any copy of x and Write(x) by writing all copies of x. When a failure occurs, the DBS resorts to QC. After the failure is repaired, it returns to reading any copy and writing all copies. Thus, it only pays the cost of QC during periods in which there is a site or communications failure.

Each transaction executes in one of two modes: *normal* mode, in which it reads any copy and writes all copies, or *failure* mode, in which it uses QC. A transaction must use failure mode if it is "aware of missing writes." Otherwise, it can use normal mode.

A transaction is aware of missing writes (MWs) if it knows that a copy x_A does not contain updates that have been applied to other copies of x. For example, if a transaction sends a Write to x_A but receives no acknowledgment, then it becomes aware of MWs. More precisely, transaction T_i *is aware of an MW for copy* x_A in some execution if either T_i writes x but is unable to write x_A, or some transaction T_j is aware of an MW for x_A and there is a path from T_j to T_i in the SG of that execution.

Suppose T_i is aware of an MW for x_A. Then the failure of x_A must precede T_i. But if T_i reads x_A, then T_i precedes the failure of x_A. Since T_i has an inconsistent view of the failure of x_A, it risks producing a non-1SR execution. Consequently, if T_i ever becomes aware of an MW for a copy it read, it must abort.

If T_i is aware of an MW for x_A, it still can read x. But by the preceding argument, it must read a copy of x that isn't missing any Writes. To ensure this, the DBS uses QC. That is, if a transaction that reads (or writes) x is aware of MWs, then it must read (or write) a read (or write) quorum of x.

If T_i begins running in normal mode and becomes aware of an MW as it runs, the DBS can abort T_i and reexecute it in failure mode. Alternatively, it can try to upgrade to failure mode on the fly. That is, for each x that T_i read, the DBS accesses a read quorum R and checks that the value that T_i read is at least as up-to-date as all copies in R. For each x that T_i wrote, the DBS checks that T_i wrote a write quorum of x (see Exercise 8.21).

To implement the algorithm, we need a mechanism whereby a transaction becomes aware of MWs. If a transaction T_i times out on an acknowledgment to one of its Writes, then it immediately becomes aware of an MW. But what if T_j is aware of an MW and $T_j \rightarrow T_i$? The definition of MW awareness requires that T_i become aware of the MWs that T_j is aware of. To do this, T_j should attach a list L of the MWs it is aware of to each copy y_B that it accesses. It tags L to indicate whether it read or (possibly read and) wrote y_B. When T_i accesses y_B in a mode that conflicts with L's tag, it becomes aware of those MWs. The

DM should acknowledge T_i's access to y_B by returning a copy of L. T_i can now propagate L, along with other such lists it received, to all of the copies that *it* accesses. This way a transaction T_j propagates MWs that it's aware of to all transactions that follow T_j in the SG, as required by the definition of MW awareness.

After recovering from failure, the DBS at site A has two jobs to do. First, it must bring each newly recovered copy x_A up-to-date. This is easy to do with a copier transaction. The copier simply reads a quorum of copies of x, and writes into all of those copies the most up-to-date value that it read. Version numbers can be used to determine this value, as before.

Second, after a copy x_A has been brought up-to-date, the DBS should delete x_A from the lists of MWs on all copies, so that eventually transactions that access those copies no longer incur the overhead of QC. This entails sending a message to all sites, invalidating entries for x_A on their lists of MWs. The problem is that while these messages are being processed, x_A may fail again and some Write $w_i[x_A]$ may not be applied. Since this MW occurred *after* the recovery of x_A that caused MW entries for x_A to be invalidated, this MW should not itself be invalidated. However, if the new MW is added to an MW list before the old x_A entry in that list was removed, it risks being removed too. To avoid this error, entries in MW lists should contain version numbers. We leave the algorithm for properly interpreting these version numbers as an exercise (see Exercise 8.22).

We can prove the correctness of the MW algorithm using RDSGs, much as we did for QC. As in QC, the SG in MW induces a write order. However, it does not necessarily induce a read order, which makes the proof more complex than for QC.

For example, suppose we have three copies $\{y_A, x_A, x_B\}$, with weight(y_A) = 1, weight(x_A) = 2, and weight(x_B) = 1. The read and write thresholds are: RT(x) = WT(x) = 2, RT(y) = WT(y) = 1. Consider the following history.

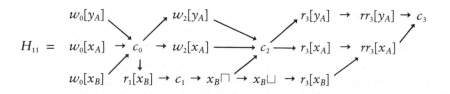

In H_{11}, T_0 and T_1 are not aware of MWs and therefore run in normal mode. T_2 is aware of its MW on x_B, and so runs in failure mode. Although x_B recovers before T_3 begins, T_3 is still aware of the MW on x_B and therefore runs in failure mode.

T_1 reads-x-from T_0, T_2 writes x, and $T_0 \rightarrow T_2$ is in SG(H_{11}). To induce a read order, we need $T_1 \rightarrow T_2$ in RDSG(H_{11}). But $T_1 \rightarrow T_2$ is not in SG(H_{11}), so we need to add it to the SG to make it an RDSG. It turns out that in all such cases where the SG of a history generated by the MW algorithm is missing an edge that is needed to create a read order, we can simply add the necessary edge to the RDSG without creating a cycle. This is the main step in proving every such history has an acyclic RDSG and therefore is 1SR (see Exercise 8.23).

8.10 THE VIRTUAL PARTITION ALGORITHM

As we have seen, the major drawback of the quorum consensus algorithm is that it requires access to multiple, remote copies of x in order to process a Read(x), even when a copy of x is available at the site where the Read is issued. This defeats one of the motivations for data replication, namely, to make data available "near" the place where it is needed. The missing writes algorithm mitigates this problem by using quorum consensus only when site or communication failures exist. The *virtual partition (VP) algorithm*, studied in this section, is designed so that a transaction *never* has to access more than one copy to read a data item. Thus, the closest copy available to a transaction can always be used for reading.

As in quorum consensus, each copy of x has a non-negative weight, and each data item has read and write thresholds (RT and WT, respectively) with the properties described at the beginning of Section 8.9. Read and write quorums are defined as before. However, these serve a different purpose in VP than in QC, as we'll see presently.

The basic idea of VP is for each site A to maintain a *view*, consisting of the sites with which A "believes" it can communicate. We denote this set by $v(A)$. As usual, each transaction T has a home site, $home(T)$, where it was initiated. The view of a transaction, $v(T)$, is the view of its home site, $v(home(T))$, at the time T starts. As we will see shortly, if $v(home(T))$ changes before T commits, then T will be aborted.

A transaction T executes as if the network consisted just of the sites in its view. However, for the DBS to process a Read(x) (or Write(x)) of T, $v(T)$ *must* contain a read (or write) quorum for x. If that is not the case, the DBS must abort T. Note that the DBS can determine if it can process Read(x) or Write(x) from information available at $home(T)$. It need not actually try to access a read or write quorum of x's copies.

Within the view in which T executes, the DBS uses the write-all approach. That is, it translates Write(x) into Writes on all copies of x in $v(T)$; it translates Read(x) into a Read of *any* copy of x in $v(T)$.

A good illustration of how this idea works is provided if we examine how VP avoids H_7 — our archetype of a problematic history in the presence of communication failures.

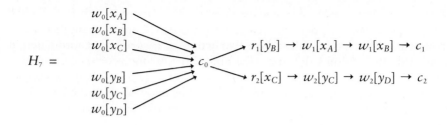

$$H_7 = \begin{array}{l} w_0[x_A] \\ w_0[x_B] \\ w_0[x_C] \\ w_0[y_B] \\ w_0[y_C] \\ w_0[y_D] \end{array} \to c_0 \begin{array}{l} r_1[y_B] \to w_1[x_A] \to w_1[x_B] \to c_1 \\ r_2[x_C] \to w_2[y_C] \to w_2[y_D] \to c_2 \end{array}$$

Recall that in this example, the network is partitioned into two components, $\{A, B\}$ and $\{C, D\}$. Suppose $home(T_1) = A$ and $home(T_2) = C$. If each site has a correct view of the sites with which it can communicate, $v(A) = \{A, B\}$ and $v(C) = \{C, D\}$. If the DBS allows T_1 to commit in H_7, $v(A)$ must have a read quorum of y (and a write quorum of x), and therefore $v(C)$ can't have a write quorum of y (or a read quorum of x). Hence the VP algorithm will not allow T_2 to commit.

Views of sites change, as site and communication failures cause the network to be reconfigured. Hence, a transaction T may attempt to communicate with a site whose view is different from T's. Or, T may attempt but fail to communicate with a site in its view. (A transaction communicates with a site to access a copy stored there or send a VOTE-REC during its commitment). These situations indicate that $home(T)$'s view is not accurate. T must abort and $home(T)$'s view must be adjusted, as explained next. Moreover, whenever a site A's view changes, all active transactions whose home is A must abort. They can all then be restarted and try to run within A's new view.

Maintaining the views in a consistent manner is not a simple matter, because site and communication failures occur spontaneously. VP surmounts this difficulty by using a special *View Update transaction*. This is issued by the DBS itself, rather than by users. In spirit it is analogous to the Include and Exclude transactions used by the directory-oriented available copies algorithm to maintain a consistent view among all sites of the copies and directories that are available (cf. Section 8.7).

When a site detects a difference between its present view and the set of sites it can actually communicate with, it initiates a View Update transaction whose purpose is:

1. to adjust the views of all the sites in the new view, and

2. to bring up-to-date all copies of all data items for which there is a read quorum in the new view.

In adjusting the views of the sites in a new view, View Updates must be coordinated to avoid problems like the one exemplified by the following scenario. Consider a network with four sites A, B, C, D such that at some point $v(B) = \{B\}; v(D) = \{D\}$, and $v(A) = v(C) = \{A, C\}$. Later, B discovers that it can communicate with A and C (but not with D) and, at the same time,

D discovers that it can communicate with A and C (but not with B).[18] Thus B will initiate a View Update to create view $\{A, B, C\}$ and D a similar one to create view $\{A, C, D\}$. Unless these two activities are properly coordinated, it is possible that A joins the first view and C the second, creating a situation where $v(A) = v(B) = \{A, B, C\}$ and $v(C) = v(D) = \{A, C, D\}$. If such inconsistent views were allowed to form, H_7 *would* be allowed since the views of A and C (home sites of T_1 and T_2, respectively) would both contain read and write quorums for x and y!

To avoid such inconsistencies, VP uses a *view formation protocol*. Associated with each view is a unique *view identifier* (*VID*). When a site A wishes to form a new view, say v, it generates a VID, newVID, greater than its present VID. A then initiates a two phase protocol to establish the new view:

- $\square$ A sends a JOIN-VIEW message to each site in v and waits for acknowledgments. This message contains newVID.

- $\square$ Receipt of JOIN-VIEW by site B constitutes an invitation for B to join the new view being created by A. B accepts the invitation provided its present VID is less than the newVID contained in JOIN-VIEW; otherwise, it rejects the invitation. Accepting the invitation means sending a positive acknowledgment; rejecting it means sending a negative acknowledgment (or nothing at all).

- $\square$ After receiving acknowledgments, A can proceed in one of two ways. It may abort the creation of the new view (either by sending explicit messages to that effect or by not sending any messages at all). In this event, A may attempt to restart the protocol using a greater newVID, hoping it will convince more sites to accept the invitation. Alternatively, A may ignore any rejected invitations and proceed to form a new view consisting only of the set of sites v' ($v' \subseteq v$) that accepted the invitation. It does this by sending a VIEW-FORMED message to each site in v' and attaching the set v' to that message. Any site that receives that message adopts v' as its view and newVID (which it had received in the JOIN-VIEW message) as its present VID. It need not acknowledge the receipt of VIEW-FORMED.

Returning to our example, if this protocol is followed, A and C will make a consistent choice: Both will join either the view initiated by B ($\{A, B, C\}$) or the view initiated by D ($\{A, C, D\}$), depending on which of the two had a greater VID. A third possibility, namely, that neither A nor C joins either new view, would obtain if the present VID of A and C is greater than the VIDs of the views B and D are attempting to create.

To ensure network-wide uniqueness, VIDs are pairs (c, s) where s is a site identifier and c is a counter stored at s and incremented each time s tries to

---

[18]Recall that timeout failures can give rise to such anomalous situations (cf. Section 7.2).

create a new view. Thus VIDs created by different sites differ in the second component, while VIDs created by the same site differ in the first component. Pairs are compared in the usual way: $(c, s) < (c', s')$ if $c < c'$, or $c = c'$ and $s < s'$.

When a new view is created, all copies of data items for which there is a read quorum in the view must be brought up-to-date. This is because, in the new view, any such copy might be read. The task of updating such copies is also carried out by the View Update transaction. It is done as follows. When a site A creates a new view v, it reads a read quorum of each data item x (for which there is a read quorum in v). It then writes all copies of x in v, using the most recent value it read. Version numbers can be used to determine the most recent value, as in QC. This procedure need not be carried out for copies that A can tell are up-to-date (see Exercise 8.24). The entire process of updating copies can be combined with the view formation protocol (see Exercise 8.25). This whole activity comprises what we called before a View Update transaction. It should be emphasized that the activity of a View Update is carried out like that of an ordinary (distributed) transaction. In particular, Reads and Writes issued in the process of bringing copies of the new view up-to-date are synchronized using the DBS's standard concurrency control mechanism. In the VP algorithm we described, the set of copies of each data item is fixed. Adding new copies of a data item x alters the quorum of x. Therefore, as in QC, it requires special synchronization (see Exercise 8.26).

VP guarantees that an execution is 1SR by ensuring that all transactions see failures and recoveries in the same order. Informally, we can argue this as follows.

1. Each transaction executes entirely within a single view.

2. For any two transactions T_i and T_j, if $T_i \rightarrow T_j$, then T_i executed in a view whose VID is less than or equal to T_j's.

3. From (2), there is a serial history H_s that is equivalent to the one that actually occurred in which transactions in the same view are grouped into contiguous subsequences, ordered by their VIDs.

Within a VP, all transactions have the same view of which copies are functioning and which are down. So if we imagine site failures and recoveries to occur at the beginning of each segment in H_s, then all transactions have a consistent view of those failures and recoveries. And this, as we know, implies that the execution is 1SR (see Exercise 8.27).

BIBLIOGRAPHIC NOTES

Since the earliest work on distributed databases, replication has been regarded as an important feature [Rothnie, Goodman 77] and [Shapiro, Millstein 77b]. Some early algorithms include primary site [Alsberg, Day 76] [Alsberg et al. 76], majority consensus [Thomas 79], primary copy [Stonebraker 79b], and a TO-based write-all-available algorithm in SDD-1 [Bernstein, Shipman, Rothnie 80] and [Rothnie et al. 80].

The concept of one copy serializability was introduced in [Attar, Bernstein, Goodman 84]. The theory of 1SR histories was developed in [Bernstein, Goodman 86a] and [Bernstein, Goodman 86b].

Available copies algorithms are described in [Bernstein, Goodman 84], [Chan, Skeen 86], and [Goodman et al. 83]. Weak consistency for queries is discussed in [Garcia-Molina, Wiederhold 82]. Majority consensus was generalized to quorum consensus in [Gifford 79]. Other majority and quorum based algorithms are presented in [Breit-wieser, Leszak 82], [Herlihy 86], and [Sequin, Sargeant, Wilnes 79]. The missing writes algorithm was introduced in [Eager 81] and [Eager, Sevcik 83]. The virtual partition algorithm was introduced in [El Abbadi, Skeen, Cristian 85] and [El Abbadi, Toueg 86].

[Davidson, Garcia-Molina, Skeen 85] gives a survey of approaches to replication, including some methods not described in this chapter: [Skeen, Wright 84], which describes a method for analyzing transaction conflicts to determine when a partition cannot lead to a non-1SR execution (see Exercise 8.19); [Davidson 84], which shows how to analyze logs to determine which transactions must be undone after a network partition is repaired; and [Blaustein et al. 83] and [Garcia-Molina et al. 83b], which describe methods for recovering an inconsistent database after a partition is repaired by exploiting semantics of transactions.

EXERCISES

8.1   The primary copy approach to the distribution of replicated Writes is useful for avoiding deadlocks in 2PL. Explain why it eliminates deadlocks resulting from write-write conflicts. Is it helpful in reducing other types of deadlock, too?

8.2   Suppose we use 2PL with the primary copy and write-all approaches to the distribution of Writes. Assume there are no failures or recoveries. Must updaters set write locks on non-primary copies? How would you change your answer if queries are allowed to read non-primary copies?

8.3   Consider an algorithm for creating new copies that satisfies the following three conditions:

  a. it produces serializable executions (its RD histories have acyclic SGs),
  b. no transaction can read a copy until it has been written into at least once, and
  c. once a transaction T_i has written into a new copy x_A, all transactions that write into x and come after T_i in the SG also write into x_A.

Prove or disprove that such an algorithm produces only 1SR executions.

8.4   Consider the following algorithm for creating a new copy x_A of x. The DBS uses primary copy for distributing Writes. The DBS produces serializable executions (its RD histories have acyclic SGs). The scheduler that controls x_A does not allow x_A to be read until it has been written into at least once. Once the primary copy's DBS has sent a Write on x to x_A, it will send to x_A all subsequent Writes on x that it receives. Assuming that copies never fail, prove that this algorithm produces 1SR histories.

8.5 Suppose a site A fails for a short period. Most data items at A that are replicated elsewhere were probably not updated by any other site while A was down. If other sites can determine the earliest time τ that A might have failed, then using τ they can examine their logs to produce a list of data items that were updated while A was down. These are the only data items at A that must be reinitialized when A recovers. Propose a protocol that sites can use to calculate τ.

8.6 One way to avoid copiers on all data items is for a site B to step in as A's *spooler* after A fails. B spools to a log the Writes destined for A (which A can't process, since it's down). When A recovers, it uses a Restart procedure based on logging to process the log at B (cf. Section 6.4). What properties must B's spooler and A's Restart procedure satisfy for this approach to work correctly? Given those properties, how should A respond to Reads while it is processing B's log?

8.7 A serial RD history H is called *1-serial* if, for all i, j, and x, if T_j reads-x-from T_i $(i \neq j)$, then T_i is the last transaction preceding T_j that writes into any copy of x. Prove that if an RD history is 1-serial, then it is 1SR.

8.8* Let H be an RD history over T. Let $G(H)$ be a directed graph whose nodes are in one-to-one correspondence with the transactions in T. $G(H)$ *contains a reads-from order* if, whenever T_j reads-x-from T_i,

  a. if $(i \neq j)$, then $T_i \ll T_j$, and
  b. if for some copy x_A, $w_i[x_A] < r_j[x_A]$, $w_k[x_A] \in H$ and $T_k \ll T_i$ then $w_k[x_A] < w_i[x_A]$.

$G(H)$ is a *weak replicated data serialization graph* (*weak RDSG*) for H if it contains a write order, a reads-from order, and a read order. Prove that H has the same reads-from relationships as a serial 1C history over T if *and only if* H has an acyclic weak RDSG. Give an example of an RD history that does not have an acyclic RDSG but *does* have an acyclic weak RDSG.

Since a weak RDSG need not contain SG(H), Theorem 8.3 does not apply. Thus, we are not justified in dropping final writes from a proof that H is equivalent to a serial 1C history. Prove or disprove that H is 1SR iff it has an acyclic weak RDSG.

8.9* In the definition of FRSGs, we assumed that each copy is created once, fails once, and then never recovers. Suppose we drop the assumption that failed copies never recover. To cope with multiple failures and recoveries of a copy, we extend an FRSG to be allowed to include more than one pair of nodes {create$_i[x_A]$, fail$_i[x_A]$} for each copy x_A, where the subscripts on create and fail are used to relate matching create/fail pairs. Redefine the edge set of an FRSG to make use of these multiple create/fail pairs. Prove Theorem 8.5 for this new definition of FRSG.

8.10* Suppose we add the following set of edges to an FRSG:

$$E2' = \{T_i \rightarrow \text{fail}[x_A] \mid T_i \text{ writes } x_A\}.$$

An *augmented FRSG* is an FRSG that includes the edges defined by E2'.

    a. Give an example history that has an acyclic FRSG, but has no acyclic augmented FRSG.

    b. Suppose a concurrency control algorithm only produces histories that have acyclic augmented FRSGs. Explain intuitively what effect this has on the state of a copy after it recovers from a failure.

    c. Does the available copies algorithm of Section 8.6 produce histories that have acyclic augmented FRSGs? If not, modify the algorithm so that it does.

8.11 Give an example of a non-1SR execution that would be allowed by the simple available copies algorithm of Section 8.6, if the missing writes validation and the access validation steps were done at the same time (i.e., the validation protocol sent the AVAILABLE and UNAVAILABLE messages at the same time).

8.12* Give a proof of correctness for the simple available copies algorithm (Section 8.6) based on Theorem 8.4. That is, list conditions satisfied by histories produced by that algorithm, justify why they must be satisfied, and prove that any history that satisfies them must have an acyclic RDSG.

8.13 When all copies of a data item fail, we say the item has suffered a total failure. In available copies algorithms special care must be taken in recovering from a total failure of a data item: The copier transaction that brings copies up-to-date must read the value of the copy that failed last. Describe methods for recovering from such total failures, for available copies algorithms.

8.14 How do the quorum consensus, missing writes, and virtual partition algorithms handle total failures of data items?

8.15 In the directory-oriented available copies algorithm, a transaction can perform access validation by checking that all directories from which it read contain the copies it accessed. Why is this so? That is, why is it not necessary to access the copies themselves? Also, if the scheduler uses Strict 2PL, show that access validation requires merely to check that the directories read by the transaction are still available (their contents need not be considered).

8.16* Formalize the correctness argument given in Section 8.7 to derive a proof that the directory-oriented available copies algorithm produces only 1SR executions.

8.17* Give a correctness proof for the directory-oriented available copies algorithm, based on Theorem 8.4. That is, prove that any history representing an execution produced by that algorithm must have an acyclic RDSG.

8.18 Describe, in some detail, an algorithm that allows the creation and destruction of directory copies, using a (replicated) master directory.

8.19* Suppose each site is assigned a set of classes and can only execute transactions that are in its classes. (See Section 4.2 for a description of classes.) Assume that the readset of each class contains its writeset.

Suppose the network has partitioned. Define a directed graph G each of whose nodes represents the occurrence of a given class in a given partition. For each pair of nodes C_i, C_j where readset(C_i) $\cap$ writeset(C_j) $\neq$ { }, G contains the edge $C_i \rightarrow C_j$ and, if C_i and C_j are in the same partition, $C_j \rightarrow C_i$. A *multipartition cycle* in G is a cycle that contains two or more nodes whose sites are in different partitions.

Assume that the partitioned network experiences no site or communication failures or recoveries. Suppose the DBS in each partition uses the write-all approach with respect to the copies in its partition. Prove that if G has no multipartition cycles, and SG(H) is acyclic for RD history H, then H is 1SR.

8.20 Describe a method whereby the weights of copies can be changed dynamically in the quorum consensus algorithm.

8.21 In the missing writes algorithm a transaction begins by using the write-all approach. If it should ever become aware of missing writes, it can abort and rerun using quorum consensus. Alternatively, it can try to switch to quorum consensus "on the fly." Describe, in some detail, the latter option. (Hint: Consider doing some extra work during the atomic commitment protocol.)

8.22 Describe, in some detail, a technique whereby missing writes to a copy are "forgotten" when all such Writes have actually been applied to the copy. Make sure your algorithm can handle correctly the situation where a copy misses (again) some updates while (old) missing updates to that copy are being "forgotten."

8.23* Give a precise proof of correctness for the missing writes algorithm by giving a list of properties satisfied by histories that represent executions of that algorithm and then proving that any history that satisfies these conditions must have an acyclic RDSG.

8.24 Consider the formation of a new view in the virtual partition algorithm. Which copies of items for which there is a read quorum in the new view are guaranteed to be up-to-date?

8.25 Describe, in some detail, a View Update transaction, by integrating the view formation protocol and the copy update process. Take into account your answer to the previous exercise to optimize the latter. Explore the round and message complexity of a View Update transaction.

8.26 Describe a method whereby the weights of copies can be changed dynamically in the virtual partition algorithm.

8.27* Give a formal proof of correctness for the virtual partition algorithm.

APPENDIX

This appendix presents the definitions and elementary properties of graphs, digraphs and partial orders used in the book. Since we anticipate that most of these will be familiar to most readers, we have organized the appendix to facilitate its use as a reference.

A.1 GRAPHS

An *undirected graph* $G = (N, E)$ consists of a set N of elements called *nodes* and a set E of unordered pairs of nodes called *edges*. Diagramatically a graph is usually drawn with its nodes as points and its edges as line segments connecting the corresponding pair of nodes, as in Fig. A-1.

A *path* in a graph $G = (N, E)$ is a sequence of nodes $v_1, v_2, ..., v_k$ such that $[v_i, v_{i+1}] \in E$ for $1 \le i < k$. Such a path is said to connect v_1 and v_k. For example, 1, 2, 4, 3, 6, 5 is a path connecting 1 and 5 in Fig. A-1.

A graph $G = (N, E)$ is *connected* if there is a path connecting every pair of nodes. The graph in Fig. A-1 is connected. Fig. A-2 illustrates an unconnected graph.

A graph $G' = (N', E')$ is a *subgraph* of G if $N' \subseteq N$ and $E' \subseteq E$. For example, the graph of Fig. A–2 is a subgraph of that in Fig. A–1.

A *partition* of G is a collection $G_1 = (N_1, E_1), ..., G_k = (N_k, E_k)$ of subgraphs of G such that each G_i is connected and the node sets of these subgraphs are pairwise disjoint; i.e., $N_i \cap N_j = \{\}$ for $1 \le i \ne j \le k$. (We use "$\{\}$" to denote the empty set.) Each G_i in the collection is called a *component* of the partition. In this definition we do *not* require $\bigcup_{i=1}^{k} N_i = N$ or $\bigcup_{i=1}^{n}$

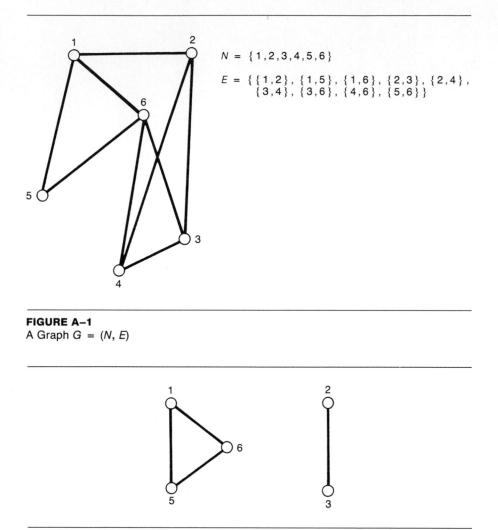

$$N = \{1,2,3,4,5,6\}$$

$$E = \{\{1,2\}, \{1,5\}, \{1,6\}, \{2,3\}, \{2,4\}, \{3,4\}, \{3,6\}, \{4,6\}, \{5,6\}\}$$

FIGURE A–1
A Graph $G = (N, E)$

FIGURE A–2
Unconnected Gráph

$E_i = E$ (but $\bigcup_{i=1}^{n} N_i \subseteq N$ and $\bigcup_{i=1}^{n} E_i \subseteq E$). Thus the graph in Fig. A–2 is a partition of the graph in Fig. A–1, consisting of two components.

A.2 DIRECTED GRAPHS

A *directed graph* (or *digraph*) $G = (N, E)$ consists of a set N of elements called *nodes* and a set E of ordered pairs of nodes, called *edges*. Diagrammatically a digraph is drawn with points representing the nodes and an arrow from point *a*

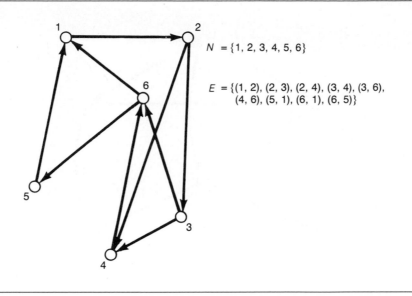

$N = \{1, 2, 3, 4, 5, 6\}$

$E = \{(1, 2), (2, 3), (2, 4), (3, 4), (3, 6), (4, 6), (5, 1), (6, 1), (6, 5)\}$

FIGURE A–3
A Digraph

to point b representing the edge (a, b). An example of a digraph is shown in Fig. A–3.

A *path* in a digraph G is a sequence of nodes n_1, n_2, ..., n_k such that $(n_i, n_{i+1}) \in E$ for $1 \le i < k$. Such a path is said to be *from n_1 to n_k*. By convention a single node n constitutes a *trivial path*. (This is different from an edge from n to itself, which is a path from n to n.) A path is *simple* if all nodes, except possibly the first and last in the sequence, are distinct. A *cycle* is a simple non-trivial path where the first and last nodes are identical. For example, 1, 2, 3, 4, 6, 5, 1 is a cycle in the digraph of Fig. A–3. If n_1, n_2, ..., n_k, n_1 is a cycle, then each edge (n_i, n_{i+1}) for $1 \le i < k$ and (n_k, n_1) is said to be *a member of* or *in* the cycle. A cycle is *minimal* if for every two nodes n_i and n_j in the cycle, if $(n_i, n_j) \in E$, then (n_i, n_j) is in the cycle. The previous example is not a minimal cycle because 1, 2, 3, 6, 1 is a subsequence of it that is also a cycle (indeed a minimal one).

A.3 DIRECTED ACYCLIC GRAPHS

A *directed acyclic graph* or *dag* is a digraph that contains no cycles. Examples of dags are shown in Fig. A–4 and Fig. A–5. A *source* is a node with no incoming edges. A dag must necessarily contain at least one source (why?). A dag with a unique source is called a *rooted dag* and the source is called the dag's *root*. The dag in Fig. A–4 is rooted while that in Fig. A–5 is not.

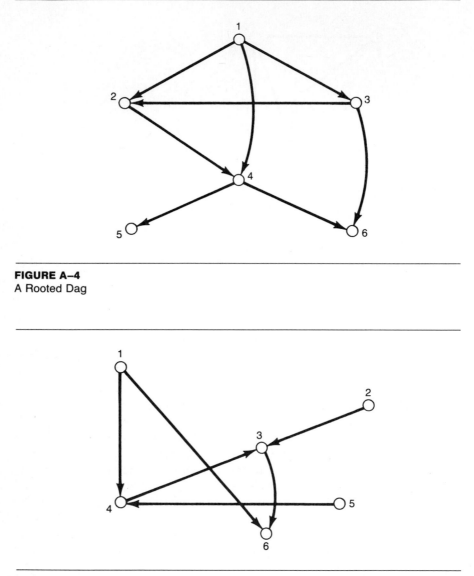

FIGURE A–4
A Rooted Dag

FIGURE A–5
A Dag With Many Sources

If (a, b) is an edge in a dag, a is called a *parent* of b and b is a *child* of a. If there is a path from a to b, then a is an *ancestor* of b and b a *descendant* of a. a is a *proper ancestor* of b if it is an ancestor of b and $a \neq b$; "*proper descendant*" is defined analogously. Note that the acyclicity of a dag implies that a node cannot be both a proper ancestor and a proper descendant of another. If

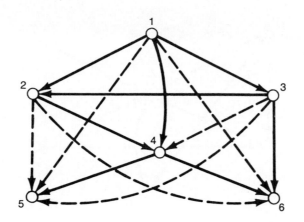

FIGURE A–6
Transitive Closure of a Rooted Dag

a and b are distinct nodes neither of which is an ancestor of the other, we say that a is *unrelated* to b.

A *topological sort* of a digraph G is a sequence of (all) the nodes of G such that if a appears before b in the sequence, there is no path from b to a in G. A fundamental characterization of dags is provided by Proposition A.1.

Proposition A.1: A digraph can be topologically sorted iff it is a dag. □

For a given dag, there may exist several topological sorts. For example, the dag in Fig. A–4 has two topological sorts, namely,

$$1, 3, 2, 4, 5, 6 \text{ and } 1, 3, 2, 4, 6, 5.$$

The *transitive closure* of a digraph $G = (N, E)$ is a digraph $G+ = (N, E+)$ such that $(a, b) \in E+$ iff there is a non-trivial path from a to b in G. Informally, $G+$ has an edge anywhere G has a (non-trivial) path. It is easy to show that

Proposition A.2: $G+$ is a dag iff G is a dag. □

A more "procedural" definition of transitive closure of a digraph G is:

    begin
        G+ := G;
        while G+ contains edges (a, b) and (b, c) but not (a, c) for some a, b, c
            in N do add edge (a, c) to G+
    end

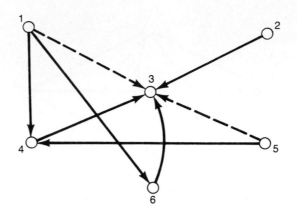

FIGURE A–7
Transitive Closure of a Dag with Many Sources

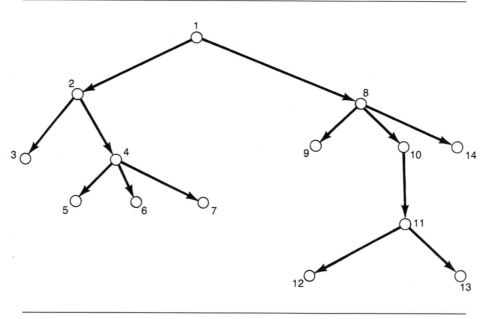

FIGURE A–8
A Tree

The transitive closures of the dags in Fig. A–4 and Fig. A–5 are shown, respectively, in Fig. A–6 and Fig. A–7. The added edges are drawn in broken lines. A digraph is *transitively closed* if it is equal to its own transitive closure (i.e., $G = G+$). Obviously, the transitive closure of any graph is transitively closed.

A *tree* is a rooted dag with the additional property that there is a unique path from the root to each node. Figure A–8 shows a tree. Ordinarily tree edges are drawn without arrows; the implicit direction is "away from the root." Since there is a unique path from the root to each node, this convention is unambiguous.

Also, the uniqueness of the path from the root to a node implies that in a tree each node has a *unique* parent, except for the root, which has no parent at all. A node may have several children, however.

A.4 PARTIAL ORDERS

A *partial order* $L = (\Sigma, <)$ consists of a set Σ called the *domain* of the partial order and an irreflexive, transitive binary relation $<$ on Σ.[1]

If $a < b$ we say that *a precedes b* and that *b follows a* in the partial order. If neither of two distinct elements precedes the other, the two elements are *incomparable* in the partial order.

A partial order $L' = (\Sigma', <')$ is a *restriction* of L on domain Σ' if $\Sigma' \subseteq \Sigma$ and for all $a, b \in \Sigma'$, $a <' b$ iff $a < b$. L' is a *prefix* of L, written $L' \leq L$, if L' is a restriction of L and for each $a \in \Sigma'$, all predecessors of a in L (i.e., all elements $b \in \Sigma$ such that $b < a$) are also in Σ'.

A partial order $L = (\Sigma, <)$ can be naturally viewed as a dag $G = (N, E)$ where $N = \Sigma$ and $(a, b) \in E$ iff $a < b$. That G is acyclic follows from the irreflexivity and transitivity of $<$. To see this, suppose G had a cycle $a_1, a_2, \ldots, a_k, a_1$. By construction of G, $a_1 < a_2, a_2 < a_3, \ldots, a_k < a_1$; by transitivity of $<$, $a_1 < a_1$, contradicting the irreflexivity of $<$. Moreover, the transitivity of $<$ implies that G is a transitively closed graph.

Conversely, we can construct a partial order $L = (\Sigma, <)$ from a given dag $G = (N, E)$ by taking $\Sigma = N$ and $a < b$ iff $(a, b) \in E+$, where $G+ = (N, E+)$ is the transitive closure of G. To verify that L is indeed a partial order, note that $<$ is irreflexive (because $(a, a) \notin E+$ for any $a \in N$, since G is acyclic), and $<$ is transitive (because $G+$ is transitivity closed).

Thus we can regard a partial order as a dag and vice versa.

---

[1] A binary relation $<$ on Σ *is irreflexive* if, for all $a \in \Sigma$, $a \not< a$ (i.e., "$a < a$" is false); it is *transitive* if, for all $a, b, c \in \Sigma$, and $a < b$ and $b < c$ imply $a < c$.

GLOSSARY

Abort. The transaction operation that a program uses to indicate that the transaction it is currently executing has terminated abnormally and its effects should be obliterated.

aborted. (Informal) The state of a transaction after the DBS has processed the transaction's Abort operation.

aborted. (Formal) Transaction T_i is aborted in history H if $a_i \in H$.

abort list. A list of the identifiers of the set of committed transactions, stored in stable storage.

abort record. A log record that says that a particular transaction has aborted.

ACA. Acronym for "avoids cascading aborts."

ACP. Acronym for "atomic commitment protocol."

active. (Informal) The state of a transaction that has started but has not yet become committed or aborted.

active. (Formal) Transaction T_i is active in H if there exists some $p_i \in H$ but $a_i \notin H$ and $c_i \notin H$.

active list. A list of the identifiers of the set of active transactions, stored in stable storage.

after image. The after image of data item x with respect to transaction T_i is the (last) value written into x by T_i.

aggressive scheduler. A scheduler that tends to avoid delaying operations by trying to schedule them immediately, possibly at the expense of rejecting other operations later on.

ancestor. In a dag, if there is a path from a to b then a is an *ancestor* of b.

archive checkpoint record. A checkpoint record written by an archive checkpointing procedure.

archive checkpointing. Checkpointing performed on the archive database.

archive database. The backup copy of a database used for media failure handling.

321

1. $H = \bigcup_{i=1}^{n} T_i$,
2. $<_H \supseteq \bigcup_{i=1}^{n} <_i$, and
3. for any two conflicting operations $p, q \in H$, either $p <_H q$ or $q <_H p$.

component. A set of operational sites that, due to a network partition, can communicate with each other, but with no other operational sites.

conflict. Two operations conflict if their order of execution affects either the state of the database or the value that one of them returns. In the Read-Write model, two operations conflict if they operate on the same data item and at least one of them is a Write.

conflict-based. A scheduler is conflict-based if it bases all of its decisions on ordering conflicting operations in a consistent way. Conflict-based schedulers produce only conflict serializable histories.

conflict equivalence. See equivalence.

conflict serializable. See serializable.

connected. A graph $G = (N, E)$ is *connected* if there is a path connecting every pair of nodes.

conservative scheduler. A scheduler that tends to delay operations, in order to avoid rejecting other operations later on.

conservative SGT. An SGT scheduler that uses predeclaration to help it determine which operations to delay in order to avoid rejecting other operations later on.

conservative TO. A type of TO scheduler that delays operations that could be run without violating the TO Rule, in order to reduce the chance that it will have to reject other conflicting operations with smaller timestamps later on.

Conservative 2PL. A two phase locking protocol in which each transaction obtains all of the locks it needs before any of its operations are submitted to the DM.

consistent state. A state of the database that satisfies the database's consistency predicates. Intuitively, this means that data item values are internally consistent with each other.

conversion. Upgrading a lock to a stronger lock type, such as upgrading a read lock on a data item to a write lock on the same data item.

cooperative termination protocol. The termination protocol in which all processes are consulted as to whether the decision is Commit or Abort.

coordinator. The process that supervises an atomic commitment protocol.

copier. A transaction that initializes a new copy, say x_A, by reading an existing copy x_B of x and writing the value of x_B into x_A.

critical section. A shared program that should be executed by at most one process at a time.

CSR. Acronym for "conflict serializable."

cycle. A cycle is a simple path where the first and last nodes are identical.

cyclic restart. A situation in which a transaction is continually aborted (e.g. selected as a victim of a deadlock) and restarted, but is never given the opportunity to terminate normally.

dag. Acronym for "directed acyclic graph."

dag locking. A generalization of tree locking to directed acyclic graphs.

database. A set of data items.

database state. The values of the data items in a database at a particular time.

data contention. A situation where transactions are delayed in queues because of lock conflicts.

data manager. The data manager (DM) is a composite module of the database system, consisting of a cache manager (CM) and recovery manager (RM).

database operations. Operations on data items that are supported by a database system, typically Read and Write.

database system. A database system (DBS) is a collection of hardware and software modules that support database operations and transaction operations. In our model, a centralized DBS consists of a cache manager (CM), recovery manager (RM), scheduler, and transaction manager (TM).

data item. A named memory area that can contain a value.

data tree. A tree structured collection of data items used to direct a tree locking protocol.

DBS. Acronym for "database system."

DC-thrashing. Thrashing in an idealized system with data contention but no resource contention.

DC-workload. $k^2 N / D$ where k is the number of locks a transaction requires, N is the multiprogramming level, and D is the number of data items in the database.

deadlock. A situation in which each transaction in a set of transactions is blocked waiting for another transaction in the set, and therefore none will become unblocked unless there is external intervention.

decentralized two phase commit. The two phase commit protocol in which all processes are in direct communication with each other, and therefore exchange messages directly instead of through a coordinator.

deferred output. A transaction T's output statements that the DBS postpones processing until after T commits.

deferred writing. In processing Write(x), the DBS delays distributing Writes to the replicated copies of x until the transaction commits.

delayed commit. The heuristic of delaying the commitment of a transaction so that the log buffer occupied by its commit record can fill up before being flushed.

descendant. In a dag, if there is a path from a to b then b is a *descendant* of a.

digraph. A directed graph.

directed acyclic graph. A directed acyclic graph is a digraph that contains no cycles.

directed graph. A directed graph $G = (N, E)$ consists of a set N of elements called *nodes* and a set E of ordered pairs of nodes, called *edges*.

directory. (For stable storage management) A mapping of data items to stable storage locations, used in shadowing.

(For replicated data) A mapping of data items to sites that store copies of those data items.

directory-oriented available copies. The available copies algorithm that uses directories to keep track of which copies are operational.

dirty. A slot whose dirty bit is set is called dirty.

dirty bit. A bit associated with each cache slot that is set iff the value of the data item stored in the cache slot was updated since it was last flushed.

distributed database system. A collection of sites connected by a computer network, where each site is a centralized database system that stores a portion of the database.

distributed deadlock. A deadlock in which two or more of the waiting situations occur at different sites.

distributed transaction log. A stable log in which the coordinator and participants in an atomic commitment protocol record information about distributed transactions.

DL. Acronym for "dag locking."

DM. Acronym for "data manager."

down. The state of a site that has failed (and not yet recovered).

election protocol. A protocol by which a set of processes select a unique coordinator.

EOF. An end-of-file marker.

equivalence. Two histories are (conflict) equivalent, denoted $\equiv$, if they are defined over the same transactions, have the same operations, and order conflicting operations of nonaborted transactions in the same way.

An MV history H is equivalent to an MV or 1V history H' if the operations of H and H' are in one-to-one correspondence, and H and H' have the same reads-from relationships.

Two RD histories over T are equivalent if they are view equivalent, that is, if they have the same reads-from relationships and final writes.

An RD history H over T is equivalent to a 1C history H_{1C} over T if

1. H and H_{1C} have the same reads-from relationships *on data items* (i.e., T_j reads-x-from T_i in H iff the same holds in H_{1C}), and

2. for final write $w_i[x]$ in H_{1C}, $w_i[x_A]$ is a final write in H for some copy x_A of x.

Exclude (EX). A transaction that updates directories to record the failure of a copy in the directory-oriented available copies algorithm.

execution. An informal term denoting the effects of operations issued by programs and performed by a computer.

fail-stop. Sites only fail by stopping. That is, they never perform incorrect actions.

failure-recovery serialization graph. Given an RD history H over transactions $\{T_0, ..., T_n\}$, a *failure-recovery serialization graph* (*FRSG*) for H is a directed graph with nodes N and edges E where:

$N = \{T_0, ..., T_n\} \cup \{\text{create}[x_A] \mid x \text{ is a data item and } x_A \text{ is a copy of } x\}$
$\quad \cup \{\text{fail}[x_A] \mid x \text{ is a data item and } x_A \text{ is a copy of } x\}$
$E = \{T_i \rightarrow T_j \mid T_i \rightarrow T_j \text{ is an edge of SG}(H)\} \cup E1 \cup E2 \cup E3$
$\quad$ where
$\quad E1 = \{\text{create}[x_A] \rightarrow T_i \mid T_i \text{ reads or writes } x_A\}$
$\quad E2 = \{T_i \rightarrow \text{fail}[x_A] \mid T_i \text{ reads } x_A\}$
$\quad E3 = \{T_i \rightarrow \text{create}[x_A] \text{ or fail}[x_A] \rightarrow T_i \mid T_i \text{ writes some copy of } x, \text{ but not } x_A\}$

Fetch. The cache manager operation that reads a data item from stable storage into cache.

final write. A Write operation $w_i[x]$ in history H is a final write if $a_i \notin H$ and for any $w_j[x] \in H$ ($j \neq i$), either $w_j[x] < w_i[x]$ or $a_j \in H$.

Given RD history H, $w_i[x_A]$ is a final write for x_A in H if $a_i \notin H$ and for all $w_j[x_A]$ in H ($j \neq i$), either $w_j[x_A] < w_i[x_A]$ or $a_j \in H$.

Flush. The cache manager operation that writes a data item from a (dirty) cache slot to stable storage.

FRSG. Acronym for "failure-recovery serialization graph."

fuzzy checkpointing. The checkpointing scheme that stops processing new operations (leaving active transactions in a blocked state), waits for in-progress operations to complete, and appends to the commit and abort lists a list of the data items stored in dirty cache slots.

Garbage Collection Rule. The Garbage Collection Rule states that an entry $[T_i, x, v]$ can be removed from the log iff (1) T_i has aborted or (2) T_i has committed but some other committed transaction wrote into x after T_i did (hence v is not the last committed value of x).

global deadlock detector. In a distributed database system, a single process that detects deadlocks by finding cycles in a global waits-for graph.

global waits-for graph. In a distributed database system, it consists of the union of the edges in the waits-for graph at every site.

granularity (of a data item). The amount of data contained in a data item, e.g., a word of memory, a page of a disk, or a record of a file.

granularity curve. Transaction throughput as a function of lock granularity.

group commit. See delayed commit.

growing phase. In two phase locking, the phase during which a transaction obtains locks.

handshake. The sequence of events of passing an operation to a module, waiting for an acknowledgment, and passing another operation. A handshake is used to control the order in which a module executes operations.

history. A prefix of a complete history.

home site. The site where a distributed transaction T originated and that is therefore the coordinator of T's atomic commitment protocol.

hot spot. A portion of the database that is accessed especially frequently.

idempotent. The property of Restart that any sequence of incomplete executions of Restart followed by a complete execution of Restart has the same effect as just one complete execution of Restart.

iff. Abbreviation for "if and only if."

immediate writing. The DBS processes Write(x) by distributing Writes to replicated copies of x at the moment it receives Write(x) from the transaction.

Include (IN). A transaction that updates directories to record the creation or recovery of a copy in the directory-oriented available copies algorithm.

incomparable. In a partial order, if neither of two distinct elements precedes the other, the two elements are incomparable.

inconsistent retrieval. A situation where a retrieval program reads some data item x before an update program writes x, but reads another data item y after that same update program writes y.

independent failure modes. Two or more storage devices have independent failure modes if no single failure event can destroy data on more than one device.

independent recovery. In an atomic commitment protocol, the ability of a recovering process to reach a decision without communicating with other processes.

index. A data structure consisting of a set of index entries that map field values into pointers to records with those field values.

index entry. A field value and a list of pointers to records with that field value.

index locking. A locking method for avoiding phantoms that sets locks on index entries to prevent accesses to records with the field values indicated by those entries.

in-place updating. The DM maintains exactly one copy of each data item in stable storage and that copy is overwritten by each Write.

integrated scheduler. A scheduler obtained by integrating an rw synchronizer with a ww synchronizer.

intentions list. The list of update records for a transaction, which is applied after a transaction commits, using a no-undo/redo recovery manager algorithm.

intention lock. A coarse granularity lock that indicates the owner of the lock has a certain type of lock for a finer granularity data item. For example, an intention read lock on a file indicates that the owner may have a read lock on one or more records of that file.

interfere. Loosely speaking, two concurrently executing programs interfere if they interact in undesirable ways. We deliberately leave the definition of this term imprecise.

interleaved. The operations of two programs (or transactions) are interleaved if an operation of one program executes in between two operations of the other program.

invalidated. In multiversion TO, if the scheduler rejects $w_i[x]$ because it already processed some $r_j[x_k]$ where $ts(T_k) < ts(T_i) < ts(T_j)$, then we say that $w_i[x]$ would have invalidated $r_j[x_k]$.

last committed value. The last committed value of a data item x in some execution is the value last written into x in that execution by a committed transaction.

least recently used. The replacement strategy that replaces the cache slot least recently accessed.

linear two phase commit. The two phase commit protocol in which processes are linearly ordered and can only communicate with their left and right neighbors.

LM. Acronym for "Lock Manager."

lock. (Noun) A reservation that prevents other transactions from obtaining certain other (conflicting) locks.
(Verb) The operation of setting or obtaining a lock.

lock coupling. The tree locking technique whereby a transaction obtains locks on a node N's children before releasing its lock on N.

lock escalation. A locking method used in conjunction with multigranularity locking whereby if a transaction obtains too many locks at one granularity, it increases the granularity of its subsequent lock requests.

lock instance graph. A set of data items structured according to a lock type graph.

lock manager. The software module that services the Lock and Unlock operations.

lock type graph. A directed acyclic graph that specifies the relative coarseness of granularity of locks in multigranularity locking.

locked point. In two phase locking, any moment at which a transaction owns all of its locks.

log.   A representation of the history of execution, stored in stable storage and used by the recovery manager to restore the last committed values of data items.

log sequence number.   The address of a log entry in the log.

logical log.   A log whose entries describe higher level operations than Write.

lost update.   An update that is overwritten before being read, thereby producing a nonserializable result. The canonical example of a lost update is when two transactions read the old value of a data item and then subsequently both write a new value for that data item.

LSN.   Acronym for "log sequence number."

LSN-based logging algorithm.   The partial data item logging algorithm where each data item contains the LSN of the update record whose corresponding operation was the last operation to write into that data item.

majority.   More than half of a set.

master record.   In the no-undo/no-redo algorithm, the master record indicates which of two copies of the database in stable storage contains the committed state.

media failure.   A failure in which a portion of the contents of stable storage is lost.

message.   A block of data transferred from one transaction to another. We assume that messages are exchanged by being written to and read from the database.

MGL.   Acronym for "multigranularity locking."

minimal cycle.   A cycle is *minimal* if, for every two nodes n_i and n_j in the cycle, (n_i, n_j) $\in E$ implies (n_i, n_j) is in the cycle.

mirroring.   The technique of storing the same data in the same locations of two storage devices to protect against the failure of one of the two devices.

missing writes.   In the available copies algorithm, a transaction T_i's Write(x_A) is missing if T_i wrote x but not x_A.

missing writes algorithm.   The algorithm for replicated data in which the DBS uses the write-all approach in the absence of failures, and uses the quorum consensus algorithm in the presence of failures.

mixed scheduler.   An integrated scheduler where different scheduling rules (i.e. 2PL, TO, SGT) are used for rw and ww synchronization.

MPL.   Acronym for "multiprogramming level."

multigranularity locking.   A locking method whereby different transactions can lock different granularity data items.

multiprogramming level.   The number of active transactions.

multiversion concurrency control.   A concurrency control algorithm in which each Write on x produces a new version, and when processing a Read, the scheduler must select which version to read.

multiversion history.   A partial order $H <$ over T with ordering relation $<$ such that

1. $H = h(\cup_{i=1}^{n} T_i)$ for some translation function h,
2. for each T_i and all operations p_i, q_i in T_i, if $p_i <_i q_i$ then $h(p_i) < h(q_i)$, and
3. if $h(r_j[x]) = r_j[x_i]$, then $w_i[x_i] < r_j[x_i]$;
4. if $w_i[x] <_i r_i[x]$ then $h(r_i[x]) = r_i[x_i]$.

multiversion serialization graph.   The multiversion serialization graph for MV history H and version order $\ll$, MVSG$(H, \ll)$, is SG(H) with the following *version order edges* added: for each $r_k[x_j]$ and $w_i[x_i]$ in H where $i, j,$ and k are distinct, if $x_i \ll x_j$ then include $T_i \rightarrow T_j$; otherwise, include $T_k \rightarrow T_i$.

multiversion TO. A TO scheduler that processes operations first-come-first-served. It translates $r_i[x]$ into $r_i[x_k]$, where x_k is the version of x with largest timestamp $\leq$ ts(T_i). It rejects $w_i[x]$ if it has already processed some $r_j[x_k]$ where ts$(T_k) <$ ts$(T_i) <$ ts(T_j); otherwise, it translates $w_i[x]$ into $w_i[x_i]$.

mutual exclusion. Ensuring that at most one process executes a particular shared program, called a critical section.

MV. Acronym for "multiversion."

MVSG. Acronym for "multiversion serialization graph."

MVTO. Acronym for "multiversion TO."

network partition. A combination of site and communication failures that divides up the operational sites into two or more components, where every two sites within a component can communicate, but sites in different components cannot.

one-copy history. See history.

one-copy serial. A serial MV history H is one-copy serial (1-serial) if for all $i, j,$ and x, if T_i reads x from T_j, then $i = j$ or T_j is the last transaction preceding T_i that writes into any version of x.

one-copy serializable. An MV history is one-copy serializable (1SR) if it is equivalent to a one-serial MV history. An RD history is one-copy serializable if it is equivalent to a serial one-copy history.

one version history. See history.

operational. The state of a site that is functioning correctly.

optimistic scheduler. See certifier.

page. The fixed-sized unit of data that can be atomically written to disk storage.

parent. If (a, b) is an edge in a dag, a is called a *parent* of b.

partial data item logging. A physical logging algorithm that logs the before and/or after images of just those portions of data items that were updated.

partial data item logging algorithm. The recovery manager algorithm in Section 6.4 that logs partial data items, uses fuzzy checkpointing, and uses a Restart algorithm that recovers from a system failure by doing a backward scan of the log for undo followed by a forward scan for redo.

partial failure. In a distributed system, the situation in which some sites are operational while others are down.

partial order. A partial order $L = (\Sigma, <)$ consists of a set Σ called the *domain* of the partial order and an irreflexive, transitive binary relation $<$ on Σ.

participant. A process that participates in an atomic commitment protocol, but does not supervise it.

partition. A partition of a graph G is a collection $G_1 = (N_1, E_1), \ldots, G_k = (N_k, E_k)$ of subgraphs of G such that each G_i is connected and the node sets of these subgraphs are pairwise disjoint; i.e., $N_i \cap N_j = \{\}$ for $1 \leq i \neq j \leq k$.

path. A path in a (directed or undirected) graph $G = (N, E)$ is a sequence of nodes $v_1, v_2, \ldots, v_k$ such that $[v_i, v_{i+1}] \in E$ for $1 \leq i < k$.

path pushing. A distributed deadlock detection algorithm where each site exchanges lists of paths in waits-for graphs with other sites in order to find a cycle in the union of those graphs.

penultimate. Second to last.

phantom deadlock. A situation in which the deadlock detector believes there is a deadlock, but the deadlock doesn't really exist.

phantom problem. The concurrency control problem for dynamic databases, that is, where transactions can insert and delete data items.

physical log. A type of log that contains information about the values of data items written by transactions.

piggybacking. The communication technique whereby two or more messages are packaged as one large message, in order to reduce message transmission cost.

Pin(c). The cache manager operation that makes a cache slot c unavailable for flushing.

predeclaration. Using predeclaration, transactions "predeclare" their readsets and writesets, meaning that the scheduler learns (a superset of) the readset and writeset of each transaction before processing any of the transaction's operations.

predicate locking. A locking method for avoiding phantoms that sets locks on predicates to prevent accesses to records that satisfy those predicates.

prefix commit-closed. A property of histories that, whenever it is true of a history H, is also true of the committed projection $C(H')$ of every prefix H' of H. Recoverability, cascadelessness, strictness, and serializability (see Theorem 2.3) are prefix commit-closed.

prefix of a partial order. L' is a *prefix* of a partial order $L = (\Sigma, <)$, written $L' \le L$, if L' is a restriction of L and for each $a \in \Sigma'$, all predecessors of a in L are also in Σ'.

preserves reflexive reads-from. A multiversion history preserves reflexive reads-froms if whenever $w_i[x] <_i r_i[x]$, then $h(r_i[x]) = r_i[x_i]$.

primary copy. The variation of deferred writing in which all transactions use the same copy of each data item while they are executing.

process. The operating system abstraction that corresponds to the independent execution of a sequential program.

proper ancestor. In a dag, a is a *proper ancestor* of b if it is an ancestor of b and $a \ne b$.

pure restart policy. A scheduling policy in which a transaction is aborted whenever it encounters a lock already held by another transaction.

pure scheduler. An integrated scheduler where possibly different versions of the same scheduling rule (i.e., 2PL, TO, or SGT) are used for both rw and ww synchronization.

Purge. The operation that deletes obsolete entries from a timestamp table. Used by TO schedulers.

QC. Acronym for "quorum consensus."

query. A transaction that reads one or more data items but does not write any data items.

quorum. Each object o (typically a site or copy) in a set O is assigned a non-negative weight. A quorum of O is a subset of O that has more than half the total weight.

quorum consensus (QC). The replicated data algorithm in which the DBS processes a Read(x) by reading a read quorum of copies of x and selecting the most up-to-date copy, and processes a Write(x) by writing a write quorum of copies of x.

RC. Acronym for "recoverable."

RC-thrashing. Thrashing in an idealized system with resource contention but no data contention.

RD. Acronym for "replicated data."

RDSG. Acronym for "replicated data serialization graph."

Read(x). The database operation that returns the current value of data item x.

read lock. A reservation to read a data item. Ordinarily (for rw synchronization), if transaction T_i owns a read lock on x, denoted $rl_i[x]$, then no other transaction can obtain a write lock on x.

read order. See replicated data serialization graph.

readset. The set of data items a transaction reads.

reads-from. (Informal) Transaction T_j reads data item x from transaction T_i in an execution if

1. T_j reads x after T_i has written it,
2. T_i does not abort before T_j reads x, and
3. every transaction (if any) that writes x between the time T_i writes it and T_j reads it aborts before T_j reads it.

reads-from. (Formal) Transaction T_i reads x from transaction T_j in history H if $w_j[x] < r_i[x]$, $a_j \not< r_i[x]$, and if there is some $w_k[x]$ such that $w_j[x] < w_k[x] < r_i[x]$, then $a_k < r_i[x]$. T_i reads from T_j in H if it reads some data item from T_j in H.

recoverable. (Informal) An execution is recoverable if, for every transaction T that commits, T's Commit follows the Commit of every transaction from which T read.

recoverable. (Formal) History H is recoverable (RC) if, whenever T_i reads from T_j in H and $c_i \in H$, $c_j < c_i$.

recovery manager. The database system module that is responsible for the commitment and abortion of transactions. It processes the operations Read, Write, Commit, Abort, and Restart.

recovery procedure. A procedure that a site (i.e., a DBS) executes after recovering from failure to bring itself to a consistent state so it can resume normal processing.

Redo Rule. The Redo Rule states that before a transaction can commit, the value it produced for each data item it wrote must be in stable storage (e.g. in the stable database or the log).

reflexive reads-from. A reads-from relationship where a transaction reads the value it previously wrote.

replacement strategy. The criterion according to which the cache manager chooses a slot to flush to make room for a data item being fetched.

replicated data (RD) history. A *replicated data (RD) history* H over $T = \{T_0, ..., T_n\}$ is a partial order with ordering relation $<$ where

1. $H = h(\bigcup_{i=0}^{n} T_i)$ for some translation function h;
2. for each T_i and all operations p_i, q_i in T_i, if $p_i <_i q_i$, then every operation in $h(p_i)$ is related by $<$ to every operation in $h(q_i)$;
3. for every $r_j[x_A]$, there is at least one $w_i[x_A]$ such that $w_i[x_A] < r_j[x_A]$;
4. all pairs of conflicting operations are related by $<$, where two operations *conflict* if they operate on the same *copy* and at least one of them is a Write; and
5. if $w_i[x] <_i r_i[x]$ and $h(r_i[x]) = r_i[x_A]$, then $w_i[x_A] \in h(w_i[x])$.

replicated data serialization graph (RDSG). Given a history H, an RDSG G for H is a graph containing $SG(H)$ and including enough edges such that

1. if T_i and T_k write x, then either $T_i \ll T_k$ or $T_k \ll T_i$, and

2. if T_j reads-x-from T_i, T_k writes some copy of x ($k \neq i$, $k \neq j$), and $T_i \ll T_k$, then $T_j \ll T_k$,

where $n_i \ll n_j$ means there is a path from n_i to n_j. If G satisfies (1), it induces a *write order*. If it satisfies (2), it induces a *read order*.

requires redo. A recovery manager requires redo if it allows a transaction to commit before all the values it wrote are recorded in the stable database.

requires undo. A recovery manager requires undo if it allows an uncommitted transaction to record in the stable database values it wrote.

resource contention. A situation where transactions are delayed in queues while trying to obtain the use of certain resources (such as processor, memory, or I/O) because other transactions are presently using those resources.

Restart. The RM operation that performs a DBS's recovery procedure.

restriction of a partial order. A partial order $L' = (\Sigma', <')$ is a restriction of $L = (\Sigma, <)$ on domain Σ' if $\Sigma' \subseteq \Sigma$ and for all $a, b \in \Sigma'$, $a <' b$ iff $a < b$.

RM. Acronym for "recovery manager."

rooted dag. A dag with a unique source, called its root.

round. In an atomic commitment protocol, the maximum time for a message to reach its destination.

rw serialization graph. A serialization graph that only contains an edge $T_i \rightarrow T_j$ if $r_i[x] < w_j[x]$ or $w_i[x] < r_j[x]$ for some data item x.

rw synchronization. Controlling the order in which Reads execute with respect to conflicting Writes.

rw synchronizer. A scheduler that only performs rw synchronization.

scheduler. The database system module that controls the relative order in which database operations and transaction operations execute, by delaying or rejecting some of those operations.

serial execution. An execution in which for every pair of transactions, all of the operations of one transaction execute before any of the operations of the other.

serial history. A complete (1V, MV, or RD) history H is serial if for every two transactions T_i and T_j that appear in H, either all operations of T_i appear before all operations of T_j or vice versa.

Serializability Theorem. Theorem 2.1, which says that a history H is serializable iff $SG(H)$ is acyclic.

serializable execution. An execution E that produces the same output and has the same effect on the database as some serial execution of the same transactions that appeared in E.

serializable history. A history is serializable (SR) if its committed projection is (conflict) equivalent to a serial history.

serialization graph. The serialization graph (SG) for history H over transactions $T = \{T_1 ..., T_n\}$, denoted $SG(H)$, is a directed graph whose nodes are the transactions in T that are committed in H and whose edges are all $T_i \rightarrow T_j$ such that one of T_i's operations precedes and conflicts with one of T_j's operations in H.

The serialization graph of a multiversion history H over T includes edges $T_i \rightarrow T_j$ $(i \neq j)$ such that for some x, T_j reads x from T_i.

serialization graph testing. The scheduling method that explicitly maintains a serialization graph and avoids nonserializable executions by checking for cycles in that graph.

SG. Acronym for "serialization graph."

SGT. Acronym for "serialization graph testing."

SGT certifier. An SGT scheduler that only checks for serialization graph cycles when it receives a transaction's Commit.

shadow copy. An old version of a data item.

shadowing. The DM maintains more than one copy of each data item in stable storage, so it may write a data item to stable storage without destroying older (shadow) versions of that data item.

shadow page algorithm. The no-undo/no-redo algorithm described in Section 6.7.

shrinking phase. In two phase locking, the phase during which a transaction releases locks.

simple path. A path in a graph is simple if all nodes, except possibly the first and last in the sequence, are distinct.

site failure. The event in which a site stops abruptly and the contents of volatile storage are destroyed.

site quorums. The approach to handling communication failures in a replicated database in which the connected component of the network that contains a quorum of sites is the only component that can process transactions that access replicated data.

slot. See cache slot.

source. In a directed acyclic graph, a source is a node with no incoming edges.

SR. Acronym for "serializable."

SSG. Acronym for "stored serialization graph."

ST. Acronym for "strict."

stable database. The state of the database in stable storage.

stable-LSN. The stable-LSN of a cache slot storing x marks a point in the log where it is known that the value of the stable database copy of x reflects (at least) all of the log records up to that LSN.

stable storage. An area of memory that is resistant to processor and operating system failures. It models secondary storage media, such as disk and tape, on typical computer systems.

Start. The transaction operation that a program uses to indicate that it wishes to begin executing a new transaction.

start-2PC record. In the two phase commit protocol, the record in the coordinator's distributed transaction log that indicates it has begun the protocol.

Static 2PL. See Conservative 2PL.

stored serialization graph. The serialization graph maintained by an SGT scheduler.

strength of locks. Lock type p is stronger than lock type q if for every lock type o, $ol_i[x]$ conflicts with $ql_j[x]$ implies $ol_i[x]$ conflicts with $pl_j[x]$.

strict. (Informal) A DBS is strict if it delays each Read(x) and Write(x) until all transactions that had previously issued Write(x) have either committed or aborted.

strict. (Formal) History H is strict (ST) if whenever $w_j[x] < o_i[x]$, either $a_j < o_i[x]$ or $c_j < o_i[x]$, where $o_i[x]$ is $r_i[x]$ or $w_i[x]$.

Strict TO. The TO scheduler behaves like Basic TO, except that it delays each Write $w_i[x]$ until there is no active transaction that issued a Write on x.

Strict 2PL. A two phase locking protocol where the scheduler releases all of a transaction's locks together, after the transaction commits or aborts.

subgraph. A graph $G' = (N', E')$ is a *subgraph* of $G = (N, E)$ if $N' \subseteq N$ and $E' \subseteq E$.

system failure. A failure in which the entire contents of volatile storage is lost.

termination protocol. A protocol invoked by a process when it fails to receive an anticipated message while in its uncertainty period.

Thomas' Write Rule. A TO ww synchronizer that acknowledges but does not process any Write that arrives too late to be processed in timestamp order.

thrashing. A situation where increasing the number of transactions in the system causes the throughput to drop.

three phase commit. A nonblocking atomic commitment protocol that can tolerate site failures but not communication failures.

timeout. An alarm that indicates to a process that a predefined time interval has elapsed.

timeout action. The action that a process must take if its waiting for an event (typically a message) is interrupted by a timeout.

timeout failure. A communication failure in which a site believes it cannot communicate with another site because it is using a timeout period that is too short.

timestamp-based deadlock prevention. A deadlock prevention technique where a transaction T_i can wait for another transaction T_j only if T_i has higher priority than T_j.

timestamp ordering. The scheduling method where each transaction is assigned a unique timestamp and conflicting operations from different transactions are scheduled to execute in timestamp order.

timestamps. Values drawn from a totally ordered domain. In concurrency control algorithms, timestamps are usually assigned to transactions such that no two transactions have the same timestamp.

TL. Acronym for "tree locking."

TM. Acronym for "transaction manager."

TO. Acronym for "timestamp ordering."

topological sort. In a digraph G, a sequence of (all) the nodes of G such that if a appears before b in the sequence, there is no path from b to a in G.

TO Rule. If $p_i[x]$ and $q_j[x]$ are conflicting operations and $i \neq j$, then the DM processes $p_i[x]$ before $q_j[x]$ iff T_i's timestamp is less than T_j's timestamp.

total failure. In a distributed system, the situation in which all sites are down. In replicated databases, total failure of a data item occurs when all copies of the data item are down.

transaction. (Informal) The execution of one or more programs that include database and transaction operations, beginning with the operation Start, and ending with operation Commit or Abort.

transaction. (Formal) A transaction T_i is a partial order with ordering relation $<_i$ where

1. $T_i \subseteq \{r_i[x], w_i[x] \mid x \text{ is a data item}\} \cup \{a_i, c_i\}$;
2. $a_i \in T_i$ iff $c_i \notin T_i$;
3. if t is a_i or c_i (whichever is in T_i), for any $p \in T_i$, $p <_i t$; and
4. if $r_i[x], w_i[x] \in T_i$ then either $r_i[x] <_i w_i[x]$ or $w_i[x] <_i r_i[x]$.

transaction class. A class is defined by a readset and writeset. A transaction is in a class if its readset and writeset are in the class's readset and writeset (respectively).

transaction failure. The event of a transaction issuing an Abort.

transaction manager. The database system module that is the interface between transactions and the rest of the database system. It receives each operation from the transaction, performs any necessary preprocessing of the operation (such as appending a transaction identifier to the operation), and then forwards the operation to the appropriate database system module.

transaction operations. The operations Start, Commit, and Abort, which are supported by a database system.

transaction-oriented shadowing. The recovery manager scheme for undo/no-redo where a transaction's updated data items are written as new versions in stable storage, and the new versions replace the shadow versions after the transaction commits.

transitive closure. The transitive closure of a digraph $G = (N, E)$ is the digraph $G+ = (N, E+)$ such that $(a, b) \in E+$ iff there is a non-trivial path from a to b in G.

transitively closed. A digraph is *transitively closed* if it is equal to its own transitive closure (i.e., $G = G+$).

tree. A *tree* is a rooted dag with the additional property that there is a unique path from the root to each node.

tree locking. The non-two-phase locking protocol in which a transaction can release a lock on a node N of the tree as soon as it has obtained all of the locks it will need on children of N.

two phase commit (2PC). The atomic commitment protocol that, in the absence of failures, behaves roughly as follows: The coordinator asks all participants to vote; if any participant votes No, the coordinator tells all participants to decide Abort; if all participants vote Yes, then the coordinator tells all participants to decide Commit.

two phase locking (2PL). The locking protocol in which each transaction obtains a read (or write) lock on each data item before it reads (or writes) that data item, and does not obtain any locks after it has released some lock.

two phase rule. The rule in two phase locking that requires a transaction to set all of its locks before releasing any of them.

two version 2PL. A multiversion scheduler that uses 2PL. See Section 5.4 for complete definition.

TWR. Acronym for "Thomas' Write Rule."

uncertain. In an atomic commitment protocol, the state of a process while it is in its uncertainty period.

uncertainty period. In an atomic commitment protocol, the period between the moment a process votes Yes and the moment it has received sufficient information to know what the decision will be.

undirected graph. An undirected graph $G = (N, E)$ consists of a set N of elements called *nodes* and a set E of unordered pairs of nodes called *edges*.

Undo Rule. The Undo Rule states that if x's location in the stable database presently contains the last committed value of x, then that value must be saved in stable storage *before* being overwritten in the stable database by an uncommitted value.

uninterpreted. The aspects of an execution that are left unspecified, and can therefore be arbitrary.

unlock. The operation of releasing a lock.

Unpin(c). The cache manager operation that makes a previously pinned slot again available for flushing.

updater. A transaction that can read and write data items.

update record. A log record that documents a Write operation of a transaction.

validation protocol. The protocol used by an available copies algorithm to ensure correctness by checking that certain copies are still operational or down just before a transaction commits.

version number. In the quorum consensus algorithm, each replicated copy is given a version number, which the DBS uses to select the most up-to-date copy to read.

version order. A version order $\ll$ for data item x in MV history H is a total order of versions of x in H.

version order edge. See multiversion serialization graph.

victim. A transaction that is aborted in order to break a deadlock.

view equivalence. Two histories H and H' are view equivalent if

1. they are over the same set of transactions and have the same operations;

2. for any T_i, T_j such that a_i, $a_j \notin H$ (hence a_i, $a_j \notin H'$) and any x, if T_i reads x from T_j in H then T_i reads x from T_j in H' and

3. for each x, if $w_i[x]$ is the final write of x in H then it is also the final write of x in H'.

view serializable. A history H is view serializable if for any prefix H' of H, $C(H')$ is view equivalent to some serial history.

view update transaction. In the virtual partition algorithm, a view update transaction updates each site's view of the members of a component (i.e. of a virtual partition).

virtual partition algorithm. An algorithm for replicated data. After a communication failure, the DBS can access a data item x only if it is executing in a component that contains a quorum of copies of x. Within a component, the DBS uses the write-all approach with respect to the set of copies of x within its component.

volatile storage. An area of memory that is vulnerable to hardware and operating system failures. It models main memory on typical computer systems.

VSR. Acronym for "view serializable."

Wait-Die. A timestamp-based deadlock prevention technique whereby a transaction aborts if it tries to lock a data item currently locked by a higher priority transaction.

waits-for graph. A graph whose nodes are labelled by transaction names, and that contains an edge $T_i \rightarrow T_j$ whenever T_i is waiting for T_j to release some lock.

workspace model. Transactions write into a workspace, not the database. When they are ready to commit, the Writes are propagated to the database.

[Andler et al. 82] Andler, S., Ding, I., Eswaran, K., Hauser, C., Kim, W., Mehl, J., Williams, R. System D: A Distributed System for Availability. In *Proc. 8th Int'l Conf. on Very Large Data Bases*, pages 33–44. Mexico City, September, 1982.

[Attar, Bernstein, Goodman 84] Attar, R., Bernstein, P.A., Goodman, N. Site Initialization, Recovery and Back-up in a Distributed Database System. *IEEE Trans. on Software Engineering* SE-10(6):645–650, November, 1984.

[Badal 79] Badal, D.Z. Correctness of Concurrency Control and Implications in Distributed Databases. In *Proc. IEEE COMPSAC Conf.*, pages 588–593. November, 1979.

[Badal 80a] Badal, D.Z. On the Degree of Concurrency Provided by Concurrency Control Mechanisms for Distributed Databases. In *Proc. Int'l Symp. Distributed Databases*, pages 35–48. North-Holland, Amsterdam, March, 1980.

[Badal 80b] Badal, D.Z. The Analysis of the Effects of Concurrency Control on Distributed Data Management and Computer Networks. In *Proc. 6th Int'l Conf. on Very Large Data Bases*. Montreal, 1980.

[Badal 81] Badal, D.Z. Concurrency Control Overhead or Closer Look at Blocking vs. Nonblocking Concurrency Control Mechanisms. In *5th Int'l Conf. on Distributed Data Management and Computer Networks*. 1981. Originally published as Technical Report No. NPS52-81-005, Naval Postgraduate School, Monterey, CA, June, 1981.

[Badal, Popek 78] Badal, D.Z., Popek, G.J. A Proposal for Distributed Concurrency Control for Partially Redundant Distributed Database Systems. In *Proc. 3rd Berkeley Workshop on Distributed Data Management and Computer Networks*, pages 273–288. ACM/IEEE, 1978.

[Balter, Berard, Decitre 82] Balter, R., Berard, P., Decitre, P. Why Control of Concurrency Level in Distributed Systems is More Fundamental than Deadlock Management. In *Proc. 1st ACM SIGACT-SIGOPS Symp. on Principles of Distributed Computing*, pages 183–193. Ottawa, August, 1982.

[Barbara, Garcia-Molina 84] Barbara, D., Garcia-Molina, H. The Vulnerability of Voting Mechanisms. In *Proc. 4th Symp. on Reliability in Distributed Software and Database Systems*, pages 45–53. IEEE, Silver Spring, MD, 1984.

[Bartlett 82] Bartlett, J.F. A "NonStop" Operating System. *The Theory and Practice of Reliable System Design*. Digital Press, Bedford, MA, 1982, pages 453–460. D. Siewiorek and R. Swarz (eds.).

[Bayer 83] Bayer, R. Database System Design for High Performance. In *Proc. IFIP 9th World Computer Congress*, pages 146–155. North-Holland, Amsterdam, September, 1983.

[Bayer et al. 80a] Bayer, R., Elhardt, E., Heller, H., Reiser, A. Distributed Concurrency Control in Database Systems. In *Proc. 6th Int'l Conf. on Very Large Data Bases*, pages 275–284. Montreal, 1980.

[Bayer, Heller, Reiser 80b] Bayer, R., Heller, H., Reiser, A. Parallelism and Recovery in Database Systems. *ACM Trans. on Database Systems* 5(2):139–156, June, 1980.

[Bayer, McCreight 72] Bayer, R., McCreight, E. Organization and Maintenance of Large Ordered Indices. *Acta Informatica* 1(3):173–189, 1972.

[Bayer, Schkolnick 77] Bayer, R., Schkolnick, M. Concurrency of Operations on B-trees. *Acta Informatica* 9:1–21, 1977.

[Beeri et al. 83] Beeri, C., Bernstein, P.A., Goodman, N., Lai, M.Y., Shasha, D.E. A Concurrency Control Theory for Nested Transactions. In *Proc. 2nd ACM SIGACT-SIGOPS Symp. on Principles of Distributed Computing*, pages 45–62. Montreal, August, 1983.

[Beeri, Obermarck 81] Beeri, C., Obermarck, R. A Resource Class Independent Deadlock Detection Algorithm. In *Proc. 7th Int'l Conf. on Very Large Databases*, pages 166–178. Cannes, France, September, 1981.

[Belford, Schwartz, Sluizer 76] Belford, G.G., Schwartz, P.M., Sluizer, S. *The Effect of Back-up Strategy on Database Availability.* Technical Report CAC Document No. 181, CCTCWAD Document No. 5515, Center for Advanced Computation, University of Illinois at Urbana-Champaign, February, 1976.

[Ben-Ari 82] Ben-Ari, M. *Principles of Concurrent Programming*. Prentice-Hall, Englewood Cliffs, N.J., 1982.

[Bernstein et al. 78] Bernstein, P.A., Rothnie, J.B., Jr., Goodman, N., Papadimitriou, C.H. The Concurrency Control Mechanism of SDD-1: A System for Distributed Databases (The Fully Redundant Case). *IEEE Trans. on Software Engineering* SE-4(3):154–168, May, 1978.

[Bernstein, Goodman 79] Bernstein, P.A., Goodman, N. Approaches to Concurrency Control in Distributed Databases. In *Proc. Nat'l Computer Conf.*, pages 813–821. AFIPS Press, Arlington, VA, June, 1979.

[Bernstein, Goodman 81] Bernstein, P.A., Goodman, N. Concurrency Control in Distributed Database Systems. *ACM Computing Surveys* 13(2):185–221, June, 1981.

[Bernstein, Goodman 82] Bernstein, P.A., Goodman, N. A Sophisticate's Introduction to Distributed Database Concurrency Control. In *Proc. 8th Int'l Conf. on Very Large Data Bases*, pages 62–76. Mexico City, September, 1982.

[Bernstein, Goodman 83] Bernstein, P.A., Goodman, N. Multiversion Concurrency Control-Theory and Algorithms. *ACM Trans. on Database Systems* 8(4):465–483, December, 1983.

[Bernstein, Goodman 84] Bernstein, P.A., Goodman, N. An Algorithm for Concurrency Control and Recovery in Replicated Distributed Databases. *ACM Trans. on Database Systems* 9(4):596–615, December, 1984.

[Bernstein, Goodman 86a] Bernstein, P.A., Goodman, N. Serializability Theory for Replicated Databases. *Journal of Computer and System Sciences* 31(3):355–374, December, 1986.

[Bernstein, Goodman 86b] Bernstein, P.A., Goodman, N. A Proof Technique for Concurrency Control and Recovery Algorithms for Replicated Databases. *Distributing Computing* 1, Springer-Verlag, 1986.

[Bernstein, Goodman, Hadzilacos 83] Bernstein, P.A., Goodman, N., Hadzilacos, V. Recovery Algorithms for Database Systems. In *Proc. IFIP 9th World Computer Congress*, pages 799–807. North-Holland, Amsterdam, September, 1983.

[Bernstein, Goodman, Lai 83] Bernstein, P.A., Goodman, N., Lai, M.Y. Analyzing Concurrency Control when User and System Operations Differ. *IEEE Trans. on Software Engineering* SE-9(3):233–239, May, 1983.

[Bernstein, Shipman 80] .Bernstein, P.A., Shipman, D. The Correctness of Concurrency Mechanisms in a System for Distributed Databases (SDD-1). *ACM Trans. on Database Systems* 5(1):52–68, March, 1980.

[Bernstein, Shipman, Rothnie 80]   Bernstein, P.A., Shipman, D.W., Rothnie, J.B., Jr. Concurrency Control in a System for Distributed Databases (SDD-1). *ACM Trans. on Database Systems* 5(1):18–51, March, 1980.

[Bernstein, Shipman, Wong 79]   Bernstein, P.A., Shipman, D.W., Wong, W.S. Formal Aspects of Serializability in Database Concurrency Control. *IEEE Trans. on Software Engineering* 5(3):203–216, May, 1979.

[Bhargava 82]   Bhargava, B. Performance Evaluation of the Optimistic Approach to Distributed Database Systems and Its Comparison to Locking. In *Proc. 3rd Int'l Conf. on Distributed Computer Systems*, pages 466–473. IEEE, October, 1982.

[Birman 86]   Birman, K.P. *ISIS: A System for Fault-Tolerant Distributed Computing*. Technical Report 86-744, Department of Computer Science, Cornell University, Ithaca, NY, April, 1986.

[Birman et al. 84]   Birman, K.P., Joseph, T.A., Rauchie, T., El-Abbadi, A. Implementing Fault-Tolerant Distributed Objects. In *Proc. 4th Symp. on Reliability in Distributed Software and Database Systems*, pages 124–133. IEEE, Silver Spring, MD, October, 1984.

[Bjork 73]   Bjork, L.A. Recovery Scenario for a DB/DC System. In *Proc. ACM National Conf.*, pages 142–146. ACM, 1973.

[Bjork, Davies 72]   Bjork, L.A., Davies, C.T. *The Semantics of the Preservation and Recovery of Integrity in a Data System*. Technical Report TR-02.540, IBM, December, 1972.

[Blasgen et al. 79]   Blasgen, M.W., Gray, J.N., Mitoma, M., Price, T. The Convoy Phenomenon. *ACM Operating Systems Review* 14(2):20–25, April, 1979.

[Blaustein et al. 83]   Blaustein, B.T., Garcia-Molina, H., Ries, D.R., Chilenskas, R.M., Kaufman, C.W. *Maintaining Replicated Databases Even in the Presence of Network Partitions*. EASCON, 1983.

[Borr 81]   Borr, A.J. Transaction Monitoring in Encompass: Reliable Distributed Transaction Processing. In *Proc. 7th Int'l Conf. on Very Large Databases*, pages 155–165. Cannes, France, September, 1981.

[Breitwieser, Kersen 79]   Breitwieser, H., Kersen, U. Transaction and Catalog Management of the Distributed File Management System DISCO. In *Proc. 5th Int'l Conf. on Very Large Data Bases*, pages 340–350. Rio de Janeiro, 1979.

[Breitwieser, Leszak 82]   Breitwieser, H., Leszak, M. A Distributed Transaction Processing Protocol Based on Majority Consensus. In *Proc. 1st ACM SIGACT-SIGOPS Symp. on Principles of Distributed Computing*, pages 224–237. Ottawa, August, 1982.

[Briatico, Ciuffoletti, Simoncini 84]   Briatico, D., Ciuffoletti, A., Simoncini, L. A Distributed Domino-Effect Free Recovery Algorithm. In *Proc. 4th Symp. on Reliability in Distributed Software and Database Systems*, pages 207–217. IEEE, Silver Spring, MD, October, 1984.

[Brinch Hansen 73]   Brinch Hansen, P. *Operating System Principles*. Prentice-Hall, Englewood Cliffs, NJ, 1973.

[Buckley, Silberschatz 84]   Buckley, G.N., Silberschatz, A. Concurrency Control in Graph Protocols by Using Edge Locks. In *Proc. 3rd ACM SIGACT-SIGMOD Symp. on Principles of Database Systems*, pages 45–50. Waterloo, Ontario, April, 1984.

[Carey 83]   Carey, M.J. Granularity Hierarchies in Concurrency Control. In *Proc. 2nd ACM SIGACT-SIGMOD Symp. on Principles of Database Systems*, pages 156–164. Atlanta, GA, March, 1983.

[Carey, Stonebraker 84]   Carey, M., Stonebraker, M. The Performance of Concurrency Control Algorithms for DBMSs. In *Proc. 10th Int'l Conf. on Very Large Data Bases*, pages 107–118. Singapore, August, 1984.

[Casanova 81]   Casanova, M.A. *Lecture Notes in Computer Science*. Volume 116: *The Concurrency Control Problem of Database Systems*, Springer-Verlag, Berlin, 1981.

[Casanova, Bernstein 80]   Casanova, M.A., Bernstein, P.A. General Purpose Schedulers for Database Systems. *Acta Informatica* 14:195–220, 1980.

[Casanova, Moura, Tucherman 85]   Casanova, M.A., Moura, A.V., Tucherman, L. On the Correctness of a Local Storage Subsystem (Extended Abstract). In *Proc. 4th ACM SIGACT-SIGMOD Symp. on Principles of Database Systems*, pages 123–133. Portland, Oregon, March, 1985.

[Ceri, Owicki 82]   Ceri, S., Owicki, S. On the Use of Optimistic Methods for Concurrency Control in Distributed Databases. In *Proc. 6th Berkeley Workshop on Distributed Data Management and Computer Networks*. ACM/IEEE, February, 1982.

[Ceri, Pelagatti 84]   Ceri, S., Pelagatti, G. *Distributed Databases—Principles and Systems*. McGraw-Hill, New York, 1984.

[Chamberlin, Boyce, Traiger 74]   Chamberlin, D.D., Boyce, R.F., Traiger, I.L. A Deadlock-free Scheme for Resource Allocation in a Database Environment. In *Info. Proc. 74*. North-Holland, Amsterdam, 1974.

[Chan et al. 82]   Chan, A., Fox, S., Lin, W.T.K., Nori, A., Ries, D.R. The Implementation of an Integrated Concurrency Control and Recovery Scheme. In *Proc. ACM SIGMOD Conf. on Management of Data*, pages 184–191. Orlando, FL, June, 1982.

[Chan, Gray 85]   Chan, A., Gray, R. Implementing Distributed Read-Only Transactions. *IEEE Trans. on Software Engineering* SE-11(2):205–212, February, 1985.

[Chan, Skeen 86]   Chan, A., Skeen, D. *The Reliability Subsystem of a Distributed Database Manager*. Technical Report CCA-85-02, Computer Corporation of America, 1986.

[Chandy, Lamport 85]   Chandy, K.M., Lamport, L. Distributed Snapshots: Determining Global States of Distributed Systems. *ACM Trans. on Computer Systems* 3(1):63–75, February, 1985.

[Chandy, Misra 82]   Chandy, K.M., Misra, J. A Distributed Algorithm for Detecting Resource Deadlocks in Distributed Systems. In *Proc. 1st ACM SIGACT-SIGOPS Symp. on the Principles of Distributed Computing*, pages 157–164. Ottawa, August, 1982.

[Chandy, Misra, Haas 83]   Chandy, K.M., Misra, J., Haas, L.M. Distributed Deadlock Detection. *ACM Trans. on Computer Systems* 1(2):144–156, May, 1983.

[Cheng, Belford 80]   Cheng, W.K., Belford, G.G. Update Synchronization in Distributed Databases. In *Proc. 6th Int'l Conf. on Very Large Data Bases*, pages 301–308. Montreal, October, 1980.

[Cheng, Belford 82]   Cheng, W.K., Belford, G.G. The Resiliency of Fully Replicated Distributed Databases. In *Proc. 6th Berkeley Workshop on Distributed Data Management and Computer Networks*, pages 23–44. ACM/IEEE, February, 1982.

[Chesnais, Gelenbe, Mitrani 83]   Chesnais, A., Gelenbe, E., Mitrani, I. On The Modelling of Parallel Access to Shared Data. *Comm. ACM* 26(3):196–202, March, 1983.

[Cheung, Kameda 85]   Cheung, D., Kameda, T. Site-Optimal Termination Protocols for a Distributed Database under Networking Partitioning. In *Proc. 4th ACM SIGACT-SIGOPS Symp. on Principles of Distributed Computing*, pages 111–121. Minaki, Ontario, August, 1985.

[Chin, Ramarao 83]   Chin, F., Ramarao, K.V.S. Optimal Termination Protocols for Network Partitioning. In *Proc. 2nd ACM SIGACT-SIGMOD Symp. on Principles of Database Systems*, pages 25–35. Atlanta, GA, March, 1983.

[Chu, Ohlmacher 74]   Chu, W.W., Ohlmacher, G. Avoiding Deadlock in Distributed Data Bases. In *Proc. ACM National Conf.*, pages 150–160. November, 1974.

[Coffman, Elphick, Shoshani 71]   Coffman, E.G., Jr., Elphick, M., Shoshani, A. System Deadlocks. *Computing Surveys* 3(2):67–78, June, 1971.

[Coffman 81]   Coffman, E.G., Gelenbe, E., Plateau, B. Optimization of the Number of Copies in a Distributed Database. *IEEE Trans. on Software Eng.* 7(1):78–84, January, 1981.

[Comer 79]   Comer, D. The Ubiquitous B-Tree. *ACM Computing Surveys* 11(2):121–139, June, 1979.

[Cooper 82]   Cooper, E.C. Analysis of Distributed Commit Protocols. In *Proc. ACM SIGMOD Conf. on Management of Data*, pages 175–183. Orlando, FL, June, 1982.

[Croker, Maier 86]   Croker, A., Maier, D. A Dynamic Tree-Locking Protocol. In *Proc. Int'l Conf. on Data Engineering*, pages 49–56. IEEE, Los Angeles, CA, February, 1986.

[Crus 84]   Crus, R.A. Data Recovery in IBM Database 2. *IBM Systems Journal* 23(2):178–188, 1984.

[Dadam, Schlageter 80]   Dadam, P., Schlageter, G. Recovery in Distributed Databases Based on Non-Synchronized Local Checkpoints. *Information Processing 80*, 1980. North-Holland, Amsterdam.

[Daniels, Spector 83]   Daniels, D., Spector, A.Z. An Algorithm for Replicated Directories. In *Proc. 2nd ACM SIGACT-SIGOPS Symp. on Principles of Distributed Computing*, pages 104–113. Montreal, August, 1983.

[Date 85]   Date, C.J. *An Introduction to Database Systems, Volume 1*. Addison-Wesley, Reading, MA, 1985. 4th Edition.

[Davidson 84]   Davidson, S.B. Optimism and Consistency in Partitioned Distributed Database Systems. *ACM Trans. on Database Systems* 9(3):456–481, September, 1984.

[Davidson, Garcia-Molina, Skeen 85]   Davidson, S.B., Garcia-Molina, H., Skeen, D. Consistency in Partitioned Networks. *ACM Computing Surveys* 17(3):341–370, September, 1985.

[Davies 73]   Davies, C.T. Recovery Semantics for a DB/DC System. In *Proc. ACM National Conf.*, pages 136–141. ACM, 1973.

[Deppe, Fry 76]   Deppe, M.E., Fry, J.P. Distributed Databases: A Summary of Research. *Computer Networks* 1(2), September, 1976.

[Devor, Carlson 82]   Devor, C., Carlson, C.R. Structural Locking Mechanisms and Their Effect on Database Management System Performance. *Information Systems* 7(4):345–358, 1982.

[Dijkstra 71]   Dijkstra, E.W. Hierarchical Ordering of Sequential Processes. *Acta Informatica* 1(2):115–138, 1971.

[Dubourdieu 82] Dubourdieu, D.J. Implementation of Distributed Transactions. In *Proc. 6th Berkeley Workshop on Distributed Data Management and Computer Networks*, pages 81–94. ACM/IEEE, 1982.

[Dwork, Skeen 83] Dwork, C., Skeen, D. The Inherent Cost of Nonblocking Commitment. In *Proc. 2nd ACM SIGACT-SIGOPS Symp. on Principles of Distributed Computing*, pages 1–11. Montreal, August, 1983.

[Eager 81] Eager, D.L. *Robust Concurrency Control in Distributed Databases*. Technical Report CSRG #135, Computer Systems Research Group, University of Toronto, October, 1981.

[Eager, Sevcik 83] Eager, D.L., Sevcik, K.C. Achieving Robustness in Distributed Database Systems. *ACM Trans. Database Syst.* 8(3):354–381, September, 1983.

[Effelsberg, Haerder 84] Effelsberg, W., Haerder, T. Principles of Database Buffer Management. *ACM Trans. on Database Systems* 9(4):560–595, December, 1984.

[El Abbadi, Skeen, Cristian 85] El Abbadi, A., Skeen, D., Cristian, F. An Efficient, Fault-Tolerant Protocol for Replicated Data Management. In *Proc. 4th ACM SIGACT-SIGMOD Symp. on Principles of Database Systems*, pages 215–228. Portland, Oregon, March, 1985.

[El Abbadi, Toueg 86] El Abbadi, A., Toueg, S. Availability in Partitioned Replicated Databases. In *Proc. 5th ACM SIGACT-SIGMOD Symp. on Principles of Database Systems*, pages 240–251. Cambridge, MA, March, 1986.

[Elhardt, Bayer 84] Elhardt, K., Bayer, R. A Database Cache for High Performance and Fast Restart in Database Systems. *ACM Trans. on Database Systems* 9(4):503–525, December, 1984.

[Ellis 77] Ellis, C.A. A Robust Algorithm for Updating Duplicate Databases. In *Proc. 2nd Berkeley Workshop on Distributed Databases and Computer Networks*. ACM/IEEE, May, 1977.

[Ellis 80] Ellis, C.S. Concurrent Search and Inserts in 2-3 Trees. *Acta Informatica* 14(1):63–86, 1980.

[Ellis 83] Ellis, C.S. Extendible Hashing for Concurrent Operations and Distributed Data. In *Proc. 2nd ACM SIGACT-SIGMOD Symp. on Principles of Database Systems*, pages 106–116. Atlanta, GA, March, 1983.

[Elmagarmid, Sheth, Liu 86] Elmagarmid, A.K., Sheth, A.P., Liu, M.T. Deadlock Detection Algorithm in Distributed Database Systems. In *Proc. Int'l Conf. on Data Engineering*, pages 556–564. IEEE, Los Angeles, February, 1986.

[Eswaran et al. 76] Eswaran, K.P., Gray, J.N., Lorie, R.A., Traiger, I.L. The Notions of Consistency and Predicate Locks in a Database System. *Comm. ACM* 19(11):624–633, November, 1976.

[Fischer 83] Fischer, M.J. *The Consensus Problem in Unreliable Distributed Systems (A Brief Survey)*. Technical Report YALEU/DCS/RR-273, Department of Computer Science, Yale University, June, 1983.

[Fischer, Griffeth, Lynch 81] Fischer, M.J., Griffeth, N.D., Lynch, N.A. Global States of a Distributed System. In *Proc. 1st Symp. on Reliability in Distributed Software and Database Systems*, pages 31–38. IEEE, Pittsburgh, PA, 1981.

[Fischer, Lynch 82] Fischer, M.J., Lynch, N.A. A Lower Bound for the Time to Assure Interactive Consistency. *Information Processing Letters* 14(4):183–186, June, 1982.

[Fischer, Lynch, Paterson 83] Fischer, M.J., Lynch, N.A., Paterson, M.S. Impossibility of Distributed Consensus with One Faulty Process. In *Proc. 2nd ACM*

SIGACT-SIGMOD Symp. on Principles of Database Systems, pages 1–7. Atlanta, GA, March, 1983.

[Fischer, Michael 82] Fischer, M.J., Michael, A. Sacrificing Serializability to Attain High Availability of Data in an Unreliable Network. In *Proc. 1st ACM SIGACT-SIGMOD Symp. on Principles of Database Systems*, pages 70–75. Los Angeles, March, 1982.

[Ford, Calhoun 84] Ford, R., Calhoun, J. Concurrency Control Mechanisms and the Serializability of Concurrent Tree Algorithms. In *Proc. 3rd ACM SIGACT-SIGMOD Symp. on Principles of Database Systems*, pages 51–59. Waterloo, Ontario, April, 1984.

[Ford, Schultz, Jipping 84] Ford, R., Schultz, R., Jipping, M. Performance Evaluation of Distributed Concurrency Control Mechanisms. In *Proc. 4th Symp. on Reliability in Distributed Software and Database Systems*, pages 84–89. IEEE, Silver Spring, MD, October, 1984.

[Franaszek, Robinson 85] Franaszek, P., Robinson, J.T. Limitations of Concurrency in Transaction Processing. *ACM Trans. on Database Systems* 10(1):1–28, March, 1985.

[Fussell, Kedem, Silberschatz 81a] Fussell, D.S., Kedem, Z.M., Silberschatz, A. A Theory of Correct Locking Protocols for Database Systems. In *Proc. 7th Int'l Conf. on Very Large Data Bases*, pages 112–124. Cannes, France, 1981.

[Fussell, Kedem, Silberschatz 81b] Fussell, D.S., Kedem, Z.M., Silberschatz, A. Deadlock Removal Using Partial Rollback in Database Systems. In *Proc. ACM-SIGMOD Int'l Conf. on Management of Data*, pages 65–73. Ann Arbor, MI, April, 1981.

[Gafni 85] Gafni, E. Improvements in the Time Complexity of Two Message-Optimal Election Algorithms. In *Proc. 4th ACM SIGACT-SIGOPS Symp. on Principles of Distributed Computing*, pages 175–185. Minaki, Ontario, August, 1985.

[Galler 82] Galler, B.I. *Concurrency Control Performance Issues*. Technical Report CSRG-147, Computer Systems Research Group, University of Toronto, September, 1982.

[Galler, Bos 83] Galler, B.I., Bos, L. A Model of Transaction Blocking in Databases. *Performance Evaluation* 3:95–122, 1983.

[Garcia-Molina 78] Garcia-Molina, H. Performance Comparisons of Two Update Algorithms for Distributed Databases. In *Proc. 3rd Berkeley Workshop Distributed Databases and Computer Networks*, pages 108–118. ACM/IEEE, August, 1978.

[Garcia-Molina 79a] Garcia-Molina, H. A Concurrency Control Mechanism for Distributed Databases which Use Centralized Locking Controllers. In *Proc. 4th Berkeley Workshop on Distributed Databases and Computer Networks*, pages 113–122. ACM/IEEE, August, 1979.

[Garcia-Molina 79b] Garcia-Molina, H. *Performance of Update Algorithms for Replicated Data in a Distributed Database*. Tech. Rep. STAN-CS-79-744, Department of Computer Science, Stanford University, June, 1979.

[Garcia-Molina 82] Garcia-Molina, H. Elections in a Distributed Computing System. *IEEE Trans. on Computers* C-31(1):48–59, January, 1982.

[Garcia-Molina 83] Garcia-Molina, H. Using Semantic Knowledge for Transaction Processing in a Distributed Database. *ACM Trans. on Database Systems* 8(2):186–213, June, 1983.

[Garcia-Molina 86]   Garcia-Molina, H. The Future of Data Replication. In *5th Symp. on Reliability in Distributed Software and Data Base Systems*, pages 13–19. IEEE, Los Angeles, January, 1986.

[Garcia-Molina et al. 83]   Garcia-Molina, H., Allen, T., Blaustein, B., Chilenskas, R.M., Ries, D.R. Data-Patch: Integrating Inconsistent Copies of a Database after a Partition. In *Proc. 3rd IEEE Symp. on Reliability in Dist. Software and Database Systems*, pages 38–48. Clearwater Beach, FL, October, 1983.

[Garcia-Molina, Barbara 83]   Garcia-Molina, H., Barbara, D. *How to Assign Votes in a Distributed System*. Technical Report TR 311-3/1983, Department of Electrical Engineering and Computer Science, Princeton University, 1983.

[Garcia-Molina, Kent, Chung 85]   Garcia-Molina, H., Kent, J., Chung, J. An Experimental Evaluation of Crash Recovery Mechanisms. In *Proc. 4th ACM SIGACT-SIGMOD Symp. on Principles of Database Systems*, pages 113–122. Portland, Oregon, March, 1985.

[Garcia-Molina, Pittelli, Davidson 86]   Garcia-Molina, H., Pittelli, F., Davidson, S. Applications of Byzantine Agreement in Database Systems. *ACM Trans. on Database Systems* 11(1):27–47, March, 1986.

[Garcia-Molina, Wiederhold 82]   Garcia-Molina, H., Wiederhold, G. Read-Only Transactions in a Distributed Database. *ACM Trans. on Database Systems* 7(2):209–234, June, 1982.

[Gardarin, Chu 79]   Gardarin, G., Chu, W.W. A Reliable Distributed Control Algorithm for Updating Replicated Data. In *Proc. 6th Data Communication Symp*. IEEE, 1979.

[Gardarin, Chu 80]   Gardarin, G., Chu, W.W. A Distributed Control Algorithm for Reliably and Consistently Updating Replicated Databases. *IEEE Trans. on Computers* C-29(12):1060–1068, December, 1980.

[Gardarin, Lebaux 79]   Gardarin, G., Lebaux, P. Centralized Control Update Algorithms for Fully Redundant Distributed Databases. In *Proc. 1st Int'l Conf. on Distributed Computing Systems*, pages 699–705. IEEE, October, 1979.

[Garey, Johnson 79]   Garey, M.R., Johnson, D.S. *Computers and Intractability: A Guide to the Theory of NP-Completeness*. W.H. Freeman, San Francisco, 1979.

[Gawlick, Kinkade 85]   Gawlick, D., Kinkade, D. *Varieties of Concurrency Control in IMS/VS Fast Path*. Technical Report TR85.6, Tandem Computers, Cupertino, CA, 1985.

[Gelenbe, Hebrail 86]   Gelenbe, E., Hebrail, G. A Probability Model of Uncertainty in Data Bases. In *Proc. Int'l Conf. on Data Engineering*, pages 328–333. IEEE, Los Angeles, February, 1986.

[Gelenbe, Sevcik 78]   Gelenbe, E., Sevcik, K. Analysis of Update Synchronization for Multiple Copy Databases. In *Proc. 3rd Berkeley Workshop on Distributed Databases and Computer Networks*, pages 69–88. ACM/IEEE, August, 1978.

[Gifford 79]   Gifford, D.K. Weighted Voting for Replicated Data. In *Proc. 7th ACM SIGOPS Symp. on Operating Systems Principles*, pages 150–159. Pacific Grove, CA, December, 1979.

[Gligor, Shattuck 80]   Gligor, V.D., Shattuck, S.H. On Deadlock Detection in Distributed Systems. *IEEE Trans. on Software Engineering* 6(5):435–440, September, 1980.

[Gold, Boral 86]   Gold, I., Boral, H. The Power of the Private Workspace Model. *Information Systems* 11(1):1–9, 1986.

[Goodman, Shasha 85]   Goodman, N., Shasha, D. Semantically-based Concurrency Control for Search Structures. In *Proc. 4th ACM SIGACT-SIGMOD Symp. on Principles of Database Systems*. Portland, OR, March, 1985.

[Goodman et al. 83]   Goodman, N., Skeen, D., Chan, A., Dayal, U., Fox, S. Ries, D. A Recovery Algorithm for a Distributed Database System. In *Proc. 2nd ACM SIGACT-SIGMOD Symp. on Principles of Database Systems*, pages 8–15. Atlanta, GA, March, 1983.

[Goodman, Suri, Tay 83]   Goodman, N., Suri, R., Tay, Y.C. A Simple Analytic Model for Performance of Exclusive Locking in Database Systems. In *Proc. 2nd ACM SIGACT-SIGMOD Symp. on Principles of Database Systems*, pages 203–215. Atlanta, GA, March, 1983.

[Graham, Griffeth 84]   Graham, M.H., Griffeth, N. Reliable Scheduling of Database Transactions for Unreliable Systems. In *Proc. 3rd ACM SIGACT-SIGMOD Symp. on Principles of Database Systems*, pages 300–312. Waterloo, Ontario, April, 1984.

[Gray 78]   Gray, J.N. Notes on Database Operating Systems. *Operating Systems: An Advanced Course, Lecture Notes in Computer Science* 60:393–481, Springer-Verlag, Berlin, 1978.

[Gray 80]   Gray, J.N. A Transaction Model. *Lecture Notes in Computer Science* 85:282–298, Springer-Verlag, Berlin, 1980. G. Goos and J. Hartmanis (eds.).

[Gray 81]   Gray, J.N. The Transaction Concept: Virtues and Limitations. In *Proc. 7th Int'l Conf. on Very Large Data Bases*, pages 144–154. Cannes, France, September, 1981.

[Gray 86]   Gray, J.N. Why Do Computers Stop and What Can Be Done about It? In *5th Symp. on Reliability in Distributed Software and Data Base Systems*, pages 3–12. IEEE, Los Angeles, January, 1986.

[Gray et al. 75]   Gray, J.N., Lorie, R.A., Putzulo, G.R., Traiger, I.L. *Granularity of Locks and Degrees of Consistency in a Shared Database*. Research Report RJ1654, IBM , September, 1975.

[Gray et al. 81a]   Gray, J.N., McJones, P., Blasgen, M., Lindsay, B., Lorie, R., Price, T., Putzulo, F., Traiger, I. The Recovery Manager of the System R Database Manager. *ACM Computing Surveys* 13(2):223–242, June, 1981.

[Gray et al. 81b]   Gray, J., Homan, P., Korth, H., Obermarck, R. *A Straw Man Analysis of the Probability of Waiting and Deadlock in a Database System*. Technical Report RJ3066, IBM Research, San Jose, CA, February, 1981.

[Gray, Lorie, Putzolu 75]   Gray, J.N., Lorie, R.A., Putzolu, G.R. Granularity of Locks in a Shared Data Base. In *Proc. 1st Int'l Conf. on Very Large Data Bases*, pages 428–451. Framingham, MA, September, 1975.

[Griffeth, Miller 84]   Griffeth, N., Miller, J.A. Performance Modeling of Database Recovery Protocols. In *Proc. 4th Symp. on Reliability in Distributed Software and Database Systems*, pages 75–83. IEEE, Silver Spring, MD, October, 1984.

[Hadzilacos, Papadimitriou 85]   Hadzilacos, T., Papadimitriou, C.H. Algorithmic Aspects of Multiversion Concurrency Control. In *Proc. 4th ACM SIGACT-SIGMOD Symp. on Principles of Database Systems*, pages 96–104. Portland, OR, March, 1985.

[Hadzilacos, Yannakakis 86]   Hadzilacos, T., Yannakakis, M. Deleting Completed Transactions. In *Proc. 5th ACM SIGACT-SIGMOD Symp. on Principles of Database Systems*, pages 43–47. Cambridge, MA, March, 1986.

[Hadzilacos 82]   Hadzilacos, V. An Algorithm for Minimizing Roll Back Cost. In *Proc. 1st ACM SIGACT-SIGMOD Symp. on Principles of Database Systems*, pages 93–97. Los Angeles, March, 1982.

[Hadzilacos 83]   Hadzilacos, V. An Operational Model for Database System Reliability. In *Proc. 2nd ACM SIGACT-SIGMOD Symp. on Principles of Database Systems*, pages 244–256. Atlanta, GA, March, 1983.

[Hadzilacos 86]   Hadzilacos, V. A Theory of Reliability in Database Systems. 1986. Submitted for publication.

[Haerder 84]   Haerder, T. Observations on Optimistic Concurrency Control Schemes. *Information Systems* 9(2):111–120, October, 1984.

[Haerder, Reuter 79]   Haerder, T., Reuter, A. Optimization of Logging and Recovery in a Database System. *Database Architecture*:151–168, 1979. North Holland, Amsterdam, G. Bracchi and G.M. Nijssen (eds.).

[Haerder, Reuter 83]   Haerder, T., Reuter, A. Principles of Transaction-Oriented Database Recovery. *ACM Computing Surveys* 15(4):287–317, December, 1983.

[Hammer, Shipman 80]   Hammer, M., Shipman, D.W. Reliability Mechanisms for SDD-1: A System for Distributed Databases. *ACM Trans. on Database Systems* 5(4):431–466, December, 1980.

[Herlihy 86]   Herlihy, M. A Quorum-Consensus Replication Method for Abstract Data Types. *ACM Trans. on Computer Systems* 4(1):32–53, February, 1986.

[Hewitt 74]   Hewitt, C.E. *Protection and Synchronization in Actor Systems*. Working Paper No. 83, M.I.T. Intelligence Lab., Cambridge, MA, November, 1974.

[Hoare 74]   Hoare, C.A.R. Monitors: An Operating System Structuring Concept. *Comm. ACM* 17(10):549–557, October, 1974.

[Holt 72]   Holt, R.C. Some Deadlock Properties in Computer Systems. *ACM Computing Surveys* 4(3):179–196, September, 1972.

[Holt 83]   Holt, R.C. *Concurrent Euclid, the Unix System and Tunis*. Addison-Wesley, Reading, MA, 1983.

[Holt et al. 78]   Holt, R.C., Graham, G.S., Lazowska, E.D., Scott, M.A. *Structured Concurrent Programming with Operating Systems Applications*. Addison-Wesley, Reading, MA, 1978.

[Horning et al. 74]   Horning, J.J., Lauer, H.C., Melliar-Smith, P.M., Randell, B. A Program Structure for Error Detection and Recovery. *Lecture Notes in Computer Science* 16:171–187, E. Gelenbe and C. Kaiser (eds.). Springer-Verlag, Berlin, 1974.

[Hua, Bhargava 82]   Hua, C., Bhargava, B. Classes of Serializable Histories and Synchronization Algorithms In Distributed Database Systems. In *Proc. 3rd Int'l Conf. on Distributed Computer Systems*. Miami, FL, October, 1982.

[Hunt, Rosenkrantz 79]   Hunt, H.B., Rosenkrantz, D.J. The Complexity of Testing Predicate Locks. In *Proc. ACM-SIGMOD Int'l Conf. on Management of Data*, pages 127–133. Boston, MA, May, 1979.

[Ibaraki, Kameda 83]   Ibaraki, T., Kameda, T. *Multiversion vs. Single Version Serializability*. Technical Report 83–1, Laboratory for Computer and Communications Research, Simon Fraser University, 1983.

[Irani, Lin 79]   Irani, K.B., Lin, H.L. Queueing Network Models for Concurrent Transaction Processing in a Database System. In *Proc. ACM SIGMOD Int'l Conf. on Management of Data*, pages 134–142. Boston, MA, May, 1979.

[Isloor, Marsland 80]   Isloor, S.S., Marsland, T.A. The Deadlock Problem: An Overview. *Computer* 13(9):58–77, September, 1980.

[Jefferson, Motro 86]   Jefferson, D., Motro, A. The Time Warp Mechanism for Database Concurrency Control. In *Proc. Int'l Conf. on Data Engineering*, pages 474–481. IEEE, Los Angeles, CA, February, 1986.

[Jordan, Banerjee, Batman 81]   Jordan, J.R., Banerjee, J., Batman, R.B. Precision Locks. In *Proc. ACM-SIGMOD Int'l Conf. on Management of Data*, pages 143–147. Ann Arbor, MI, April, 1981.

[Joseph, Birman 86]   Joseph, T.A., Birman, K.P. Low Cost Management of Replicated Data in Fault-Tolerant Distributed Systems. *ACM Trans. on Computer Systems* 4(1):54–70, February, 1986.

[Kaneko et al. 79]   Kaneko, A., Nishihara, Y., Tsuruoka, K., Hattori, M. Logical Clock Synchronization Method for Duplicated Datbase Control. In *Proc. 1st Int'l Conf. Distributed Computing Systems*, pages 601–611. IEEE, October, 1979.

[Kanellakis, Papadimitriou 81]   Kanellakis, P., Papadimitriou, C.H. The Complexity of Distributed Concurrency Control. In *Proc. 22nd Conf. on Foundations of Computer Science*, pages 185–197. IEEE, New York, 1981.

[Kanellakis, Papadimitriou 82]   Kanellakis, P., Papadimitriou, C.H. Is Distributed Locking Harder? In *Proc. 1st ACM SIGACT-SIGMOD Symp. on Principles of Database Systems*, pages 98–107. Los Angeles, March, 1982.

[Kawazu et al. 79]   Kawazu, S., Minami, S., Itoh, S., Teranaka, K. Two-Phase Deadlock Detection Algorithm in Distributed Databases. In *Proc. 5th Int'l Conf. on Very Large Data Bases*, pages 360–367. Rio de Janeiro, 1979.

[Kedem 83]   Kedem, Z.M. Locking Protocols: From Exclusive to Shared Locks. *Journal of the ACM* 30(4):787–804, October, 1983.

[Kedem, Silberschatz 81]   Kedem, Z.M., Silberschatz, A. A Characterization of Database Graphs Admitting a Simple Locking Protocol. *Acta Informatica* 16:1–13, 1981.

[Kersten, Tebra 84]   Kersten, M., Tebra, H. Application of an Optimistic Concurrency Control Method. *Software Practice and Experience* 14, February, 1984.

[Kiessling, Landherr 83]   Kiessling, W., Landherr, G. A Quantitative Comparison of Lockprotocols for Centralized Databases. In *Proc. 9th Int'l Conf. on Very Large Data Bases*, pages 120–130. Florence, Italy, October, 1983.

[Kim 79]   Kim, K.H. Error Detection, Reconfiguration and Recovery in Distributed Processing Systems. In *Proc. 1st Int'l Conf. on Distributed Computing*, pages 284–294. IEEE, 1979.

[King, Collmeyer 74]   King, P.F., Collmeyer, A.J. Database Sharing—An Efficient Mechanism for Supporting Concurrent Processes. In *Proc. 1974 NCC*. AFIPS Press, Montvale, NJ, 1974.

[Klahold et al. 85]   Klahold, P., Schlageter, G., Unland, R., Wilkes, W. A Transaction Model Supporting Complex Applications in Integrated Information Systems. In *Proc. ACM-SIGMOD Int'l Conf. on Management of Data*, pages 388–401. Austin, TX, May, 1985.

[Kohler 81]   Kohler, W. A Survey of Techniques for Synchronization and Recovery in Decentralized Computer Systems. *ACM Computing Surveys* 13(2):149–184, June, 1981.

[Koon, Ozsu 86]   Koon, T., Ozsu, M. T. Performance Comparison of Resilient Concurrency Control Algorithms for Distributed Databases. In *Proc. Int'l Conf. on Data Engineering*, pages 565–573. IEEE, Los Angeles, February, 1986.

[Korth 82]   Korth, H.F. Deadlock Freedom Using Edge Locks. *ACM Trans. on Database Systems* 7(4):632–652, December, 1982.

[Korth 83]   Korth, H.F. Locking Primitives in a Database System. *Journal of the ACM* 30(1):55–79, January, 1983.

[Korth et al. 83]   Korth, H.F., Krishnamurthy, R., Nigam, A., Robinson, J.T. A Framework for Understanding Distributed (Deadlock Detection) Algorithms. In *Proc. 2nd ACM SIGACT-SIGMOD Symp. on Principles of Database Systems*, pages 192–201. Atlanta, GA, March, 1983.

[Krishnamurthy, Dayal 82]   Krishnamurthy, R., Dayal, U. Theory of Serializability for a Parallel Model Of Transactions. In *Proc. 1st ACM SIGACT-SIGMOD Symp. on Principles of Database Systems*, pages 293–305. Los Angeles, March, 1982.

[Kung, Lehman 80]   Kung, H.T., Lehman, P.L. Concurrent Manipulation of Binary Search Trees. *ACM Trans. on Database Systems* 5(3):339–353, 1980.

[Kung, Papadimitriou 79]   Kung, H.T., Papadimitriou, C.H. An Optimality Theory of Concurrency Control for Databases. In *Proc. ACM-SIGMOD Int'l Conf. Management of Data*, pages 116–125. May, 1979. Also, *Acta Informatica* 19(1):1–11, 1983.

[Kung, Robinson 81]   Kung, H.T., Robinson, J.T. On Optimistic Methods for Concurrency Control. *ACM Trans. on Database Systems* 6(2):213–226, June, 1981.

[Kuss 82]   Kuss, H. On Totally Ordering Checkpoints in Distributed Databases. In *Proc. ACM-SIGMOD Int'l Conf. on Management of Data Bases*. Orlando, FL, Page 174, June, 1982.

[Kwong, Wood 82]   Kwong, Y.S., Wood, D. Method for Concurrency in B-Trees. *IEEE Trans. on Software Engineering* SE-8(3):211–223, 1982.

[Lai, Wilkinson 84]   Lai, M.Y., Wilkinson, W.K. Distributed Transaction Management in JASMIN. In *Proc. 10th Int'l Conf. on Very Large Data Bases*, pages 466–472. Singapore, August, 1984.

[Lakshman, Agrawala 86]   Lakshman, T.V., Agrawala, A.K. O(N $\sqrt{N}$) Decentralized Commit Protocols. In *5th Symp. on Reliability in Distributed Software and Data Base Systems*, pages 104–112. IEEE, Los Angeles, January, 1986.

[Lamport 78a]   Lamport, L. The Implementation of Reliable Distributed Multi-process Systems. *Computer Networks* 1(2):95–114, 1978.

[Lamport 78b]   Lamport, L. Time, Clocks, and the Ordering of Events in a Distributed System. *Comm. ACM* 21(7):558–565, July, 1978.

[Lampson 81]   Lampson, B.W. Atomic Transactions. *Distributed Systems— Architecture and Implementation: An Advanced Course*. Springer-Verlag, Berlin, 1981, pages 246–265, Chapter 11. G. Goos and J. Hartmanis (eds.).

[Lampson, Sturgis 76]   Lampson, B., Sturgis, H. *Crash Recovery in a Distributed Data Storage System*. Technical Report, Computer Science Laboratory, Xerox, Palo Alto Research Center, Palo Alto, CA, 1976.

[Langer, Shum 82]   Langer, A.M., Shum, A.W. The Distribution of Granule Accesses Made by Database Transactions. *Comm. ACM* 25(11):831–832, November, 1982.

[Lausen 81] Lausen, G. Serializability Problems of Interleaved Database Transactions. In *Proc. of 3rd Conf. European Cooperation in Informatics, Lecture Notes in Computer Science*, Vol. 123, pages 252–265. Springer-Verlag, Berlin, October, 1981.

[Lausen 83] Lausen, G. Formal Aspects of Optimistic Concurrency Control in a Multiple Version Database System. *Information Systems* 8(4):291–300, February, 1983.

[Lausen, Soisalon-Soininen, Widmayer 84] Lausen, G., Soisalon-Soininen, E., Widmayer, P. Maximal Concurrency by Locking. In *Proc. 3rd ACM SIGACT-SIGMOD Symp. on Principles of Database Systems*, pages 38–43. Waterloo, Ontario, April, 1984.

[Lavenberg 84] Lavenberg, S.S. A Simple Analysis of Exclusive and Shared Lock Contention in a Database System. In *Proc. ACM SIGMETRICS Conf. on Measurement and Modeling of Computer Systems*. Boston, MA, August, 1984.

[Lee 80] Lee, H. Queueing Analysis of Global Synchronization Schemes for Multicopy Databases. *IEEE Trans. on Computers* 29(5), May, 1980.

[Lehman, Yao 81] Lehman, P.L., Yao, S.B. Efficient Locking for Concurrent Operations on B-Trees. *ACM Trans. on Database Systems* 6(4):650–670, December, 1981.

[LeLann 78] LeLann, G. Algorithms for Distributed Data-Sharing Systems Which Use Tickets. In *Proc. 3rd Berkeley Workshop Distributed Databases and Computer Networks*, pages 259–272. ACM/IEEE, August, 1978.

[LeLann 81] LeLann, G. Error Recovery. *Distributed Systems—Architecture and Implementation: An Advanced Course*. Springer-Verlag, Berlin, 1981. B.W. Lampson, M. Paul, H.J. Siegert (eds.).

[Leu, Bhargava 86] Leu, P., Bhargava, B. Multidimensional Timestamp Protocols for Concurrency Control. In *Proc. Int'l Conf. on Data Engineering*, pages 482–489. IEEE, Los Angeles, February, 1986.

[Lien, Weinberger 78] Lien, Y.E., Weinberger, P.J. Consistency, Concurrency and Crash Recovery. In *Proc. ACM-SIGMOD Conf. on Management of Data*, pages 9–14. Austin, TX, 1978.

[Lin 79] Lin, W.K. Concurrency Control in a Multiple Copy Distributed Data Base System. In *Proc. 4th Berkeley Workshop on Distributed Data Management and Computer Networks*, pages 207–219. ACM/IEEE, August, 1979.

[Lin 81] Lin, W.K. Performance Evaluation of Two Concurrency Control Mechanisms in a Distributed Database System. In *Proc. ACM-SIGMOD Int'l Conf. on Management of Data*, pages 84–92. Ann Arbor, MI, April, 1981.

[Lin et al. 82] Lin, W.K., et al. *Distributed Database Control and Allocation: Semi-Annual Report*. Technical Report, Computer Corporation of America, Cambridge, MA, January, 1982.

[Lin, Nolte 82a] Lin, W.K., Nolte, J. Read Only Transactions and Two Phase Locking. In *Proc. 2nd Symp. on Reliability in Distributed Software and Database Systems*, pages 85–93. IEEE, Pittsburgh, PA, 1982.

[Lin, Nolte 82b] Lin, W.K., Nolte, J. Performance of Two Phase Locking. In *Proc. 6th Berkeley Workshop on Distributed Data Management and Computer Networks*, pages 131–160. ACM/IEEE, February, 1982.

[Lindsay 79] Lindsay, B.G. *Notes on Distributed Databases*. Research Report RJ2517, IBM San Jose, CA, July, 1979.

[Lindsay 80]   Lindsay, B.G. Single and Multi-Site Recovery Facilities. *Distributed Data Bases*. Cambridge University Press, Cambridge, U.K., 1980, pages 247–284, Chapter 10. Also available as IBM Research Report RJ2517, San Jose, CA, July 1979.

[Lindsay et al. 84]   Lindsay, B.G., Haas, L.M., Mohan, C., Wilms, P.F., Yost, R.A. Computation and Communication in R*: A Distributed Database Manager. *ACM Trans. on Computer Systems* 2(1):24–38, February, 1984.

[Liskov 81]   Liskov, B. On Linguistic Support for Distributed Programs. In *Proc. 1st Symp. on Reliability in Distributed Software and Database Systems*, pages 53–60. Pittsburgh, PA, July, 1981.

[Liskov, Scheifler 83]   Liskov, B., Scheifler, R. Guardians and Actions: Linguistic Support for Robust, Distributed Programs. *ACM Trans. on Programming Languages and Systems* 5(3):381–404, July, 1983.

[Lomet 77a]   Lomet, D.B. A Practical Deadlock Avoidance Algorithm for Data Base Systems. In *Proc. ACM SIGMOD Int'l Conf. on Management of Data*, pages 122–127. Toronto, 1977.

[Lomet 77b]   Lomet, D.B. Process Structuring, Synchronization and Recovery Using Atomic Actions. *ACM SIGPLAN Notices* 12(3):128–137, March, 1977.

[Lomet 78]   Lomet, D.B. Multi-Level Locking with Deadlock Avoidance. In *Proc. Annual Conf. of the ACM*, pages 862–867, 1978.

[Lomet 79]   Lomet, D.B. Coping with Deadlock in Distributed Systems. *Data Base Architecture*. Von Nostrand Reinhold, 1979, pages 95–105. G. Bracchi and G.M. Nijssen (eds.).

[Lomet 80a]   Lomet, D.B. Subsystems of Processes with Deadlock Avoidance. *IEEE Trans. on Software Eng.* 6(3):297–304, May, 1980.

[Lomet 80b]   Lomet, D.B. *The Ordering of Activities in Distributed Systems*. Technical Report RC8450, IBM T.J. Watson Research Center, September, 1980.

[Lorie 77]   Lorie, R.A. Physical Integrity in a Large Segmented Database. *ACM Trans. on Database Systems* 2(1):91–104, March, 1977.

[Lynch 83a]   Lynch, N.A. Concurrency Control for Resilient Nested Transactions. In *Proc. 2nd ACM SIGACT-SIGMOD Symp. on Principles of Database Systems*, pages 166–181. Atlanta, GA, March, 1983.

[Lynch 83b]   Lynch, N.A. Multilevel Atomicity—A New Correctness Criterion for Database Concurrency Control. *ACM Trans. on Database Systems* 8(4):484–502, December, 1983.

[Lynch, Fischer 81]   Lynch, N.A., Fischer, M.J. On Describing the Behavior and Implementation of Distributed Systems. *Theoretical Computer Science* 13(1):17–43, 1981.

[Macri 76]   Macri, P.M. Deadlock Detection and Resolution in a CODASYL Based Data Management System. In *Proc. ACM SIGMOD Int'l Conf. on Management of Data*, pages 45–49. Washington, D.C., June, 1976.

[Malcolm, Vasudevan 84]   Malcolm, M.A., Vasudevan, R. Coping with Network Partitions and Processor Failures in a Distributed System. In *Proc. 4th Symp. on Reliability in Distributed Software and Data Base Systems*, pages 36–42. IEEE, Silver Spring, MD, October, 1984.

[Manber, Ladner 84]   Manber, U., Ladner, R.E. Concurrency Control in a Dynamic Search Structure. *ACM Trans. on Database Systems* 9(3):439–455, September, 1984.

[Parker et al. 83]   Parker Jr., D.S., Popek, G.J., Rudisin, G., Stoughton, A., Walker, B.J., Walton, E., Chow, J.M., Edwards, D., Kiser, S., Kline, C. Detection of Mutual Inconsistency in Distributed Systems. *IEEE Trans. on Software Engineering* SE-9(3):240–247, May, 1983.

[Parker, Ramas 82]   Parker, D.S., Ramas, R.A. A Distributed File System Architecture Supporting High Availability. In *Proc. 8th Int'l Conf. on Very Large Data Bases*, pages 161–184. Mexico City, September, 1982.

[Peinl, Reuter 83]   Peinl, P., Reuter, A. Empirical Comparison of Database Concurrency Control Schemes. In *Proc. 9th Int'l Conf. on Very Large Data Bases*, pages 97–108. Florence, Italy, October, 1983.

[Peterson, Strickland 83]   Peterson, R.J., Strickland, J.P. Log Write-Ahead Protocols and IMS/VS Logging. In *Proc. 2nd ACM SIGACT-SIGMOD Symp. on Principles of Database Systems*, pages 216–242. Atlanta, GA, March, 1983.

[Pittelli, Garcia-Molina 86]   Pittelli, F., Garcia-Molina, H. Database Processing with Triple Modular Redundancy. In *Proc. 5th Symp. on Reliability in Distributed Software and Data Base Systems*, pages 95–103. IEEE, Los Angeles, January, 1986.

[Popek et al. 81]   Popek, G., Walker, B., Chow, J., Edwards, D., Kline, C., Rudisin, G., Thiel, G. Locus: A Network Transparent, High Reliability Distributed System. In *Proc. 8th ACM SIGOPS Symp. on Operating Systems Principles*, pages 169–177. December, 1981.

[Potier, Leblanc 80]   Potier, D., Leblanc, Ph. Analysis of Locking Policies in Database Management Systems. *Comm. ACM* 23(10):584–593, October, 1980.

[Pradel, Schlageter, Unland 86]   Pradel, U., Schlageter, G., Unland, R. Redesign of Optimistic Methods: Improving Performance and Applicability. In *Proc. Int'l Conf. on Data Engineering*, pages 466–473. IEEE, Los Angeles, February, 1986.

[Pun, Belford 86]   Pun, K.H., Belford, G.G. Optimal Granularity and Degree of Multiprogramming in a Distributed Database System. In *Proc. Int'l Conf. on Data Engineering*, pages 13–20. IEEE, Los Angeles, February, 1986.

[Rahimi, Frants 79]   Rahimi, S.K., Frants, W.R. A Posted Update Approach to Concurrency Control in Distributed Database Systems. In *Proc. 1st Int'l Conf. Distributed Computing Systems*, pages 632–641. IEEE, October, 1979.

[Ramarao 85]   Ramarao, K.V.S. On the Complexity of Commit Protocols. In *Proc. 4th ACM SIGACT-SIGMOD Symp. on Principles of Database Systems*, pages 235–244. Portland, OR, March, 1985.

[Ramirez, Santoro 79]   Ramirez, R.J., Santoro, N. Distributed Control of Updates in Multiple-Copy Data Bases: A Time Optimal Algorithm. In *Proc. 4th Berkeley Workshop on Distributed Data Management and Computer Networks*, pages 191–205. ACM/IEEE, August, 1979.

[Rappaport 75]   Rappaport, R.L. File Structure Design to Facilitate On-Line Instantaneous Updating. In *Proc. ACM SIGMOD Conf. on Management of Data*, pages 1–14. San Jose, CA, 1975.

[Reed 78]   Reed, D.P. *Naming and Synchronization in a Decentralized Computer System*. PhD thesis, M.I.T. Dept. of Electrical Engineering, 1978.

[Reed 79]   Reed, D.P. Implementing Atomic Actions. In *Proc. 7th ACM SIGOPS Symp. on Operating Systems Principles*. December, 1979.

[Reed 83]   Reed, D.P. Implementing Atomic Actions on Decentralized Data. *ACM Trans. on Computer Systems* 1(1):3–23, February, 1983.

[Reuter 80]   Reuter, A. A Fast Transaction-Oriented Logging Scheme for UNDO Recovery. *IEEE Trans. on Software Engineering* 6:348–356, July, 1980.

[Reuter 82]   Reuter, A. Concurrency on High-Traffic Data Elements. In *Proc. 1st ACM SIGACT-SIGMOD Symp. on Principles of Database Systems*, pages 83–92. Los Angeles, March, 1982.

[Reuter 84]   Reuter, A. Performance Analysis of Recovery. *ACM Trans. on Database Systems* 9(4):526–559, December, 1984.

[Ries 79a]   Ries, D.R. *The Effect of Concurrency Control on Database Management System Performance*. PhD thesis, Computer Science Dept., University of California, Berkeley, April, 1979.

[Ries 79b]   Ries, D.R. The Effects of Concurrency Control on the Performance of a Distributed Data Management System. In *Proc. 4th Berkeley Workshop on Distributed Data Management and Computer Networks*, pages 75–112. ACM/IEEE, August, 1979.

[Ries, Stonebraker 77]   Ries, D.R., Stonebraker, M. Effects of Locking Granularity in a Database Management System. *ACM Trans. on Database Systems* 2(3):233–246, September, 1977.

[Ries, Stonebraker 79]   Ries, D.R., Stonebraker, M. Locking Granularity Revisited. *ACM Trans. on Database Systems* 4(2):210–227, June, 1979.

[Robinson 82]   Robinson, J.T. *Design of Concurrency Controls for Transaction Processing Systems*. PhD thesis, Carnegie-Mellon University, 1982.

[Roome 82]   Roome, W.D. The Intelligent Store: A Content-Addressable Page Manager. *Bell System Technical Journal* 61(9, Part 2):2567–2596, November, 1982.

[Rosen 79]   Rosen, E.C. The Updating Protocol of the ARPANET's New Routing Algorithm: A Case Study in Maintaining Identical Copies of a Changing Distributed Data Base. In *Proc. 4th Berkeley Workshop on Distributed Data Management and Computer Networks*, pages 260–274. ACM/IEEE, August, 1979.

[Rosenkrantz, Stearns, Lewis 78]   Rosenkrantz, D.J., Stearns, R.E., Lewis, P.M., II System Level Concurrency Control for Distributed Database Systems. *ACM Trans. on Database Systems* 3(2):178–198, June, 1978.

[Rothnie et al. 80]   Rothnie, J.B., Jr., Bernstein, P.A., Fox, S., Goodman, N., Hammer, M., Landers, T.A., Reeve, C., Shipman, D.W., Wong, E. Introduction to a System for Distributed Databases (SDD-1). *ACM Trans. on Database Systems* 5(1):1–17, March, 1980.

[Rothnie, Goodman 77]   Rothnie, J.B., Jr., Goodman, N. A Survey of Research and Development in Distributed Databases Systems. In *Proc. 3rd Int'l Conf. on Very Large Data Bases*, pages 48–59. Tokyo, October, 1977.

[Ryu, Thomasian 86]   Ryu, I.K., Thomasian, A. Analysis of Database Performance with Dynamic Locking. Manuscript in preparation, 1986.

[Samadi 76]   Samadi, B. B-Trees in a System with Multiple Users. *Inform. Proc. Letters* 5(4):107–112, 1976.

[Schlageter 78]   Schlageter, G. Process Synchronization in Database Systems. *ACM Trans. on Database Systems* 3(3):248–271, September, 1978.

[Schlageter 79]   Schlageter, G. Enhancement of Concurrency in DBS by the Use of Special Rollback Methods. *Database Architecture*. Von Nostrand Reinhold, 1979, pages 141–149. G. Bracchi and G.M. Nijssen (eds.).

[Schlageter 81]   Schlageter, G. Optimistic Methods for Concurrency Control in Distributed Database Systems. In *Proc. 7th Int'l Conf. on Very Large Databases*, pages 125–130. Cannes, France, September, 1981.

[Schlageter, Dadam 80]   Schlageter, G., Dadam, P. Reconstruction of Consistent Global States in Distributed Databases. In *Proc. Int'l Symp. on Distributed Databases*, pages 191–200. North-Holland, Amsterdam, 1980.

[Schwarz, Spector 84]   Schwarz, P.M., Spector, A.Z. Synchronizing Shared Abstract Types. *ACM Trans. on Computer Systems* 2(3):223–250, August, 1984.

[Sequin, Sargeant, Wilnes 79]   Sequin, J., Sargeant, G., Wilnes, P. A Majority Consensus Algorithm for the Consistency of Duplicated and Distributed Information. In *Proc. 1st Int'l Conf. on Distributed Computing Systems*, pages 617–624. IEEE, October, 1979.

[Sevcik 83]   Sevcik, K.C. Comparison of Concurrency Control Methods Using Analytic Models. *Information Processing 83*:847–858, 1983. R.E.A. Mason (ed.).

[Shapiro, Millstein 77a]   Shapiro, R.M., Millstein, R.E. *NSW Reliability Plan*. Technical Report 7701–1411, Computer Associates, Wakefield, MA., June, 1977.

[Shapiro, Millstein 77b]   Shapiro, R.M., Millstein, R.E. Reliability and Fault Recovery in Distributed Processing. In *Oceans '77 Conf. Record*. Vol. II, Los Angeles, 1977.

[Shrivastava 85]   Shrivastava, S.K. *Reliable Computer Systems*. Springer-Verlag, Berlin, 1985.

[Shum 81]   Shum, A.W., Spirakis, P.G. Performance Analysis of Concurrency Control Methods in Database Systems. *Performance '81*:1–19, 1981. F.J. Kylstra (ed.).

[Siewiorek, Swarz 82]   Siewiorek, D.P., Swarz, R.S. *The Theory and Practice of Reliable System Design*. Digital Press, Bedford, MA, 1982.

[Silberschatz 82]   Silberschatz, A. A Multi-version Concurrency Control Scheme with No Rollbacks. In *Proc. 1st ACM SIGACT-SIGOPS Symp. on Principles of Distributed Computing*, pages 216–233. Ottawa, August, 1982.

[Silberschatz, Kedem 80]   Silberschatz, A., Kedem, Z. Consistency in Hierarchical Database Systems. *Journal of the ACM* 27(1):72–80, January, 1980.

[Sinha, Nandikar, Mehndiratta 85]   Sinha, M. K., Nandikar, P. D., Mehndiratta, S. L. Timestamp Based Certification Schemes for Transactions in Distributed Databases. In *Proc. ACM-SIGMOD Int'l Conf. on Management of Data*, pages 402–413. Austin, TX, May, 1985.

[Skeen 81]   Skeen, D. A Decentralized Termination Protocol. In *Proc. 1st IEEE Symp. on Reliability in Distributed Software and Database Systems*, pages 27–32. IEEE, Pittsburgh, PA, July, 1981.

[Skeen 82a]   Skeen, D. Nonblocking Commit Protocols. In *Proc. ACM SIGMOD Conf. on Management of Data*, pages 133–147. Orlando, FL, June, 1982.

[Skeen 82b]   Skeen, D. A Quorum Based Commit Protocol. In *Proc. 6th Berkeley Workshop on Distributed Data Management and Computer Networks*, pages 69–80. ACM/IEEE, February, 1982.

[Skeen 82c]   Skeen, D. *Crash Recovery in a Distributed Database System*. Technical Report, Memorandum No. UCB/ERL M82/45, Electronics Research Laboratory, University of California at Berkeley, 1982.

[Skeen 85]   Skeen, D. Determining the Last Process to Fail. *ACM Trans. on Computer Systems* 3(1):15–30, February, 1985.

[Skeen, Stonebraker 81] Skeen, D., Stonebraker, M. A Formal Model of Crash Recovery in a Distributed System. In *Proc. 5th Berkeley Workshop on Distributed Data Management and Computer Networks*, pages 129–142. ACM/IEEE, 1981.

[Skeen, Wright 84] Skeen, D., Wright, D. Increasing Availability in Partitioned Database Systems. In *Proc. 3rd ACM SIGACT-SIGMOD Symp. on Principles of Database Systems*, pages 290–296. Waterloo, Ontario, April, 1984.

[Sockut, Krishnamurthy 84] Socket, G.H., Krishnamurthy, R. *Concurrency Control in Office-by-Example (OBE)*. Research Report RC 10545, IBM Research, May, 1984.

[Soisalon-Soininen, Wood 82] Soisalon-Soininen, E., Wood, D. An Optimal Algorithm for Testing Safety and Detecting Deadlocks in Locked Transaction Systems. In *Proc. 1st ACM SIGACT-SIGMOD Symp. on Principles of Database Systems*, pages 108–116. Los Angeles, March, 1982.

[Spector et al. 84] Spector, A.Z., Butcher, J., Daniels, D.S., Duchamp, D.J., Eppinger, J.L., Fineman, C.E., Heddaya, A., Schwartz, P.M. Support for Distributed Transactions in the TABS Prototype. In *Proc. 4th Symp. on Reliability in Distributed Software and Database Systems*, pages 186–206. IEEE, Silver Spring, MD, October, 1984.

[Spector, Schwarz 83] Spector, A.Z., Schwarz, P.M. Transactions: A Construct for Reliable Distributed Computing. *ACM Operating Systems Review* 14(2):18–35, April, 1983.

[Stearns, Lewis, Rosenkrantz 76] Stearns, R.E., Lewis, P.M., II, Rosenkrantz, D.J. Concurrency Controls for Database Systems. In *Proc. 17th Symp. on Foundations of Computer Science*, pages 19–32. IEEE, 1976.

[Stearns, Rosenkrantz 81] Stearns, R.E., Rosenkrantz, D.J. Distributed Database Concurrency Controls Using Before-Values. In *Proc. ACM-SIGMOD Conf. on Management of Data*, pages 74–83. 1981.

[Stonebraker 79] Stonebraker, M. Concurrency Control and Consistency of Multiple Copies of Data in Distributed INGRES. *IEEE Trans. on Software Engineering* 3(3):188–194, May, 1979.

[Stonebraker 81] Stonebraker, M. Operating System Support for Data Management. *Comm. ACM* 24(7):412–418, July, 1981.

[Stonebraker, Neuhold 77] Stonebraker, M., Neuhold, E. A Distributed Database Version of INGRES. In *Proc. 2nd Berkeley Workshop on Distributed Data Management and Computer Networks*. ACM/IEEE, May, 1977.

[Strom 81] Strom, B.I. Consistency of Redundant Databases in a Weakly Coupled Distributed Computer System. In *Proc. 5th Berkeley Workshop on Distributed Data Management and Computer Networks*, pages 143–153. ACM/IEEE, 1981.

[Su 86] Su, J. Safety of Non-well-locked Transaction Systems. In *Proc. 5th ACM SIGACT-SIGMOD Symp. on Principles of Database Systems*, pages 47–52. Cambridge, MA, March, 1986.

[Sugihara et al. 84] Sugihara, K., Kikuno, T., Yoshida, N., Ogata, M. A Distributed Algorithm for Deadlock Detection and Resolution. In *Proc. 4th Symp. on Reliability in Distributed Software and Database Systems*, pages 169–176. IEEE, Silver Spring, MD, October, 1984.

[Tanenbaum 81] Tanenbaum, A.S. *Computer Networks*. Prentice-Hall, Englewood Cliffs, NJ, 1981.

[Tay, Goodman, Suri 84] Tay, Y.C., Goodman, N., Suri, R. *Performance Evaluation of Locking in Databases: A Survey.* Technical Report 17–84, Aiken Computation Laboratory, Harvard University, October, 1984.

[Tay, Goodman, Suri 85] Tay, Y.C., Goodman, N., Suri, R. Locking Performance in Centralized Databases. *ACM Trans. on Database Systems* 10(4):415–462, December, 1985.

[Tay, Suri, Goodman 84] Tay, Y.C., Suri, R., Goodman, N. A Mean Value Performance Model for Locking in Databases: The Waiting Case. In *Proc. 3rd ACM SIGACT-SIGMOD Symp. on Principles of Database Systems*, pages 311–322. Waterloo, Ontario, April, 1984.

[Tay, Suri, Goodman 85] Tay, Y.C., Suri, R., Goodman, N. A Mean Value Performance Model for Locking in Databases: The No Waiting Case. *Journal of the ACM* 32(3):618–651, July, 1985.

[Thanos, Carlesi, Bertino 81] Thanos, C., Carlesi, C., Bertino, E. Performance Evaluation of Two Concurrency Control Mechanisms in a Distributed Database System. *Lecture Notes in Computer Science.* Springer-Verlag, Berlin, 1981, pages 266–279. G. Goos and J. Hartmanis (eds.).

[Thomas 79] Thomas, R.H. A Majority Consensus Approach to Concurrency Control for Multiple Copy Databases. *ACM Trans. on Database Systems* 4(2):180–209, June, 1979.

[Thomasian 82] Thomasian, A. An Iterative Solution to the Queueing Network Model of a DBMS with Dynamic Locking. In *Proc. 13th Computer Measurement Group Conf.*, pages 252–261. Computer Measurement Group, San Diego, CA, December, 1982.

[Thomasian, Ryu 83] Thomasian, A., Ryu, I.K. A Decomposition Solution to the Queueing Network Model of the Centralized DBMS with Static Locking. In *Proc. ACM SIGMETRICS Conf. on Measurement and Modelling of Computer Systems*, pages 82–92. Minneapolis, August, 1983.

[Tirri 83] Tirri, H. Freedom from Deadlock of Locked Transactions in a Distributed Database. In *Proc. 2nd ACM SIGACT-SIGOPS Symp. on Principles of Distributed Computing*, pages 267–276. Montreal, 1983.

[Traiger 82] Traiger, I.L. Virtual Memory Management for Data Base Systems. *Operating Systems Review* 16(4):26–48, October, 1982.

[Traiger et al. 82] Traiger, I.L., Gray, J., Galtier, C.A., Lindsay, B.G. Transactions and Consistency in Distributed Database Systems. *ACM Trans. on Database Systems* 7(3):323–342, September, 1982.

[Ullman 82] Ullman, J.D. *Principles of Database Systems.* Computer Science Press, Rockville, MD, 1982. 2nd Edition.

[Unland, Praedel, Schlageter 83] Unland, R., Praedel, U., Schlageter, G. Design Alternatives for Optimistic Concurrency Control Schemes. In *Proc. 2nd Int'l Conf. on Databases*, pages 288–297. Wiley, New York, September, 1983.

[Verhofstad 77] Verhofstad, J.S.M. Recovery and Crash Resistance in a Filing System. In *Proc. ACM-SIGMOD Int'l Conf. Management of Data*, pages 158–167. Toronto, 1977.

[Verhofstad 78] Verhofstad, J.S.M. Recovery Techniques for Database Systems. *ACM Computing Surveys* 10(2):167–196, 1978.

[Verhofstad 79] Verhofstad, J.S.M. Recovery Based on Types. *Data Base Architecture*: 125–139, 1979. North-Holland, Amsterdam, G. Bracchi and G.M. Nijssen (eds.).

[Walter 82]   Walter, B. A Robust and Efficient Protocol for Checking the Availability of Remote Sites. In *Proc. 6th Berkeley Workshop on Distributed Data Management and Computer Networks*, pages 45–68. ACM/IEEE, February, 1982.

[Weihl 83]   Weihl, W.E. Data-Dependent Concurrency Control and Recovery. In *Proc. 2nd ACM SIGACT-SIGOPS Symp. on Principles of Distributed Computing*, pages 63–75. Montreal, August, 1983.

[Weihl 85]   Weihl, W. E. Distributed Version Management for Read-Only Actions. In *Proc. 4th ACM SIGACT-SIGOPS Symp. on Principles of Distributed Computing*, pages 122–135. Minaki, Ontario, August, 1985.

[Weikum 86]   Weikum, G. A Theoretical Foundation of Multi-Level Concurrency Control. In *Proc. 5th ACM SIGACT-SIGMOD Symp. on Principles of Database Systems*, pages 31–42. Cambridge, MA, March, 1986.

[Weinberger 82]   Weinberger, P.J. Making UNIX Operating Systems Safe for Databases. *Bell System Technical Journal* 61(9):2407–2422, November, 1982.

[Wilkinson, Lai 84]   Wilkinson, W.K., Lai, M.Y. Managing Replicated Data in JASMIN. In *Proc. 4th Symp. on Reliability in Distributed Software and Database Systems*, pages 54–60. IEEE, Silver Spring, MD, October, 1984.

[Wolfson, Yannakakis 85]   Wolfson, O., Yannakakis, M. Deadlock-Freedom (and Safety) of Transactions in a Distributed Database. In *Proc. 4th ACM SIGACT-SIGMOD Symp. on Principles of Database Systems*, pages 105–112. Portland, OR, March, 1985.

[Wong, Edelberg 77]   Wong, K.C., Edelberg, M. Interval Hierarchies and Their Application to Predicate Files. *ACM Trans. on Database Systems* 2(3):223–232, September, 1977.

[Xu 82]   Xu, J. A Formal Model for Maximum Concurrency in Transaction Systems with Predeclared Writesets. In *Proc. 8th Int'l Conf. on Very Large Data Bases*, pages 77–90. Mexico City, 1982.

[Yannakakis 81]   Yannakakis, M. Issues of Correctness in Database Concurrency Control by Locking. In *Proc. 13th ACM SIGACT Symp. on Theory of Computing*, pages 363–367. Milwaukee, 1981.

[Yannakakis 82a]   Yannakakis, M. Freedom from Deadlock of Safe Locking Policies. *SIAM J. Comput.* 11(2):391–407, May, 1982.

[Yannakakis 82b]   Yannakakis, M. A Theory of Safe Locking Policies in Database Systems. *Journal of the ACM* 29(3):718–740, July, 1982.

[Yannakakis 84]   Yannakakis, M. Serializability by Locking. *Journal of the ACM* 31(2):227–244, 1984.

[Yannakakis, Papadimitriou, Kung 79]   Yannakakis, M., Papadimitriou, C.H., Kung, H.T. Locking Policies: Safety and Freedom from Deadlock. In *Proc. 29th IEEE Symp. on Foundations of Computer Science*, pages 286–297, 1979.

[Zhou, Yeh, Ng 84]   Zhou, B., Yeh, R.T., Ng, P.A.B. An Algebraic System for Deadlock. In *Proc. 4th Symp. on Reliability in Distributed Software and Database Systems*, pages 177–185. IEEE, Silver Spring, MD, October, 1984.

[Zobel 83]   Zobel, D.D. The Deadlock Problem: A Classifying Bibliography. *ACM SIGOPS Operating Systems Review* 17(2):6–15, October, 1983.

INDEX